MEMORIES OF LIFE IN LHASA UNDER CHINESE RULE

MEMORIES OF LIFE

TUBTEN KHÉTSUN

TRANSLATED AND WITH AN INTRODUCTION

BY MATTHEW AKESTER

ASA UNDER CHINESE RULE

 COLUMBIA UNIVERSITY PRESS   NEW YORK

Columbia University Press
Publishers Since 1893
New York   Chichester, West Sussex
Translation copyright © 2008 Columbia University Press

Panorama of Lhasa on pages 2–3 from Demo Wangchuk Dorje, *Visual Culture Photos of the Land of Snows* (China Tibetology Press, 2005). Photo taken by Demo Rinpoche in 1942.
Except for the bottom photograph on page 221, all those reproduced by permission from Woeser are from her book *Forbidden Memory: Tibet During the Cultural Revolution* (text by Woeser; photos by Tsering Dorje) (Taiwan: Locus Publications, 2006).

Library of Congress Cataloging-in-Publication Data
Khétsun, Tubten, 1941–
[Dka' sdug 'og gi byung ba brjod pa. English]
Memories of life in Lhasa under Chinese rule / Tubten Khétsun ; translated by Matthew Akester.
      p.   cm.
ISBN 978-0-231-14286-1 (cloth : alk. paper)
1. Khétsun, Tubten, 1941– 2. Tibet (China)—Biography. 3. Political prisoners—China—Tibet—Biography. I. Akester, Matthew. II. Title.
DS786.T48613   2008
951'.5—dc22
[B]   (Khetsun)
  2007011003

Contents

Translator's Introduction

WHAT WENT ON in Tibet during the twenty years of Maoist rule between 1959 and 1979 is still only vaguely known to the outside world, and even to most Tibetans born in exile. The history of the period has yet to be written in depth, and the memories of those who lived through it are one of the few available sources. Tubten Khétsun's autobiography is so vividly self-explanatory that further introduction seems superfluous, but it is hoped that a brief survey of the historical background and related literature may be of service to the reader.

History

The modern history of Tibet is usually thought to have begun with the British invasion of 1904, the subsequent missions of reconquest by Sichuanese and imperial troops from 1905 to 1911, the final collapse of the Manchu empire in 1911, the return of His Holiness the Thirteenth Dalai Lama from exile, and the reestablishment of a national government in 1913. There followed a brief era of top-down reform, initiated by the Dalai Lama, who sought to introduce the modern institutions needed to guarantee the country's integrity, chiefly a national army. This involved dependence on British India, the former enemy, which had brokered unsuccessful negotiations on Tibet's status with Nationalist China at Simla in 1913, and intervened again when British-trained and -equipped Tibetan troops repulsed Sichuanese advances in 1917–18. Western influence and moves toward modern statehood were opposed, however, by the conservative establishment, particularly the great monasteries, unable to countenance an end to ecclesiastical power and international isolationism, and while trade and communication with India inevitably broadened Tibet's exposure to modernity, the reformist agenda was largely stifled. It also provoked a rift in 1923 between the Lhasa government and the Panchen Lama's court at Shika-tsé (historically rival provinces) that was to undermine national unity.

Shortly before his premature death in 1933, the Dalai Lama warned his subjects that Tibet would suffer the same fate as Mongolia, where Buddhist monasteries had been destroyed wholesale by Communist troops, unless they were able to defend themselves. The regency governments that ruled the country for the next seventeen years (Reteng Rinpoché 1934–41, Takdra Rinpoché 1941–50) showed no such initiative, and were characterized by factionalism, intolerance, and corruption. The former's main achievement by far in office was overseeing the search for the infant Fourteenth Dalai Lama (who was found in the far northeast, in a Tibetan village on the traditional border with China) and his enthronement in Lhasa at the age of five (1940).

For Chinese Nationalists and Communists alike, the multinational Chinese republic including Tibet, east Turkestan, and Mongolia was (indeed still is) an unquestionable goal, and colonization of these countries was part of the sacred duty of reclaiming territory lost to foreign imperialist powers in the late Manchu era. During the 1930s, the Hui Muslim warlords of Xining enforced military control over much of northeastern Tibet, while the Sichuan warlords held firmly onto the eastern half of Kham province (east of the Yangtse river) and laid claim to the western half. These regions were notionally constituted by the Nanking government as Chinese provinces called "Qinghai" (the Tibetan regions of Amdo, Golok, Tsaidam, and Nangchen), for which there was some Manchu administrative precedent, and "Xikang" (most of Kham, Powo, and Kongpo), which had no such precedent and was abandoned by the Communists soon after coming to power.

The British Government of India reestablished a permanent diplomatic mission in Lhasa in 1936, trade between the two countries boomed, noble families sent their children to school in India, Tibetans in Lhasa sipped sweet tea and hummed songs from the latest Bombay films, but Tibet was never more than peripheral to British imperial interests, which in any case were history once India gained independence in 1947. As elsewhere in decolonizing Asia, the former colonial power's role was taken up by the United States, which extended discreet diplomatic support to the Lhasa government and went as far as training and equipping Khampa resistance fighters in the 1950s, but these interventions were essentially opportunistic, and it is most unlikely that the kind of military and political commitment needed to support a real resistance war was ever seriously considered in Washington. For the new government of independent India, warm relations with the People's Republic of China (PRC) were essential to the nonaligned movement of developing countries, and it was ready to concede Tibet as a Chinese sphere of interest, provided that local autonomy was respected. Even so, there was consternation at the speed with which the People's Liberation Army (PLA) took over the country and pushed into its Himalayan borders.

The occupation of Tibet was led by the southwest command of the PLA in the summer of 1950. The main advance followed the highway from Dartsédo to Kandze, across the Yangtse and on to Chamdo, seat of the Lhasa government's eastern commissioner, which fell with little resistance in October. The Beijing government then called on Lhasa to send delegates for talks on "Peaceful Liberation," undertaking to halt the military advance while these took place. The Tibetan delegates were presented with a Seventeen-Point Agreement stating that all Tibet was Chinese territory, that the Tibetan government should allow Chinese troops to enter the country unopposed, but the traditional government would remain in place with limited powers of administration alongside the regional military authority. It was made clear that the alternative was invasion on less benign terms. Advance units of the Sichuan-based armies under the southwest command started to reach Lhasa in summer 1951 and were joined several months later by an army under the northwest command that had advanced through western Qinghai and Nakchu-ka, laying the route of Tibet's main supply line (later highway, and now railway) as they went.

Communist rule in Tibet can be periodized quite simply as follows: Liberal 1950–58, Maoist 1959–79, Liberal 1980–89, each phase turning on a pivotal event: the 1959 uprising, the 1979 reforms in China, the 1989 protest movement. A different term might be needed to describe the period 1990 to the present (economic privatization, political repression, and hyper-constructionism), but that is not our concern here, for this book is mainly about the second phase.

In the first phase, 1950–58, PLA soldiers had orders to win over the population, not to impose on them or offend their beliefs. The United Front had exceptional authorization and funding to co-opt former nobles and religious figures, many children of the former elite were sent for schooling in mainland China, model schools and hospitals were built, "poor families" were given cash handouts, children were given sweets. Still, the arrival of thousands of troops in Lhasa and other towns led to huge economic inflation and political encroachment, which was not popular. The military authorities insisted that the Tibetan government arrest leaders of protest groups in Lhasa and Shika-tsé, and in 1952 requested the prime minister's resignation because they found him too outspoken. This approach was "liberal" only in the context of Chinese Communist Party (CCP) Nationality policy, which argued that Tibet's "special characteristics" should be respected and that efforts should be made to build up a local cadre force capable of managing regional affairs. At that time, for example, Tibet was allowed its own time zone (two hours behind Beijing time; it was withdrawn in 1959 and never reinstated). As in other colonial regimes, quite a few of the early Communist administrators were earnest idealists seeking to uplift what they saw as a hopelessly backward society, although most fell victim to the 1957–58 Antirightist campaign or the "cleansing" campaigns of the early 1960s.

In 1956 a committee was established, including members of the now largely symbolic Tibetan government, to prepare for an "autonomous region" comprising central and western Tibet and western Kham, the eastern half of the country having been divided into "autonomous prefectures" in four neighboring Chinese provinces. The Dalai Lama and his entourage took the opportunity of a Buddhist anniversary to visit India, apparently with a view to eliciting Indian pressure on the PRC to respect Tibet's autonomy. The attempt was unsuccessful, though serious enough for foreign minister Chou Enlai to stage an unscheduled appearance in Delhi, and His Holiness elected to return the following year, against the better judgment of many of his subjects. Chinese leaders had repeatedly offered assurances that socialist reforms (collectivization, expropriation, and persecution of "class enemies") would not be forced on Tibet, but this did not apply to eastern areas outside the "autonomous region," where their direct imposition sparked a war of resistance and brutal counterinsurgency. This continued throughout 1957, and worsened in 1958 when nomadic areas across eastern Tibet became affected. Guerrilla resistance prompted military assaults on civilian populations, and refugees flooded into Lhasa. These developments coincided with the rise of Maoism at the center, the purge of "rightist" officials, and the launch of the Great Leap Forward. As armed insurgency spread to central Tibet, the military authorities prepared to respond in full measure, and the liberal policy phase was at an end.

The turning point came in March 1959, when rumors that the Dalai Lama was to visit the Chinese army camp in Lhasa unaccompanied drew large crowds to gather outside the walls of the Summer Palace (*Nor bu gling ka*), denounce the senior ministers as collaborators, and appoint their own guards for his protection. In the chaos of the following days, as the agitated public held demonstrations and passed resolutions, the Dalai Lama and his immediate entourage fled through rebel-held territory to the Indian border, where he was granted exile. The PLA garrison waited nearly a week before launching an artillery barrage, then moved into the city to restore order. Across central Tibet, tens of thousands were killed, tens of thousands fled as best they could through the Himalayan passes into India, and hundreds of thousands were arrested as "counterrevolutionaries" over the following months, most of whom were forced to labor in prison camps for the next two decades, if they survived that long.

The authorities lost no time in imposing "Democratic Reform" through-out the country; monasteries were disbanded and closed, castles and estates were looted and vandalized, former nobles and land owners were subjected to "class struggle" and their property confiscated. The population was reg-istered, categorized by class, and reorganized into local committees run by newly recruited Tibetan officials, which dictated much of the people's everyday lives and held compulsory political reeducation meetings most evenings. One group of former nobles and lamas, so-called "progressives" who had gone over to the Communist Party in the 1950s and denounced the uprising, were rewarded with government salaries and not dispos-sessed during Democratic Reform. The Shika-tsé faction, whose quarrel with Lhasa had been well exploited by Beijing, also denounced the uprising and retained their privileges. The campaign was followed by another, called "Reexamination" (1960), which broadened the criteria for including indi-viduals in the persecuted upper-class categories and intensified the inquisi-tion into hidden weapons and property.

In 1961 there was a slight relaxation, corresponding with Liu Shaoqi's rise to power at the center; class categorization was revised and wronged individuals were given compensation, some private trade was permitted, and key Tibetan monuments were given state protection. China was then in the grip of its worst-ever famine, induced by three years of disastrous Maoist policies, and many thousands of Tibetans inside and outside prison also died of starvation in those years, but Tibet was run by the military, and official personnel and their dependents continued to eat as usual. Thus internal economic and humanitarian crisis did not prevent the PRC from inviting a border war with India in summer 1962, fighting simultaneously on two fronts at opposite ends of the Himalaya and winning convincingly. The victory set the seal on China's control of Tibet, led to the militarization of the Indian Himalaya, and dealt Sino-Indian relations a blow from which they have yet to recover.

The relaxation was soon over, and as Mao Zedong swiftly regained control of the Party leadership, more punitive campaigns were launched in Tibet (like the "Three Big Educations" and "Four Cleanups"). The main Tibetan victim of Mao's new antirightist purge was the Panchen Lama, the most senior religious figure still in Tibet, whom the Party had been grooming as a figurehead, but who had dared to speak out during the brief premiership of Liu Shaoqi, against the oppressive rule of Tibetan areas since the uprising. His denunciation and imprisonment in 1964 were accompanied by a harsh campaign aimed at rooting out "little Panchens" in society at large. In 1965 the Tibet Autonomous Region (TAR) was finally inaugurated, the first flagship projects like the Lhasa airport and Ba-yi yarn factory were completed, and the onerous commune system began to be introduced in rural areas.

Then came the Great Proletarian Cultural Revolution, a radical campaign launched by Mao to unseat suspected opponents in the leadership that turned into a violent and chaotic mass inquisition. With its launch in Tibet in September 1966, Party activists and Red Guard youth militia set about desecrating whatever remained of the country's heritage, subjected formerly "progressive" Tibetan officials and other non-Maoist figures of authority to public humiliation, and forced everyone else to destroy anything associated with the "old society," from statues and books to clothing and eating utensils. For most of the next three years, people lived in terror as Red Guard factions battled for control of the administration, though the military remained sufficiently aloof to ensure the maintenance of essential networks and institutions. Things came to a head in the summer of 1969, when popular revolts broke out in several areas and the PLA moved to crush them and then reimpose order under martial law in 1970–71. Civilian government was reestablished under a unified Party committee in Lhasa, as in many homeland provinces, one committed to "leftist" goals and vigilant attention to security, and Tibet was governed accordingly until 1979. The eyewitness account of the political campaigns of the early 1970s in this book is perhaps the most detailed to have appeared.

The post-Maoist reforms in China began to have an impact in 1979: class labels were removed, prison camps were disbanded, the ban on visible manifestations of Tibetan culture was lifted, and representatives of the exile government were permitted to make an inspection tour. The third phase had begun, and was formalized by the visit to Lhasa in 1980 of Party Secretary Hu Yaobang, who issued the first and only apology by the central government for decades of misrule and announced a package of reforms for the Tibetanization of the local administration and implementation of the autonomy measures envisaged by the 1979 constitution. Tibetan society began to revive with remarkable determination: monasteries and temples were restored, traditional crafts resumed, education and language reforms drafted, and tentative negotiations held with leaders in exile. These developments faced considerable resistance within the Party at both central and regional levels, however. Hu himself was forced from office in 1987, and nationalist protests in Lhasa led to the imposition of martial law in March 1989, months before it was imposed nationwide in response to the momentous pro-democracy movement of that year.

Autobiography

Autobiography as a means of narrating personal experience of historical events is, as far as we know, a recent development in Tibetan literature, at least when written by those of undistinguished status or achievement. Under the influence of modern literary forms, it has emerged largely as an attempt to register Tibetan perceptions of the catastrophic twentieth-century history of their country, often in contestation of official Chinese interpretations. The memoirs of aristocrats, lamas, and former government officials account for a good deal of what has been published in Tibetan; most recall personal involvement in the events of the second quarter of the century and evoke a way of life that came to an abrupt end with the 1959 flight into exile.[1] This group includes several memoirs by grandees of the exile community ghostwritten in English, and their description of pre-Communist Lhasa society, aimed at non-Tibetan readers, has become the most familiar.[2] These works have some parallel in the brief histories of noble families commissioned and published by various United Front presses in occupied Tibet, although virtually no voluntarily written Tibetan autobiography has been published inside the PRC.[3]

Tibetan accounts of life under Maoist rule after 1959 tend to be prison memoirs, many of which were originally ghostwritten in English. These include the stories of Palden Gyatso, an ordinary monk imprisoned for twenty years and then rearrested for political activism in the 1980s; Adhe Tapontsang, who spent twenty years in the labor camps of eastern Tibet; Ani Pa-chen, the Khampa princess who led resistance fighters against Communist troops and spent her adult life in prison; and Tendzin Choedrak, who survived twenty years in Chinese prisons to become a leading physician in exile. The recent autobiography of Ba-pa Puntsok Wang-gyé is so far the only such work by a senior Communist official.[4]

One other group of memoirs is concerned with Tibetan armed resistance to the occupation in the 1950s and 1960s. Otherwise, there are precious few published accounts of life in eastern Tibet in that period.[5]

This Book

Tubten Khétsun was born into a respectable Lhasa family in 1941, and at the time of the 1959 uprising he had just completed the rigorous examinations that qualified young men of his background to enter government service. Caught up in the dramatic events of that year—the flight of the Dalai Lama and his court into exile, PLA bombardment of Lhasa and imposition of Democratic Reform in central Tibet—he was arrested along with thousands of others, and spent the next two decades being subjected to forced labor and political reeducation, first as a prisoner and then as a "class enemy" in civil society.

His memoir, first published in Tibetan in 1998 (*dKa' sdug 'og gi byung ba brjod pa*, Tibet Cultural Press, Dharamsala), has the quiet integrity of an everyman's tale, with a careful recollection of detail full of poignant images that give the reader something of the texture of everyday life. Unlike most of the material so far published in English, it is primarily addressed to the author's generation, recalling the sufferings undergone by all in restrained and occasionally humorous language, and has been well received as such by Tibetan readers in exile.

Khétsun-la gives his own vivid accounts of the main events, well known among Lhasa people, although seldom articulated in writing—the 1959 uprising, the 1966 launch of the Cultural Revolution, the mass executions of 1969–70, the destruction of Ganden monastery—and touches on others less known, the failed attempt to relocate the regional government in 1965, for instance, or the punitive "cleansing" campaigns of 1973–74. In particular, the narrative is peppered with tales of work accidents, such as the infamous Nga-chen landslide and the Tölung power station canal leak, which were evidently a common feature of socialist construction. There are fascinating asides on matters such as the fate of Lhasa's Muslim communities, public health, and rural taxation. There are dispassionate and insightful portraits of Tibetan collaborators. Ultimately, it is the evocation of the petty cruelties of Maoist rule that gives the book its power: the images of

barefoot prisoners carrying their guards piggyback across icy rivers, of local officials having "class enemies" lay out Chinese slogans in white pebbles
on the mountainside, of soldiers burning harvested swamp grass for fun or
hounding invalids from their beds in the middle of the night. Its publication in English will be a heavyweight addition to the literature, and I hope
it will go some way toward fulfilling the author's intention.

I would like to express my thanks to those who have helped bring
Tubten Khétsun's story to the English-reading world, especially Robbie Bar-
nett of Columbia University, Tashi Tséring of the Amnye Machen Institute,
and Warren Smith of Radio Free Asia for their encouragement, and our
editor, Anne Routon, for her enthusiastic and diligent support.

Notes

1. E.g.: *rGas po'i lo rgyus 'bel gtam* by Khe smad bSod nams dbang 'dus (Dharamsala: Library of Tibetan Works and Archives, 1982); *Mi tshe'i rba rlabs 'khrugs po* by bSam
pho bsTan 'dzin don grub (Delhi: Privately published, 1987); *lHa'u rta ra'i lo rgyus* by
rTse mgron bsTan 'dzin rgyal mtshan (Dharamsala: Tibet Cultural Press, 1988); *Mi tshe'i
lo rgyus dang 'brel yod sna tshogs* by rNam sras gling dPal 'byor 'jigs med (Dharamsala:
Library of Tibetan Works and Archives, 1988); *Rang gi lo rgyus lhad med rang byung
zangs* by Shan kha ba 'Gyur med bsod nams stobs rgyal (Dharamsala: LTWA, 1990);
lHa rgya ri'i gdung rabs rin chen phreng ba by Khri chen rNam rgyal rgya mtsho (Delhi:
Paljor, 1999); *Mi tshe'i lo rgyus las 'phros pa'i gtam thabs byus snying stobs kyi 'bras bu*
by Kun bde gling 'Od zer rgyal mtshan, 2 vols. (Mysore: Privately published, 2001); *The
View from My Window: Memoirs of a Young Noble Girl's Days in Lhasa* by Tsha rong
dByangs can sgrol dkar (Dharamsala: Amnye Machen, 2006). Numerous memoirs and
short biographies of former nobles and officials in exile have appeared in the LTWA
Oral History series (17 vols., 1996–2002). English titles of this type include *Born in Tibet*
by Chogyam Trungpa (Boulder: Shambhala, 1977) (first published by Allen and Unwin,
London, 1966); *My Life and Lives: The Story of a Tibetan Incarnation* by Rato Khyongla
Rinpoche (New York: Dutton, 1977) and *In the Presence of My Enemies: Memoirs of
Tibetan Nobleman Tsipon Shuguba* by Sumner Carnahan with Lama Kunga Rinpoche
(Santa Fe: Heartsfire, 1998).

2. E.g.: Rinchen Dolma Taring, *Daughter of Tibet* (Boston: Wisdom, 1987) (first
published by John Murray, London, 1970); Dorje Yudon Yuthok, *House of the Turquoise
Roof* (Ithaca, NY: Snow Lion, 1990); Jamyang Sakya, *Princess in the Land of Snow* (Boston: Shambhala, 1990); Jetsun Pema, *Tibet, My Story* (Shaftesbury, England: Element
Books, 1997); Dundul Namgyal Tsarong, *In the Service of His Country: The Biography of*

Dasang Damdul Tsarong, Commander General of Tibet (Ithaca, NY: Snow Lion, 2000); Namgyal Lhamo Taklha, *Born in Lhasa* (Ithaca, NY: Snow Lion, 2003).

3. E.g.: histories of the bShad sgra, Hor khang, lHa klu, lHa rgya ri, lHa smon, and lHa'u rta ra families in the Collected Materials on Tibetan Culture and History series published by the TAR Chinese Peoples' Political Consultative Conference (CPPCC) since the mid-1980s. Profiles of "patriotic" officials and religious figures appear regularly in official publications. *Gangs ri'i pang gi lang tsho'i rol mo* by gSer tshang Phun tshogs bkra shis (interpreter at the 1951 negotiations and later central government official) is apparently the first book-length memoir to have been published in Tibetan in the PRC (Beijing: China Tibetology Publishing House, 2003). Tashi Tsering's *The Struggle for Modern Tibet* (an autobiography coauthored by M. Goldstein and W. Siebenschuh, University of California Press, 1997) is perhaps the only such foreign publication to have enjoyed legal distribution there.

4. *Fire Under the Snow: The Testimony of a Tibetan Prisoner* by Palden Gyatso with Tsering Shakya (London: Harvill Press, 1998); *Ama Adhe: The Voice That Remembers* by Adhe Tapontsang with Joy Blakeslee (Boston: Wisdom, 2000) (a story already told in *A Strange Liberation* by David Patt [Ithaca, NY: Snow Lion, 1993]); *Sorrow Mountain: The Journey of a Tibetan Warrior Nun* by Ani Pachen with Adelaide Donnelly (Tokyo: Kodansha International, 2000); *The Rainbow Palace* by Tenzin Choedrak with Giles von Grassdorf (London: Bantam, 2000) (a story already told in *In Exile from the Land of Snows* by John Avedon [Boston: Wisdom, 1984]); *A Tibetan Revolutionary* by M. Goldstein, W. Siebenschuh, and Dawei Sherap (Berkeley: University of California Press, 2004). There are other prison memoirs in English by Ke'u-tsang Lama Jampel Yeshe (*Memoirs of Keutsang Lama* [Delhi: Paljor, 2001]) and Losang Yonten (*The Fire of Hell* [Utrecht: Pantau, 2001]), and a series in Tibetan published by the Gu-chu-sum ex-political prisoners' association in Dharamsala. Accounts of life outside prison include Dhondub Choedon's *Life in the Red Flag People's Commune* (Dharamsala: H.H. the Dalai Lama's Information and Publicity Office, 1978), Rimbur Rinpoché's Tibetan-language autobiography (*dGe sdig las kyi myong ba* vol. 2 [Dharamsala: Tibet Cultural Press, 1989]), and *A Tailor's Tale* by Namsa Chenmo Gyeten Namgyal (in *Chöyang* [Department of Religion and Culture, Dharamsala] no. 6 [1994]: 28–63).

5. E.g.: Gonpo Tashi Andrugtsang, *Four Rivers, Six Ranges: Reminiscences of the Resistance Movement in Tibet* (Dharamsala: Information and Publicity Office of H.H. the Dalai Lama, 1973); Jamyang Norbu, *Warriors of Tibet: The Story of Aten and the Khampas' Fight for the Freedom of Their Country* (Boston: Wisdom, 1986) (first published as *Horseman in the Snow* by Tibet Information Office, Dharamsala, 1979); Kunga Samten Dewatsang, *Flight at the Cuckoo's Behest: Life and Times of a Tibetan Freedom Fighter* (Delhi: Paljor, 1997); *Gangs can bstan srung dang blangs dmag* by Phu pa Tshe ring stobs rgyas (Dharamsala: Nartang, 1998); the *bTsan rgol rgyal skyob* series by Tsong kha lHa

mo tshe ring (Dharamsala: Amnye Machen, 1992–2003); *Khrag gi mig chu* by rDo gcod dKon mchog bstan dar (Dharamsala: Privately published, 2002); *A mdo rDo thar gyi mi tshe mthong thos myong gi gtam* by Sa dkar 'Od zer rgya mtsho (Delhi: Privately published, 2002). Autobiographical accounts of ordinary life in eastern Tibet after 1959 include *Under the Blue Sky* by Hortsang Jigme (Dharamsala: Privately published, 1998), and *Six Stars with a Crooked Neck* by Pema Bhum (trans. Lauren Hartley) (Dharamsala: Tibet Times, 2001).

Preface

H omage to the supremely enlightened Tendzin Gyatso
A valokitesvara, embodiment of the compassion of all the buddhas
I ngenious propagator of the Buddhist teachings
L ord of the Buddhist polity and protector of the land of snows.

WITH THIS WORSHIPFUL invocation of the noble object of refuge, I shall begin. In 1959, after the brazen military invasion and subjugation of our independent country, Tibet, the land of snows, by the Red Chinese, some of His Holiness the Dalai Lama's disciples and followers among the peoples of the three great districts of Tibet fled as refugees to the neighboring land of India and other countries, while those of us who were less fortunate remained behind and experienced unbearable suffering under the rule of the aggressors. No single person could thoroughly or comprehensively describe the inexpressible destruction of the country and way of life of the Tibetan people by the Chinese invaders, but it is up to all those who experienced the various aspects of this [destruction] at different times and in different areas to tell whatever they know and recall. I had long wanted to write an account of my own story, but since the sufferings I had experienced were quite ordinary, I doubted if it would have much value. My own level of innate and acquired knowledge is extremely low, and thinking how difficult it would be to put my memories into writing, I remained hesitant and discouraged.

Then, during the commemoration of the March 10, 1959 uprising in 1988, His Holiness the Dalai Lama told us that concerning the situation of occupied Tibet, truth was on our side, but it was not enough for us to realize and know that only for ourselves. It was very important to put the truths of our experiences into writing. It would not do [just] to say that with the imposition of Chinese rule in Tibet in recent times, both our land and our people have been entirely decimated and those who actually experienced this have died. He said that these experiences should be articulated in a form that could be clearly seen and heard about, so that in future the world could be shown, a clear historical record could be written, and the next generation could understand what happened. Therefore it was very important for us all to write a frank and direct account of the sufferings we had actually experienced individually, based on what we had seen and heard for ourselves, without depending on what others may have said. Otherwise, all who had actually experienced such suffering would gradually pass away, and without the direct, detailed transmission of their stories to the new generation, there was a danger that nothing more would be known about it in the future than the general statement that some great suffering took place at that time. We should try to produce many different written accounts of people's actual experience, whether in summary or in detail. A few people had already written accounts of their personal history and a few more were still being written; if the volume of such writings could be increased, particularly by those still in Tibet, that would be a good thing. Because of the impossibility of publishing and publicizing them inside Tibet, such writings could be brought out and published here in exile.

Hearing this advice, I made up my mind, because of my recurrent thoughts of writing as well as the opportunity of having arrived in a free country, to put down the story of how I lost my youth to suffering, an unadulterated and untiring account of what I heard and saw for myself, whatever I knew or could remember.

MEMORIES OF LIFE IN LHASA UNDER CHINESE RULE

CHAPTER 1

The Story of My Family

OUR HOUSEHOLD IS known as Gyatso Tashi, and was so named after the builder of our family house, in the Banak-shöl area of Lhasa. Our forebears were farmers from Nyémo district who settled in Lhasa after two successive family members served as officials in the palace bursary (*rTse phyag las khung*) of the Ganden Po-trang government. One of them, Sonam Rabten-la, married Tsewang Sangmo, daughter of the Lhasa resident Ba-pa Changdzö-la, and they had one son and one daughter. Their son, Tubten Changchup, the elder of the two, became a novice monk in the Tsangpa Khen-chen's residence in Drépung monastery's Loséling college, and later entered government service as a monk-official (*rTse drung*). Their daughter, Pema Drölkar, was my mother. Following social convention, my father, Changchup Lo-dro of Lhasa Gyéché-ling, joined the household as her husband (*Mag pa*). His father came from the Lha-khang-teng family from Rinchen-gang in Tromo, and had joined Lhasa Gyéché-ling through marriage (*Mag pa*). He served as a clerk (*Jo lags*) in the government Labrang Bursary (*Bla phyag las khung*), and passed away while on the annual grain procurement mission to Tingkyé. My grandfather Sonam Rabten-la retired at the age of sixty after an exemplary career in the palace bursary and took full monastic vows, dedicating the rest of his life to religion.

My father, Changchup Lo-dro, was duly appointed in his stead to the bursary, where he served as a clerk. He worked diligently in recognition of the government's kindness, and was the *Jo-la* selected to supervise the mission organized every four years to visit Nepal and make offerings to the three great *stupa*s there, offer religious objects to the Nepalese king, and procure official supplies such as rice (*Bal yul rten bzhengs*). He fulfilled this task on two successive occasions. Later on, in the earth mouse year 1948,

Panorama of Lhasa in 1942, with the Potala Palace at the upper left, by Demo Rinpoche Tendzin Gyatso. *After Wangchuk Dorje 2005.*

when he was forty-two, he was appointed government trade officer in west Tibet, but tragically, he came down with a fever and did not survive.

My eldest brother, Jampa Tsultrim, was serving as a palace steward (*rTse mgron*) at the time of the 1959 uprising against the unacceptable subjection of the Tibetan people by the Red Chinese invaders. He was arrested at the Summer Palace (*Nor bu gling ka*) and subjected to twenty years of torture and imprisonment. After his release, he worked in the research department at the TAR teacher training college, and in 1983 he traveled to India to seek an audience with His Holiness the Dalai Lama and took up employment in His Holiness's private office. The next eldest, my sister Losang Chönyi, a nun, was imprisoned for three years by the Chinese and later went to settle in India, together with my two younger nun sisters and younger brother Jampun. My elder sister Yangchen Drölkar, younger sister Tendröl, and younger brother Nga-nam have remained in Lhasa. My elder brother Yéshé Khédrup was a monk-scholar at Drépung at the time of the uprising. He escaped to India, where he worked for the exile government teacher recruitment program and the Mussoorie school, before requesting leave to join the Mongolian Géshé Wangyel-la in New Jersey in America, where he now works for the [Voice of America] Tibetan-language broadcasting service.

My mother, Pema Drölkar, dedicated herself to the service of others, had great faith in the Three Jewels [of Buddhist refuge], and always strove

to be virtuous. In 1959, when the popular uprising broke out, she joined the Womens' Association when it was first established at Shöl (below the Potala). She participated in the demonstrations and was one of the association's delegates to the parliament (*gZhung dmangs tshogs 'dus*), and one of the delegates sent to plead the truth of Tibet's case with the resident Indian trade representative, the Nepalese and Bhutanese representatives, and leaders of the Muslim community. Following the violent suppression of the uprising by the Chinese authorities, they summoned my mother, while she was severely ill, to the Tsémön-ling Reeducation Center that they had set up for the systematic investigation and interrogation of participants in the uprising. Only when her illness worsened was she permitted to return home, and even as she approached death, Chinese officials repeatedly came to search the house and harangue us, saying that her imprisonment could not be delayed further. But before long, later the same year, she passed away. This was our kind mother, a courageous and unselfish patriot who had loved and cared for us so tenderly, and to be separated from her by imprisonment while she was still with us, only to be separated by death straight after, oppressed us with tremendous sorrow, especially as we never had the opportunity to commemorate everything she had done for us. I continually pray and beseech Arya Lokesvara never to forsake her throughout all her future lives, in memory of her great kindness and exemplary conduct.

The Gyatso Tashi family house in Lhasa, 1998. *Photo by Andre Alexander*

My mother's elder brother, my uncle Tubten Changchup-la, studied at the Tarpo-ling primary school before becoming a monk at Drépung, where he voluntarily and earnestly continued his studies. His father, Sonam Rabten-la, performed a divination (*Pra phab*) to discover whether he would complete his academic studies, and the response came clearly expressed in a four-line stanza. I was not able to discover the first two lines, but the last two said: "Despite aspirations for the religious life, external factors will cause obstacles / To perform service beneath the golden throne is excellent!"

To give a brief account of his service in the Tibetan Ganden Po-trang government: his father was sent to India several times to procure supplies on behalf of the great Thirteenth Dalai Lama, which he did well, and the Dalai Lama showed His pleasure at this by asking about his son. Later, after he had returned from another supply mission to India, they were suddenly notified that Tubten Changchup, then aged eighteen, had been appointed as a monk-official to the palace secretariat (*Yig tshang las khung*). While serving there, he worked on the collection of pastoral taxes at Uyuk Lingkar, served as sacristan of the Eleventh Dalai Lama's (*Phan bde 'od 'bar*) reliquary *stupa* in the Potala, and assisted in the construction of the Thirteenth Dalai Lama's reliquary *stupa* (*dGe legs 'dod 'jo*). He was an estate manager in the Ön valley, was a librarian, and accompanied the

Khendrung Tubten Changchup. *Photo taken in the mid-1940s when he was serving as governor of Lho-ka.*

former Purbu-chok incarnation on a mission to the northern territories to identify candidates for the recognition of the Fourteenth Dalai Lama. He served as a steward of the fifth rank under the Taktra regent, and when the fourth-rank senior monk-official (*mKhan chung*) was promoted to governor of Lho-ka province (*lHo spyi*), he managed the ongoing office work for the next five years. Then he worked for a short time in the foreign ministry, and took charge of the office that organized special government-sponsored *pujas* (*Zhabs 'phar*) for a few years. Then he was appointed state monastic representative (*mKhan nang*) in Nakchu, as counterpart of the fourth-rank [lay] official Mönkyi-lingpa, and again as governor of the northern provinces (*Byang spyi*) for three years. During that time, the new Preparatory Committee for the Tibet Autonomous Region (PCART) was set up and established an Animal Husbandry Bureau (in replacement of the former office) of which he took charge. In 1957 he was appointed chief secretary of the palace secretariat (*mKhan drung*), and he continued his duties right up until the [1959] uprising, not only as an official who benefited both state and society while ascending the various levels of the bureaucracy but also as a *bhikshu* who was an indefatigable religious practitioner. He guided us with loving kindness and skillfully trained us with exceptional generosity.

Lhasa 1979: the author's three nun sisters, from left to right: Losang Chödzom, Losang Chönyi, Losang Dékyong. In the back row: sister-in-law Lochö Doyontsang holding nephew Tendzin Jikmé, younger sister Tendzin Drölkar. *Author's collection*

At the time of the 1959 uprising, he was among the elected deputies to the parliament, and it was he who took charge of fulfilling a request written by the Dalai Lama when departing the Norbu Lingka to rescue as many sacred images as possible from all over the palace, and he continued in his efforts even during the artillery bombardment. After the Chinese had forcibly suppressed the uprising, he was arrested at the Norbu Lingka and imprisoned at the Chinese military headquarters. After a series of interrogations, they suspended their decision on his case and kept him in leg irons for a long period for not showing the required attitude during questioning. In 1963 he was transferred to Drapchi prison, became very sick, became

Losang Dékyong, Losang Chödzom, and Losang Chönyi in Dharamsala, India, 1985.
Author's collection

worse after incorrect medical treatment, and died later that year. It is one
of my greatest misfortunes that I was unable to meet this immeasurably
kind teacher again before his death. However, one can see that even if he
had lived a few more years, his suffering would only have intensified under
the conditions of heightened cruelty, torture, and enslavement that were to
come, and I console myself with the thought that during his lifetime he not
only pursued a blameless career in government service but also encountered the Dalai Lama and many other high lamas, as well as perfecting his
own religious practice, and with the certainty that he will reap the karmic
rewards of his virtuous conduct.

My mother's elder stepbrother Jampel Khétsun-la, the former Kalachakra teacher (*Dus 'khor slob zur*) of Namgyel Dra-tsang college, was
taken to the Tsukla-khang temple after the suppression of the uprising to
join the group that the Chinese called the "Buddhist Association," who
were obliged to attend frequent "study" sessions on Chinese government
policy. When they were told to recognize the outrageous claim that Tibet
is an inseparable part of China, he told them openly that since relations

between the two countries were like the relations between lama and bene-factor (*mChod yon*), Tibet could not be incorporated by China in this way, and spoke about history, for which he was criticized and viciously denounced. Not long after, at the start of the so-called Cultural Revolution, he was sent to Drépung monastery, which was like the number two prison, where the conditions of his detention were such that even when he became sick his relatives were not permitted to visit him, and that is where he passed away.

CHAPTER 2

My Childhood

I WAS BORN in the iron snake year 1941. In the earth rat year 1948, when I was eight, my elder brother Yéshé Khédrup and I were sent to the Nyarong-shak school, and we joined the Loséling college of Drépung monastery not long after. At that time, our grandfather Sonam Rabten had retired from government service and taken monastic vows, and he took a special interest in the physical and mental development of his grandsons. Before we were sent to school, he had taught us to read and write the alphabet, and he took full responsibility for overseeing our schoolwork. I clearly remember Grandfather coming on our first day of school to discuss our education with the headmaster.

The headmaster at the Nyarong-shak school was a well-known doctor of Tibetan medicine, and his name, Lhundrup Peljor, was respectfully prefaced in our schoolbooks with the title "Master of the Healing Science" (*'Tsho byed rig 'dzin*). Nyarong-shak was among the best-known private schools in the country in those days, and there were around two hundred students at the time I started. It was run along progressive lines: the students were divided into four classes, although there were no separate classrooms, led by four inspectors with one assistant each and two supervisors, and they ensured that school discipline and class work did not suffer in the headmaster's absence. As well as drills in literacy, our school exercises included the explanation of many different types of official documents. As for the timetable, we had to reach school at dawn, summer and winter, and begin by melodiously chanting the "Hundred deities of Tushita" (*dGa' ldan lha brgya ma*), the Manjusri (*Gang blo ma*), or Tara prayers from our prayer books. We also had to recite the spelling and arithmetic tables [we had memorized]. After a brief reading practice, once the sun had risen, we went inside for morning tea. Then, apart from the midday recess, we spent the whole day learning to write, until school finished at sunset. There was also a group of students learning Tibetan medicine, and they spent their time memorizing medical treatises and learning about medical practice.

This type of school suited the needs of the society at that time, and drew its students from all social strata. In the school register, the students were classified according to family background in three divisions, which were seated slightly differently. There was no set fee to be paid as a condition of attending the school, and students paid different rates according to their means. Thus, when children from the wealthy noble families joined the school, they would make abundant offerings to the headmaster; most children would present him with a gift of rice and tea, or money; and those from deprived backgrounds would offer a simple greeting scarf (*Kha btags*) rather than come empty-handed, but this was sufficient for them to be accepted. Although those who could not pay their dues (*Zhugs ja*) may have been cursed for it by their schoolfellows, the school gave exactly the same instruction to all students, regardless of the offerings they had made. So it was that if a child from a noble family was studying in the same class as a child of his family's servants, and the servant child got better marks on the twice-monthly tests, school tradition required the servant child to give the son of his master a rap on the knuckles with a cane.

In the Chinese Communist propaganda distributed both internally and externally, it is forcefully stated that formerly only the Tibetan aristocracy had the opportunity of a formal education and that this was completely denied the ordinary people. Some foreigners have been misled by this without checking the facts for themselves and the allegation has been repeated in some foreign publications, and although the younger generation of Tibetans do not necessarily believe it, the fact that some foreigner has said so makes them doubtful, and if they lack determination to seek the truth, they do not bother to question those of us with direct experience of Tibetan society at that time about what it was really like.

In 1949, after I had been at school for two years, the Communists seized power in China and the news gradually spread that they had started to invade Tibet. The government announced measures for military conscription to supplement the existing garrison, and each division sent group after group of soldiers for the defense of the northeast (*mDo smad*), but before long the Communist troops reached Chamdo in the east (*mDo stod*). Ngapö (Ngawang Jikmé), the Eastern Commissioner (*mDo spyi*), set fire to the

Chamdo armory [to prevent the Chinese acquiring the weapons, and fled] but was arrested not far away and taken prisoner.

As these terrible reports came in quick succession, we children, who had no idea [of the political situation], were terrified. It was during this time of fear that many Lhasa people made their way to the Potala palace over the course of a few days during the eleventh month of the iron tiger year [1950] to greet the Dalai Lama. One day Yéshé Khédrup and I decided to do the same, but when we reached the [Phun tshogs 'du lam] gate of the palace, a crowd of people was coming out and we learned from them that His Holiness and the most important members of His entourage had departed the previous day. We greatly regretted not having been able to come a few days earlier. Once His Holiness had departed, the families of about three quarters of the two hundred students at our school withdrew their children. Some sought refuge in India, but most returned to their estates in the countryside. Our family had no place of refuge outside Lhasa and we stayed with the remainder of fifty or so students, supposedly continuing our studies, but given the dreadful situation the Tibetan population was facing, our school maintained the appearance of functioning but not the teaching and discipline we were used to.

After a few months, when the news came of the completion of the "Seventeen-Point Agreement on peaceful liberation" between Tibet and China and of His Holiness's return to the capital from Tromo, the number of students increased again. At that time, there was a lot of talk about a group of Communists who had come by sea, traveled through India, and were about to reach Lhasa. I had never seen a Communist and didn't know how to recognize one. Before that, people used to talk about how the Red Army faced such difficulties during the Long March that they were forced to eat their leather belts and shoe soles, and not knowing how to understand this, we imagined that those who ate leather belts and soles must be fearsome, evil spirits. So with a mixture of curiosity and fear, I went out on the day they were due to arrive and waited to see them. When they arrived at about four o'clock in the afternoon, accompanied by an escort of twenty-five Tibetan soldiers (lDing khag gcig) and two representatives of the Tibetan government [one monk and one layman], I saw the three Chinese leaders dressed, quite contrary to my expectations, in clean, light blue uniforms, with flower garlands draped around their necks, riding on horseback and smiling and waving to the crowd of onlookers.

On that occasion, arrangements were made for them to stay at the Wongshing Tri-mön house in Lhasa. The most senior of those three Chinese leaders was the central government's resident representative in Tibet, Zhang Jinwu, and he was accompanied by his colleague Alo Bu-zhang and a translator. As soon as they arrived at the accommodation provided by the Tibetan government, even before removing their flower garlands, they threw sweets and other little gifts out the windows of the house to the children looking in, and a great number of children then gathered under their windows. In retrospect, it seems to me that the bribery they used to disguise their occupation started then and there.

His Holiness returned to Lhasa from Tromo, and before long the first of the invading troops, a large group from the advance guard of the 18th Army led by Wang Qimei, arrived. For a few days before entering the city, they pitched their tents near the river on its east side, between Kumbum-tang and Trung-lha, and many of my school friends went to have a look at them. When I also went to look at the expeditionary force, I saw one soldier on guard within shouting distance of the tents, wearing a padded cotton uniform and large goggles strapped to his helmet and holding a rifle fitted with a bayonet, as if on high alert. He had rounds of bullets, a hand grenade, and a water bottle fastened to his waist and wore a thin cotton ration bag over his shoulder. It was disturbing just to look at his darkened face, cracked and wrinkled by hardship and sunburn, and unlike the false impression given by the three Chinese leaders, his expression was a harsh one of unfeigned malice, and there was no question of us schoolchildren being allowed any closer to the camp. A few days later, the soldiers from that camp entered Lhasa in procession, carrying brightly colored flags and large portraits of Mao Zedong, Zhu De, Liu Shaoqi, and Zhou Enlai, playing an anthem called "The Three Great Disciplines and the Eight Responsibilities." For us children it was a great spectacle, but the elders couldn't stop exclaiming, "Now we have really seen the sign of impending disaster!"

A few months later, the 18th Army, led by General Zhang Guohua and Political Commissar Tang Guansan, arrived in Lhasa. That day, a temporary stage was set up in the fields to the east of the city for a ceremonial welcome by the cabinet ministers in the government. This event was like a big meeting where the Chinese leaders made speeches, and afterward the soldiers marched around the Lhasa Parkor street carrying the pictures of the four leaders and multicolored flags and playing drums and cymbals, then proceeded to the new army headquarters, the Yamen army camp, and other places where accommodations had been prepared for them. Not long after that, the advance cavalry and camel brigades of the army advancing through Qinghai under Fan Ming arrived, and in addition a constant stream of Chinese soldiers kept coming, visibly in daylight or surreptitiously by night, until within the space of a year Lhasa was completely filled with Chinese, both military and civilian, and the price of commodities in the market multiplied, and ordinary householders had nothing but curses for them.

Then, in typical colonialist fashion, and in order to appease Tibetan sentiment, the Chinese established a "People's Hospital" at Pomsur-nang in the Lubu area and a primary school at the former Séshim house. They recruited children from all social classes, did not require fees, and even offered a monthly allowance of ten white *dayuan* [Chinese silver coins]. Students from poor families were provided with summer and winter clothing and their families given income support, and in this crude way the Chinese sought to win people's loyalty through financial largesse. There was a vulgar saying that "The Chinese Communists are our kind parents / Their silver coins fall like rain," and so many families withdrew their children from the Nyarong-shak school and sent them to the Séshim primary school instead that the number of pupils was halved. In the course of their attempts to recruit the remainder, the Chinese invited the private Tibetan schools to join a picnic to be held on the first of June, which they had designated "Children's Day." That day, after a short speech by the director of the Chinese primary school, a group of pupils gave a performance of a play they had been rehearsing. We Tibetan schoolchildren were given big bags of sweets and cookies, provided with balls and skipping ropes and other toys, and encouraged to play whatever games we liked; they used many such enticements to overwhelm us, as well as instructing the Chinese school pupils to pass on their propaganda about the school organization and the different kinds of classes they attended when they spoke with us and to encourage us to transfer.

Of course, under such influence I also wanted to attend the Chinese school, but our family was extremely stubborn, and not only was there no chance of our being sent there, due to resentment against the activities of the Chinese, we had no chance to even express our wish to go. In Tibetan society at that time, those who did attend were disparaged as "fed students" (*lTogs gla'i slob grva ba*). So we continued attending our private Tibetan school, but due to numerous current influences the program there declined, and in 1952 my elder brother and I withdrew altogether and continued our studies at home.

At that time, as the Chinese were consolidating their presence, they gathered together a group of youths and set up another school in Trungchi Lingka, called the Social School (*sPyi tshogs slob grva*), for those who were above the age limit to attend middle school. Since the parents of some of the students also attended, Lhasa people sarcastically called it "the parents' school." Likewise, they sent as many Tibetan students as possible to study in China at the Beijing Nationalities College, Southwest Nationalities College, and [other institutions]. Just like the proverb about growing horns on one's head that eventually put out one's eyes, many of them were returned to Tibet at the time of the imposition of Democratic Reform in 1959 to become accomplices in the urgent task of crushing Tibetan resistance.

Thus, in those years the Chinese bribed the best-off with gifts and the worst-off with assistance, and beguiled the youth with shows, picnics, and parties and the children with cookies, candies, and toys. In particular, they began to form associations of leading figures or personalities from each social class who were taken to China on tours arranged every year to witness the progress made there since "Liberation" in "building a new motherland." They were shown the best factories and the nicest places, taken to banquets, picnics, and parties, and invited to watch dance and theater performances and films.

At the same time, to split up the territory under the authority of the Ganden Po-trang government, which had ruled the whole country under successive Dalai Lamas, and exploit historical feuds to set the Tibetans in internal conflict, the two provinces of Ü and Tsang were divided, each with its own local government. Similarly, there was a local government authority at Chamdo in Kham (*mDo stod*), called the Chamdo Liberation Committee. It controlled the area previously under the nominal authority of the Eastern Commissioner of the Tibetan government, consisting of ten districts (*rDzong*). [In fact,] except for one or two, most of them had to be "discounted" [as not governable], and even those remaining one or two not only paid no tax whatsoever to the Tibetan government but also were given to rebelling against its representatives whenever the opportunity arose. Some weak-hearted government officials used to resign from service when they were appointed to those districts, rather than have to go there.

In Lhasa, apart from the Chinese army headquarters and the office of the Communist Party Tibet Work Committee, the most visible public institutions were the hospital, school, supply office and shop, bank, and post office and, most importantly, what was officially known as the United Front Bureau, which was actually the Public [Affairs] Bureau (*Phyi tshogs pu'u*), the office for spies and informers. The office allocated them to work within particular social classes, and according to some former United Front Bureau officials, those who lavished the most money on cultivating their links in Tibetan society were considered the most capable and praiseworthy.

One of the principal aims of the Chinese in this period was the construction of the Sichuan-Tibet highway, and since their position depended on it, they spent no end of their white *dayuan* to achieve it.

In the wood horse year 1954, news spread of the invitation of His Holiness to attend the inauguration of the Chinese National People's Congress. Tibetans in general regarded the idea of His Holiness going to China as a serious threat to His well-being and that of the state, and it caused them unbearable concern. At that time, it became the main subject of conversation, and the government functionaries had a special meeting to discuss whether the invitation should be accepted or not. After a debate, two irreconcilable viewpoints emerged: one emphasized the advantages of accepting, and the other asserted that this would entail serious harm not only to His Holiness's well-being but also to His government, and called for a refusal. My uncle was serving as Northern Commissioner, but he was in Lhasa at the time of that meeting, where he forcefully expressed the view that His Holiness should not go to China; I clearly remember once hearing his account of it at home.

Anyway, finally His Holiness agreed to go, and on the day of His departure, May 11, 1954, I went to offer farewell greetings at the Trung-lha coracle ferry outside Lhasa. The Lhasa Kyi-chu river, swollen by the spring rains, was a dark, murky color, churned by crashing waves, and as His Holiness climbed into one of two coracles lashed together, I felt an inconsolable sorrow. The people lining the [man-made] river embankments let out an anguished wail, and until He reached the Lha-dong Shenka ferry dock on the far shore, they made prostrations in His direction. I waited on the bank until He left Lha-dong Shenka, and as I went home with a resoundingly empty feeling, all the other people walking away had gloomy expressions on their faces and hung their heads, as if they had just witnessed a calamity. In the hope that His Holiness would one day return to His capital, but also to attract publicity, His Tibetan subjects, both monastics and laypeople, submitted petitions that His Holiness should kindly return swiftly to the religious sanctuary of the land of snows, to His Holiness and the Chinese government, one after the other, as well as sending emissaries. Since ensuring His Holiness's speedy return was the most urgent matter facing the Tibetan people, there was a great deal of concern, and that year His absence was felt more deeply than ever.

He returned to Lhasa on May 11 in the wood sheep year 1955, completing the final stretch from Tsé Kungtang in a mounted procession, and from the time it set out in the morning until it reached the Norbu Lingka summer palace there was a very heavy rainfall. Some said this indicated the joy of the Tibetan gods, *nagas*, and territorial spirits, but others worried that it threatened instability. Either way, although everyone, officials, monks, and laypeople, had been requested to turn out in their best clothes, all one could see was the reddish woolen cloth that everyone used to keep off the rain, which made the monks indistinguishable from the laity. That day, I clearly beheld His golden countenance sometime before He reached the [new] Lhasa bridge and felt boundless joy, for at that moment, nothing could have brought the Tibetan people greater happiness than His safe return.

That year, the monks of the Three Great Seats were each presented with ten *dayuan*, a molded clay figure (*Phyag tshva*) of Yamantaka, and a yellow rosary to mark His Holiness's safe return from China, and my uncle was appointed as the representative in charge of extending this distribution to the monastic communities of Tashi-lhunpo and Ganden Chökor-ling [in the Shang valley in Tsang]. There was provision for an assistant to accompany him, so he took my elder brother Jam-tsul, who had become an official in the palace secretariat by then, and I got to go along with them. We left Lhasa just at the beginning of autumn, when the weather is neither too hot nor too cold, and having plentiful provisions, we had a most pleasant journey. But passing through Gyantsé on our outward journey, we saw for ourselves the terrible damage done by the flood in that area the previous year, and since the bridges had not yet been repaired and the roads were in poor condition, we had to make our way through wild and trackless stretches of country. After reaching Shika-tsé and completing the distribution of gifts satisfactorily, we had an excellent tour of the sacred images in the monastery. On the way to Shang, we visited and made offerings at the Serdok-chen monastery founded by Shakya Chokden and at Wen-gön Ri-trö, the seat of Gyelwa Wensa-pa Losang Döndrup. Then, after crossing the Tsangpo river, we reached the Ganden Chökor-ling monastery in the Shang valley. We very successfully made similar offerings before the sacred images there, traveled on through the Lha-pu valley in upper Shang, then the Uyuk and Nyémo valleys, and returned to Lhasa by the end of autumn.

Not long after, the Chinese Deputy Prime Minister Chen Yi came to Lhasa for the inauguration of the PCART, the central institution of Chinese rule in Tibet, made up of prominent people drawn from the Tibetan government, the lamas, and Khampa representatives [people from the Kham region]. Since my uncle was still serving as Northern Commissioner [of the Tibetan government] at the time, he was given the title of Bureau Chief in

the Animal Husbandry Bureau of the PCART. When prefectural committees were being established all over China, he had to attend the ceremonial
inauguration of the Nakchu prefectural committee, and I went along. Just
as the ceremony was ending, a letter came with the news that His Holiness
had confirmed His intention to accept the invitation of the Mahabodhi Society of India to attend the celebrations for the 2,500th anniversary of the
Buddha's nirvana. It had also been announced by the government of India
that Buddhist pilgrims attending the celebrations could travel at half-price
on Indian railways, and it was said that a great many Tibetans intended to
go. My own kind parents, three elder nun sisters, and two younger sisters
were among them, and as my uncle was also keen to go, he returned to
Lhasa shortly after receiving that letter. My parents and sisters completed
all the arrangements, but my uncle was delayed for quite some time waiting
for leave from the government and could not come with us.

Although our rights had been so reduced by that time that the Chinese
authorities required Tibetans traveling to India to apply for a reentry permit
before leaving, most Tibetans innocently assumed that previous conditions
would continue to prevail, and although the eight members of our family
could have left for India permanently, they stuck to the ostensible purpose
of making a pilgrimage to holy places and then returning, and never considered the idea of leaving Tibet in view of the overall situation. Taking only
the necessary funds and provisions for the journey, we left Lhasa during
the ninth lunar month in a Chinese truck, and traveled through Shika-tsé,
Gyantsé, Pa-ri, and Tromo, down to Kalimpong. After resting there for a
few days, we hired a translator and went on a tour of the holy places, returning to Kalimpong in the eleventh lunar month. We spent another few weeks
of leisure there, and returned to Tibet in the twelfth month.

That trip was one of the most important and valuable experiences in my
life. However, the first Tibetan resistance group seems to have been established in Kalimpong at that time, and as many of its members came to visit
my uncle during his stay there and the Chinese later came to know about it,
that issue caused me the worst problems of all during my time in prison, as
will be seen. In any case, our pilgrimage party consisted of ten people, the
eight of us and two servants, and from the day we left Lhasa until our safe
return on the first day of the new Tibetan year, we suffered no setbacks or
losses whatsoever, met with no disagreeable situations, and neither lost nor
were robbed of any of our possessions.

His Holiness returned to Lhasa from India (*Arya-bhumi*) not long after
that, and gave teachings at the Norbu Lingka on the condensed exposition

of the "Gradual Path," followed by the [public] Kalachakra initiation requested by Do-mépa Jinpa Gyatso, all of which I received.

At that time, the Chinese tried occasionally to give the impression that they respected Tibetan self-rule or that they had only come to give assistance, and they announced that the Democratic Reform that had already been launched in the rest of the country could be postponed in central Tibet for another six, or even ten or fifteen years, that if the Tibetan upper class were against it, the reforms should wait; and they cut back the number of officials at the PCART and other offices. However, in the east of the country, where Democratic Reform had been introduced, they first announced the confiscation of weapons from the people, then imposed a tax on the monasteries, demanding large amounts of money and taking the monasteries' valuables in payment, and many other such previously unheard-of actions. Even worse, they organized groups of vagrants and work-shy beggars to make false accusations against the law-abiding majority of the religious and lay communities and subject them to endless "struggle" and torture. Unable to bear the vicious behavior of the Chinese, the monasteries rebelled, for which many of them were entirely destroyed by artillery or aerial bombardment. At that point, the people gave up on the idea [of coexistence] altogether, formed a guerrilla organization, and withdrew to the mountains and wilderness areas, and all over Kham (mDo stod) and Amdo (mDo smad) there was an upsurge of guerrilla attacks on the Chinese army.

Now that their military forces in Ü-tsang were in a state of readiness, the Chinese stepped up their oppression. They withdrew the currency notes and postage stamps guaranteed by the Tibetan government, and openly criticized and repudiated the Buddhist religion and lamas and monks in the *Red Flag* and some other periodicals and newspapers. They issued a warning to eastern Tibetans living in Ü-tsang and Chinese residents with independent livelihood that unless they returned to their native areas within a specified period, they would be arrested. The Chinese entrepreneurs were arrested suddenly and sent back to China with nothing but the clothes on their backs, and the easterners were subjected to official registration, harassment, and sudden arrest, so that they were driven to desperation. [From their point of view,] it was indisputable that Tibet was historically an independent nation, and the Chinese had invaded us using the sheer force at their disposal to maximum effect, just as bigger insects eat up smaller ones, and while there was no way they could be repulsed, the eastern Tibetans could no longer stand their abusive treatment. Thus, under the leadership of Li-tang A-druk Gönpo Tashi, then resident in Lhasa, they established the

"Four Rivers and Six Ranges" Volunteer Army in Defense of Religion, with headquarters at Drigu Dzong in Lho-ka, and lit the flame of a sporadic war of resistance [in central Tibet].

Although the status of our own government had by then been reduced to that of a local authority, its officials had retained their titles, and the work of the various government departments as well as provincial representatives carried on. It was just as the Chinese had demanded a reduction of the Tibetan government personnel serving in the newly constituted PCART that my turn came to be nominated for the annual procedure of appointing new functionaries. When those arrangements were made, at the time of the Ngamchö (*lNga mchod*) festival in the fire bird year (1957), there was an announcement directing me to attend the entrance examination for the palace secretariat. Those who had been so notified had to write their examination paper under the direct supervision of the [*Yig tshang gnyer pa, Yig tshags dbu mdzad ri mo ba*, and a couple of other] senior secretariat staff, and we were instructed not to write our names or family background on the paper. These measures had been adopted because there was talk that some recent entrants had submitted false exam papers and others had had their exam results overlooked after paying private visits to the secretariat officials.

I passed the exam and, as specified in the notification, went at once to the office, where the approval form was signed and I was admitted to the Ngamchö inaugural ceremony. Once I started working in the secretariat office, my main task was copying documents. Two junior monk officials called "incense bearers" were required on ceremonial occasions to stand near His Holiness holding a censer, and not long after my arrival, when the previous ones were moved elsewhere, another boy and I were appointed to replace them. Although that seemed like a dull formality, it was actually the most fortunate experience of my life, since my appointment coincided with the ceremony at which His Holiness the Dalai Lama demonstrated mastery of five volumes of canonical scripture before the monastic assembly (*Grva skor dam bca' chen mo*). This auspicious ceremony occurs only once in the Dalai Lama's career, and in the case of this fourteenth incarnation, it took place at a time of disquiet, when Tibet's Buddhist polity was in dire straits, and as Tibet's human and divine beings made desperate appeals to His infinite compassion as the only one capable of assuming the responsibility of head of state. In spite of the extreme and unremitting difficulties, He began to exercise His skill in wisdom and compassion with the utmost kindness by taking on the task of assuring the immediate and ultimate well-being of the country out of compassion for His subjects. At the same time, He had achieved mastery over the Buddhist canonical scriptures of India and Tibet through great efforts and constant, dutiful study with His two tutors, and at the series of ceremonies at which He demonstrated His achievement of having crossed the ocean of Buddhist and non-Buddhist doctrines, in front of the monks of Séra, Drépung, and Ganden, and at Gémpel Ri-trö, Gémpel Ü-tsé, Pabong-ka, Tsé Kungtang, and so on, I too experienced the nectar of His presence, and to have had such wonderfully good fortune can only be the result of my having accumulated more than a little merit in previous lives.

The situation in Tibet by that time was critical. The resistance army (*Chu bzhi sgang drug*) had grown with the influx of some novices and non-scholastic monks from the great monasteries, as well as ordinary people of Ü-tsang and soldiers in the Tibetan army who brought their government-issued weapons with them. They launched attacks on the Chinese troops at Gongkar, Tsétang, and Dra-nang in Lho-ka and at Yangpa-chen, Mar-kyang, Takdru-ka, and many other places, and it was said that five Chinese army divisions had been dispatched against them. In particular, the resis-tance troops managed to carry off a cache of firearms from a government weapons depot at Shang Ganden Chökor-ling monastery, and when the Chinese military found out, they pursued them and fought a terrible battle with them in the Nyémo area, with heavy losses on both sides. After that, the Chinese prepared to enforce their control of the whole country, and in the city of Lhasa they set up a large number of fortified military posts and defenses at street intersections.

At the same time they leveled exaggerated accusations against the Ti-betan cabinet ministers that they not only had ties to but also were the prin-cipal sponsors and inciters of the rebel army. They repeatedly summoned all the senior ministers to the Chinese army camp in order to harangue them, demanding that if there were really no connection between the gov-ernment and the rebels, then the government should send its own troops to put down the rebellion. While the chief government officers were un-able to implement the Chinese demand, they were concerned that unless they found a way to calm the situation it would become polarized, and they summoned all the government representatives, monk and lay officials, and representatives of the three great monasteries to a plenary meeting of the National Assembly at the Norbu Lingka to discuss immediate measures for the pacification of the revolt. They made a detailed presentation to the as-sembly of the accusations made by the Chinese against the cabinet, the an-nouncements that had been issued, and the requests made to the cabinet by the rebels and the replies it had given, and opened a discussion on "ways of setting the central government's mind at rest and bringing the revolt under control." The debate sessions were separated according to official rank, and at the end of the discussions when spokesmen for each division reported their conclusions, those with high rank (such as *Dza sag* and *The'i ji*) called for "prudence, stability, and control," while those of the fourth rank and lower called for unified opposition to the Chinese. The army officers' and lay officials' delegates made some particularly incisive contributions, and I can remember the military delegate (*dMag sgar gyi ru brgya*) Késang Dramdul, who is now a veteran official of the exile government, declaring: "The government has been providing for and promoting our Tibetan army up to now for a reason, and if this milk-fed baby conch is of no use when hurled into the jaws of the threatening sea monster, then it serves no purpose at all. We soldiers are ready to fight whenever the government gives the order, and we will give our lives in defense of the Buddhist polity." The cabinet secretary Késang-la, the lay officials' delegate, suggested, "His Holiness can temporarily reside in Europe or some such place, while we recruit every able-bodied Tibetan to fight for our freedom." [These speakers] proposed only the use of force to drive back the Chinese, in total opposition to the conclusions reached by the highest officials.

At that point, many ordinary people like me felt that since Tibet was unquestionably an independent country with a rich national history, we were sure to receive support from the international community, and especially that India would help us through both diplomatic and military means. We also heard a lot of rumors and half-truths about the heavy losses being inflicted on the Chinese army by the (*Chu bzhi sgang drug*) guerrilla fighters and had a high degree of confidence in these reports. Anyway, we quite unjustifiably reckoned that our own strength supplemented by external assistance would suffice. We wondered why the cabinet ministers found it so necessary to make face-saving gestures to China, but in reality Tibet had drifted apart even from India, a neighboring country with whom we had a thousand years of cultural and religious ties, not to mention other states, as can be seen from careful examination of the present Dalai Lama's autobiography. There is no doubt that if the leading figures in the government had openly declared the actual state of internal and external affairs at that time, the people's confidence would have been shattered and the Chinese could have swallowed up Tibet at an even quicker pace. Moreover, His Holiness spared no effort in the difficult task of impressing on the principal [Tibetan] leaders that the idiotic strategy of relying on armed force was tantamount to suicide, and it seems to me that it was His ability to follow a policy of avoiding both extremes that inspired the present [favorable] international view of the Tibet issue.

Of course, there were Chinese spies at every level of society at the time, but I particularly recall how during the session of the assembly that produced the two opposing statements, the statement by the monk officials was actually stolen from the meeting while it was in progress. That statement was a sizeable scroll of Tibetan paper, not like the easy-to-handle documents we have today, so the audacity of those spies who carried it off from the very center of the meeting must have been great indeed. Anyway, as soon as the monk officials discovered the theft they became very indignant, although even before any investigations were made, there could have been no doubt that the statement, which was a record of the frank views expressed at the meeting, had fallen into enemy hands. Whether as a deliberate policy of the Volunteer Defense Army in Lho-ka or merely as a boast, another statement was sent to the Chinese, saying that unless the invaders retreated to their own country at once, every single one that remained would be wiped out. Because of that, the Chinese military and civilian installations in Lhasa were put on a state of alert, and many people reported seeing troop reinforcements, armored vehicles, and a lot of other military hardware arriving along the road from Qinghai.

Then, following the intensification of Chinese suppression in Gyéku-do and Nangchen in the east, large numbers of those people left their homeland and arrived in Lhasa as refugees, where they found some relief, lodging secretly with whichever relatives or fellow countrymen would take them in. Gradually, as many of these people came to stay in Lhasa, where they planned on watching the latest developments, the Chinese concentrated on watching their movements, and if there was even slight cause for suspicion, they would wait until the suspect left town on a journey and then follow him and secretly arrest him. One time when Samten-la of Tréhor Chakdzö-tsang and Chimé Dorjé of Tréhor Gyanak-tsang went on a trading trip to India, Samten-la was suddenly arrested as they reached the nomad area of Mar-kyang, and disappeared. After making numerous inquiries with their various contacts, the family finally discovered that he was being held in the army headquarters prison. Similarly, the husband of the Gonjo Chösur-tsang family's daughter, a Chinese trader from Beijing who had lived in Lhasa for a long time, was secretly arrested on the road, on his way to the Siu-tang (Se'u thang) festival at Ganden monastery, and imprisoned at the army headquarters.

At the same time, a small number of contemptible, mercenary Tibetans, induced by the generous rewards offered secretly by the Chinese, carried out bandit robberies and all kinds of other crimes in the rural areas around Lhasa, posing as members of the Volunteer Defense Army. This succeeded in creating antagonism between ordinary Tibetan people and the rebel army, and many villagers living in scattered settlements suffered terrible violence. Although the Chinese were waiting for a convenient opportunity to crush the resistance, our government behaved so unobjectionably that it was not forthcoming that year. But in early 1959, during the Great Prayer festival, when His Holiness was due to take His final (*lHa rams pa*) examination before the monastic assembly in the Tsukla-khang temple, there was an unprecedentedly large congregation of people, and a high risk that trouble would break out in and around the city. Some time previously, there had been many stories of a Chinese dressed in civilian clothes taking explosives into the Potala palace, and after the Chinese made an enclosure of sandbags around the upper window and roof of the Kyi-tö house, a building they had occupied right in front of the Sungchö-ra courtyard [where the examination was to take place], turning it into a watchtower, the Tibetans were out of their minds with worry about threats to His Holiness. For His security, He was always accompanied by members of the "Bodyguard Regiment," reinforced by a hand-picked group from other regiments, and during the *Lha-rampa* examination ceremony a voluntary group of monk officials organized themselves to mingle with the general monastic assembly as incognito security assistants.

Thanks to the merciful blessings of the main participant, the ceremony went off without problems from start to finish. I had the great fortune to be serving as incense bearer in His Holiness's presence during the greater and lesser ceremonies of His examination. After their successful completion, His Holiness had also agreed to visit the three southern colleges (*mNga' Dvags rGyal gsum*), and as preparations for the journey were under way, I was provisionally selected to join the group of attendants who would travel with Him. We were waiting for the departure date to be fixed when there was a sudden turn in the course of events.

CHAPTER 3

The March 10th Uprising

ON THE MORNING of March 10, 1959, as we were about to attend the morning tea service for officials at the Norbu Lingka summer palace, one of our relatives, the monk official Ngawang Chöpel-la, came to our room [in the family house in Lhasa] to discuss an important matter with my uncle (then chief secretary) and elder brother (a palace steward). He had an easygoing manner and liked to joke, but that day his behavior was quite different: he seemed anxious, and even told me not to go empty-handed but to carry some kind of weapon. I asked him what had happened, but all he would say was, "We have to go quickly now. You will find out." Tension between Tibetans and Chinese was very high at the time, but since our neighborhood was peaceful as usual, I wondered if there had been some internal government disagreement. In that state of anticipation, as my brother and I rode our bicycles toward the Norbu Lingka, we came across a large group of people on the main road in front of the Tsukla-khang temple, also heading west. As we got closer, we saw that they carried greeting scarves and the older people among them were crying as if something terrible had happened. At the head of the crowd was the old white-haired [government] coracle supervisor (*Ko dpon gnyer pa*) Wangchuk, and as soon as he saw us he called out, "You gentlemen hurry on ahead, we will catch up with you as quickly as we can!" Both Ngawang Chöpel-la and Wangchuk clearly knew what was up, and Wangchuk assumed that we did too, but I felt even more bewildered. When we arrived in front of the Potala palace, we found another crowd of people in the same state heading for the Norbu Lingka. Their leader was Tamdrin, who worked in the palace storeroom. When we reached the main gate of the summer palace, there was no one to be seen except a few people from the neighborhood, but within a few moments the group led by Tamdrin arrived, followed by Wangchuk's group, and immediately they prostrated themselves as one in the direction of the summer palace, like a great tree bending in the wind, filling the air with their cry: "The wish-fulfilling jewel [His Holiness] is Tibet's only savior, don't let the nobles exchange Him for Chinese silver!"

I was with a group of other junior officials, discussing among ourselves what had brought on this disturbance, and I can still remember hearing Khenchung Tara-wa Do-ngak Tarchin of the Nangma-gang office explain that it was because the Chinese army headquarters had issued an unusual invitation on the thirtieth of the first Tibetan month (March 9) for His Holiness to attend a cultural show at their camp, with many outlandishly suspicious and previously unheard-of conditions, such as saying that they would take responsibility for His security and that He was not to be accompanied by His bodyguards. Meanwhile, the shouts of the crowd grew louder, and more and more people kept arriving from Lhasa to join them. I later heard that the marketplace and the shops had opened as usual that morning, until around ten o'clock ("Lhasa time," as it was then called) when people heard the rumor, there was a big commotion, and everyone closed up their shops and went to the summer palace. When I myself discovered the reason behind the disturbance, I was incredulous.

Thereupon, instead of proceeding to the morning tea service, we followed Tara-wa's instruction to attend to the situation by backing up the security personnel and offering whatever services were needed, and I stayed with those guarding the main entrance against both Chinese using trickery to take His Holiness, heart jewel of the Tibetans, into custody and members of the crowd entering the boundary wall of the Norbu Lingka and causing trouble. A group of us young officials together with the men from the bodyguard regiment held the main door firmly closed, and admitted only those who had good reason to enter the palace, once they had pushed their way through the crowd.

By eleven o'clock that morning there were around 10,000 people gathered in front of the main gate of the summer palace. At that point, the general (dMag spyi) and cabinet minister (bKa' blon) Samdrup Po-trang arrived, and seemed to be trying to stay out of sight, inside his car. Since he had the rank of vice commander in the army, he had a Chinese military bodyguard and a Chinese driver. The crowd threw stones at them, one of which hit Sam-po's head and knocked him unconscious, and he was immediately taken to the hospital run by the Indian mission. Therefore, when Ka-lön Surkhang arrived soon after, a couple of monk officials who had

Crowds outside the Norbu Lingka gates on March 10, 1959. *Department of Information and International Relations, Central Tibetan Administration, Dharamsala*

studied in China were sent out from the main gate to request him not to approach by vehicle. After they had explained the situation to Surkhang and spoken to his Chinese driver in Chinese, the minister proceeded on foot as we made way for him through the crowd up to the main gate. To have approached inside his vehicle like Sam-po would have been to put his life at risk, and as it was, the crowd filled the air with their desperate shouted appeals to the cabinet ministers: "Don't trade our lama for Chinese silver!" Surkhang was very contrite and kept saying "Excuse me" as he struggled to get through the main gate.

Then, when a small car belonging to the Tibetan government tried to leave from the main gate to go and pick up His Holiness's mother, the crowd suspected that His Holiness might be inside, pulled out the driver, who was a member of the bodyguard regiment, and searched it entirely, even lifting up the seats to check underneath, while others lay down in its path, saying they would die rather than allow it to leave. Eventually, the car couldn't go anywhere and was pushed back inside the gate without the driver. After that, having secured the door and retreated, we heard angry shouts of "Ki!" and "Kill him!" coming from outside the wall. We looked from the windows to either side of the main gate and saw the crowd beating a man to death with stones, clubs, and knives. At once, we opened the door slightly and went out, and when inquiries were made as to who the man was, we were told he was a Chinese spy. In fact, we could tell that it was Khen-chung Sonam Gyatso, elder brother of the Chamdo Pakpa-la Rinpoché, whom I myself had seen earlier that morning on his way to the tea service as usual. It seemed that he had gone back out [of the summer palace] shortly after and then returned on a bicycle, wearing lay clothes and a Chinese-style dust mask, and as he approached the gate, the crowd took him for a Chinese spy. Later it was widely supposed to have started just because an old woman said, "That man looks like a Chinese!" Anyway, when he was seized by the crowd they found that he was carrying a pistol, and because he also had a pale complexion like a Chinese and was wearing the dust mask, there is some doubt that he was targeted because of his real identity. Although he had quite strong links with the Chinese government, no one has mentioned any evidence or proof that he was actually a spy. It is possible that he too deplored the threat to His Holiness's well-being and was coming to His defense. Anyhow, we had a very immediate demonstration of the fact that if one gives even the slight appearance of belonging to the opposition at a time of such tense confrontation, when there is no chance of careful discrimination, one can certainly be killed. When I saw the corpse it was already beaten beyond recognition, but people continued to pelt it with stones in their unrequited anger, while the old people spat on it.

As the situation thus drastically worsened, the senior members of the government had no choice but to inform His Holiness, and following His order that the common people be told they had no business staging disturbances and should pacify the situation by returning to their homes at once, the cabinet ministers, chiefs of palace staff, chief secretaries, chamberlains, and officers of the bodyguard regiment came out to address the crowd from the parapet over the main gate. A delegation of about sixty representatives was then summoned inside the gate, where Ka-lön Surkhang told them that until that day the cabinet ministers had no knowledge of the invitation to the army camp differing from previous invitations and giving rise to suspicions, and that they had arrived at the Norbu Lingka as a matter of normal routine. He said that the common people were not to blame for instigating the situation, that His Holiness had decided not to accept the invitation, and that they themselves would go to the army headquarters to inform the Chinese of His decision. He then requested as diplomatically as he could that in view of His Holiness's command, the crowds gathered outside should call off their agitation at once and return to their homes; it was up to the representatives to convey this news to the people. As soon as he had finished, many of the delegates stood up and impatiently remonstrated on various issues. The most incisive speaker among them was a man in his forties with light-speckled hair like a Caucasian, called Shöl-pa Ta-tongwa. He began respectfully, pointing out that the Chinese authorities did not keep their word and going into some detail about how in the Amdo region of east Tibet in particular they had invited high lamas to banquets, shows, and so on and then kept them as hostages in order to prevent popular unrest. He concluded more defiantly by saying that His Holiness was the patron deity and life force of the land of Tibet, and from that day on not only was there no question of His accepting any invitation to the Chinese army camp, but the public should be informed about His every movement outside the palace and should establish safeguards. The cabinet ministers responded that the existing bodyguard regiment reinforced by other military personnel was sufficient, that additional safeguards instituted by the public would create unnecessary interference, and that the crowd should withdraw by all means. [The speaker] replied that the people had already made up their minds to assign a bodyguard of their own.

When the delegates were admitted at the main gate, they had not brought their weapons inside, and when we searched them, we put to one side the guns and knives we found on a few of them, which they reclaimed as they left. Then the ministers went to the army headquarters to report on what had taken place that day. The delegates allotted a piece of land for the accommodation of a people's bodyguard, and the crowd returned to Lhasa shouting, "Tibet is independent! Chinese quit Tibet!" At the main bottlenecks along the way, the foremen continued to address the procession until, after going around the Lhasa Parkor, they all dispersed and went home. Throughout this demonstration, they dragged the corpse of Pakpala's brother by a rope tied around its ankle, like a dead dog, and when it was over, they dumped it in a shed called the Om-khang, where the unclaimed bodies of dead prisoners were usually left. Later on, members of his family estate and Labrang recovered the body and cremated it at the mouth of the Nyang-tren valley near Lhasa. They made votive tablets (*Tshva tshva*) with the ashes and built a shrine (*Tshva khang*) to contain them, which I used to see when, later on as a prisoner, I was sent to work in that area. That day, the young junior officials present at the Norbu Lingka were hurriedly allotted security duties, but as I was given none, I went home. That was the 10th of March, which we now commemorate annually.

After that, although we had no particular duties, it was impossible to remain inactive, and I set off for the summer palace as usual next day, in the spirit of volunteering wherever needed. On the way there I found that the Chinese had set up barricades at strategic points along the main road, which were occupied by Chinese soldiers in combat uniform and at the ready to resist attack. Similarly on our side, the normal bodyguard contingent at the palace was reinforced by soldiers from other regiments, and by the volunteer security force of members of the public, who wore their own clothes, carried their own guns, whether rifles or pistols, and brought their own rations. Those government officials who were still in Lhasa as well as the people's representatives all came to the summer palace.

Once the morning tea service was over, they convened a session of the assembly at the *puja* hall (*Zhabs brtan lha khang*) in the Norbu Lingka grounds, presided over by the cabinet and chief secretaries, who reported on their discussions at the army camp the previous day, saying that these were continuing and emphasizing the need for stability meanwhile. But the people's representatives and the younger officials spoke at length about how Tibet was fundamentally an independent country with a rich history going back to the first king of the Yarlung dynasty (*gNya' khri btsan po*), how the Chinese government had forced an unequal treaty on the Tibetans and even failed to abide by its provisions themselves as their greed increased to the maximum, arguing that since it was now impossible for the two peoples to coexist, there was a pressing need for practical measures to restore unity between the Tibetan leaders and the people. I particularly remember Khen-drung Bum-tang Tubten Chöpel-la telling those speakers, "Whether in terms of population, economy, military strength, or war experience, we Tibetans are as far removed from the Chinese as the earth is from the sky. Other than by sticking to wholly peaceful means, how can we think of taking on the Chinese?"

Shöl-pa Ta-tongwa answered, "We have nothing to encourage us to take on the Chinese except the facts of history. I am suggesting only that we request them to return to China while humbly prostrating ourselves, not while standing upright with rocks in our hands seeking to fight them. In any case, if we carry on like this, acting too proud to start swimming even after being swept away by water, what has already happened in the east of Tibet will happen here too. From today onward, the Tibetans should draw a clear line between themselves and the Chinese. Whether they are government officials who have been appointed to Chinese government offices or people who have joined the Chinese of their own accord, unless they take a clear stand from now on against the make-believe assessment [that political coexistence between the traditional government and the Chinese military authority was possible] that has so far prevailed, there will be no way to escape the fate of Pakpa-la's brother Khen-chung Sonam Gyatso yesterday. We will not attempt to persuade those who want to join the Chinese side to stay with us. Equally, we will welcome those who turn back from the abyss in cognizance of the government's mercy and return to the Tibetan camp, provided that they have the support of two guarantors."

In view of this demand, most of those working in Chinese government offices named their own friends and relatives as guarantors, and the majority of the government officials present added their signatures to the list of self-proclaimed "*tsampa* eaters" approving the resolution to clearly demarcate the Chinese and Tibetan camps. I also made up my mind to sign my name there. Then, the officials revised the appointment of their representatives in each subcommittee as necessary, and the senior delegates reconvened the assembly in the hall of the palace printery (*Zhol bka' 'gyur par khang*). An emergency headquarters was set up at the Norbu Lingka to implement decisions reached by the assembly, which appointed the younger officials to security duties there, at the Potala, and at the Tsukla-khang temple, set up an emergency system for paying military wages, and distributed a large number of guns from government armories to unarmed volunteers and young officials on security duty.

Likewise, Tibetan women gave up their normal exclusive concern with domestic matters and took part in the popular uprising, establishing the Tibetan Womens' Association at a meeting held on March 12 at the Drébu-ling threshing ground in front of the main gate of Shöl, attended by more than 10,000 women from the Lhasa area. Kundé-ling Gur-teng Kunsang-la was one of 10 women representatives elected to run the organization. Under their leadership, another meeting was held the following day, as well as a demonstration; incense was offered, flagpoles were erected, and inaugural ceremonies were held. Then the representatives led a delegation of their members to the Indian mission, Nepalese consulate, and Bhutanese representative (*Lo phyag*) to urge them to uphold the righteousness of the Ti-

Tibetan Women's Association Rally, March 12, 1959. *Department of Information and International Relations, Central Tibetan Administration, Dharamsala*

betan struggle among the international community, and appealed to them emphatically to serve as neutral witnesses to Chinese oppression of the Tibetans and, in particular, to the circumstances of the present uprising.

Meanwhile, the Chinese side were building or reinforcing defensive barricades of sandbags around the roofs, doors, and windows not just at their army bases but also in civilian offices, schools, shops, and hospitals. Chinese people, military and civilian, moved around town carrying weapons, inciting fear among ordinary citizens. By night, the noise and electric lights of the soldiers and military transport vehicles could be heard and seen in the streets and from the army bases, terrifying the people of Lhasa. Armed Chinese came repeatedly around the Norbu Lingka to survey and take measurements, on the pretext of repairing electricity cables and telephone lines. Then, on March 17, several cannon were fired in the direction of the summer palace from the truck depot on its north side. Luckily two shells that landed in a common thoroughfare beyond the outer boundary wall failed to explode, but with no hope of peaceful reconciliation, it was only a matter of time before open confrontation broke out. On the 13th, I had been appointed to security duty at the door of the Khamsum Silnön palace, and as my uncle, the chief secretary, had been elected leader of the standing assembly and was required to stay permanently in the Norbu

Lingka compound, I also stayed there from that day on. Also on duty at the entrance to the Khamsum Silnön palace were the monk officials Ngawang Khyenrab, Tsultrim Chöpel, Tenpa Gyeltsen, and five members of the body-guard regiment. Armed with a non-army issue Sten gun (*Lan khru'u*) and 150 cartridges, I stayed on guard with absolute dedication, prudence, and alertness. Half of our number remained on duty by day on alternate shifts, and by night we all stayed there, changing shifts every two hours.

On the eighth day of the Tibetan month, March 17, around nine o'clock in the evening, Ka-lön Surkhang, Sha-sur, and Liushar came around on patrol wearing ordinary clothes, and none of us was suspicious when Surkhang told us by way of encouragement, "It is customary for the Chinese to attack under cover of darkness in the early hours of the morning, and they are very ac-complished at doing that. So you should be on highest alert at that time, and for the moment you can all relax at your posts." When a truck pulled up at the (*Nyi 'od 'gag*) entrance to the summer palace, we thought it must be the one that occasionally delivered ammunition from the Shöl armory. But when ten rounds of machine-gun fire came from the direction of Rama-gang, south of the palace, everyone became apprehensive and went to the temporary head-quarters to ask what was going on. We were told that no delivery of ammuni-tion was due and that we were not to be alarmed by the sound of gunfire and should return to our posts. On the way back, the troop of elite bodyguards who were supposed to accompany His Holiness everywhere and had been on guard with us for the last few days were suddenly withdrawn. I did wonder why at the time, but the actual reason never occurred to me.

When I passed by my uncle's quarters at around eleven o'clock that night, neither he nor my elder brother had returned yet. When they came, they were behaving unusually, speaking to each other in low voices, and broke off their conversation when I approached. They just asked me what was being said, and when I replied that apart from the unusual occurrences earlier on I had heard no particular news, they repeated what the staff at headquarters had said, that there was no cause for alarm. Then I realized that something strange was going on, but when I asked them what was up, they would only say that I would find out in due course. I returned to my own post with my mind racing. As soon as I awoke next morning and went to my uncle's place, his attendant Lekden told me the news that His Holi-ness had left the Norbu Lingka the previous night and fled toward Lho-ka.

Of course, at the earlier meetings some people had called for His Holi-ness to seek sanctuary in another country, and while those of us who were called upon to protect Him were prepared to lay down our lives, the military capabilities of the Chinese and Tibetan sides were as far apart as the earth and the sky. The senior government officers were obviously concerned that He could not remain [in His palace] at the center of the Norbu Lingka compound indefinitely, and even in my own childish mind I was terribly anxious that He could be harmed in the event of a conflict. Nonetheless, the idea that He might have suddenly left the previous night had not occurred to me. This demonstrates not only the naïve state of my mind [at that time] but also the secrecy surrounding an enterprise that would have been disastrous had it failed. Its successful accomplishment is certainly one of our fundamental victories. On hearing the news, I had an indescribable feeling of joy mixed with sorrow. The summer palace and its surroundings seemed resoundingly empty, and whoever I looked at seemed languid and subdued, but this was only my imagination, for most people did not come to know until after the [following] ninth day [of the Tibetan month]. My uncle and elder brother kept up their secrecy and said nothing to me, but my relative, the monk official Ngawang Chöpel, who was an assembly delegate and had been a member of a secret [political] organization, gave me a clear account.

That day I felt ill at ease and wanted to go back to our family house in Lhasa to spend a moment with my dear mother, but there was extremely tight security at all the entrances to the Norbu Lingka to prevent movement between the palace and the city, lest the secret should become known, and I was unable to leave. Gradually, the news spread by word of mouth through the summer palace, and a meeting of the full assembly was held in the *puja* hall in the spirit of assessing what to do next, but no direct announcement was made of the escape. None could be made the next day either, as it was astrologically inauspicious (*Yan kong*), and although they arranged a meeting on the following day, the eleventh of the Tibetan month, and encouraged people to attend, fighting broke out that morning, so the assembly never found the right time to make the announcement. From what I heard later, it was considered too risky on the ninth when His Holiness had departed only on the evening of the eighth, and by the eleventh, we security workers and volunteers were returning to our homes and planning to maintain whatever stability possible until negotiations could be held between the Chinese and the Tibetans. In any case, whether they knew of these plans or not, having prepared themselves for war, the Chinese began their armed reprisal on the morning of the eleventh [March 20] by firing artillery shells, and open conflict broke out.

CHAPTER 4

The Chinese Fan the Flames of War

AROUND FOUR O'CLOCK Lhasa time on the morning of March 20, all the Chinese army bases and settlements in the surrounding area trained their cannon on the Norbu Lingka summer palace and began to fire. Even now, recalling that sound evokes a distinct sensation of despair. At that point, I was still guarding the entrance to the Khamsum Silnön palace. As soon as I heard the cannon, I knew that fighting had broken out and was terrified at the thought that I could not expect to survive the day ahead. But the two regular members of the bodyguard regiment on duty with me were not so frightened, and seeing their air of determination, I felt a little more sanguine. As it was still dark, there was nothing to do but stay where we were and remain alert, and headquarters gave us no particular instructions. The volunteers staying outside the southern boundary wall of the summer palace could be heard shouting "Ki!" and returning fire. I imagined that the Chinese soldiers had advanced under artillery cover and engaged the volunteers in fighting at close quarters, and fully expected those of us inside to come under attack if they could not hold the Chinese back, but no Chinese came and the shouts of "Ki!" gradually receded. [Then] I imagined that the Chinese soldiers had been unable to break through on their first try and had withdrawn, and even that, judging by the fierce shouting and firing we had heard, a large number of them could have been killed or wounded. As dawn arrived, I was curious to look outside, but when I went to do so, there was not even the whiff of a Chinese nearby. It turned out that the gunfire and war cries during the early hours had been quite arbitrary.

Then, as the sun rose, the artillery fire became heavier. To either side of our post, I could see many unexploded shells. There was a tremendous noise as some of our cannon in the bodyguard regiment camp were fired toward the Chinese encampment at Nor-tö Lingka [a short distance to the west], in the hope that they might make some impact, but almost instantly enemy shells fell near that gun emplacement, killing and wounding the gunners, and thus we lost the use of our cannon. The Gyantsé soldiers near the Chinese truck depot on the north side of the Norbu Lingka, the Amdo unit stationed near Nor-tö Lingka, and the Tibetan army and volunteers at Bongwa-ri and Chakpo-ri had a clear view of the Chinese and engaged them in exchanges of fire for some time, but those of us in the summer palace and on the south side of Chakpo-ri could do nothing but stay where we were and be pounded by enemy fire. We had absolutely no experience of warfare, and since we also had no experienced commanders, by about ten o'clock that morning we were all disorganized, and instead of staying in our shelters, we began running here and there trying to avoid the falling shells, making our casualties even heavier.

Returning to my uncle's room, I got the message that remaining officials were to gather at the palace secretariat office, and went there. There were twenty-odd monastic and lay officials, as well as an Amdo-wa chief and representatives from the Upper Tantric College. The commander of the emergency headquarters, Khenchung Tara-wa of the Nangma-gang, had had to retreat from heavy fighting with the Chinese at Chakpo-ri after running out of ammunition, but he was determined to go back and appealed to us, saying, "They say, 'The time has come for smart young people [to get out], now no trace is left where Lhasa was,' but since His Holiness has not fallen into enemy hands we still have a chance! Which of you will join me?" The monk official Gyeltsen Tashi declared, "I will go!" but the others remained silent. He spoke again decisively, saying, "Staying inside the Norbu Lingka, you have no way to fight back and will just be slaughtered. It would be better to find a way to get outside, and you should combine your strength to do that by any means," then went back to Chakpo-ri with Tsédrung Gyeltsen Tashi and his brother Tara Sonam Tséring. But there was no discussion about how to unite among the rest of us, and as everyone looked for his own place to shelter, I went back to my uncle's room. He was there, and I appealed to him, "People are fleeing! How can we stay here any longer?" but he said, "That is just your idea. If you want to leave you can do as you please, but we have work to do!" and set off again to the Chensel Po-trang palace to procure weapons. Meanwhile, I waited for my elder brother, whom he had sent with Khenchung Gyeltsen-la to the protector chapel to request a divination (*Zan brtags*), and as soon as he got back, we set off together for the Chensel Po-trang. By this time it was about three o'clock in the afternoon, the bombardment was at its height, and we ran this way and that trying to avoid the falling shells.

When we got there, the treasurer, Lha-ding Khen-chen Ngawang Drak-pa-la, my uncle, and the palace steward Losang Dondrup-la were handing over the rifles and pistols they had removed from the Nyiwö and Késang Dékyil apartments at Chensel Po-trang to the ex-monk official Losang Yéshé and Gönsar-pa, a former officer of the "Ga" (third) regiment [based in Shika-tsé], to be sent to the rebel army in Lho-ka. The cannon shells started to fall like rain, and several landed within the yellow [inner] boundary wall. Thinking it would be safer to shelter in a building, we went inside the Lu-khang palace and waited there. We removed some blessed substances from the amulet boxes we carried with us everywhere and ate them. Then the building was hit by a shell and badly damaged, the windows shattering from the force of the explosion.

We had to retreat once again, and as we did so, more shells exploded nearby, and we lost sight of one another and became separated. My left thigh was hit by fragments in one of the explosions, and although I was not seriously wounded, it became difficult for me to move. As I tried to crawl outside the boundary wall, there was another explosion and my right cheek was hit, again not seriously, but maybe a vein was severed, because I was soaked with blood, even inside my shoes. I was still doggedly trying to get outside by going through the inner section of the stables when the main door of that building was hit by a shell and it collapsed instantly, crushing several of the people inside. Many people inside the stables, as well as horses and mules, were killed or injured, and those still alive shouted for others to help pull them out of the wreckage. By then, my throat was absolutely dry with thirst [from blood loss] and all I could think about was finding water to quench it. I went into the nearby living quarters of several of the sweepers and stablehands but found no one there. Finally, I went into the room in the basement of the "stables palace" (*Chibs rva pho brang*) that was the stablemaster's office, and the stablemaster himself was there. When I asked if I might also come inside, he recognized me and urged me, "Come in, sit down, it should be slightly safer than outside." When I asked him for water, he at once tore open a paper packet of blessed pills, poured a few into a cup of water, and handed it to me, and that sensation of relieving my terrible thirst is something I remember even now.

The two of us stayed in that basement for some time, while the noise of the bombardment outside was as loud as could be. When I reluctantly re-emerged, I saw a pet monkey tied to a wooden post in the stable courtyard that no one had thought to release, and it was scampering up and down in terror, holding the cotton awning from a nearby doorway, which it wrapped around its head for protection when it heard another explosion, just like a human. When there was a lull in the firing, it stared around wide-eyed at the dead and wounded people and horses and became more terrified still. I looked for a way to release it from its chain, but as it did not know me, it ran back to the top of the post as I approached. Fearing that worse was to come, I made no further attempt to save the monkey and left the stables.

It was about six o'clock by then. Many people were leaving from the west gate on the southern side of the Norbu Lingka and heading toward Rama-gang. This seemed the best direction in which to escape because there were no Chinese military bases or camps on that side, and I also followed people going that way, but after I had crossed a stream in front of that gate and started crawling on across the open plain toward the Kyi-chu river, my wet shoes and clothes were caked in mud and sand and became extremely heavy. And after getting wet in the stream, the wound on my leg became very painful. One group of those fleeing carried their weapons with them, while another group abandoned them and waved sticks to which they had tied white scarves as they walked, as a sign of surrender that could be seen from afar. At first, as we left the west gate, gunfire could be heard in all directions, but it did not seem to be aimed at this area, and people were heading for the hills behind Rama-gang thinking that no Chinese soldiers were there. But shortly after, many machine guns began firing simultaneously from the hills behind Rama-gang, and a great many of those walking across the river plain were killed. Some were hit from behind as they fled, some kept going forward, but as the firing continued, many more were killed and wounded. It was terrifying to see this happen right in front of me, but as I was mostly crawling along, I did not get hit; whereas had I gone farther, it would have been the same as committing suicide.

It was getting dark, and I resolved to turn back, return to the Norbu Lingka, and try to find my uncle and elder brother. It was dusk by the time I got there, my search proved futile, and just as night fell, Chinese troops approaching from all sides entered the summer palace. They fired or threw grenades at anything that moved, and shouted in Chinese that we should stand still, not move, and give up our weapons. Those of us sheltering inside the palace stables surrendered together. One group of soldiers kept their guns trained on us from a distance, while another group searched us for weapons before leading us outside the yellow boundary wall. We were grouped together with others being led out by the soldiers, in the open area between the main gate and the entrance to Késang Po-trang. Eventually, all of the four or five thousand people arrested in the Norbu Lingka or its environs that night were assembled there. Chinese soldiers stood around the perimeter with various kinds of weapons, guarding us so strictly that we were not allowed to get up even to urinate.

One Ba-pa Késang Yang-ga, who seemed to be a Chinese army officer, effectively instilled us with fear by telling us that the People's Liberation Army (PLA) would not hesitate to shoot if we made any untoward movement or sign of resistance. Then, gradually, Tibetans serving as Chinese officials, and in particular officials of the United Front Bureau, arrived and began to pick out officials of the Tibetan government from among the crowd; they were loaded into prisoner transport trucks and sent off. I imagined that the government officials had been separated from the crowd because they were going to be shot, and did my best not to be recognized, putting on a wool hat that covered my eyes and trying to look as ordinary as possible, so that night I was not identified and stayed among the common people. But I had the wounds on my leg and cheek, my clothes were wet from crossing the stream by the southern gate while trying to flee, and the ground we were made to sit on was frozen at that time of year, so I suffered more from the cold that night than at any other time in my life.

Anyway, we got through the night suffering from cold, hunger, thirst, and fear, and the next morning, army officers from the so-called Tibet Military District (TMD) headquarters arrived, accompanied by photographers and reporters. They checked again to see if there were any remaining government officials, and among the Tibetans working as Chinese officials, there was one, Shölkhang Jédrung Tubten Nyima, whom I recognized. He was checking carefully among the crowd and picking out officials, but he could not recognize me, as he had been with the Chinese side since their arrival in Tibet and had largely withdrawn from government service, so he was not familiar with the newly inducted officials. However, there was a United Front Bureau official called Kung Ping who had formerly served as UF representative and been in contact with most government departments, and he recognized me and picked me out. There were about seven of us remaining officials identified that day, and although we generally didn't look like very strong individuals, we were bound together with a cotton rope, not close together but at some distance from each other, and those reporters and photographers took a lot of photos of us.

That day they gave out the food they had collected from the Norbu Lingka and the voluntary security people's camp, but people had gone without food for two days and there was a great crush, so only the stronger ones managed to get a morsel while the weak and the wounded got nothing. Those of us who had been picked out were not only denied food, we were not even allowed to drink from the small water channel running behind us. We were put in the *puja* hall, where the seriously wounded were gathered, and around five o'clock in the evening we were taken to the quarters of the chief monk official (*mKhan po tshang*) in the Norbu Lingka, which had become a makeshift Chinese army canteen. There they gave us *tsampa* and a white, milky liquid that the Chinese themselves drank, but our hands were still tied behind our backs and we did not know how we should eat. A young soldier untied my hands and told me to make *tsampa* dough (*sPags*) and feed it to the others, so I prepared the *tsampa* in a large enamel food container (*ku'u rtsi*) and gave it to them, but they did not eat more than a mouthful, and although I had gone two days without any food, I too could eat no more than a mouthful.

After that, my hands were tied behind my back once more, and after waiting a while in the courtyard, we were loaded like sacks of flour into a big army truck with a canvas top and taken away. Gunfire had not yet ceased at the Potala and around Lhasa, and our truck was fired on from the Potala. The guards told us not to squat but to lie down. The truck passed Dékyi Lingka and went south along the river and into the west gate of the TMD headquarters. All along that road there were a great number of corpses. At that point, I no longer feared summary execution, but since I had been recognized as a government official, I knew I was in for some bad treatment.

CHAPTER 5

Imprisoned at the Tibet
Military District Headquarters

AS SOON AS we got inside the gate of the army headquarters, a large group of soldiers gathered around the truck we were riding in and searched it, and many of the soldiers occupying the shelters around the entrance came out to take a look at us. Amazingly, their wives were also there, carrying their children on their backs and guns or grenades in front, glaring and shouting at us. It seemed that the guards who had brought us didn't know where we were to be taken, and we had to wait there for half an hour before a soldier was sent to accompany us. We came to realize that they had been preparing for conflict for a long time, for only ten days had passed between the invitation to His Holiness to visit the army camp and the outbreak of fighting, and they could not have set up such formidable defenses inside the camp in such a short space of time. I remember thinking that they must have long since resolved to impose their rule by force, on the pretext that the Tibetans had gone against the [Seventeen-Point] agreement. We were then taken to the prison, which was an extremely fearsome place even to look at, with two-story circular surveillance towers in the middle of the courtyard and at each corner of the boundary wall, iron grilles on all the cell windows, and coiled barbed wire, supposedly electrified, all around the windows and atop the boundary wall. It had been built in the place where the palace stewards used to go for picnics.

After we got down from the truck, the ropes binding our hands were untied and we were thoroughly searched and locked together in pairs with either handcuffs or leg irons, and allocated to [one of] several cells. I was handcuffed with my relative, the monk official Ngawang Chöpel, and put in cell number 11. That room was no more than two square yards in size, but there were already fourteen people inside. Since they were officials who had been picked out of the crowd at the Norbu Lingka summer palace the night before, I knew that if they had not been executed, my uncle and elder brother should also be alive. We were packed in there day and night, squatting on our haunches, unable to stretch our arms or legs, and Ngawang Chöpel-la and I being chained together made movement even more difficult, especially going to the toilet.

Among those whom I can remember being locked in that cell were: an elderly Géshé (and *mTshan zhabs* or debate partner of a high lama) from Gya-rong, the cabinet secretary (*bKa' drung*) Gégyé-pa Tendzin Dorjé, the cabinet steward (*bKa' mgron*) Sarjung-sé, the lay officials (*Shod drung*) Kyarsip-pa and Wolön, and the palace cook (*gSol thab pa*) Losang Pelden. Among the officials who were arrested in Lhasa and brought there the following day, the elderly ex-cabinet minister (*bKa' zur*) Tashi-lingpa was put in our cell. He was already suffering from a nervous disorder (*Srog rlung*), but after the sudden, devastating events we had all been through, his illness worsened and he started babbling nonsense.

Those who brought us our food were the older prisoners already in Chinese military custody, including the Chinese trader mentioned earlier, from the "Beijing store" (*Bar 'khor Pad cing tshong khang*), married to the daughter of Gonjo Chösur-tsang. He had been arrested without warning the previous year on the way to Ganden with a group of others to see the Siu-tang festival and put in this prison, without anyone knowing where he had gone. He now brought us our food and drinking water, and commiserated with us a great deal. There was also a group of young vagabonds from the Lhasa area who had been caught stealing from the camp. At that time they fed us twice a day, mostly steamed corn buns with a little bit of fermented garlic leaf or fermented bean curd. It was passed into the room through a circular hole in the door. The prisoners were taken out to the toilet twice a day. Most of us who had been arrested at the summer palace were chained.

After three or four days, the soldiers went to each cell and called for the wounded prisoners to go for medical treatment at the hospital. We were tied together in line with a long rope and led off. As the gunfire in Lhasa had still not come to an end, we had to walk along in a ditch, and since some of us were quite unable to walk in any case, it took nearly two hours to get there. At the hospital were members of the Yabshi Langdün household, Chamdo Pakpa-la's mother, and others. Pakpa-la's mother couldn't help referring to us as "the killers of my son," although we were hardly to blame. Wangdü and Peljor of the Langdün family and a group of other Tibetans carrying arms who worked as officials for the Chinese came over to stare at us for their amusement. As we were already defeated, wounded, and forlorn, having to suffer their infuriating behavior as well was miserable indeed. In any case, that day, far from receiving medical treatment, we were simply shouted at and then taken back.

About seven days later, we were summoned to what served as the prison meeting hall, where the Chinese officer with a harelip who was in charge of the prison told us through an interpreter that if we followed prison regulations he would release a group of us from our handcuffs and leg irons that day, but if we broke the regulations he would not only chain us but also tie us up, after which most of the younger prisoners had their chains removed. At that meeting, Mön-ling Dzasa was by my side and looking at the wound on my cheek; he asked me how it had happened. As I was replying, the harelipped Chinese officer heard me, and as a punishment for talking, he took the kind of elasticized wire he always carried in his hand and twisted it around my head two or three times. I felt more fear than pain, but after the meeting was over and I touched my palm to my skull, I could feel that a long swelling had come up, and that night it was extremely painful. However, it was a tremendous relief to get out of the handcuffs we had been wearing constantly. That was the first time during my ordeal that I was assaulted.

One day, a group of aristocrat collaborators including Tsi-pön Tsogowa Dondrup Tséring; Wangchuk Gyelpo, son of Rimshi Changlo-chen; Tétong Khen-chung Losang Namgyel; and Tsédrung Tendzin Trinlé came to visit and talk to those of us in custody. Tétong Khen-chung told us, "You people really took the wrong path. From the beginning, the People's government took the trouble to offer education and future prospects to all, but you didn't listen and have now committed the heinous crime of rebelling against the state. Even if you regret it now, it is no use. The way out for you now is to give clear answers when the People's government questions you about your crimes," and many other cruel things.

About two weeks later, we were led out of our cells and into the courtyard to attend a kind of meeting. There were about three hundred of us, lamas, government officials, staff of the great monasteries, and army officers who had been arrested at the Norbu Lingka, at the Potala, or in the city, and at that point we got some idea of who had died in the fighting or had fled. At that meeting they read a list of names and told those people to come forward. Most were officials below the fifth rank, as well as monastery staff and lamas in general. We were taken immediately to the Traldé Lingka, a park where the palace bursary workers used to hold picnics and where later there had been a carpet factory under joint Chinese and Tibetan management, and we were accommodated temporarily in those buildings. There were about twelve rooms of different sizes, and I was one of seven people put in a one-pillar [one pillar = about 3 square yards] room in a Tibetan-style building. Compared to (*gNyer tshang gling kha / rGya'u gling kha*) [the TMD prison where we had been] previously, it was relaxed, although we had only the clothes on our backs and no bedding at all, and we had a hard time making it through the cold spring nights. They fed us and took us out to the toilet twice a day.

By that time, the fighting in Lhasa was over, there was no armed resistance left, and most males over the age of seventeen had been taken into custody. As for those of us who had gone armed to defend the Norbu Ling-ka, Potala, or Tsukla-khang temple, our relatives began trying to find out whether we were still alive by going to the area where we were supposed to have been on duty and examining the corpses there. If they did not recognize their loved ones, there was some hope that they were still alive, and they then went around all the different prisons, often spending many days standing outside the gates trying to confirm the presence of their relatives there, and if they were able to do so, bring bedding and food for them. If they were not able to confirm their presence, they could only hope that the missing people had escaped into exile. The large number of relatives gathered at the entrance to the military headquarters were given slips of paper confirming that we were held there, and in that way my family members too were able to bring me bedding and food. At that time, the soldiers would give us whatever food had been delivered, regardless of its quality or quantity, at the twice-daily feeding times. The bedding brought by our relatives was even more important, since we had none whatsoever.

Then they started questioning us. Since there were many of us, several groups of officials did the questioning, but mostly it was Chinese students who had been learning Tibetan at the Central Nationalities Institute in Beijing who acted as interpreters. To begin with, they questioned us only in outline: name, age, occupation since age eight, where we had been during the fighting and whether we had taken part, whether we were members of an underground organization, whether we had killed any PLA soldiers, how much we had fired guns, and so on. One day, all the lay officials had their hair ornaments removed and their long hair cut, and at the same time we all had to wait with our heads bowed in submission as they took frontal and profile photos of each of us, to be attached to prison documents.

While I was in the Traldé Lingka prison, there was a serious epidemic of stomach disease [dysentery?], which spread easily due to the poor medical care and nutrition and the lack of bedding to keep us warm, and those affected had continual diarrhea. The doors were locked so we could not get to the toilet, and they taunted us by saying that we should do it out of the window. When some of the slightly kinder Chinese soldiers were on duty, they would take us on extra visits to the toilet, but the bad ones, far from unlocking the door, would scold us harshly just for calling out. The sick prisoners would be obliged to soil their pants and even to use their clay eating bowls, the whole place was filled with the stench, and several died from the disease.

One day, all those being held at the Traldé Lingka were suddenly called out to attend a meeting, where we were addressed by Kung Ping, the official who had identified me at the summer palace. Holding a newspaper in his hands, he told us that the meeting had been called to give us the good news reported in the *People's Daily* that the heroic PLA fighters had thoroughly eliminated the Khampa reactionaries in Lho-ka. He also announced that although the Dalai Lama had now arrived in India after being kidnapped by the reactionary clique of upper-class Tibetans, He had always belonged to the "patriotic and progressive" faction. That really was good news. At that time, four or five aircraft were taking off every day and heading south, and imagining that they might be pursuing His Holiness, we were disturbed by thoughts of them endangering His life by dropping bombs and so on, so the announcement came as a relief.

We were being interrogated, but "struggle" sessions and such had not yet begun, and except for a few occasions, neither had forced labor. My first experience of prison labor was when one of Kundé-ling Dzasa's attendants called Gyelpo, who knew a little Chinese, and I were called to work as servants in the prison officials' kitchen. In the morning we had to sweep the area around the entrance and chop firewood. In the afternoon, they made us empty their toilet. Unlike in a Tibetan toilet, their shit was all red, and because the Chinese always ate garlic and pickled vegetables, the smell was so bad that as a free man I would not even have approached the toilet, but as prisoners, we had no choice but to empty it. Later, I remember thinking that I would rather die than continually have to do that job.

One day, they read another list of names, and most of us were put into a group called the "training brigade" (*sByong brdar ru khag*) and moved to the Tsédrung Lingka [next to the Traldé Lingka]. Except for one or two fourth-rank officials, we were all people of regular status; most of the higher-status people and those facing specific charges were being held at the Gyawu Lingka detention center (*lTa srung khang*). Unlike before, our cells at Tsédrung

Lingka were not locked, and during the day we were free to go to the toilet unaccompanied. In the morning, they took us to the river nearby to wash our hands and faces. Then we had to study the *Tibet Daily* [Party newspaper] and Communist texts for four hours every morning and four hours every afternoon. After the evening meal, we were put to work until it got dark, followed by a further study session until ten o'clock at night. The main work we were given at that time was dismantling the barricades that had been constructed in all the Chinese army camps before the outbreak of fighting. Thereby we confirmed not only that the Chinese had been stealthily preparing for a confrontation for some time, and that the hastily built barricades put up by our side at the Norbu Lingka were like child's play in comparison, but also how fortunate it was that the fighting had been brought to an end within three days. Had we attempted sudden attacks on the Chinese army bases, it would have amounted to suicide, for these barricades were so strong that none of us could have got past them.

About a month after our arrest, a group of us younger prisoners were taken out to work. Since we spent most of our time cooped up, going out to do various jobs was something of a relief, and moreover, leaving the army camp gave us some hope of meeting our relatives. The task we were given that day was to burn the unidentified corpses of those killed in the vicinity of the summer palace during the fighting. First we went to the west gate of the Norbu Lingka to exhume all the bodies that had been dumped in the trenches dug by the Amdo people who had been defending that gate, and loaded them onto a truck. Those bodies were not only unrecognizable but also completely rotten; even with two layers of cotton wrapped around our mouths, the smell made us retch. There was still a group of Lhasa women whose husbands or sons had been volunteers at the summer palace during the fighting and had not been seen since, and who had come looking for their bodies. They picked through the putrid corpses, turning them this way and that without caring about nausea or the stain of pollution, which demonstrates the very loving attitude that Tibetan women typically have toward their husbands, as well as the commonly stated claim that we Tibetans have a psychological attitude [to such things] quite distinct from other kinds of people. We gathered all the rotten corpses, as well as those scattered across the meadow south of the Norbu Lingka, on the south side of the Mani Lhakhang [chapel]. They amounted to four or five large piles, which we threw gasoline over and burned. The acrid smoke and stench of burning flesh hung in the air over the city, and the miserable thought occurred to me that had I been killed that day, I would now be one of those corpses.

Then our so-called training brigade was moved back to the central [TMD] prison at Gyawu Lingka, which was organized into inner and outer divisions. The high-ranking officials and special suspects were kept in the [inner] detention center. They were mostly in leg irons and were kept in locked cells even during the day. The members of our training brigade were put in buildings near the inner division that were not purpose-built cells and were usually occupied by the guards. It was only a short distance from there to the central prison, and because the prisoners in the inner division were brought out every morning to a round patch of open land by the entrance, where they walked around for exercise and there was a well where they could wash their hands and faces, I was able to see my uncle from a distance every morning. He had still not been released from his leg irons, and his hair and complexion seemed to get paler every day, but as a loving gesture of encouragement to my elder brother and me, he kept smiling.

Our training brigade was divided into three work teams (*Ru khag*), each subdivided into four groups (*Tshogs chung*) of 11 members, which adds up to about 150 people in total. We had the same kitchen and diet as the inner-division prisoners, but except for the rest day on Sundays, when we were fed twice, we were fed three times a day and regardless of the quality of the food, this was enough to fill our stomachs. We could also receive the food and clean clothes delivered by our family members. We could go to the toilet as we pleased during the day, but if we needed to go at night we had to call out in Chinese loudly enough for the guards to hear. Other than various tasks such as dismantling barricades or preparing vegetable gardens, we had no regular work allotted to us. The main requirement was that we should each make a statement admitting our participation in the uprising. But first of all, as a preparatory stage, for many days we were taught and urged to accept the Chinese government's version of history: that, due to the relations between Tibet and China starting with the invitation of Princess Wen-ch'eng Konjo [to marry the Tibetan king; seventh century] right up to the Qing dynasty, Tibet was indisputably an inseparable part of the glorious Chinese motherland. After that we were required to identify those who had participated in the uprising. Most of us said that at the very beginning of the fighting there had been gunfire and cannon fire on the west side of the Norbu Lingka, but we couldn't say exactly who might have been responsible. They told us repeatedly that this was not clear enough, and in the end we had to repeat what they said in their propaganda: that the uprising had been started by the upper-class Tibetan reactionaries in collusion with foreign imperialists and Indian counterrevolutionaries.

Then, the denunciation (*Byur bkag*) of our crimes began at a series of general meetings about the "policy of seizing the guilty," "leniency for those who confess and severity for those who refuse," [the need to] "atone for crimes with worthy deeds" (i.e., confession and informing on others), [and the declaration that] "those who were deceived by the reactionaries have done no wrong," and so on, where we once more had to give an account of our lives from age eight onward, and in particular, give a written statement of our involvement in the fighting, which was scrutinized and queried by the group leaders. The officials of each team also did their own investigations. The team-level officials set about investigating the serious situations and problematic cases, and their method of internal investigation and cross-examination was vicious and accusatory. The officials also held a separate meeting for some of the keener [to collaborate] young prisoners and repeatedly enticed them by telling them, "Atone for crimes with worthy deeds," and "Every confession means a corresponding reduction of your sentence," and there were some who succumbed and agreed to report whatever they had "seen, heard, or suspected" of others in exchange for their own records being overlooked. Some even confessed to things they had never done, and were praised for clearly acknowledging their guilt and presented as a model for others, but when the time came for them to be sentenced, there was no corresponding reduction, and some people had much cause for regret. For example, Shödrung Tséwang Dramdul, son of the Lhasa headman Ko-karwa, confessed many things he pretended to have done during the uprising, and when the time came, he was sentenced to fourteen years on the basis of all his false confessions. He was only seventeen at the time.

The leader (*Tsu'u krang*) of our group was Losang Chöjor, also called Peljor, formerly an attendant at Trijang Labrang and later a monk official, indeed assembly delegate of the ordinary monk officials, as well as a secretary in the emergency headquarters [during the uprising]. As one of the ordinary monk officials most heavily implicated in the fighting, he traded his own integrity for a lenient sentence and not only reported everything he "saw, heard, or suspected" of others but also cross-examined other members of the group very harshly and thoroughly. Worst of all, in the hope of being rewarded [by his superiors], he went to the group members individually and tried to get their stories out of them, whether through gentle coaxing or fierce intimidation. However, as most of the group members behaved with great restraint, we had no incidents of people being beaten or bound.

Special investigators also came from the intelligence office known as the Public [Affairs] Bureau. They dealt with special cases, members of underground organizations, suspected spies, and foreigners, and the groups paid special attention to people under their investigation. One time, a Public Affairs Bureau official with the family name Wang, who spoke Tibetan extremely well, sought me out. At that time I had admitted only to having signed the assembly declaration and served as an armed guard, so I wondered if he had the wrong name, but as he led me into the interrogation room, he told me, "You are a relative of the Gyatso Tashi chief secretary." He sat down in the chair at the desk in front of him, sat me down on a squat chair two or three paces away, then took out an unholstered pistol from his waist and put it on the table in front of him, took a cigarette from his shirt pocket and lit it, and also lit one that he passed to me.

He asked me, "Do you want to get out of prison?"

"Naturally," I replied.

"So what is the Party's policy?" he asked.

"Leniency for those who confess their guilt and severity for those who refuse, atone for crimes with worthy deeds, and so on."

"But have you given all the facts?"

"I have given an account of my history since the age of eight, and particularly a detailed [account of] my situation during the uprising in writing, and spoken about it many times in group meetings."

"I don't mean your situation," he said. "Your release from prison doesn't depend on confessing the facts in your own case. You have to tell the facts about your uncle, the chief secretary. For instance, you need to tell us which members of the welfare association he met in Kalimpong when you all went to India in 1956, and what political activities he engaged in on his return to Lhasa."

This was something I had not even imagined, much less thought over. I replied by saying, "I did go to India with my uncle, but I was so young that I just enjoyed myself and had no idea about who might or might not have come to see him, and after returning to Lhasa I paid no attention to his activities. Since my uncle is still in prison, you can ask him about it directly."

"If he would tell us straight, there would be no point in asking you," he said, "but your uncle's thinking is highly reactionary, and instead of admitting the facts, he insists that he has done no wrong."

"Are you fond of your uncle or not?" he continued. "He is in a very dangerous situation, and if you care about him, this is the time to come to his aid. That means telling everything you know about him. One of your relatives has already told us that he must have mentioned the main things that went on at that time to you. I can give you a signed guarantee that you will be released as soon as you tell us everything about it. If not, there will be no hope for your uncle and the outcome for you also will be uncertain, just like 'both losing hold of the reins and getting dragged along behind [a galloping horse].' You should make the right choice and speak out."

"A few different people came to visit while we were in Kalimpong, but I don't know who any of them were. And I don't know anything about his political activities after returning to Lhasa," I replied, "but some propaganda materials from the Kalimpong Tibetan Welfare Association that had come into my uncle's possession were discovered when our house was confiscated by the state. That's all I know."

"You can't get away with such a convenient summary," he said as he dismissed me. "You must think more carefully. It is not yet too late, we can wait [for you to speak], but time is limited."

He questioned me on several subsequent occasions, and when I repeated what I had said earlier without adding a single word, he either went into a rage, waving his arms and stamping his feet, or cunningly tried to entice me by pretending to give me confidential advice.

When my group leader Peljor came to know that I had been investigated by the Public Affairs Bureau, he was convinced that it was a serious matter. But he didn't know what it was about, and without being ordered to participate in a special investigation, he could not make his own inquiries, as this would have exceeded the limit of his responsibility; there were some such matters about which information was restricted. Anyway, he wanted to know more about my case, figuring that there could be an opportunity for his own advancement if he was able to discover something about it. While pretending to have great concern for me, he told me, "The Party's policy is really very correct. For example, in my own case, I wasn't just someone who signed the declaration or served as a guard, I was an eminent ringleader, not only representing the monk officials in the assembly but serving as a secretary in the emergency headquarters, and if you consider the serious nature of my crimes, what I said during the uprising and the false rumors I spread about the Party, I could barely have survived this far. But because of the Party's correct policy, I am not even in the same situation as you and most others, but have been put in charge of the group. This is due to having taken the Party into confidence concerning my own crimes and whatever I have 'seen, heard, or suspected' of others. If you want to be like me, you need to speak clearly about any misdeeds you may have committed in your youth, or concerning your family members, and especially concerning your ongoing investigation by the Public Affairs Bureau."

"The Public Affairs Bureau are questioning me about my uncle, the chief secretary," I replied, "but I really don't know anything about it."

He told me, "Since you were always in his company, no one will believe that you don't know. You don't have to know all about it, suspicions and incidental stories are enough—not necessarily in a written report, but preferably as an embarrassing accusation (*gDong gzhi ra sprod*), which indicates that you have done some thinking. Soon they plan to hold a big meeting where the older government officials will be confronted with embarrassing accusations. If you take that opportunity to stand up and expose your uncle, that would be very good. I can make arrangements." He mentioned many other reasons informing on my uncle could benefit me.

Some time before that, at a combined meeting of the inner and outer divisions of the prison, one of the Chinese leaders had issued a warning that the Gyatso Tashi chief secretary and Rimshi Sa-lungpa were being extremely obstinate, and there would be trouble unless they improved. After that, at a reeducation meeting of our team, number 3, Tashi Topgyel, the son of Shödrung Nam-pön, echoed that Chinese leader's words by saying that the Gyatso Tashi chief secretary and Tsi-pön Shu-küpa were among those chiefly responsible for the uprising, aping what the Chinese had said, which got me really worried. Because of all this, I was beside myself with fear for my uncle.

Then, one day there was a big meeting of all the prisoners where Shölkhang-sé Sonam Targyé and Khyung-ram Rikdzin Namgyel, who were among the leaders and "activists" of the training brigade, stood up and called the names of elder former government officials such as Khendrung Tubten Tendar, Mak-chi Khen-chung Lo-dro Késang, Khen-chung Késang Ngawang, Tsi-pön Shu-küpa Jamyang Khédrup, and Rimshi Mentöpa, making them stand up and telling them that they had to take full responsibility for the uprising, while subjecting them to cruel treatment like slapping and punching them, spitting at them, and pushing them down by the neck. Worse, both Shölkhang-sé Sonam Targyé and Khyung-ram Rikdzin Namgyel held long-legged boots with iron nails in the heels, which they used to beat them. I was dreading the prospect of their doing the same to my uncle, and the idea of Peljor and Nam-pön Tashi Topgyel specifically calling on me to make accusations was terrifying, but that day the meeting ended in uproar.

In the evening, a generally more peaceful team-level meeting was held where we were told to state our views on the earlier meeting. No doubt the officials and those responsible for the beatings wanted to hold such meetings more frequently, but the members of the groups protested forcefully about the earlier meeting. Like many others in teams 1 and 2, many of the people in team 3 said that it was absolutely in violation of Party policy, and that even if it was necessary to subject one or two obstinate individuals to struggle, that kind of physical brutality was never justified. The Communist Party was reforming the thinking of old minds patiently through reeducation, whereas those couple of people at today's meeting had conducted themselves despicably and without regard to their responsibility, physically abusing people on any pretext, in contradiction to Party policy. They also said that regardless of their differing backgrounds and offenses, all the prisoners in both divisions of the prison should be treated equally, and made such strong criticisms that the authorities had no choice but to stop holding such meetings.

By thus using the policy of the Communist Party itself to counteract this corrupt and loutish minority, the prisoners were able to halt some of the direct physical abuse, but the same aggressive style of interrogation continued in the group meetings. Over the next five months, I didn't suffer badly for lack of food or clothing, nor from compulsory labor, nor even on account of my own offenses. It was concern for my uncle that disturbed me the most.

Meanwhile, outside prison, the "Three Rejections and Two Reductions" campaign (*Ngo rgol gsum dang chag yang gnyis*) was going on. The Three Rejections were: reject the reactionary uprising, reject feudalism, reject the three big oppressors (the state, the church, and the land owners). The Two Reductions were reduction of high-interest loans and reduction of land rent. To conduct this campaign, the Chinese gathered those who either had been born blind, crippled, or with missing limbs due to their karma or had previously suffered mutilation as a legal punishment for serious crimes such as murder and horse rustling, and persuaded them to testify that their physical defects were the result of cruel mistreatment at the hands of the "three big oppressors." They held public meetings at which the people were required to "remember the sufferings of the old society," and in Lhasa, they arranged exhibitions in the former prisons at Nangtsé-shak and Shöl by filling them with skeletons, which they had to bring from elsewhere, and lots of scorpions, and calling on people from each neighborhood committee to come and see, and they made propaganda films and magazine articles about it for distribution at home and abroad. According to those who were under the Shöl neighborhood committee at the time, the scorpions used for the display in the Shöl prison had been collected by the children from the Shöl

People's school, but when they tried to film, the scorpions would not stay on top of the corpses where they had been placed and kept escaping into cracks in the walls, so they had to be held in place with invisible threads attached to their limbs.

They also pressured workers, servants, and poor dependents of the government, noble houses, and monasteries (*gZhung sger chos gsum*) to struggle against their former masters, and for a time these struggle meetings were going on every day, and people were taken from the prisons to be struggled against in the city. One time, Tsédrung Ngawang Tashi-la, the Norbu Lingka steward (*Khang gnyer*) who was in our section, and the Shöl steward Rimshi Mu-jawa from the inner division of the prison were taken out to a struggle meeting, and when they were brought back in the evening, Tsédrung Ngawang Tashi's face and eyes were swollen and his ears were almost dangling off his head. They had assembled people from Gyatso, near Norbu Lingka, Jar-rak, Chabgo, and other areas previously under the authority of the Shöl and Norbu Lingka stewards for the meeting, and he said that the cruel mistreatment visited on Shöl-nyér Mu-jawa was worse than his own injuries. They had loaded a sack full of sand on his back and forced him to go to work on the river embankments until he was half-dead with exhaustion.

Then when another prisoner in our section, Trinlé Gyelpo (the son-in-law of the Changdong-tsang house in Banak-shöl) was taken for a struggle meeting, he came back in the evening with a lot of food and fresh clothes and told us that many of his family members and relatives had come to meet him, bringing tea and beer. He was a target for struggle because he had been a people's representative at the time of the uprising and had led the people on, but although he had had to stand submissively for a long time, which made his waist a little sore, he hadn't suffered any beatings. Thus we anticipated our fate with hopes for the best as well as fear of the worst.

While I was in that training brigade, Khen-chung Losang Tendzin of Namgyel Dra-tsang college jumped into the Kyi-chu river and drowned himself. Then there were those who died of disease, and in this way our numbers decreased somewhat in a short time.

Since we had never experienced these kind of things before, very few of us were capable of grasping the deceitful nature of Chinese strategy, so a few wrongly motivated and feebly committed individuals, who betrayed their people and country, were able to stir up internal squabbles on the pretext of some flaws in our former system of government, while some other small-minded people did whatever the Chinese told them in order to save themselves. Because of this there was so much internal contradiction [among the Tibetans] that the Chinese did not even have to show their real intentions.

It was at this time that training brigade prisoners were taken to remove sewage from the drains on either side of the Mön-drong bridge [in east Lhasa], to be used as fertilizer. Since that work was not done regularly, we experienced great hardship wading in the sewers and digging out muck, the evil smell was overpowering, and we were bitten by swamp insects, which was so irritating that we could not sleep at night. Nonetheless, this was the first time since imprisonment that we had been taken to work in the city, and during our three days there, many of the prisoners' families—wives, children, parents, siblings, and other relatives—came to visit them, bringing food and fresh clothes. In addition, many other people would come to us with gifts of tobacco or snuff, and we were so encouraged by the commiseration and determination of the ordinary people that we ignored the difficulty and the smell and worked joyfully.

Since we took our midday meal there at the work site, the prisoners' families could bring them food, Tibetan tea, sweet tea, and so on, for them to eat their fill. More importantly, hitherto they had only been able to pass things to their imprisoned relatives indirectly using the paper slips issued by the prison authorities, and this was the first time the prisoners and their relatives had met at close quarters and seen one another's condition for themselves.

Those days coincided with my mother's release, due to illness, from the prison known as "Tsémön-ling Reeducation," where the investigation and interrogation concerning secondary incidents in the uprising was taking place. One day she came, supported on both sides by my brothers and sisters, to visit my elder brother and me, and we saw her from a distance. Our kind mother smiled lovingly toward us, clenching her jaw and blinking her eyes, as a way of encouraging us to be brave. She left me feeling affectionate joy and looking forward to our next meeting, and I never imagined that that was the last time I would ever see her.

One day not long after, following the celebration of the [tenth] anniversary of the founding of the Chinese People's Republic on October 1, 1959, the training brigade prisoners were suddenly transferred to the Norbu Lingka prison.

CHAPTER 6

Imprisoned at the Norbu Lingka Barracks

IT IS WELL known to those who spent time in the Norbu Lingka prison and their relatives and acquaintances, but those unfamiliar with that period and those both in and outside Tibet who grew up later may be interested to know how control of the prison passed from Tibetan into Chinese hands. The Chinese fabricated false stories about the former [Tibetan government] prisons at the Potala, Norbu Lingka, Lhasa Nangtsé-shak, and Shöl, saying that this was where the laboring masses were put to death, and used them for internal and external propaganda. So maybe I should explain a little about the Norbu Lingka prison to clarify the situation for the reader: it was located on the southwest side of the Norbu Lingka grounds and formerly served as the barracks of the Dalai Lamas' bodyguard regiment (*sKu srung dmag sgar*). As for how the Chinese used it as a place to incarcerate Tibetans: at the time of the uprising, the fiercest armed resistance to the Chinese was concentrated around the summer palace, and since the Norbu Lingka was also the center of the suppression of the fighting, most people were arrested from that area. For a few days, they were held inside the boundary wall of the Norbu Lingka under armed guard. Then the bodyguard regiment barracks were stripped of their former contents and used to hold the detainees. Later, most of those taken prisoner by the army in Lho-ka were detained there, with the exception of a few notables. It thus became known as the "Norbu Lingka prison." Similarly, as will be explained below, the so-called "Drapchi prison" was formerly the location of the Drapchi [Tibetan] military base, and once the Chinese established the most extensive of their "Reform Through Labor" prisons there, people called it "Drapchi prison."

It was autumn when we were taken to the Norbu Lingka prison, around the eighth [Tibetan] month, just as the trees start to shed their leaves. We were not put together with the other prisoners, but in a separate group of rooms that had been arranged for us. The prison population was 1,500. There was a separate canteen for each team (*Ru khag*). Before eating, the prisoners had to line up in order, holding their eating bowls and spoons, and sing revolutionary songs. At those times, the great yard of the barracks was completely filled with people. Those of us transferred from the TMD prison did not need our own kitchen but ate at the canteen of a team with relatively fewer members. Compared with the army headquarters prison, the food was a little worse, but we could receive food and clothes from our relatives once a week.

The people held at that prison were former soldiers in the Tibetan army, regular monks from Séra and Drépung, and other Lhasa people who had not been in government service. So the Chinese officials told them that "the prisoners who came from the TMD prison are not like you, they are ringleaders of the uprising as well as representatives of the historically exploitative ruling class; they will not work alongside you, and apart from watching them, you should have nothing to do with them." Meanwhile they told us, "So far the other prisoners have not even studied the Party's policies," and other disparaging things, as a way of enhancing their control by inciting disagreements and divisions among us.

One day, after we had been there for about three weeks, the list of names of the prisoners sent from TMD was read out and we were divided into four groups. I was in a group of about fourteen that was assembled for a separate meeting where the officials told us pleasantly, "Since you have committed lighter offenses, there is a chance that you will be released soon. But for the moment you will be doing compulsory labor on the construction of the Nga-chen power station. This is like taking an exam in school, so you should make your best effort when you join in that noble work." The names that had been called were those of former government officials with no political responsibility, such as official physicians (*Bla sman*), doormen (*gZim 'gag*), a few junior officials like me, and a couple of ordinary people. The highest in rank was Shölkhang-sé Sonam Targyé. That he was not accused of involvement in the fighting seemed to be because he had sold all his integrity to the Communist Party while in the TMD prison and become one of the internal accusers, and had his sentence reduced.

One of the other three groups was sent to the Téring prison in Lhasa; another was sent to China. The rest remained at the TMD prison. Our group was taken off to labor the very next day, in a prisoner transport truck. We arrived at the Nga-chen work site with hopes of being released soon, but it turned out to be quite the opposite, for working there was just the start of the ordeal of hunger, thirst, exhaustion, and torment that I was to go through.

CHAPTER 7

At the Nga-chen Power Station Construction Site

IN NOVEMBER 1959, our group of prisoners was loaded on a transport truck and taken to the prison at the Nga-chen power station building site. There I met up with my elder sister Losang Chönyi, who was in one of the women prisoner teams. As soon as we got down from the truck, she came with a thermos of hot salted tea. The weather was foul that day, and we had had nothing but hot water. The delicious taste of my loving sister's hot tea warming and reviving me is something I have not forgotten even now. To suddenly see the face of my sister, who could have been dead for all I knew, was of course a joy. Having arrived at that work site a few days earlier, she had seen for herself how rough and dangerous the work was, and she was full of concern that I would have to suffer such hardship and especially danger. Before we had any chance to tell each other in detail about what we had been through, I had to go and help set up the tents we were to live in. Afterward, the new arrivals were assembled for a meeting where the main leader of the prison, a military officer, spoke to us about what was to be done.

That Chinese officer was the one who had earlier been appointed by the central government as a bodyguard for Ka-lön Samdrup Po-trang. In a very lengthy speech, he told us that the old Tibetan society was extremely cruel, barbaric, dark, and backward, and the reactionary upper strata of the Tibetan local government had not voluntarily accepted reforms, so the heroic PLA had put down their revolt, and now the reconstruction of Tibet could begin. Since the generation of electric power was the foundation of that reconstruction, building the Nga-chen power station had a noble purpose and meaning. "You people not only exploited the masses for generation after generation," he said, "you are also guilty of opposing the state and the masses by participating in an uprising. However, in accordance with the correct policy of the Party, you will be dealt with in a humanitarian way by being given the opportunity to become new people through labor reform by working on projects such as this, which is something glorious. The other prisoners at this work site are quite different from you. Apart from some minor involvement in the uprising, they are not guilty of historical oppression, and they will watch you and scrutinize your behavior. If, instead of regretting and accounting for your past actions, you resist and show no enthusiasm for work, you will be strictly punished according to regulations." Having made this distinction, he called on the other prisoners to keep their eye on us.

Then senior and junior leaders (*bCu dpon*) were appointed among our group of 10. Sonam Targyé, the son of Rimshi Shölkhang, was the senior, and Shödrung Lhundrup Peljor of Chakri-shar was the junior. This was because Shölkhang-sé's elder brother Tubten Nyima was one of the famous revolutionary nobles in the Chinese camp, while Lhundrup Peljor had previously served in Ka-lön Sam-po's security retinue and was known to the Chinese officer. The construction site prison was located between the canal for the power station and the Kyi-chu river, and the prisoners' tents were arranged team by team. Some of them were worn-out military-style tents of quilted cotton, others were made of canvas, and in the middle of the encampment was a group of good-quality quilted cotton tents for the officials in charge. Of the five teams in that work camp prison, the first consisted of prisoners sent from Téring prison in Lhasa, the second was prisoners from the Norbu Lingka prison, the third consisted only of monks from Séra and Drépung, the fourth was those of us from the TMD prison plus a few latecomers from Téring, and the fifth was prisoners from Taktsé Dzong in the upper Kyi-chu valley who had been held temporarily at Ganden monastery. As there were a good 400 people in each team, there must have been over 2,000 of us, but the prison was known as Gya-shok number 7 (*brGya shog* = group of 100), because at the time when prisoners were organized in a large number of Gya-shoks, this was the site of number 7, and the name stayed in use. Instead of a boundary wall, there was a barbed-wire fence about 2 yards high around the perimeter, with a few stone-walled circular towers at intervals for the soldiers on guard duty. At that time there must have been tens of thousands of people working at Nga-chen, and it was under the nominal administration of the TMD authority.

We were given food four times a day, twice in our own camp, in the morning and evening, and twice at the work site. It was rice or wheat with some watery residue of boiled cabbage. At work, the eating periods were no longer than fifteen minutes, and latecomers would miss out. Near the eating place there was a big blackboard used for displaying big-character bulletins. No one who was imprisoned there then could have forgotten it, because the Chinese officials would use it sometimes for fearsome threats to make the prisoners work harder and sometimes for beguiling exhortations about the noble significance of building the New Tibet at Nga-chen power station. More spitefully still, they used that blackboard to record the scores in a thoroughly resented competition among the different teams to exceed their work quotas. Being obliged to record our scores there caused the greatest of difficulties for all the competitors. Among ourselves, my comrades and I called that notice board "the governor." On the way to work, we had to line up in team order and sing "revolutionary songs" in a loud and clear voice. The most common song at the time was "Socialism Is Great, Socialism Is Good!" and everyone, young and old, had to know it well. At the beginning of our meetings, the teams would have to compete in singing these songs. That was another kind of torment in addition to the labor.

The Gya-shok 7 prisoners were not sent to work at the same time but had to alternate day and night shifts. The morning I arrived, a group of night workers had just returned from their shift. They were dressed in worn-out army uniforms of quilted cotton covered with patches. Their faces were white with dust, most of their eyes were bloodshot from the dust, and they walked as if they were seventy or eighty years old. I remember wondering why only old people had been recruited for such rough work. But many among them behaved as if they recognized us and smiled, and it was only because of their changed appearance, with dusty faces and uniforms, that I did not know them at first. A moment later, when we went to the canteen together, I realized that most of them were young men, and those who had smiled were former acquaintances of mine. In the course of exchanging greetings, they told me to be very alert about safety, and asked me did I have a pad for my back? Were my shoes good? Did I have a strong pair of gloves? On reflection, I realized that this was their way of warning me that the work we had to do was extremely dangerous and hard, as it was not permitted for older prisoners to speak plainly about this with new arrivals. Those people had become so physically reduced in less than a year, and although I had been incarcerated in the imposingly named TMD prison, I had not been exposed to such hardship, so it was evident simply from our physical condition that we had just arrived and they had been there for some time. Before reaching that power station, I had been confident enough to think that wherever we were sent we would be given [the same] "corrective labor" (*Ngal rtsol sbyong brdar*), but on the very day of my arrival I was shaken by much of what I saw.

The best thing about the building site prison was that we were allowed to visit with our relatives once every two weeks. While I was in the TMD prison, we could only occasionally catch a glimpse of our relatives from a distance and almost never had the opportunity to actually meet and speak with them. So after getting to Nga-chen I became very conscious of the calendar, in order to keep track of the meeting days. On the Saturday night before the fortnightly meeting I could not sleep and spent the whole night wondering how it would feel when I saw my family, and since we would have no more than a few minutes, thinking what we would talk about in that time. When we got up on Sunday morning and went for our morning meal, peoples' families were already there, outside the perimeter fence, kindling fires in the icy morning wind to boil water for tea. I could see my sister Tendzin Dékyong and my younger brother Jam-pun among them. When we had finished eating, a prison official registered the relatives' names and they were called in turn. When our relatives' turn came, they read my name and the name of my eldest sister Losang Chönyi, calling us to meet them.

My brother and sister held our hands tightly, their eyes full of tears, and asked us with choking voices if we were all right. When I asked them about our mother and the other brothers and sisters, they replied that Mother was seriously ill and could not come to visit us, but had she not been so ill, she would have been put in prison long ago. "Because the two of you were arrested," they continued, "the contents of our house were declared state property, the door was sealed, and we inhabitants given just a minimal allowance of tea, *tsampa*, and clothing to last for a few days." After briefly explaining the situation, they said, "You two look after yourselves! We can come whenever we are allowed to see you." "Please keep taking good care of Mother," I said, but even before I could think of more to say, the meeting period was over and we were abruptly separated.

The prison officials had their day off on Sundays, and for the fortnightly Sunday visits they were there only in the morning, so the prisoners' relatives had to reach the gate of the prison early. That meant that they had to leave their homes in Lhasa in the middle of the night to make the four-hour walk and reach the prison gate at sunrise. Then, since it is the Tibetan custom that when you go to greet someone you pour hot tea for them, they had to kindle fires in the icy morning wind, and since there were no villages nearby where they might have bought firewood, they had to carry it on their backs all the way from home. When I thought carefully about the thousand difficulties our relatives willingly undertook to look after us in this way, it seemed to me that as long as I lived I should try to repay their kindness. Anyway, the night before each meeting, and for several days after, I could hardly sleep.

I arrived at the construction site prison just when the Chinese launched a campaign for all the workers to forge ahead, called "Fifty Days of Fierce Struggle." Besides spending 13 hours a day on the job, we had sundry "duties" to do when we got back to our camp, and including the meetings that we had to attend every evening, we worked 15 hours a day. The job given to the prisoners in Gya-shok 7 was to cut through the mountain spur known as the Nga-chen defile (*rNga chen 'phrang*) at the center of the site where the power station's turbines were to be installed. Of all the work sites in the construction area, this was the toughest and most dangerous, because we had to blast the mountain spur with dynamite and the rock shrapnel from the explosions caused a lot of damage. Worse, the blasts loosened the rocks on the mountainside so that even a strong gust of wind could cause a devastating rockfall. There was a group of prisoners from China setting the dynamite, and we had to remove the rubble left by their blasting. Since the place was extremely narrow and all the prisoners in the team could not fit in at one time, they were continually rotated, day and night, so that the work site was never empty. The work target for each member in a group of 10 was to remove 200 basketfuls of rock per day, with two members of the group filling the baskets, one digging the rubble with a pick, and the rest carrying. If you failed to meet this target once or twice, that would be enough for the group to investigate, but if it kept happening, you would have to face struggle at the team level.

I was just eighteen and had not been prepared for this kind of work at the TMD prison, so even with a maximum of effort the target was very hard to meet, and I received criticism and scolding at several nightly group meetings. Most of the older prisoners managed to meet the quota, and I assumed that this was due to their strength and training, but then I started to wonder whether there might not also be some technique. When I asked those I knew, they told me that if you managed to pick up the bigger stones, the basket would count for two [regular loads], and instead of just waiting in line for the team members to fill your basket, you should use that time to do it by your own effort. By thus taking the bigger rocks myself and doing my best to fill my own basket when the basket fillers were busy, I managed to meet the target. But we got wounds on our backs from carrying those big stones, and our fingertips split open after a single day of loading our own baskets with crushed rock. We were given new gloves once a week, and our families also brought them for us on visiting days, but they did not last even one day of continually loading broken rock. Just touching it with our raw fingers would make our very hearts tingle with pain, and the only way to heal the wounds on our backs was to stop carrying loads for a few months, or so the older prisoners said.

Under those conditions, it was hard to keep meeting the target, but since we had no choice, I had to trade the food brought to me by my family with the stronger prisoners in exchange for work points (*Thel rtse*), instead of eating it myself. The Chinese gave everyone tokens in various denominations of points, representing work completed, when we filled our baskets. The person with whom I traded most often was a former monk from Ganden Jangtsé who had an astoundingly plentiful supply of work points, even though he did not look strong enough to have earned them himself. He was extremely useful to me at the time, but I never dared ask him if he had really earned these in excess of the required quota. I met him again about eighteen years later, when he was working in one of the main granaries in Lhasa. He had been released not long after we worked together at the power station prison, gotten married, and had children. We reminisced about our time at the power station, and I asked him about the extra work points; he said that if he had really tried to meet that target day by day the strain would have killed him, but he had resorted to a couple of ways to acquire a surplus. One of them was to exchange the tokens for individual points with the bigger tokens of 20, 50, or 100 points, which could be done surreptitiously when the old people who gave out the tokens were dealing with a lot of people. At those times, they were too distracted to count, and we could tell them "Hurry up! Our time is being wasted!" throwing a wad of 50 small tokens into their lap and bluffing them that there were 100. "Another way was that when the markings on the tokens became unclear, we could double the numbers by cutting them in half and hand in as many as we could, making them smaller every day, while those with clear markings could be traded with people like you who were able to meet their relatives."

One day, during the time when I was having to trade all the food and clothing brought by my family, one of the old people who could not work and instead handed out tokens at the place where we dumped our loads of rock just handed the tokens to me without counting and put them in my shirt pocket, making me wonder what he was up to. When I got back to my tent in the evening after work and counted how many tokens I had received, to my amazement I found a 50-point token among them. When I thought carefully, I realized it could only have come from the old man, for I had not dumped enough baskets that day to earn it, and I could not help pondering what had made him give me extra. If the officials had gotten him to do it as a test and I were to use the extra points, all the targets I had genuinely achieved would be canceled, and I would undoubtedly have to face struggle at a big meeting. If the old man had given them for my benefit, it was a real boon. That night, I resolved not only not to use them but also, if asked, to make out that I had not met the target, to make sure that the officials had not put him up to it. If they had, I would still be able to deny that any such thing had happened. But even after I'd waited for a few days, no one checked.

Then I started to think that the old man must be a former acquaintance and really wanted to find out who he might be, but he was only occasionally on duty, and in any case he wore goggles, a cotton dust mask, and a woolen hat covering his face. He was a frail old man, his gown tied with a bulky belt, wearing felt shoes from China, who needed a walking stick to get around, but I did not get to see his face and didn't dare ask who he was. Thinking that he would take off his goggles and mask once he got back to his tent from work, I repeatedly passed by the tents of that team, but except when he went to the toilet, he was always inside the tent, and I couldn't find out who he was. Then, while talking with a former schoolmate of mine called Yéshé Tenpa who was in the same team, but without asking directly about the old man, I learned that among those handing out the tokens were Shölkhang Épa Yöndak-la and Reteng Rinpoché's father. Reteng Rinpoché's father was not known to me, but I had worked together several times with Épa Yöndak-la in the office of the palace secretariat, so I decided it must be him. But several days passed before I actually got to talk to him. One day, I suddenly bumped into him at the door of the toilet. He took hold of my hand and asked after my health: "Are you well? Isn't the work too tiring?"

"I am fine," I replied, "but I haven't done this kind of work before and it's hard. In time I will shape up," and asked in turn after his health.

"Basically, there's nothing wrong with me," he said, "but as I am one of the old and decrepit, I am not required to do labor but am one of those who distribute work points. With that opportunity I have been able to benefit my comrades a little bit, but I know that those activities will be discovered one day," bravely giving me the signal that he was passing out extra tokens. I thanked him and told him I would never forget his kindness, and moreover that he need not worry, for I would not say a word about it to others.

Although we didn't speak directly about the extra tokens, we understood each other, and after that, whenever I found him on duty, he would give me extra tokens. In total, he gave me about 500 points, so during that time I didn't have to worry about not meeting my quota, and I could use the provisions my family brought myself. Épa Yöndak-la had served as a secretary since his youth during the reign of the Thirteenth Dalai Lama, and he was a great Tibetan who cared about his people and loved his comrades. His passing me extra tokens was not just an individual gesture but an act of resistance against the Chinese plot to break the spirit of the Tibetan people by enslaving them under the pretext of "Reform Through Labor." He looked after the welfare of our people and relieved the hardships of many others like me. Later, after my release, I was extremely sad to learn that he had died after being subjected to struggle in Drapchi prison.

Even though by using the extra tokens I was not in fear of failing to meet the quota, I could not sit idle, and could only catch the odd moment of rest on the night shift by pretending to go to the toilet. One had to squat, since if one sat back on the ground one would be seen by the officials who often came around to check that we were really relieving ourselves. Some of the nastier officials would bring lamps to check carefully. So if one could not go, one squatted above where someone else had been recently, and I managed to fall asleep in that position quite a few times.

Anyway, during that year of the uprising, when large numbers of people were arrested all over Tibet and imprisoned in different centers, of the six or so detention centers in the Lhasa area alone, the Nga-chen power station was the worst. The weather at the Nga-chen work site was much colder and windier than in Lhasa, and since our accommodation was miserable and we had to do difficult and very dangerous work for long hours, my hands and feet were blistered and my back was virtually covered in wounds. Under those conditions, many people of lesser endurance killed themselves in one way or another, by jumping in the river or throwing themselves off a cliff or under the wheels of a truck. At that time, a man I knew called Jampa Yönten told me that he could not stand the hardship anymore and was going to kill himself. I told him, "That will never do. Unlike us, you did not participate in the uprising; you were not employed by the government and are not one of the ruling class, so you can hope to be released soon," and said whatever else I could think of to stop him, but one day he jumped with a basket on his back off a cliff 100 steps in height, by the ravine where we deposited our loads of earth and rock. Strangely and amusingly enough, he was caught on a wire about 30 steps of the way down, and apart from some walnut-sized bruises on his head, he was unharmed, and some prisoners were able to rescue him. After that, he decided that he was not destined to die just yet. Later we were together in Drapchi prison.

The story of Jampa Yönten's imprisonment was amazingly ironic. Since he had once lived in Dartsé-do and knew a little Chinese, he started working in the Chinese supply office around 1953. During the uprising, after the assembly moved from the Norbu Lingka to the Shöl printery and registered volunteers to serve as security guards at the Norbu Lingka, he went to register of his own accord, but some people knew him as an official of the supply office and told the others that he was a Chinese spy, so he was immediately detained in the Shöl prison, which at that time was still under Tibetan control. After the uprising, when the Chinese released those held in our prisons, there was a Khampa in his cell who had been arrested during the fighting between the Chinese army and Khampa rebels in Nyémo and handed over to our side, and as the Chinese knew that he was a Khampa fighter they transferred them together, like both losing hold of the reins and getting dragged behind a galloping horse, to a Chinese prison.

As I mentioned, we prisoners of Gya-shok 7 were put to work cutting through the mountain spur where the turbines were to be installed. Every day, there were three scheduled series of blasts, with about sixty or seventy explosions each time, and it was necessary to keep count of the explosions to be sure that they had all gone off. Sometimes the person keeping count made mistakes, and before my arrival there had been a few instances when the workers had reassembled by the rubble, thinking the blasting had finished, and further explosions went off in their midst. By the time we started working there, the spur had been mostly blasted through, leaving a ravine. The workers were crowded into the middle, where even a strong gust of wind hitting the mountainside, which had been loosened by blasting, could bring down rockfalls from either side in which people were wounded or killed.

One of the worst incidents happened in the early morning, at about four o'clock. We had been working the night shift in that ravine, but luckily, once the rubble from the previous blasts had all been cleared, our team 4 was moved to another area to load rocks onto a truck. Then, since we could not see enough in the dark without lamps, we had to leave and return in daylight. After we got back to our tents and lay down to sleep, we heard a lot of shouting around the officials' tents and the truck that was used to transport the injured going back and forth through the night. I fell asleep wondering who might have been killed or wounded, and when I got up the next morning I found out that a great boulder had tumbled down where the prisoners from team 2 were at work. About seventeen people were injured, three of whom died on the spot. Among the injured was someone I knew, the husband (*Mag pa*) of the Néchung oracle's niece, who had served as a bursary official (*Shod phyag nang*), and Kundé-ling Ta-tsak Rinpoché's cook. They were all taken to the Lhasa People's Hospital. The next day, when we went to work at the site of the accident, it looked like a blood-stained battlefield. Several people had been trapped under the great boulder, and the members of team 2 told how during the hour or two it took to get them out, their screams from the pain of broken arms and legs and so on echoed terrifyingly around the ravine.

That day, all twenty-four of the ten-man units in team 4 were taken back to our encampment, where a meeting was held with the work site officials and team officials. They made a threatening announcement along these lines: "As you well know, some people have been grievously wounded, and in order to save their lives we need donations of compatible blood. Since you people are from the former exploiting class that lived exclusively on good food, your blood must be very rich and you must now make donations," and that night we were taken to the People's Hospital. When they tested our blood, mine was of no use. They drew the blood of three who had the right blood type, Sumdo Lekdrup Chödar, Losang Tenpa, one of the official physicians, and Késang Rabgyé of the Gonjo Chösur-tsang family, after which they were given about five days' rest. The rest of us went back to work at the ravine just as before. After that, they appointed someone to watch for the danger of rockfalls on either side, although in the event of a slide like the last one happening again, evacuation would be very difficult. During the two months I was in the work camp prison, that was the largest number of people injured in the ravine at one time, but every day a few people would be hit by falling rock.

Soon after, we were put onto the task of building the embankment wall of the reservoir. Sometimes we had to bring sand and pebbles from the river shore, and sometimes we had to dig and carry earth from the foot of the mountainside. The paths leading to both places were open, there was no need for any blasting, and by all appearances there was no danger. Yet, incredibly, one day a landslide came down the mountain and buried eleven people [working there]. They managed to pull two of them out, but the other nine were killed instantly. I still have a vivid memory of the scene.

After the rockfall in the ravine, each team had appointed a "safety officer," and in our team it was Tangpé Tséring, who spoke some Chinese and was in my canteen group. One morning, as soon as we arrived to dig and carry earth from the mountainside, he inspected the site for signs of danger and found that a crevice had opened above the excavated pit. This was considered dangerous, and at once a group of workers, with rope tied around their waists and using hammers and chisels, tried to force it open. But after working for half a day, they failed; the crevice had not widened at all. Then the team official and the Chinese foreman said that the crevice didn't seem to be dangerous, that since we hadn't been able to make it collapse when we tried, it shouldn't fall down by itself, and instead of wasting more time, we should carry on digging earth. At the time I was suffering from a cold and not feeling strong, so I took the job of pulling on a rope attached to the spade for digging and filling the baskets. The person digging was the former official physician and compulsory blood donor Losang Tenpa. Around four o'clock that afternoon, one of the earth carriers, Dondrup (a former servant at Shöl-shar), called out that a landslide was coming. I myself was still apprehensive after seeing the crevice that morning, and as soon as I felt a puff of wind like another person blowing on me, I started forward. When I had run a little way, I glanced back to see what seemed like the lower half of the mountainside collapsing and the group of workers being buried by the landslide. It had struck as soon as I had stepped away.

At once, everyone began calling out the names of their friends or canteen group members in confusion, but no one could really tell who had been buried under the landslide. Then we lined up in our groups of ten and were counted, so that it could be seen who was missing. Two people whose limbs stuck out were pulled out alive, but among the nine who lost their lives were my fellow digger, the physician Losang Tenpa-la, and the spade puller working at my side, a relative of Tsawa-rongpa A-ba. My elder sister Losang Chönyi was working with the women's team nearby, and as she knew I had been digging there, she assumed that I had been buried under the landslide, and she came calling my name and wailing fearfully with grief. I went to her and started to tell her I was unharmed, but in her panic, weeping and agitated, she didn't see me. Right away, our section had to line up and go back to camp. The two teams of night workers who were to extract the bodies from the rubble arrived in a state of terror. The "Lhasa volunteers" team (*lHa sa dang blangs ru khag*), who were not prisoners, and the "workers team" (*Las mi ru khag*), former prisoners who had been given work duty on the Nga-chen power station after their release, were not very far away, and because they well knew that a landslide had fallen on a brigade of prison laborers and caused heavy losses, the bad news spread through

Lhasa that same night. Then the prisoners' families were filled with anxiety, and some of them walked through the night and arrived at the prison camp gate at dawn, trying to find out whether their relatives were still alive. My own elder sister Tendzin Dékyong came, and I made sure she could see me, still alive and unharmed.

Although one or two prisoners had been getting killed or injured almost every day, their deaths were not even considered as important as those of animals, but on that occasion the rumor that a large number of people had been killed in an accident was rife in Lhasa and nearby, without the central office at Nga-chen being able to do anything about it. Since those relatives had come, they made an announcement and then allowed them to meet their family members among the surviving prisoners as a special concession, since this was not the fortnightly prison meeting day, before they had to leave. The relatives of the dead prisoners were called to the officials' tent, where [the officials] told them that the dead had given their lives for the construction of New Socialist Tibet, which was glorious, and consoled them with smooth words, like saying that the bodies could be disposed of according to local custom or however the relatives wished, which was adding insult to injury.

The physician Losang Tenpa from our group of ten who had been killed was his mother's only son and had a close bond with her. When we had been in the TMD prison earlier in 1959, his mother had come almost every day to the main gate to see how her son was doing. Even after we got to Nga-chen, the tiring journey did not discourage her from coming often, and it went without saying that she would be there for every meeting day, so we said among ourselves that she would go mad with grief. When the bedding and effects of the deceased were handed over to their families, the leader (bCu dpon) of our group had to deliver Losang Tenpa's, and when he returned, we asked how she had reacted. We were amazed to hear that she didn't weep or even speak. Actually, his mother was in shock, and I heard that as a result she developed "water in the heart" [pericardial dropsy] and passed away soon after. Relatives of the other dead prisoners were similarly afflicted.

Then the Chinese said that the safety officer for our team, Tangpé Tséring, should take responsibility for the loss of life, and he was shackled and handcuffed and placed in a small room under close guard. All the teams in the so-called Gya-shok 7 camp were suspended from work for the next three days, and the Nga-chen central office sent a work team (Las don ru khag) to determine who had been responsible for the accident. An army officer in charge of that team questioned all of the assembled members of the twenty-four groups in our team 4. He asked us who could give the clearest account, and since I had been assisting the digger who was killed, he told me, "If you saw the incident clearly you should speak up." Thereupon, I gave an honest and balanced account of the events of that day: how the safety officer Tangpé Tséring had seen a fissure, a group had been organized to try to force it open but failed after half a day's effort, how the official and the foreman had decided there was no danger, and finally how the event caught the workers unawares. The army officer asked me, "In your opinion, who should take responsibility for the loss of life?" I replied that our team's safety officer had only slight responsibility, since he had seen the signs of subsidence and reported it, and had he not done so, more people could have been affected, but chiefly responsible were those who had decided that the crevice was not dangerous. No one else among us came forward to speak.

At the end of the three days there was a big meeting where they read out the names of many people who had to speak about who should take responsibility for the landslide. The members of the other teams did not have firsthand knowledge of the incident and could not blame the official and the Chinese supervisor, and since they had been encouraged to look down on our group of "oppressors" since we first arrived at Nga-chen, some mindless people put all the blame on Tangpé Tséring. The last name called from the list of those who had to speak was my own. I had not been told anything about having to address the meeting and had not prepared myself at all. Moreover, I had never addressed a large meeting before, and what I had said in front of my group of ten directly contradicted what had already been said by members of other teams. I was shaking with fear and sweating profusely, but once one's name has been called, one has no choice but to speak, so I collected my thoughts and repeated what I had told the army officer in front of my group—that those who had decided there was no danger had the main responsibility, and the safety officer had only the lesser, unavoidable responsibility entailed by his position. Since I had contradicted the members of other teams and I was a member of the same canteen group as Tangpé Tséring, I thought that however one looked at it, the situation was not good, like both losing the reins and getting dragged behind [a galloping horse], but the meeting was reconvened [after the work team had discussed its decision], and the army officer in charge announced in conclusion that the Chinese supervisor should take full responsibility. He was clapped in irons and detained, and Tangpé Tséring was released. In reality, however, the higher officials had full responsibility because that Chinese supervisor, who had been appointed after being released from prison, had to follow whatever they said and had no authority to make decisions of his own. But the officials made use of their power to shift their own responsibility onto that unfortunate Chinese man.

The story of that landslide became known throughout Tibet, and because of a few individuals from Lhasa who managed to escape to India at that time, my elder brother Yéshé Khédrup-la heard tell that I had been buried in the landslide while he was in India. I was among those departed souls for whom he requested lamas to make prayers right up to 1979, when Tibetans began to get permission to travel back and forth and he could confirm that I was still alive.

My greatest loss in the landslide was my padded cotton jacket, which was buried. Later, one of the people retrieving the corpses gave it back to me, but he took tokens worth about 200 points out of the top pocket. Since I would have had to explain how I'd gotten hold of so many extra tokens if there were an inquiry, I had to stay silent and suffer the loss. From then on, we carried sand and pebbles for the embankment from the river shore and quit bringing earth from the mountainside where the landslide had occurred. Sand and pebbles are the heaviest of building materials, I was weakened by a bad cold, and having lost my extra work points, I had to struggle to meet the targets.

For a few days, I'd had pain in my calf muscle. There was an elementary clinic at the construction site where they would treat visible wounds, but if you had an internal injury they would consider it a ruse to get off work, and instead of rest or treatment you would be given a scolding. So I decided not to go there, hoping it would get better, but on the contrary, the pain in my calf became so severe that I couldn't walk unassisted and had to hold on to the wall. There was another former official physician in my group of ten, Yönten Tarchin-la, who told me that I had dislocated the muscle (*Nyva log*). The cure for that, he said, was to take nutritious food and a long rest, the two rarest things of all in that prison. And many of the older people in the other groups told me remedies, such as eating the egg of a black hen, that I had no means to apply. Even worse than my own suffering from the pain was that my elder sister Losang Chönyi worried about me more than ever. She made inquiries with knowledgeable people about how to treat a dislocated calf muscle, but asking on someone else's behalf under prison conditions where talking to others is difficult, who knows if black hens' eggs was the right answer? Anyway, she managed to get hold of a few eggs and some butter, and gave them to me. But I didn't get any better. Unable to sleep at night and quite incapable of going to work during the day, I approached the section leader there called Chamdowa Lha-gyel and asked to be excused. He was one of a group of new officials who had come to work at the construction site. At first he was indecisive, saying that he had only arrived a few days before and was not familiar with the routine of the place, and that they could not decide in the case of sick leave but would have to ask what the regulation was. Then suddenly he said, "Without permission from the camp clinic, you cannot take leave!"

"The clinic only accepts patients with visible injuries," I said, "and even though I have actually dislocated a muscle and can't walk straight, they will not take me, as you well know. Please have some compassion and do something to help me out." I pleaded with him pathetically, sinking to my knees and resting my forehead against his leg. At that point my condition moved him. "Poor little Lhasa kid," he said, "let's see what the doctors say," and took me over there. Because he had been asked by an official, the doctor gave me a permit (*sPa se*) for two days' medical leave, and I got to spend two whole days in bed. But there was no improvement, and by this time, my calf muscle had slipped so far it was touching my shin. There was no way to ask the team leader for further leave, and just as I was wondering what I was going to do the next day, a group of policemen from the Lhasa Public Security Bureau came to the camp prison around six o'clock, and the prison authorities read out a list of names of people from our eastern neighborhood of Lhasa, announcing that they had to roll up their bedding and move to another place. Where that was, only the officials knew. Since I was left behind in bed, I did not yet know that my name had been called, and I waited hopefully for those whose names had been called earlier. After a moment, the section official Lha-gyel, with the air of bringing good news, told me to roll up my bedding at once. "Those whose names were called out are off to Lhasa now, they are all east Lhasa people," he said, confidentially explaining, "Your cases are to be decided by the deliberations of the masses." Now I was no longer his problem.

Luckily, my elder sister's name was called out together with ours. Right away, my fellow group members helped me to roll up my bedding, and by the time we left the camp prison the sun was well over the western horizon. My companions dumped me in the truck like a piece of luggage, and we headed in the direction of Lhasa.

CHAPTER 8

In Téring Prison

IT WAS ONE of the first days of January 1960, at about six o'clock Beijing time, when our group of east Lhasa people from the Nga-chen work camp prison were loaded into two large trucks with canvas tops and driven away, through the hamlets of Garpa, Shangtap, and Rak, to the Téring (*Phreng ring*) prison. We got there at about ten o'clock that night. The prison was a simple one-story Tibetan-style building. By the electric light bulbs over the cell doors, we could clearly see that each cell had a number and a circular hole in the door, and from the electric bulbs positioned outside each window pointing inward, that each was sealed with iron bars. There were more electric lights on the roof and at the entrance, and fierce-looking guards equipped with machine guns and grenades stood around the perimeter. All else was shrouded in the still darkness of night.

Once we had gotten down from the truck and collected our baggage, there was another roll call, and we and our possessions were thoroughly searched. They didn't take away just the items normally forbidden for prisoners, but even leftover food brought by our relatives that we had been saving and any bits of rope more than a few inches long, from our belts down to the drawstrings of our underwear. Then, with our clothes hanging loose, we were put in cell number 2. This was a Tibetan-style room of six pillars that already contained sixteen prisoners, and with the addition of all the male prisoners from Nga-chen it was extremely crowded. As soon as you came through the door, there was an awful stench of urine and feces from the two large tin chamber pots that were in every cell. Everyone tried their best not to have to stay near those chamber pots, but since I had a leg injury and could barely walk there was no question of my getting a preferable spot, and I had no choice but to sit right next to them. I thought that we would be relocated the following day, but at that time prisoners were continually being brought to Téring from other prisons, as we had been, so all the cells were as crowded as ours, and I had to sit next to the chamber pots for the next month. However, once we had left Nga-chen power station, we did not have to work at all for a month while we were questioned and given time to reflect on the crimes we had committed during the uprising, and during that time my calf injury gradually healed. And after a few days, I got so used to the stench of urine that I didn't notice it anymore.

The Téring prison was located just beyond the eastern limit of the processional path (*Gling 'khor*) around Lhasa, on the site of the former Téring family house and the house of Samdrup Po-trang the younger, Tendzin Dondrup-la, and their outbuildings. These had been taken over by the Lhasa Public Security office and Public Security prison, which ordinary people referred to as the "Téring prison." There were twenty-five cells in the prison building, but of different sizes, some no more than one pillar and some six pillars in extent. Our cell had six pillars and fifty people crowded into it. Therefore it is hard to say with certainty what the total population was, especially since the time I spent there was during the political campaign called "Reexamination" (*sKyar zhib*), which was going on throughout Tibet, following Democratic Reform, and detainees were continually arriving from all over Lhasa and the surrounding area. In accordance with the superficial exercise of deciding the sentences of those guilty of involvement in the uprising through the "deliberations of the masses," all the prisoners awaiting sentence under the Lhasa municipal government were kept at Téring before being sent on to one of the Reform Through Labor prison camps (*bsGyur bkod kyi rva ba*). So I think there were more inmates at Téring then than at any other time since it had started to be used as a prison.

There were two cells of former government officials in Téring at that time. One held a group sent there from the TMD prison shortly before we arrived, including Khen-chung Késang Ngawang-la, the "Labrang bursar" Khen-chung Tubten Tenpa-la, and Tangpé Puntsok Namgyel-la. In the other cell were Shéling Tsewang Namgyel, the monk officials Lo-tsa Tubten Seng-gé and Tubten Géché, and a group of lamas and senior monks including [Séra-jé] Tsamtrul Rinpoché, the acting chant master of the upper tantric college, [Séra-mé] Chubsang Tulku, and [Séra-jé] Lawa Géshé Jampa Chöpel. Most of the other prisoners were ordinary people. Their crimes were such things as having served as local deputies or household managers or having organized *puja*s at the time of the uprising, but in any case they were mostly political prisoners, and only a very few were petty thieves, vagrants, and the like.

Although most of us were ordinary people, of all the prisons in Lhasa at that time, Téring had the worst conditions and the tightest control. The cell doors were opened only twice a day, morning and evening, for prisoners to be taken to the toilet, and at all other times they had to use the chamber pots in their cells. When they took us to the toilet in the morning and evening, they would not open all the doors at the same time, but one by one. The number of guards was increased and they enforced very strict security. When you went out, you would take your belt, bootstraps, or whatever you had left outside the cell door, since it was not permitted to keep any kind of rope longer than the palm of one's hand, and when you came back in, you would be thoroughly searched once again.

As for the food, when I arrived in January 1960 there were two meals a day, three if you worked. The diet was *tsampa*, and in the evenings we would get either a little boiled cabbage or some black tea in which they had put the acrid-tasting butter residue from the offering lamps in the Tsuklakhang temple, left over since the uprising. Before long, they cut back on the evening serving of cabbage, and the *tsampa* ration dwindled day by day until, by the time I was sent on from there to Drapchi prison, the prisoners' diet consisted of only about 3 ounces (*Srang*) of *tsampa* per day, and once a week or so a very thin gruel, both morning and evening, that may not even have been cooked. It was the color of tea tainted with verdigris, no different from the water we squeezed out of our dirty clothes, but it didn't even taste as good as copper-boiled tea, because the leftover lamp butter residue made it look and taste nauseating. The verdigris from a copper pot that has not been lined with white soda is said to be poisonous; it is very damaging to the stomach and the liver, and many of the prisoners who had spent a long time in Téring had stomach and liver ailments, but medical treatment for them was rarer than gold.

In the six months I spent there, I never saw any of my fellow prisoners being given medical care. An old cook from Drépung right next to me died of dysentery, but for a long time beforehand no one came to give him even a single dose of medicine. As prisoners were not usually given water for washing their hands and faces, there was no way to get water for washing clothes, and since they didn't provide us with prison uniforms and we were not allowed to receive fresh clothes from our relatives outside, the most abundant thing in that prison was fleas and lice. Due to the miserable diet and lack of medical attention, a great number of people suffered from lice infestation (*Shig nad*). There were even several incidents of people having lice come out of their insides.

While we were confined under these miserable conditions, the sentencing of prisoners was going on, supposedly by "the deliberations and decisions of the people," which was a way for the authorities to do their dirty work in the name of the people. Many prisoners were sentenced to fifteen, eighteen, twenty years for offenses lesser than my own, and the words I had heard after being picked out of the TMD prison about being released after a period of labor at Nga-chen vanished into thin air. My stay in Téring prison was the start of living on the edge of death from starvation, hardship, and fear, and all I could hope for was to be sentenced soon, be it light or heavy, so that I could be moved to another prison and at least get something to eat.

Fortunately, as we were sent on to a Reform Through Labor prison after sentencing, we did not have to spend a great length of time there. We had no particular daily work to do; sometimes we were given hard and dangerous jobs, but this might give us a chance to meet our relatives, and sometimes we stayed inside, to reflect on our crimes or study the *Tibet Daily* and other Communist literature. At that time, the three officials in charge of the prisoners were Norbu Dorjé, a former servant of Yabshi Taktsér from Drongtsé in Tsang; Yéshé Tenpa, son of a housekeeper from Lho-ka; and a woman called Purbu Drölma. Every day they opened and closed the doors when we were taken to the toilet or for work or at mealtimes. The names of the prisoners required for questioning were given to them, and it was their job to fetch them, but apart from dealing with those who broke the prison regulations, they had no authority to question prisoners about their crimes.

I will describe one of the incidents I remember most clearly from the six months I had to spend at Téring: the first work I had to do after arriving was at a big canal construction site north of Lhasa, near Drapchi Lingka, where all the Téring prisoners were sent to work for a few days. One day, nine of us healthier-looking prisoners were sent on a work assignment to an army camp occupying the former residence of Amdo Lekshé near Lingka Sarpa on the eastern edge of Lhasa. From there we were sent, pulling three mule carts, three of us for each, to the Drip valley on the other side of the river to collect clay (*Ar ka*) for building, accompanied by two guards. There were several clay pits on the mountainside, but it was a steep climb up to the one with the best quality Arka. There was already a truck there filling up, but since it couldn't get close to the pit, it stayed on the road and ten or so workers were carrying clay down from the pit to the truck in baskets. Our two guards instructed us to take clay from that pit, but since the space at the site was limited, we had to wait until the truck was full before we could start, and it seemed that we would not get back to Téring in time for the midday meal.

This made the guards nervous, and once the truck had gone, instead of leaving our carts on the main road, they had us push them right up to the pit. Then they told us to be quick about removing the clay and loading up the carts, so that we could get back. One of my two fellow cart pullers, who I think was called Chöpel, had been detained along with other religious people at the Tsukla-khang temple after the suppression of the uprising, and later imprisoned for refusing to denounce Trijang Rinpoché [one of His Holiness's tutors]. He was young and got along easily with his fellows, taking hardships on himself and leaving easier things for others, like a true monk. The other one was a former Tibetan soldier called Pa-wang. We decided that to get the cart back down the hill, I should go in the middle, since it was easier to steer with a taller person in the middle, while Pa-wang held the shaft down. Although smaller in stature, Gen Chöpel was very strong, and he pulled on a rope attached to the back of the cart to keep it from rolling downhill too fast.

We were the first cart to go back down the hill, because we had been the first to load up, and although the two guards shouted at us to hurry up, it was a dangerous enterprise. As prisoners, the only thing we could do was to make prayers to the Three Jewels, so ignoring the guards' coercion, I said a few Refuge and (dMigs brtse ma) prayers to Jé Rinpoché in a quiet voice while pretending to fasten my belt and shoelaces, and Gen Chöpel uttered the invocation of Mahakala. Then we carefully started to roll the cart. After about twenty-odd paces the cart broke loose; Gen Chöpel yelled at us to hold it from our end, but the two of us were powerless to stop it. Then Gen Chöpel's restraining rope snapped and the cart hurtled downhill uncontrollably; my companion Pa-wang and I were forced to run as fast as we could, thinking that the moment of death had come, almost up to the road. If we kept going once we hit the road, we would fall into a deep ravine on the far side, with no hope of survival. I called out to Pa-wang to let go of the shaft and get out, and not for his sake alone, because unless we were agreed on which way to turn the cart away from the edge, we would plunge straight into the abyss. As I called out, Pa-wang pulled off the rope around his shoulder and released the shaft, and had gotten free of the cart just as it hit the side of the road. I tried to turn the cart back toward Drip with my own strength, adopting the pose of a weight lifter, but at the same moment, the two cart shafts were wrenched uncontrollably out of my hands, and I lost consciousness. When I awoke, I had been thrown to one side of the road, and the cart was lying perfectly overturned by the boundary wall of the army camp on the left side. Once our serious accident confirmed the danger, the people pulling the two carts behind us started to come down, saying, "The same thing will surely happen to us," but the guards ordered them to go ahead and roll the other two carts down.

We had no way to refuse, but we could find a better method with the lessons of experience, so we tried to bring the next two carts down using all nine of us, most people pulling on ropes from behind and two on each side holding down the shafts, edging backward down the slope as carefully as possible, and in this way we got one of the carts safely down. But when the second one rolled onto the steep part it broke out of control; some ropes snapped, others were jerked away, the force was too great for the two holding down the cart shafts, and as it approached the road, the poles struck the ground and the team member in the middle of the cart, another Tibetan soldier and a friend of Pa-wang, was killed. He was not able to free himself from the harness of the cart and was crushed under it; they said his back and neck vertebrae were crumpled. Some also said that it was a daggerlike piece of wood on the cart shaft that had stuck in the ground [that killed him]. I was one of those pulling the cart from behind, and whether because of the strain or because of my accident, I was feeling stiff and numb, and when the cart lurched forward, forcing the rope out of my hands, it pulled me down so hard I tore my shoes and trousers.

Pa-wang and the dead man had known each other since childhood, and during the uprising and thereafter as prisoners they had made a pledge to live or die together that had helped them survive. Pa-wang took the body in his arms and let out a full-throated wail, which was echoed by the mountains surrounding that rocky gully, as if adding their voices to his lamentation. The rest of us also felt wretched, but other than embracing Pa-wang and consoling him, there was nothing we could do. The two guards paid less attention to the dead man than they would have to a dead dog and, vexed at being late for lunch, ordered us to pick up the two full carts, put the corpse in the one that had overturned, and head back immediately. We returned hurriedly, as we had been told. That morning, we had come singing a cart-pulling song all together. We sang not as a sign of our happiness but to take our minds off the work, and also to signal that we were coming, since when we were sent to work outside, ordinary city people frequently came forward to offer us small gifts, like tobacco or snuff. But on the way back that day, hanging their heads and with tears in their eyes, the workers were a sorry sight.

I was thinking that although there would be no special team to investigate the causes of this incident, as there had been for the landslide deaths
at Nga-chen power station, if there could be, and if I were to be asked
about the causes [as I had been then], I would give a forthright explanation of how the situation had arisen after the guards, thinking greedily of
their midday meal, had gotten us to pull the carts right up to a clay pit on
a precipice that was too steep, and so on. But on our return to Téring, we
were put back in our respective cells as usual, there was no inquiry into the
causes, and we didn't even find out how they disposed of the dead body.
The two guards were completely unaffected and accompanied us on work
duty just as before, which shows how little value was put on prisoners' lives
in those days.

Another time, a group of us were sent to work at a place southwest of
the city near the river, formerly a park used by ordinary monk officials and
now an army camp, where "Guest House 1" was being constructed. Our job
was to uproot the old willow trees around the new guest house, which were
to be distributed to various Chinese offices in the city, including Téring
prison, for firewood. Generally when we were sent to work for other departments, they would give us a little of their tea at lunchtime, but some of
them required us to return to the prison at midday. Since in this case we
were doing the prison's own work, we had to bring our own lunch, and I
was sent together with a guard to fetch it. That was a moment of unforgettable hardship. It was more than a mile from the prison back to the camp,
and I had to carry two metal urns of tea using a shoulder pole, as the Chinese do, and a cotton bag containing about 15 pounds (rGya ma) of tsampa
for the prisoners as well as food for the officials and guards, all by myself. It
seemed like the kind of load I could have carried on my back Tibetan-style
without too much difficulty, but carrying a shoulder pole is something one
really has to get used to, and even a very strong person will have great difficulty to begin with. By that time I had been put to many different kinds of
labor but had not yet carried a shoulder pole, and after going for thirty or
forty paces out of the prison gate, I had to stop for rest every four or five
paces. Because I didn't know the correct way to walk with a shoulder pole,
I jolted the urns of tea and spilled much of it. At first, the Chinese guard
"shook his fists and stamped his feet" at me and cursed me for it, but no
matter how fiercely he shouted, my staggering got worse and worse, until he
became enraged and kicked me and beat me with the butt of his rifle. But
just as no amount of beating can get a tired donkey to move, I lay there by
the side of the main road. The Tibetan passersby on the road couldn't bear

to see what was happening and called out to the guard asking him not to beat me, but he paid no attention and carried on. That main road ran along the Ling-khor [processional circuit] on the south side of Lhasa, so there were a few old folks walking the circuit, and they cried out from a distance, "That bloody Chinese has killed one of our people," but they couldn't approach any closer. Finally, the guard was obliged to carry the cotton bag of *tsampa* and the officials' food himself. Then I only had to carry the two tea urns, and since most of the tea had been spilled they were very light, and I was just about able to get them to the work site. By the time I got there it was two hours later than the regular eating time, and both the officials and the prisoners were feeling hungry and resentful toward me. But when they saw that I had been made to do something I could not, that my face was soaked in sweat, blood was running from my mouth, and I showed other signs of intense suffering, they sympathized and consoled me, and no one complained about having to wait for his food.

One time when they called out the prisoners in our "cell 2" for work as usual, they brought out us younger ones, and as we took our belts and bootstraps from the door and got ready to go, the prison official Norbu Dorjé told us to gather together first, as he had something to explain. "Today you will not be working with stone and earth as usual," he told us, "but sorting through valuable objects. Now, recently some people from another prison were caught pinching things while doing this work, and they were expelled and are now here in Téring prison. Therefore you all have to be alert. The group leaders (*Tsu'u krang*) will have the responsibility of seeing that no one takes even the smallest thing for himself, but you should all keep an eye on each other and report any incident of this kind at once."

We were handed over to another group of officials carrying guns, and they led us through the city and into the Sha-tra house on the south side of the Parkor, which had been occupied by the offices of the Finance Bureau. The job was to sort through the possessions of noble Lhasa families who had participated in the uprising, which had been seized by the state during Democratic Reform and collected and stored there. One of the officials told us again, "Some of the Drapchi prisoners who came to work here tried to switch the fine clothes and things with poor ones, and some of them hid things. So now it's your turn."

Most of the stuff we had to sort through were the ceremonial costumes worn by lay officials according to their rank (*rGya lu chas, Khal kha gzugs*) and the ceremonial robes worn by monk officials (*rDa gog rtse, 'Phyar gru 'phyar stod*). Then there were gowns made of different kinds of silk brocade with dragon designs (*rGyan bzhi* and *mDzod gos*), army officers' uniforms in serge and homespun wool, and everyday clothing of excellent quality made of serge and different types of woolen broadcloth (*'Go snam, sPu phrug*). We had to sort them and put them in storage trunks arranged by category. Meanwhile, prisoners at Téring were not given a single thread of clothing, nor were we allowed to receive any from our relatives, and some people who had no relatives around Lhasa were dressed in nothing more than rags, so as well as being obviously short of food we also had desperate need of clothes. In the three days that we spent putting them in order, because of the way we had been threatened, all we could do was imagine how well these clothes would fit us and remark on how lovely the gowns looked, how warm the jackets, how soft the pants, or how comfortable the boots as we handled them.

On the third day, Jampa Tendzin-la of Reteng Labrang and I were taken by an official to clean up one of the Sha-tra family's apartments. There were precious medicines and blessing pills there that an official emptied into a metal pot and told us to throw into the toilet. Not wanting to comply at once, my companion delayed by pretending to clean up another mess before moving on to the next job, then after we had moved on, he told me, "Those are pills blessed by Tromo Géshé Rinpoché and precious pills made in the time of the Thirteenth Dalai Lama, which we could scarcely have gotten hold of as free men, and now as prisoners, whatever mortal dangers we may face, or if we die before being released, there is no one to put a precious pill in our mouths at the moment of death." He told me many things about the background of those medicines and blessing pills, as a way of encouraging me to hide a few of them away, but at the time I did not get his point. I had kept a package of priceless sacred blessing pills from the things left behind by my uncle, and managed to conceal it despite all the many searches I had undergone at the TMD prison, the Nga-chen work camp prison, and especially at Téring prison by hiding it at the head of my bed, until the prison official Purbu Drölma made a thorough search of our mattresses and bedding one day while were out at work, found it, and threw the whole thing in the chamber pot. In my disappointment at not being able to use these precious pills that I had taken the risk of keeping with me, and not having found any other way of hiding such things, after thinking carefully, I resolved to swallow one or two of them there and then. We didn't discuss [our plans] openly, but we gave each other the opportunity, as I went out on the pretext of going to the toilet, and then Jampa did the same. After he had gone out, I took three of the cloth-wrapped pills from the metal pot, without being able to tell which was which. That was at about five o'clock Beijing time, and about fifteen minutes later, I had the feeling of my nerves stiffening and felt worse and worse until my whole body became numb and my legs would no longer hold me up, and I slumped over right there. At that point, we were the responsibility of the Finance Bureau officials who had brought us there, and they started talking about taking me to the hospital. I was afraid that if they did they would find out that I had eaten the pills, but I also feared that my health might be endangered if I stayed where I was. While it was clear to my companion, Jampa, that I had suddenly become ill from the pills, he couldn't ask me about it, and the official who had given us the medicines and pills to throw away obviously became suspicious that I had eaten some of it, but he couldn't actually accuse me because he himself would be suspected of failing to properly supervise us. By this time, the other prisoners had finished their work and gathered around, asking many questions about what had happened. I couldn't tell them that my condition was self-inflicted, and as I didn't know what to say, their questions were most unwanted. Then, to prevent one member bringing disgrace on the group, two of them took turns carrying me on their backs while the others huddled around us now and then, and in that way we got back to Téring prison. That evening I couldn't even drink the thin gruel we were given and became nauseated; my stomach churned and I began to vomit and have diarrhea by turns until sometime after midnight, when I finally fell asleep. When I woke up in the morning with aching eyes and emaciated flesh, my fellow prisoners told me I looked like I had been seriously ill for months, and I was obliged to stop working for a few days.

However, not only did I come to no harm, in the long run I came to believe that those pills had strengthened my body a good deal. As I have already said, the diet and especially the containers we had to use for food affected most people's health very seriously, but during my four years in prison I managed with whatever [food] I was given, whether hot or cold, wet or dry, old or new, and underwent conditions of great deprivation without becoming seriously ill, except for the occasional cold. After I had recovered, my friend Jampa Tendzin-la asked me about what pills I had actually taken. "Following your kind lengthy explanation of the excellent qualities of those pills," I replied, "I ate three of them, which proved excessive."

"I only suggested hiding one or two of them away," he told me. "I didn't think you were going to do something so stupid. For people in such poor physical condition as us, it is impossible to digest more than half a pill," and he showed me the few he had secreted. This is something that still makes me laugh, and remember how not to act.

At that time, when we were taken out to work for other departments, we were under the supervision of Tibetan guards, and they discreetly allowed us to meet our relatives and even receive food and clothing from them. I met with my brothers and sisters on several such occasions. I would always ask how Mother was, and they told me she was fine. My dearest hope at that time was to see my mother, just for a moment. One time, three prisoners including myself were employed pulling horse carts full of river pebbles from the Mön-drong bridge area to the place used as a pigsty by the Téring prison office. On the way, we passed near my house, and the guard who came with us was the traffic policeman called Tsöndru-la. We prisoners used to call him Lama, because when accompanying prisoners to work he would always discreetly allow them to meet their relatives and permit gifts of food, tobacco, snuff, and so on to be given to those who had no relatives whenever they were offered. He oversaw our work in a very tolerant way and warned us when there were dangers to watch out for. What the prisoners liked most was that he always said that the prisoners should not get injured. "Once you are injured," he used to say, "your life is over." He had worked as a construction supervisor when the first [Tibetan] monastery was built in Bodh Gaya, and was said to speak Hindi quite well. That day, it seemed that I had the optimal conditions to meet my mother, and as we were on our way, as soon as I saw the daughter of one of our neighbors, I asked Tsöndru-la for permission to send a message to my family, to which he agreed. I told the girl that today was the best opportunity for me to see my family members, and that she should by all means inform them that I was at work in the neighborhood. It took no more than five minutes to reach the place where we were working from my house, but after we had twice filled our carts, none of my relatives had come. Then one of our neighbors, an old Khampa lady we called Jomo, came carrying something wrapped up in her apron. I didn't suppose that it was me she had come for, and wondered if she was an acquaintance or relative of my two workmates. Tsöndru-la asked her, "Grandma, who have you come to see?" and moving toward me, she replied, "I have come for the son of the Gyatso Tashi house." At once I asked her, "Are my family not there?"

"I don't know if they are there or not," said old Jomo, "but as soon as I heard that you were working nearby I came to give you a little something," and saying nothing more about my family, she brought out the kettle of black tea she had in her apron and some plain *tsampa* dough in an enamel dish. As we sat in a corner drinking the tea and eating the *tsampa*, Ama Trinlé-la, the wife of a carpenter who lived in our neighborhood, also came carrying a bag of food. She too had come to see me. I asked her right away if my family members were still not back, and handing me a leather bag full of delicious *tsampa* dough and a small cotton bag of molasses, she said, "None of your family members are at home, and since I couldn't bear to see you disappointed, I came myself." In consternation, I thought that my brothers and sisters could not all have gone to work if my mother was lying ill at home, and therefore, since she had been one of the main organizers of the Women's Association and in danger of arrest and imprisonment, I began to fear that she could have been imprisoned.

Then, as we were on our way back to Téring, my younger sister Tendröl caught up with me, all out of breath. I asked her immediately, "Where is Mother?" but without answering, she hung her head, large teardrops falling on her knees, as she undid something she had for me wrapped in cotton. Realizing that something was wrong, I held my sister firmly and shook her a few times. "What has really happened to Mother?" I insisted.

"Mother died a few months ago," she said through her tears, "and we arranged whatever rituals we could for her at that time." When I heard that my mother was dead, sound reverberated in my ears and tears blurred my vision. Not only was I unable to speak, in my anxiety it seemed that my chest was so full that I could not even draw breath. My younger sister held my hand tightly, and said only "Mercy!" Trying to console me, my companions told me, "It's not only you; this has happened to so many people like us. Our sadnesses are the same. If we die in prison, we well know that there will be no one there even to give us a glass of water, so we have to be brave and look after ourselves."

The place where we met was behind the boundary wall of what is now known as the East Lhasa School. Normally when prisoners met their relatives many people would come to watch, and since my meeting with my sister seemed to be an event out of the ordinary, within moments quite a few people had gathered around some distance away and were watching us. Most of them had tears in their eyes and were evidently sympathetic. This scared Tsöndru-la and he said at once to my sister, "If you have given him what you had to give, you had better go back home. If the prison comes to know about an incident like this, I too will have to face an inquiry." And to me he said, "Hide away the food you have been given, we have to go straight back to the prison for the midday meal," and I picked up the cart and walked off.

When we reached the destination of our loads, the prisoners working at the pigsty had already left for the midday break. We stopped there for a moment, and Tsöndru-la instructed me to hide carefully the food I was carrying, dry my eyes, and act as normal. Usually when I happened to receive gifts from my relatives while out at work, I would find very ingenious ways of concealing them, but that day it was as if my life force had left me and I couldn't focus on anything, so my companions rolled up the remaining dough very thin inside a length of cotton and wrapped it around my waist, put some of the molasses and things in the inner lining of the big back pad I was wearing, and hid the rest about themselves, and off we went. When we reached the gate, the official Yéshé Tenpa briefly searched us and found nothing, and we got safely back to cell 2.

The joy and strong hope I'd had that morning about going outside for work, and going with a good guard, had turned instantly into despair and unfathomable misery, and now I felt as if I didn't have as much as a sesame seed left to live for. *Whenever I die, it will be without remorse*, I thought. As soon as the other prisoners saw my depressed demeanor, they asked what kind of calamity had occurred. After my two work companions whispered to them an explanation of what had happened that day, everyone sympathized, and especially the virtuous ones [among us] gave me a lot of commiseration and encouragement. That was one of the most depressing and miserable times in my life.

Then one evening, after the meal was over and it was time for us to read the *Tibet Daily* newspaper, the prison official Yéshé Tenpa unlocked the door of our cell and told our group leader to make space for three more people, and Norbu Dorjé came in leading three monks. It had been more than a year since we had seen monks, and for us to suddenly encounter people in robes was delightful and astounding. I guessed the elder monk was about forty; he was emaciated and had a sallow complexion; he spoke softly and his gaze fell on the tip of his nose with gentle grace. He was wearing a battered old yellow cap of the kind worn by hermits in retreat. The other two were also of gentle disposition and from their respectful service to the elder, it was clear that they were his dutiful disciples. Our group leader didn't put them together but wherever there was a space, and the youngest monk was put in a space in front of me.

I had a strong inclination to chat with them and ask where they were from, but prisoners were never supposed to ask each other more than their names, and it was forbidden to discuss how they had gotten there, so one had to find the right opportunity. I asked the youngest monk his name; it was Losang Chöden. He spoke in a strong Khampa dialect and from the way he wore his robes, one could tell he was from either Drépung or Séra. At that time our daily work was sometimes breaking up charcoal into little pieces for the stove in the guards' quarters, and sometimes cleaning up the area. When we went for work as usual the next morning, Norbu Dorjé said that the elder monk did not have to go, and I imagined he would be under tight control. The younger two came to work with us, and doing my best to find the chance to question either of them during work time, I found myself hauling water by shoulder pole together with the youngest one.

"Where have you all come from?" I asked him.

"We were sent here from the prison in Chu-shul Dzong," he replied.

"Which monastery or hermitage are you from?"

"I am a Drépung monk."

"Are the three of you a teacher and his disciples?"

"We younger two are brothers."

"So who is the elder?"

"Our scripture teacher."

"He certainly seems to have the qualities of a senior scholar (*dGe bshes*)."

"He is taking the (*dGe bshes*) degree."

"What's his name?"

"Ngawang Puntsok."

"Which college and house do you belong to?"

"Loséling college. We two are from Pomra house (*sPom ra khang tshan*) and the elder one is from Pu-khang (*Phu khang khang tshan*)."

"One of my elder brothers studies scripture at Drépung Loséling. His name is Yéshé Khédrup. He disappeared during the uprising."

"I know Yéshé Khédrup," he exclaimed, "he is in all our scripture classes," and with that he became more relaxed and started to speak more easily. "That elder teacher is also known as Pu-khang Gen Lam-rim. At the time of the uprising, we fled from Drépung and took refuge at the Longdöl hermitage in Nyétang for a while, but after a few months, the villagers living nearby came to know about it, and the local work team (*Sa gnas las don ru khag*) came there to arrest us. The name of our precious teacher is Lam-rimpa."

As soon as I heard that, I had an indescribable sensation of joy and sorrow arising together. This was because I had often heard Yéshé Khédrup mention Gen Rinpoché's name and the great qualities of his body, speech, and mind, and I really wanted to meet him. But I had never imagined the sudden changes ahead, and to be able to meet him now, as if through the power of karma, at a time when we were under such close control that we were not even free to go to the toilet when we wished, seemed to me extremely fortunate. However, under these terrible conditions, it was not permitted for me to offer him greetings or salutations, and what was worse, religion was considered to be poison and the guards were hostile to monks and lamas. From the fact that Gen Rinpoché had not been allowed to come to work, it seemed that they regarded his case as serious, and I guessed that he was in for no end of hardship.

Norbu Dorjé, the official who had announced that he was not to go to work, was very cruel and would beat the prisoners for any small thing without asking questions first, even though they had not broken any prison regulation. One time when another prisoner and I were on the way to work we had a small quarrel, and without bothering to ask who had started it, he beat me "until I cried for my mother." However, quite unimaginably, it turned out that he was preventing Gen Rinpoché from going to work not because of the seriousness of Gen Rinpoché's supposed crimes or any particular malice toward him; rather, he was using his power to spare Gen Rinpoché the hardship of physical labor.

At that time, the prisoners were given a gruel for their evening meal that sometimes contained the skin, blood, and offal from the sheep and goats slaughtered for the officials. Gen Rinpoché hadn't eaten meat for years and took nothing more than *tsampa* and boiled water. When they served gruel both morning and evening not just for one or two days at a time, but sometimes for a week or more, he went without food. This ability was plainly evident to all those who shared a cell with him, and it may be that when Norbu Dorjé found out about it he was impressed, but in any case, after that, when gruel was served, the cooks were given orders to provide hot water especially for Gen Rinpoché. Basically, the qualities of Gen Rinpoché's body, speech, and mind were beyond ordinary comprehension; he was naturally gentle and serene, maintained the seven-point meditation posture of Vairocana both day and night, and whichever way you looked at it, he was a saint among us Tibetans who had grown up in our traditional Tibetan society. You could not meet him without being amazed and developing some faith in him. Thus Norbu Dorjé had taken it on himself to protect Gen Rinpoché within the limits of his power, and my resentment at having been beaten by him vanished as a result.

As I was looking for an opportunity to talk to Gen Rinpoché, it happened that one day many of the prisoners in our cell were sentenced and sent off to Drapchi prison, and as there were very few of us left, we got the chance to talk together. When I first asked after Gen Rinpoché's health, he said that he didn't care even one sesame seed for his own well-being but was anguished over the destruction of Buddhism. "We are no more [important] than worms in the ground," he told me. "What matters is that the

Lord's teachings have come to such an end and the noble beings who are the guardians of the teachings have lost their places of residence and had to take on intolerable hardship. For myself, I cannot fret about having been imprisoned. If one is ready to purify the negative karma and obscuration that one has accumulated over many lives, it will ultimately be beneficial."

After delivering this counsel, he asked me, "Where are you actually from? I seem to have seen you before," and after asking me all about myself and my family, he was very pleased. From then on he gave me much invaluable advice when there were incidental opportunities, and without regard for the danger and effort involved, he even wrote out a complete summary of the Lam-rim [gradual path] teaching for me on my prison charge sheet and gave me oral instructions on each point as he did so. He told me to do a recitation every day, and to do the practice whenever I got the chance. I memorized it with great determination and made every effort to find opportunities to continue receiving his commentary. Since Gen Rinpoché did not have to go to work, I would fake illness in order not to have to work either, and then request his teaching, but it wasn't long before I was sentenced and sent on to Drapchi, and it was a great disappointment not to hear the last part of his commentary. Nonetheless, it seemed to me that meeting this real yogi and spiritual guide, whom I had long since heard about and been determined to meet, under such terrible conditions was the result of previously accumulated good karma.

Also, one evening at around that time, Ka-ché Gonam Marma, a man of Kashmiri descent who had formerly had a room in the Tsarong house, was brought into our cell in leg irons. It is customary for Muslims to wash their hands and faces and their clothes very often, and with the smell in that prison of many people deprived of cleanliness and sanitation, the lack of ventilation, and especially the stench of the chamber pots in each cell, he covered his nose with his chained hands as soon as he came through the door, sweating and struggling to draw breath, and looked as if he was about to pass out. Most of the prisoners in the cell were village people who had never seen someone like him with a hairy face, yellow eyes, and a big nose and did not respond to him, and since he had been brought with only the clothes he was wearing and no mattress or bedding, I responded by spreading out my own bedding and making a place for him to sleep. The next morning, when he saw the prison meal of coppery black tea and a small amount of coarse, lumpy *tsampa*, his misery worsened, and he said that he should be put in a clean cell and [be allowed to] bring food from his own home. "Please ask the officials," he requested, not realizing that there is no provision for such requests in Chinese prisons. For a few days, he didn't take the food and went hungry, but when the prison officials showed no interest whatsoever, he was obliged to eat something, and gradually he got used to the smell.

However, he was questioned repeatedly, and unlike the other prisoners, he was taken for questioning only at night. He was very scared, and each time he was questioned, he got upset, wept, and couldn't sleep. Unlike with the other prisoners, the circumstances of his arrest were very secret, and I wondered whether the Chinese suspected him of having links with foreign countries, because from talking with him it emerged that he had visited many countries in the world, had extensive contacts in [Tibetan] society, and had formerly associated with senior officials of the [Tibetan] government. He was a devout follower of his religion and he solemnly pledged that religious principles could not be abandoned for the sake of one's present life. But his debilitating fear during questioning and inability to control his aversion to the prison food and surroundings were quite pathetic. The two men in my cell with whom I associated, the Buddhist Gen Lam-rimpa of Drépung Pu-khang and this devotee of Islam, believed in and practiced different traditions, and it is not for one of lesser abilities like myself to judge the capacities of different individuals, but I saw in them the difference between great and small minds when faced with adversity.

Once the Chinese had finished questioning him, Marma became a little more relaxed and told many interesting stories from both earlier and more recent times, especially how he had been in China as a trade agent for the Reteng Labrang during the war against Japanese occupation. When the war intensified, the Tibetan government emissaries could no longer stay in China, and on the way back to Tibet, Japanese soldiers were stopping trains and searching the passengers' baggage in every station. He dressed in the costume of a native of Turkey, a country that had been allied with Germany in the [first] world war, and this exempted the Tibetan delegation from being searched. Since he had had strong connections with the great noble families and had often met with them, he spoke of many internal government affairs that had not been public knowledge. Most of all, in confirmation of the Lhasa saying, "Don't look at a Kashmiri's mouth, look at what he eats," and the idea that Kashmiri Muslims are expert in the art of preparing food and eat extremely well, he talked about the preparation, nutritional value, taste, and way of eating different foods, making his listeners' mouths water. During that time I experienced for myself what is called "food for the mind," the power of stories to substitute for physical sustenance.

Since his hands were chained for a long time, I did whatever I could to help him, to change his clothes when he had lice, to eat his food, or to arrange his bedding in the mornings and evenings, and because the two of us were the only people from Lhasa in our cell, he was very fond of me. He always used to say that if we were released, he would prepare a fine Kashmiri feast for me. He was still in Téring prison at the time I was sentenced and sent on to Drapchi, but later I heard that he was among the prisoners of foreign origin who were expelled from the country in accordance with international law, and he went abroad.

I was taken two or three times for questioning about my case by a Chinese woman official of the Higher People's Court whose family name was Wang and her translator, Yéshé Drölma from Kham Ba-tang. I had already given an account of my crimes many times while in the TMD prison and when I arrived at Téring, in written statements and before the subcommittee meetings as well as to the special investigators, and once they were satisfied that I had nothing new to say, it wasn't long before officials of the Higher People's Court and the Military Control Commission came to Téring prison, in June 1960, to take me and four others—Puntsok Wangdü, a coppersmith from Tsédong; the secretary of the Banak-shöl Tsatrul-tsang house; Aku Késang, a relative of the Lamo house; and Chimé, an officer (*lDing dpon*) of the bodyguard regiment—to be sentenced. In the beginning, prisoners had been taken with their hands chained before big public meetings where they had to stand for a long time with their heads bowed while the formal statements of their sentences were read out, but we were simply taken to one side of the prison, where three officials read out the formal statements of our sentences. I was sentenced to four years in prison with two years' deprivation of political rights, and none of the others received less. With the terrible conditions in that prison, I thought desperately that if I had to stay there for four whole years I would not survive to see my release. Each of us received similar [short] sentences, but we had to serve them [in prisons where] there was no provision for maintenance and the inmates were physically exhausted by the time their sentences had been served. As soon as we had our tea the next morning, the five of us were ordered to proceed to the Reform Through Labor prison.

CHAPTER 9

In Drapchi Prison

IT WAS IN June 1960 that the six [five] of us were sentenced, and the following morning at about ten o'clock, we put our bedding on our backs and, together with a number of others who had been sentenced in Tölung Déchen county and four Chinese soldiers as our guards, we were sent to the Reform Through Labor prison at Drapchi. It takes no more than half an hour to cover the distance from Téring prison to Drapchi prison, but even so we were taken on a short cut through the fields. Since it was during the summer rains, there was a lot of water flowing through the irrigation channels and it was very muddy in places, making the going difficult. While in Téring, we had not been allowed to keep even the drawstrings in our long underwear or our bootstraps, let alone cord to tie up our bedding, so that day we had nothing to tie our bundles with, and this gave us a lot of difficulty once we started walking. A couple of us, the coppersmith Puntsok Wangdü and the Tsatrul-tsang secretary, had a little more to carry, and their loads kept coming apart and having to be repacked. At first the guards shouted at them; then they started to kick them and beat them with their rifle butts. Those of us with lighter loads tried to help them, but the guards would not let us and told us that those two had to carry their loads by themselves. Some of our companions from Tölung had very little bedding and offered to carry some of their things, but the guards would not allow this either and forced them on. As they became weaker and weaker, they sank in the mud or, unable to jump across the water channels, they fell in, and the beatings they received were difficult for the rest of us to bear, not to mention for the victims themselves. Eventually, they were obliged to jettison most of their belongings, not selectively but arbitrarily, and by the time we approached the Drapchi prison walls they were on the verge of collapse. We encouraged them by saying that we were nearly there, but as we entered the main west gate of the prison and heard the terrifying noise of a mass struggle meeting going on, our sense of relief at having arrived suddenly dissipated and we stared at one another wide-eyed, as if we had lost our wits. It was about noon by the time we reached Drapchi.

Drapchi prison, situated between Lhasa and Séra monastery, was formerly the Drapchi military camp and headquarters of the second (*Kha*) regiment of the Tibetan army. After the uprising, the Chinese had initially put the prisoners arrested at Séra and Drépung there. Gradually they enlarged it into a Reform Through Labor prison where sentenced prisoners from all over Tibet were concentrated and relocated to many different work sites. The sign over the main gate read PRISON NO. 1—REFORM THROUGH LABOR CENTER—PUBLIC SECURITY OFFICE DEPARTMENT NO. 4. Of the three sections within Drapchi, the one with the tightest security was the Detention Center (*lTa srung khang*), where the higher-ranking prisoners from Séra and Drépung, abbots and managerial staff, had been put at first. Later on, a group of senior government officials under close guard had been transferred there, and prisoners held there were never sent out to work but kept under special scrutiny. The other two sections were the Sentenced Brigade (*Thag bcod ru khag*) and the Training Brigade (*sByong brdar ru khag*); the latter comprised the ordinary monks arrested from Séra and Drépung who had been there all along, and the former included sentenced prisoners from Drapchi or had been sent there from other prisons. At the time we got there, the number of cells occupied by both brigades was 40 to 50 altogether, with about 20 prisoners in each. There was also a women's brigade and an infirmary, and taking them into account, there must have been at least 1,500, and who knows how many in the 16 cells in the Detention Center. When we arrived as sentenced prisoners from Téring, we were put in the Sentenced Brigade cell number 24.

Since our arrival coincided with a political campaign, it was a time of high security, and besides occasionally having to go out and collect firewood from the mountain hermitages north of Lhasa, we had to do political reeducation. During the day we were not even allowed to go to the toilet except when our group was taken there, and at ten o'clock at night the guards locked the cell doors. There were no prison uniforms, so all the prisoners, both monks and laypeople, had to wear their own clothes and looked very ragged. Some who had been there longer smiled as if they recognized me, but although they were people I had been acquainted with, I was unable to identify them except that in their ragged clothes they seemed like former monks. Amusingly, when my elder sister Yangdröl-la's father-in-law, Yakdé Démön Rikdzin, greeted me, at first I could tell nothing more than that he was a monk I had once known.

The main targets of struggle in that political campaign were Ön Gyelsé Tulku Ngawang Losang-la, in the Training Brigade, for his counterrevolutionary remarks on the *Tibet Daily* newspaper, and one Késang in the Sentenced Brigade, a member of the Panam Ayarwa family and a brother of the Ga-drang chief treasurer (*sPyi khyab mkhan po*), for having been caught plotting to escape while in the Panam county prison. They were struggled against in meetings of several groups combined, and sometimes at general meetings. Otherwise, those in every group who were accused of being "rumor spreaders," harboring "empty hopes of reestablishing the old society," showing a "bad attitude to compulsory labor," and so on, were struggled against regardless of whether their offenses were great or small. However, by the time we got there, the brunt of the campaign had passed and it was being wound down. On the day we arrived, the brigade leaders introduced themselves and appointed one of our number as the group leader (*Tsu'u krang*), a former clerk (*Jo lags*) of the "Labrang bursary" called Losang Tséring, from Tölung Déchen. The brigade leaders instructed us on how political education was to be conducted, but the prisoners in our group had just arrived at Drapchi, and most did not know their fellows from their previous places of confinement and therefore could not accuse or speak against one another. So we spent the following days giving accounts of our own thoughts, instead of in accusatory struggle, until the general meeting concluding the campaign. The principal crimes dealt with during the campaign were listed and a concluding statement made; there were no executions or increased sentences, but it was said that Ön Gyelsé Tulku was moved from the Training Brigade to the Detention Center.

My elder sister Losang Chönyi was in the women's brigade at Drapchi prison then and I was overjoyed to meet up with her, but she still didn't know about our mother having passed away, and except for a slip of paper with the food parcel she received once a month saying that all the family members were fine, she had heard nothing about Mother's health for a long time and had naturally been wondering what was up. She pressed me, saying that I must know about it and should tell her whether Mother was really fine, making me feel miserable that our reunion should be marred by discussing this bad news. If I told her directly that Mother had passed away months ago, she could make final prayers for her, but since my elder sister had been very attached to our mother, there was no saying what sudden effect this could have on her, so for the moment I could only tell her that Mother was fine, and gradually break the news to her using her fellow female prisoners as intermediaries.

As I had been hoping, the food allowance and control regime at Drapchi were far better than at Téring prison. At that time, we received a pound (*rGya ma*) of *tsampa* per day, four ounces (*Srang*) in the morning, four at midday, and two in the evening with gruel. If one had relatives to bring extra food, one could meet them to receive it every fortnight. Except during the political campaign mentioned earlier, we were allowed to go to the toilet as we pleased during the day. But Drapchi was a Reform Through Labor institution where we were made to work, and except during the occasional political campaign, we had to do productive labor constantly, making adobe bricks in spring and autumn, breaking rocks in summer and winter, and collecting firewood from the mountainside at least once a week throughout. We were also given other kinds of heavy labor, such as construction and vegetable gardening, and had to meet excessively high work quotas, which was both physically and mentally exhausting.

The first work I had to do at Drapchi was collecting firewood from the mountains. I particularly remember my first day. Whatever kind of work we had to do, physical strength was not enough, experience and familiarity with the technique were also required, and in this case, the wood we had to cut was thorny and I was not only inexperienced, that day I didn't even have gloves to protect against the thorns. Before dawn, the leader of our group collected tools from the office and distributed two pieces of rope each and a sickle or hatchet to every two or three of us, and we marched off, lined up in our groups of ten with guards to either side and at the front and back of the line, and the brigade leaders carrying guns and binoculars and so on in case of any attempt to escape. We were taken through the Nyang-tren valley north of Lhasa up to the Jokpo hermitage at its head, and reached there about eleven o'clock. We rested for a moment as the guards spread out across the slopes to either side; then the officials pointed out the area in which we were to work, saying that if we went beyond it, the guards would fire on us immediately, and each of us had responsibility [for preventing this]. Then we were ordered to finish cutting the wood within a period of fifty minutes, and when the whistle blew, to reassemble at the starting point. Thereupon, the prisoners started to rush up the hill as if it were a race, and when they reached the wood, they threw their ropes or shirts or back pads over the thorn bushes to stake their claims.

Completely out of breath from running uphill and unaware of the practice of claiming a bush, I was unable to find any large thorn bush for myself, and the member of my group of ten with whom I shared tools, Dondrup from Pelnang in the Penpo valley, was nowhere to be seen. If you did it by hand, in the minute or two it took to break the bushes you would feel the pain of the thorns piercing your hand, and especially the pain of thorns under your fingernails, which seemed to assail your whole body. Carrying on like that, by the time the work period was over and the whistle was blown to call us back down the mountain, I had collected no more than a few sticks, while most of the other prisoners were heading back down with hefty loads. I thought that if all the prisoners did not return together the guards might suspect an escape and start firing, but if I went back down the hill with only a few sticks, I would be beaten or shouted at, as well as embarrassed in front of the others. As I hesitated, not knowing what to do, someone carrying a big load came from behind. As he approached I saw that it was Késang Chöpel-la, former caretaker of Nangtsé-shak, and when I asked if I could borrow his sickle, he showed concern, put down his load, and helped me to cut some of the thorn bush. Gathering up what he had cut, he told me to tie it into a load, but even that was by no means easy; it was heavier on one side than on the other, and since it was not bound tightly enough, it gradually came apart on the way down. I was planning to retie it when we got there, but the rest of the prisoners had been waiting for the few stragglers like me and began marching off as soon as we arrived. I couldn't even get my breath back before joining them and then had to repeatedly retie the load on the way down, and the one or two prisoners and I who lagged behind the main group were forced on by the guards, pushing us, kicking us, or beating us with their rifle butts.

When we finally got back to Drapchi, some officials near the gate were keeping back the prisoners with smaller loads and weighing them, and since my load was one of the smallest, I was taken aside, and when it was weighed it did not even come to 30 pounds, and they wrote down my name. The names were read out at the brigade meeting that evening, and when it was discussed at the group meeting, I had to explain first that I had never done this work before, and second that I had become separated from the companion with whom I shared tools, but without this being taken into consideration I had to give a guarantee that I would bring a full load next time. That night I fell asleep in the misery of reflecting on the hardship and fear I had been through that day and the pain of the thorns all over my hands, and that suffering is something I can clearly recall even now. As I tried to remove the thorns that evening, the more experienced ones in my group of ten advised me that even in a few days I would not finish getting them all out, but if I left them alone they would become infected, and then they would be easier to squeeze out, and this advice was invaluable. I had to do many different kinds of work in those days, but to make it simpler for the reader, I will continue with the story of collecting firewood.

After the hardship of the first day of woodcutting without experience or equipment, I learned my lesson. On my second trip, in accord with the proverb "To fall over the edge once is to increase your wisdom once," I stuck close to those I was sharing tools with, and as I was put with someone who had grown up in the forest and knew about gathering firewood, and had taken care of immediate needs like leather gloves and a back pad, the work was very easy, unlike before. Whatever kind of work was assigned, I learned from experience, and by requesting the necessary equipment from my family [visitors] or even by my elder sister getting hold of what I needed within the prison, I kept myself supplied and was able to match the loads collected by the other prisoners and moreover, to do so within the allotted time.

I will describe one other occasion, though not because of any particular difficulty it caused me. The harvests failed in China for three years running from 1959, while the differences that had emerged with Russia worsened. Russia was said to have demanded that China repay the loans it had given earlier as assistance, just as the famine was taking place. For the sake of its reputation and with no regard for the suffering of its own people, China is said to have used whatever [grain] it had to repay the debt. In any case, Tibet also experienced the horror of famine as an adjunct of China; edible oil became very tightly controlled and other basic necessities were rationed. Needless to say, the daily food allowance in prison was reduced day by day, and the firewood that we had to collect also became more scarce. When I first came, we were cutting the thorn bushes around the nearby mountain hermitages, but as those became depleted, we had to go as far as the Ga-la pass on the way from Lhasa to Penpo and the top of the mountain called Sandy Spring (*Bye ma chu mgo*), starting before dawn and not getting back before dusk. Once the bushes were finished, we had to go with picks and dig out the roots. Then, when the roots were also finished, we had to use the tools for breaking rocks to extract tree roots from rocky crevices, and dismantle the hermitage buildings. With no wood left on the mountain, their timbers were stripped, and if you came back empty-handed you would have to face struggle in the evening. Because of that, prisoners had no choice but to risk their lives, tying ropes around their waists to venture onto cliff sides where even mountain goats wouldn't go, and every time one or two would be killed or injured.

One time, we went back and forth between the top of the Canopy Mountain (*gDugs ri*), behind the Tashi Chöling hermitage north of Lhasa, and the nearby Takten hermitage. My companion that day was a former truck driver from the bodyguard regiment called Tséring Dondrup, and, contented with having taken a meager amount of wood from a cliff near Takten hermitage, we were on our way back down when we caught a glimpse of what looked like a piece of red cloth up ahead, being blown away by the wind and out of sight. After a while, we saw that many of the prisoners who had already gotten down to the foot of the mountain had huddled together on top of a rock and were standing there. My good friend, the lay official Sumdo Lekdrup Chödar, called out my name and shouted, "You better take care on the way down, one of us has been made into *momo*s [dumplings]." "Made into *momos*" is a way of saying "killed." His words echoed clearly off the mountain above in a terrifying way. My entire body stiffened and was quivering as if I had been electrified, and I felt unable to continue down the mountain. Incidents of prisoners being killed and wounded happened all the time, but none of them had made me feel anything like this. I told my companion that what stopped me from going on today was a fear I had not felt before, and since there was no saying what might happen to me as a result, I would either roll my load of wood down the mountain or divide it into smaller loads. He concurred that to feel something one has not felt before was a bad sign, but said that if we rolled the load down the mountainside we might not be able to retrieve it, and without it we would be beaten. He said it was better for me to reduce the load and he would carry the extra. When we got down to the place where we drank tea, we could adjust the loads again so that mine would be big enough. And so we reduced my load. When we got to the foot of the mountain, the elderly former disciplinarian (*Zhal zur*) of the Lawa house (*La ba khang tshan*) at Séra lay there dead, his brains splattered all around, having fallen off the mountain. Since the prisoners present could not touch his body until the officials and guards arrived, they were [just] standing around it. Once they had come, one of the prisoners divided up his load among the others so that he could carry the body.

That day we had our midday tea at the foot of the mountain, near the Chubsang hermitage. At the time, we got two ounces of *tsampa* [per day each] when we were collecting wood, and usually, in my case, I would not be able to keep it until midday but would eat it all for breakfast and have nothing left for lunch but the weak black tea. However, it was just a few days since my family had brought things for me, and I was carrying some of the *tsampa* from my sisters in a leather bag; besides being relieved to get

down from the dangerous spot where I had been frightened for the first time, I was looking forward to a decent piece of *tsampa* dough at lunchtime. Some way before the Chubsang hermitage was a narrow defile where, instead of moving freely, prisoners were continually stopping and waiting. I wondered what this was about, and as I approached, saw something I had not even imagined: the officials and guards were searching the pockets of all those with small loads and confiscating their lunchtime *tsampa*. Usually my load was heavy enough, and that day I had only reduced it because of getting frightened and planned on readjusting it once we reached the midday tea stop, when that situation came from out of the blue. My pockets were searched and my *tsampa* bag taken away.

At that, I felt more anger, sorrow, and dejection than ever before. From the prisoner's point of view, the value of one meal's worth of *tsampa* was the same as life itself. By then, the work targets and the food allowance at Drapchi prison were as far apart as the earth and the sky, so that for a period there were seven to ten prisoners dying every day, not from infectious disease but from hunger. When we went to collect wood, we would pass four or five bodies along the way, left lying on the spot where they had died. I myself was oppressed by the thought of having gained this precious human body for once, only to succumb to starvation. You had to find any way of feeding yourself, and people would disregard even prison rules and danger just to get a bite to eat. The former disciplinarian of Séra's Lawa house had fallen from the mountain and lost his life that day because of the scarcity of wood, not because it was plentiful and he had failed to collect a heavy enough load. And to take away my share of *tsampa* for the midday break in that way, at such a time, was really the height of cruelty. Those who had their *tsampa* ration confiscated that day discussed it openly and unabashedly among themselves, asking if anyone could recall anything meaner, and saying that it was worse than a hundred lashes of the whip. Some said that they felt worse about this than they had when the state confiscated all their property. Usually when our loads did not meet the target weight, they would slap us and kick us on the spot, and then in the evening we would have to face the torture of struggle at the meeting, but those things were commonplace and the prisoners ignored them. This episode, however, gave us the deep conviction that having lost their country, the Tibetan people were quietly being wiped out.

At that time, each of the Chinese and Tibetan officials who came along to supervise the prisoners collecting wood brought a full leather bag of best-quality *tsampa* for their midday meal, made with the [grain provided

for the] prisoners' edible oil allowance and mixed with butter, instead of using their own monthly ration of rice and wheat flour. Among the Drapchi
officials at the time was a woman from Rong Rinpung called Tashi, who had
a fearsome appearance, physically strong with long hair and gold teeth, and
was always smoking. She carried a Sten gun and called all prisoners both
young and old not by their names but only in derogatory terms like "Ké!"
[for men] and "Mé!" [for women], and she was among the officials who marshaled the prisoners collecting wood. Like the others, she came with a bag
of buttered *tsampa* taken from the prisoners' allowance. One of my friends
told me that if you waited in front of that official while she ate her *tsampa*
dough she would surreptitiously give you the leftovers, so one day I went
and waited in front of her like a hungry dog. At first, she gave me a mean
look and said, "I'm not putting any *tsampa* in his mouth," turning her head
in the other direction. I went to that side and kneeled down again, waiting
and watching, and after a while, after looking this way and that, the other
officials surreptitiously threw me the actual bag she had been eating out of.
From then on, whenever she came along with the prisoners gathering wood,
I would manage to get hold of the leftover *tsampa* dough at lunchtime.

She had been sent back to Tibet as an official from the Chengdu Nationalities Institute, and had initially worked at either Drépung or Séra. In 1959,
when the imprisoned monks were sent to do labor at the Nga-chen power
station, she went there as a supervisor. Prisoners were still getting rice and
wheat flour then, but because they only had a few minutes in which to eat it,
most had to jostle with the crowd to be in time, and the elderly monks got
nothing. When she came to know about this, that woman went and stood
by the rice bowl and filled the common bowl for the elder monks herself
so that they were served first. I heard about her kindness after my release
from those who had been acquainted with her, which showed the truth of
the saying, "A tiger's stripes are [visible] on the outside, but a person's stripes
are [invisible] on the inside." Among the officials working for the Chinese
were some who were well disposed toward the Tibetans and discreetly did
what they could to help, and since the outlook of the officials, and especially
those in charge of prisoners, was not uniformly hostile, it was extremely
important to be able to distinguish between them. I still believe that when
things reach a critical juncture in the future, some of the Tibetans working
as Chinese officials could prove to be an important force.

Another time, we were taken to gather wood near the Khardo hermitage, a beautiful site with a sweeping view, where formerly there was a more
abundant growth of bushes such as wild rose, barberry (*sKyer pa*), and rock-

spray (*Tshar pa*) than at the other nearby hermitages, and the sweet sound of the songbird was heard. After many previous wood-gathering trips, there were no bushes left and even the roots had all been dug up; no free person would consider going there to collect firewood, but as enslaved prisoners who were driven up there, we had no alternative, and as the folk saying goes, "You never leave your parents or the mountains empty-handed," and if we worked hard without fearing death, we could just about make a load each. However, since I wasn't feeling well at the time, I stayed in the vicinity of the hermitage and didn't climb any farther up the mountain; some prisoners were stripping the roof of the abandoned hermitage building, and I waited nearby, hoping to make up a load from their leftovers. The apparent leader of the officials supervising us was called Pao-pao; his parents were western Chinese from Qinghai, but he had grown up in Gyéku-do [in eastern Tibet], and he was a brute. He went inside the former hermitage and emerged carrying a statue in one hand and a long spear that had been kept in the protector chapel in the other, and wearing an iron helmet from the protector chapel on his head. As soon as he saw me and another prisoner, he demanded, "Where are your loads?" and seeing that the roof timbers the other prisoners had removed were not ours and we were waiting to pick up their scraps, he struck the other prisoner once with his spear and it broke into pieces. [That fellow] said, "Excuse me," and ran off. I considered explaining to Pao-pao that I was sick that day, but before I could say a word, he picked up one of the pieces of the broken spear shaft to beat me with it as best he could. I just tried to protect my head, while exposing my upper back, where he beat me repeatedly until that piece of the shaft broke as well. He threw it away, called me a vandal, and kicked me several times. One of the kicks hit me in the stomach and winded me so that I rolled on the ground, and then he laid off and went away.

When I stood up again, intending to try to collect some wood, Tsöndru Neljor of Séra's Tantric college and someone called Min-gyur Dorjé from Lho-ka Dra-nang, who were standing behind me and had watched me being beaten, sympathized, and with their help I was able to gather some firewood and did not have to return empty-handed. But that day, feeling ill and suffering from the physical pain and mental dejection of a savage beating, I returned to Drapchi thinking that although I would not have to die of starvation thanks to the support of my dear elder sisters, I didn't know how I was going to get through the remaining three years and more of my sentence under such oppressive conditions. That night, my upper back was so swollen I could barely get my shirt off.

The beatings that that official Pao-pao inflicted on prisoners were innumerable, but not long after mine, an investigation was carried out following cases of prison officials taking prisoners' belongings for themselves. The authorities looked into whether or not the cash, wristwatches, and so on belonging to prisoners had been registered upon their arrival and which officials had been responsible for it, and it was said that Pao-pao turned out to have appropriated property belonging to a large number of different prisoners. In any case, he was removed from his position and had to do some forced labor himself for a while. Those who had suffered beatings at his hands may have felt some gratification over this, but the way the prison was run remained unchanged. Firewood for the prison kitchen, as well as the officials' kitchen, still had to be brought from the nearby mountain hermitages where of course nothing growing was left, and once the roots had been dug out we had to go onto the mountains with crowbars. These were what we used for breaking rocks, and one might wonder how we were supposed to use them to gather firewood: it was to overturn or topple boulders to expose any roots and tendrils that might have been growing in the rock crevices underneath.

Once when we were overturning a boulder on the Ne'u-chung-ri mountain, where there was a nunnery, a nest of lizards was struck by a shard of rock and a large number of them were killed or injured. There was a former monk from Drépung's Go-mang college called Jampa Sonam who used to boil tea for the prisoners, and meanwhile, of his own accord, he would pick nettles growing nearby and cook them up for us. That day, after some of the prisoners had claimed that these creatures were very good for the stomach, kidneys, and so on, and could even make a tonic to strengthen the whole body, he added a few of the dead lizards to the boiling nettles. He didn't tell us about it until we had finished eating, and then he announced that it wasn't a joke, he had really done it. Most people didn't seem to mind very much, and I myself didn't feel particularly revolted. Later on, when Jampa Sonam and I spent a long time as members of the same group, he explained that he had fed us lizard flesh because he wanted to use his job as tea maker to do whatever he could to further the prisoners' welfare, and it had come about that we had been reduced to eating the flesh of such a repugnant creature in order to keep ourselves going. After all, there was no grain to fortify us for the hard work of providing the prison with firewood.

At the time, we were getting the same gruel morning and evening, and as firewood was scarcer than before, no one was going to make a fuss if the prisoners' tea and gruel was uncooked from time to time. But as the food for the officials and the guards really had to be cooked, most of the prisoners' strength and effort was spent simply on collecting firewood. Because other kinds of productive labor suffered as a result, they eventually selected a group of the fittest prisoners to stay on the mountain and stockpile wood, which ordinary prisoners would occasionally come and collect. That did spare most of the prisoners a little hardship, but I was selected as one of the fittest, which was like a special punishment for me. One day during the extremely cold winter of 1960, an official called Kun-yang read out a list of names, and the sixteen of us whose names had appeared were called to one side. They told us that we would have to stay on the mountain for some time, and tried to encourage us by saying that the work was an urgent necessity and to accomplish it was glorious and would be very helpful for us in the future, and we were each given a fleece jacket to wear.

Kun-yang was from Pema-kö and was said to be the son of Kyapjé Düjom Rinpoché. He loved to destroy life. When we went onto the mountain to collect wood, he would bring his rifle and go hunting, and when he took us to the vegetable garden or other places of work, he would kill whatever mice, birds, or even insects he laid eyes on, without mercy. He would force prisoners to work without any limit and treat them with the utmost cruelty even for small things or in ambiguous circumstances. He didn't even have the mentality of an ordinary Tibetan, and no one would believe that he could be the son of Kyapjé Düjom Rinpoché, a great Nyingma-pa religious master, but these days when I see a picture of Düjom Rinpoché their features look identical, something I cannot explain. In any case, he was the one in charge of our elite squad of prison laborers, and to be in any kind of group with him in charge made me despair, but there was nothing to be done about it.

That day we arranged for tools and other necessities, and the next day, carrying our own bedding and *tsampa* rations, as well as the cooking pot and the tools, we set off with a detachment of ten guards accompanying another group of prisoners and reached the Jokpo hermitage in the upper Nyang-tren valley. By then, except for two nomad families, there was no one at the hermitage and it had become very dilapidated, but at least we were able to stay there, rather than out in tents through those freezing winter nights. Our sixteen had been selected from three different groups, and Kun-yang appointed a leader to take responsibility for each group. Our daily work target was six loads of firewood, each weighing no less than 80 pounds. Every evening, the leader of each group had to account for the work performed, and put it in writing for the competition between the different groups in which we had to participate. Even worse, we were under tight prison discipline, not allowed to move except when ordered to by the guards, and had to listen to a lot of threatening, abusive talk [from them].

All the vegetation in that vicinity had long since been wiped out, and meeting the target was extremely difficult. The Chinese convention is that when an order comes from higher up, even if it is obvious that it cannot be fulfilled, there is no way of saying that, so in our group discussions we had to commit ourselves to succeeding. Occasionally, when there was good weather and we found a place with a lot of scrub, we could just about make adequate loads, but most of the time, even staying out on the mountain from before dawn until after dusk, that was impossible. When there was a high wind, whatever twigs we had managed to collect got blown away, and sometimes, coming back down with our loads, the wind was too strong to withstand and we would fall and roll downhill, but in spite of enduring endless difficulties and setbacks, we could never talk about them and had to spend every evening until midnight being shouted at in the meeting.

Since no one managed to meet the work target and they were obliged to shout at everyone rather than punish us selectively, it became routine after a while and everyone ignored it. Still, there was no way to avoid spending the whole day in the cold wind going up to one mountaintop or another, and especially having to touch thorns early in the morning when we could not yet see the lines on our hands, which made the whole body tingle with pain. Every few days someone would be injured, and whether because of the chilling wind or the hard work, many of us fell sick, but since no rest was permitted, we had to take them up the mountain with us.

The worst of all was when our group leader, Mindro Ngawang Puntsok of Drichu Sérka, stepped on a sharp splinter of wood one morning that pierced his shoe, went straight through his foot, and came out the other side. When we removed the splinter, his foot was covered in blood and for a while he was speechless with pain, but far from being allowed to rest or given treatment, he was sent to collect wood alongside me. Then his wound got frostbitten and after a few days his leg had swollen to the size of a beam, and the pain prevented not just him but all his comrades from sleeping at night. Thereupon, we made a request to the officials that Ngawang Puntsok and the other wounded men return to Drapchi and be replaced, and after a few days they responded by sending some of the injured back down. A week or two later, I pinched the nerve in my waist and could only walk bent over, but when I told the official about it, he said that it was psychological, that I was faking because a group of prisoners had recently been sent back to Drapchi and I hoped the same would happen to me, and although I got a day off, I had to go back up the mountain, regardless of the fact that I was unable to work. But with the help of our group members I managed to make up a load each day, and gradually I got better and did not have to go back down. A few days later, that official was replaced, and after we had been at Jokpo for about a month and a half, a larger number of prisoners were sent there for wood collection.

We moved on to the village called Jéma Chun-go [Sandy Spring] on the other side of a pass from Jokpo hermitage, where it was a little warmer. Moreover, our leader, a young man called Tséring Wangdü, did not make us work more than eight hours a day, and for the next two months things were much less onerous than before. Then, by the time all the bushes and roots in that area had been consumed, Drapchi prison's firewood duty came to an end. Eventually they started bringing loose wood by truck from Kongpo for the officials' kitchen, and since there was only tea and gruel to boil in the prisoners' kitchen, they used electricity. At that point, we were allowed to go back to Drapchi.

After that, it seemed that the hardest and most dangerous work was over for the Drapchi prisoners. In the beginning, I had suffered for my lack of experience and preparation and, like everyone else, from the hardship of the work and the beatings I received on a few occasions due to circumstances, but as my elder sisters continually provided me with such essential items as boots, gloves, and thornproof back pad, as well as warm clothing and above all sustenance, I never got injured or totally exhausted. But due to various causes, many other prisoners lost their lives in the course of that work.

Among the ornaments of the erstwhile "city of peace," the delightful places of solitude where noble beings meditated one-pointedly on the cultivation of altruism and their followers sought liberation through developing their powers of concentration, where earth and water are pure, medicinal herbs and all kinds of flowers grow untended, with the fragrance of fruit trees and the music of birdsong, where wild animals stayed comfortably, free from any harm or fear, were such perfect and excellent solitary resorts as Drépung Gémpel Ri-trö, Gönsar Ri-trö, Pa-ri Ri-trö, Jokpo Ri-trö, Ga-ri nunnery, Pabongka Ri-trö, Tashi Chöding, Takten Ri-trö, Chubsang Ri-trö, Séra-tsé Drupkhang Ri-trö, Raka-drak Ri-trö, Kyu-tsang east and west, Purbuchok Ri-trö, Khardo Ri-trö, Néuchung-ri nunnery, Ri-gya Samten-ling, Rak Ri-trö, Garpa Ri-trö, and more, sprinkled across the mountainsides like stars in the night sky. Since the institutions of the occupying Chinese state already forced prisoners to destroy their sanctuaries and the trees that surrounded them as well as any flora and fauna in the locale, the blame for this destruction can in no way be put on the Cultural Revolution or the so-called Gang of Four. Pabongka Ri-trö, for instance, was a great holy place with a long history, a meditation place of King Songtsen Gampo, the place where Tönmi Sambhota created the Tibetan alphabet, and one of the earliest surviving examples of Tibetan multistory architecture. Similarly, Séra Chöding, Raka-drak, and others were among the very blessed hermitages in which Jé Tsongka-pa stayed. At the same time, the eradication of the thorn bushes and other vegetation in the Do-dé and Nyang-tren valleys at the foot of the mountains where the hermitages were situated had a very adverse effect on the livelihood of the inhabitants of both areas. Since the cultivable part of Do-dé and Nyang-tren was small and the farmers could not live from agriculture alone, they used to supplement their income by grinding *tsampa,* and they relied on the thorn bush for fuel to roast the grain. Before it was eradicated, they used to harvest the bush with scythes, allowing it to grow back so that the supply was not depleted, but after the Drapchi prisoners dug up even the roots there was no new growth, and the income of those two communities was affected.

Concerning nutrition, when I first arrived at Drapchi prison, the food was a little better than at Téring, but before long it deteriorated. Once for quite a long period we were given nothing but a very thin gruel both morning and evening; one couldn't even tell whether it had been boiled, and if it hadn't it would make the body ache. Sometimes we even had to go without salt for long periods, so that the tea and gruel not only had no taste but also gave us stomachaches. The learned former palace steward (*Tsha rdor rtse mgron*) Jampa Tendar-la composed this verse about it:

> This thin pea gruel, clear like river water
> Lacking even salt, it makes the teeth tingle
> No solids like meat or fat, even a pale vegetable's rare as gold
> But don't say so, better keep it to yourself.

The first line tells that the gruel made with pea flour was as thin as water. The second means that however hungry one is, the pea flour gruel without salt tastes nauseatingly bland. The third says that far from containing meat or fat, even bits of vegetable yellowed with age were as rare as gold in the gruel, but since commentary on such things was not permitted, these lines had to be recited only to oneself.

Everyone knows that Tibet has inexhaustible natural deposits of salt capable of supplying the whole country and other countries too, but like telling fibs to children, they said that normal supplies had been disrupted by the poor harvests. Actually, it was during this time that the campaign known as "Maximize production, minimize expenditure, build the nation by thrift" was launched in civil society, and food and clothing were in shorter supply than ever. But we could still meet our relatives every fortnight to receive small gifts of food or fresh clothes, and my elder sisters always brought something extra to eat, regardless of the quantity, even if they had to ask others for it, and a change of clothes. I asked them for some salt, and when it came, I handed it out to friends like *jinlap* [any substance empowered with blessing by a lama, taken in minute quantity].

Since most Drapchi prisoners were from other regions, with no relatives nearby, they had to make do with prison clothing that didn't warm the body and prison food that didn't fill the stomach and moreover was inadequate nutrition for the heavy labor they had to do, so they were mostly emaciated and had bags under their eyes. At that time, the more people there were from Lhasa or nearby in one's group of ten, the happier one was, for on the day when their relatives brought provisions, as soon as they arrived the recipient would give out a piece of whatever it was to each member of his group. A piece of bread would be divided into many portions and shared, and even if it was no more than a spoonful of *tsampa*, the practice was to divide it up and share it out, so those with many comrades from the Lhasa area would receive gifts of food even though no one had come to visit them.

For those who had relatives nearby, it was difficult to use the gifts of food economically, because apart from leaving them under one's bedding, there was no secure place to put them, and with prisoners on the verge of death from starvation, they would be stolen. Also, the officials sometimes did unannounced searches of all the prisoners' belongings for articles prohibited by the regulations, and bits of food brought by relatives or leftover *tsampa* would also be confiscated. This was because they suspected escape attempts, but in any case, to have food that one was unable to enjoy confiscated by the officials was more disheartening than to have it stolen by one's fellow prisoners. Once or twice, *tsampa* in my possession that had been saved for me by my eldest sister Losang Chönyi-la was confiscated during searches. Thus, those with relatives had no chance to ration the extra food they received. One time one of the prisoners was brought a dish of dough balls in melted butter (*Bag tsha mar khu*) by his relatives, and for the reasons just mentioned, he had to eat it all at once. Being accustomed to a very poor diet, he was unable to digest it, and a little while later he vomited. The vomit was eaten by all the other starving prisoners who managed to get some.

This took place from the end of 1960 through the middle of 1961—the period of the largest number of deaths due to starvation among Tibetan prisoners. For example, we Drapchi prisoners were given secondhand uniforms of padded cotton with multicolored triangular identification tags on the upper back that were said to have come from prisoners who had died while working at Chang Tsala Karpo [the boron deposits on the northern plateau]. Those uniforms were not worn out at all, but were covered with fleas and lice both inside and out, and especially in the seams, which were so full of lice that the stitching could no longer be seen. At that time, my elder sister was in a group of women prisoners doing the prison laundry, and after she washed one for me and I flushed all the dead fleas and lice out of the seams, I could wear it. There weren't just a few dozen of these uniforms; five or six hundred of them came to Drapchi in one batch, so the number of deaths from starvation at Chang Tsala Karpo certainly wasn't small.

In the same period, a group from the Norbu Lingka prison were sent to Samyé to work on cultivating desert land, and most of them died of starvation. Among them were several people connected with or known to our family. Those who survived the experience jokingly rephrased a verse from the praise to Guru Padmasambhava that goes, "On the hill of Hépo-ri at Samyé / He subdued the eight classes of local deities and spirits," to say, "On the hill of Samyé Hépo-ri / All the 'pulu' were subdued / Some keeled over backward and died / Some fell flat on their faces and died." "Pulu" was the Chinese word for prisoners of war. Anyway, what I heard from the survivors was that two thirds of the original group had died there. Weakened by hunger, they dropped off even as they worked, or on the way to and from work. It may well be that compared with the boron mines and places like Samyé, the situation in Drapchi prison was a little better, because the prisoners from Lhasa were able to meet their relatives every fortnight and receive extra provisions, no matter how small, and since Drapchi was in close proximity to the city, the civilian population would find out and spread the word if a very large number of prisoners died from starvation, so the prison leaders and others had to be careful, as later became apparent.

Nonetheless, what we had to do in those leanest of times was to make mud bricks, which was the heaviest kind of work and the most physically demanding, with the longest shifts. This was Drapchi prison's main business then, so the level of production was the main concern, and there was no regard for the feeding, clothing, or physical condition of the prisoners. We were made to work 12 hours a day, and every group of 20 or so members had to produce 4,000 to 5,000 bricks per day, which was a very difficult quota to meet. Each group had four brick molds and selected four of the most skilled workers to operate them. The others dug the earth and mixed the mud, while the weakest members had to carry it. The work site was at the mouth of the Do-dé valley, north of Lhasa.

Although the prisoners' physical state was very poor, at the start, when the necessary earth and water were at hand, we were sometimes able to fulfill the quota, but as the extreme disparity between labor and sustenance widened, our physical strength weakened day by day, the quality of the materials worsened, the hardship increased, and by midday two or three members of each group would be laid out with exhaustion. In particular, the weakest workers carrying the mud would roll over as they dumped their loads, and even when they got back to their feet their bodies stiffened and they were unable to move, like overworked donkeys. There were many who died while on the job. But in spite of such grave hardship, at the nightly group or general meetings, many of the weaker workers were said to be "resisting labor reform" and subjected to struggle. There were those who passed away the same night after undergoing the torture of struggle.

The youngest and strongest were chosen as brick makers and the ability to meet the quota depended on them, but even if they didn't collapse from exhaustion, after molding a thousand or more bricks every day, day after day, their forearms became so swollen and numb (*rTsa dkar*) that they could no longer work and had to be replaced. At first, I was one of those mixing mud in the digging pit, but later I had to become a replacement brick molder, working without even stopping to go to the toilet, and making sometimes more, sometimes less than a thousand. Being unused to brick molding, I was unable to stand up afterward and would have to walk bent over for a while, and many times I blacked out and nearly fainted, but gradually I got used to it. After a couple of weeks or so, my forearms became swollen and numb like the earlier brick molders', so that at mealtimes I couldn't even pick up my bowl and at night I couldn't fix my own bedding and had to ask someone to help me. Rolling over during the night was the most painful of all. At the elementary clinic in Drapchi they gave us traditional Chinese-style acupuncture, ointments, and so on, but it did no good. Unable to mold bricks anymore, I went into the lowest position of carrying mud.

Since I was young and received some extra food from my relatives, I myself did not get completely exhausted or depleted, but I believe that it was during this time that the greatest number of deaths occurred among Drapchi prisoners. When malnutrition led to death from starvation, initially the prisoners' bodies became very dry and their faces swollen. Then, as their legs could no longer support their bodies, they would just sort of drag themselves along, unable even to get over a doorstep. Sometimes they would slip on stony ground and fall over, and if no one came to help they would not be able to get up again. In that case, they were generally beyond hope, and were taken to a corner of the clinic where before long they would finally die. Some died while still in their work groups, before there was a chance to take them to the sickroom. In my own group, there were instances of both. One night, Sang-gyé-la, a monastic functionary, maybe a disciplinarian or a chant leader, from a monastery in Tsang Uyuk, was on my right, and in the next space but one on my left was someone called Loga from Drikung Mangshung. During the night, their breathing stopped one after the other, and until the prison officials came in the morning, I had to lie there between two corpses. However, I was as unaffected by this as a young child, for not only were there regular deaths from starvation in every group at that time, but after such experiences as having to collect and manhandle the body of a dead Drapchi prisoner from Lhasa People's Hospital not long before and having the person next to me die during the night while I was in Téring prison, I had become accustomed to it. It was more the idea that we had to spend our lives undergoing terrible suffering due to such a turn of events that depressed me deeply, however I thought about it.

Going to collect the corpse from the People's Hospital was a job I volunteered for by mistake. It was on a day when all the prisoners were kept back from work in order to be searched, and at around midday, the young woman known as "mini-official" came to a prisoner I knew called Yönten Puntsok with a handcart, telling him to accompany a guard going to Lhasa and take one helper with him. I asked Yönten Puntsok to take me, thinking that the guard was going to pick up some supplies and there was a chance that someone would give us a little food along the way. But once we were out of the main gate, that guard asked Yönten Puntsok in Chinese if he knew someone called Tashi, and Yönten Puntsok asked which brigade and group, for there were many Tashis, and then asked what was up. "He's dead," said the guard, "we are going to collect his corpse from the hospital," a mission quite contrary to what I had hoped for. When we reached the hospital, the guard went into the main office and had us wait outside. He came out holding a slip of paper, and said, "We have to go in the morgue. If you two can recognize his corpse, that will do; otherwise we have to identify it by the number."

The morgue was a small, dilapidated building alongside the main hospital building of several stories. Inside, there was a large platform for laying out corpses, but there was only one there, and on inspection we could see that it was indeed Khampa Tashi from brigade 1. A few days before, one could have seen him alive and well, but now he was laid out on that platform naked, without a shred of covering. At the door of the hospital and nearby, there were many Lhasa people who had come for treatment, and we thought we should wrap the body in a shroud as Tibetans normally do, but the guard told us to put him on the cart just as he was. The two of us looked around [in vain] for any scraps of cloth to lessen the embarrassment and defilement of carrying a naked corpse as we loaded it on the cart, but as we headed off, the body had to be repeatedly rearranged, because it did not sit well and we had no rope to keep it in place. Whatever the cause of death had been, there was a mixture of blood and pus oozing quite disgustingly out of its eyes, mouth, and other orifices, and by the time we got back to Drapchi we had had to lay our hands on it ten times over, so that in complete opposition to my hopes for a gift of food, I ended up handling a revolting, rotten corpse.

Since the majority of deaths at that time were from hunger, there was no intense pain at the moment of death, just the cessation of breathing. There were also some whose physical condition did not degenerate that far, but who died suddenly and painfully. Those taken to the [sky burial] cemetery rather than being buried, who were examined by the doctor of the Drapchi clinic, were generally said to have died from overeating! The very idea of deaths from overeating when the majority were dying of hunger sounds preposterous, but the reason for it was this: a large quantity of sheep fleece had recently been brought from the northern plateau to be used for making winter uniforms. The fleeces had to be softened before they could be worn, so a group of prisoners with the necessary experience was arranged and put to work. Since the weather was rather cold at the time, the fleece kneaders were permitted to take a small tin of cinders from the kitchen hearth to prevent the fleeces from stiffening, so many of them grilled bits of sheepskin in the embers and ate them. After some time, it swelled in their stomachs and killed them.

Sometimes those sent to harvest the vegetable gardens would eat the raw vegetables or whatever else they could find there. On my trips to the garden I ate a great deal of raw vegetables. Cabbage was quite digestible, but turnips and such would make you feel ill for the whole day. Then there were always those who wandered constantly with their eyes on the ground, scavenging like pigs or dogs for any edible thing, and even picking [raw] barley and peas out of the nosebags of the prison's draft horses and mules. Due to the lack of nutrition, people's intestines became very thin, so that even if they got something solid to eat it was difficult to absorb, and even if absorbed it was said that the movement tore the intestinal passage and killed them. When we folded up the mattress of one deceased member of our group, a monk from Sung-rab-ling monastery in Lho-ka, we saw a heavy bag under the pillow, and when we looked inside we found old bones of animals such as horses and mules that he had dug up out of the ground, collected, and stored. It seems that in times of such severe hunger, the concept of what is edible gets adapted.

While there were only a few public executions of Tibetan prisoners at that time, loss of life due to such circumstances as these was by no means minimal. The Drapchi prison undertaker, a Khampa called Pu-sang, could not manage alone and someone had to be sent to help him. Most of the bodies were taken out behind the prison boundary wall through a small door and buried, so among ourselves we used to jokingly make the prayer that we would not have to go through that door on Pu-sang's back, and we would make it in earnest when we got up in the morning. Most of the prisoners who died untimely deaths in Drapchi were farmers and nomads from all over the country, and monks. They died because they had no relatives nearby to bring them the extra food they needed to stave off hunger.

Since the prisoners' names, ages, places of birth, and crimes were repeatedly recorded in that period, one came to know something about them. For example, many of the prisoners from upper Tsang were never told why or on what charge they had been arrested, but if they did not admit to any particular crime once in custody, they were beaten and subjected to the torture of struggle on the pretext that they were denying their guilt. Thus, when the officials recorded their offenses, many people from Tsang said "reactionary religious worship." This was a reference to the practice in some parts of Tsang of burning incense at dusk as an offering to the local deities, an ancient custom that was an expression of Buddhist faith and had nothing to do with opposing the Chinese Communists. As for the monks detained there, most were functionaries, such as heads of college houses, managers, bursars and so on, and had assumed these worldly duties only because it was required by their rank [in the monastery], not because they had actively sought such responsibilities. These were true monks, who earned their sustenance from the daily offerings of the devoted, but they were taken into custody after being labeled "monastic members of the exploiting class."

Anyway, many blameless farmers and nomads who had been toiling for generations in pursuit of their traditional livelihood died of starvation in that period, as well as innocent and committed monastics who had taken cold ground for their beds and cold rock for their pillow with no attachment to this life while teaching and serving their communities.

One day around that time the names of a large group of sentenced prisoners were read out and they were sent off to labor in the Kongpo region. Just as when I was in Téring, getting to a place where there was enough to eat, however much labor we had to do, was all I could think of. Many of my comrades' names were called out but mine was not, and I was distinctly sorry to be left behind at Drapchi, but the reality was that had I not been left behind, but for a flutter of good fortune, I would not be here now writing this story. When I later met up with some of those who had been sent to Kongpo, they said that the suffering there was much worse still than what we had gone through in Drapchi. Living on an extremely poor diet, unable to receive any extra supplies from their families to alleviate hunger, and having to do hard work with no provision for the most basic needs, two thirds of the group died, just as had happened at Chang Tsala Karpo and Lho-ka Samyé.

Most of Lhasa's Muslim business community of Kashmiri origin had returned to Kashmir after the events [of 1959], but two of their leaders, one called Gadhi, whose shop was on the ground floor of the Shékar-ling house, and Abdul Ghani, who resided in the Drapchi Shar house, were arrested by the Chinese, sentenced to ten years in prison, and sent to Kongpo. Not long after that group was sent off [from Drapchi] to Kongpo, due to special circumstances those two were suddenly brought back to Drapchi, and when they arrived they were on the verge of death. Abdul Ghani had a connection with our family, so when I found a chance to do so, I greeted him. At first he didn't recognize me and was frightened, but once I had explained clearly who I was he grasped my hand, his eyes filled with tears, and uttering "Godhar" [the name of God] he choked, unable to say anything more for a moment. Then, after drawing breath, he started to recount the hardships he had been through for the last year or so in Kongpo. Since he had been arrested as a leader of the Muslim community, before departing for Kashmir and other foreign countries their people had arranged for someone to look after the two of them and left enough funds for extra food to be brought to them periodically wherever they were, which had kept them alive. Otherwise, of the thirty-four members of the group in which he was sent to Kongpo, all but twelve were dead. As he spoke, I felt relief that, through the mercy of the Three Jewels, my name had not been among those chosen to be sent to Kongpo.

As talk of the huge numbers of dying prisoners gained force outside prison, changes in the policy of treating prisoners came within. It was said that the so-called higher-ups (*Rim pa gong ma*) had made inquiries into the large number of deaths at Drapchi prison. In any case, one day the leaders of all the groups were called to a meeting and asked the reasons for so many deaths, and bravely they explained that it was both the poor diet and the heavy workload. Then gradually the prison officials dealt with the lack of nutrition, giving us cooked lentils at first until the supply of *tsampa* came through, while a group of prisoners who had been sent earlier to work at an army camp was given a truckload of wild ass (*rKyang*) meat on their return, which was a real boon, and gradually the death rate decreased. However, the prison leaders would not admit the main reasons for the deaths and attributed them to more trivial causes such as poor hygiene, initiating a campaign in which every brigade and group had to compete in improving hygiene. They brought the former kitchen cauldrons from Séra monastery to the prison, filled the three largest with hot water, and had all the prisoners immerse themselves, one group of ten at a time, whether they wanted to or not. Since there is no habit of frequent bathing in Tibet due to the climate, and from the outset, far from having baths, there had been no provision for prisoners to wash even their hands and faces, when they changed the water after every two or three groups of ten, there was a residue of filth more than an inch thick, and they made a lot of talk about hygiene being the real reason for the high mortality rate, to lessen their responsibility for the deaths from starvation.

Nonetheless, with a basic level of control having been established, such practices as inflicting struggle without reason and forced labor with no fixed hours were phased out, the sick received attention, the regular political education session on Saturday evening was replaced with a cultural event, and after reconsideration of prisoners' crimes, a large number of those imprisoned without substantial charge during the suppression of the uprising and the imposition of Democratic Reform were released without having to complete their sentences.

One day as I returned from cutting swamp grass, I was thinking that at that point there were four members of our family in prison, the contents of our house had been seized during Democratic Reform, and my mother, two elder sisters, and three younger brothers and sisters had been evicted and moved into the basement of a ruined house where Mother had passed away in the grip of a serious illness. Now my two elder sisters were looking after the three younger ones, and they faced the difficulty of finding others to bring supplementary food to the four of us in prison at the appointed times because they were unable to come themselves. As I approached the prison walls, I was thinking with stronger feeling than usual how in this situation it would be best if I could be released early, but if not, then how great it would be if my elder sister Losang Chönyi-la were to be released. As we got inside the outer wall, one of the leaders of the women's movement for independence, Kyiré Risur Ama Yangchen-la, who was among the prisoners of the women's brigade washing there as usual, was looking out for me among the group returning with loads of swamp grass on our backs. Ama Yangchen-la had been in the same group as my mother during the independence movement, they had been comrades, and since her imprisonment she had been close to my elder sister and treated me like her own son. That day, she looked as if there had been some good news. I backed out of the line to approach her while she headed toward me and said, "Your elder sister's being released! Put your load down and go see her, she's in the workshop. I'll take care of tying up your load." I went straight there and found my elder sister with her bedding rolled up and ready to go. With her was Chimé-la of Banak-shöl Shonka Tsenkhang, who had been a kind of secretary of the women's movement, and two other women.

My elder sister's release made me happier than if I had been released myself, while she appeared sad and dejected that I had to remain in prison. She was the second eldest of our siblings, and since she was young she had helped our parents with bringing up the younger ones and taking care of household duties like a second mother. She had done as much as she could as a neighborhood organizer during the 1959 uprising, and in communicating the decisions of the assembly to the public. She was arrested by the Chinese and later sentenced to five years, but the sentence had now been favorably reviewed. Except for my time in the TMD prison, we had been imprisoned together all along, at the Nga-chen power station, in Téring, and in Drapchi, and throughout my sister, with unlimited kindness, had disregarded all difficulties in order to wash and patch my clothes, and even to give me her share of the rations brought by our brothers and sisters from home.

Maybe there was a change in the style of governance throughout China during 1962, but in any case a policy statement of "Twenty-six Points" was publicized in Tibet, and the extremely tight restrictions on trade and barter between farmers and nomads in different areas of Tibet were lifted. For those of us in prison, there was a slight improvement in all aspects of life

Risur Ama Yangchen with her grandson, after her release
from prison. *Author's collection*

compared with before, like a respite from hell. As I said, there was a process for the review of prisoners' sentences, and when those in the Training
Brigade and Detention Center at Drapchi came up for sentencing, many of
them and even some of those already sentenced were released, as my elder
sister had been, so that many of us had hopes of being released as well. I had
already completed two and a half years of my four-year sentence, and since
I had only a year and a half to go, prison conditions had improved, and I
believed that the worst was over, I became a little more relaxed. For the
next few months I was sometimes breaking rocks and sometimes working
in the vegetable gardens, but mostly I was transporting the earth and stone
required for the work of expanding the prison compound.

One day when another list of names was read out, mine was among them. It was said that we were going to Powo Tramo to work on the cultivation of vacant land. Having been told by the two Muslims about how two thirds of a large group of prisoners had met their deaths in Kongpo, when I heard my name read, I was immediately downcast. The situation in Drapchi might have improved slightly, but there was no saying whether that would be the case in Powo. Moreover, since it would be extremely difficult for my relatives to bring me the extra food required to stave off desperation, there was no doubt that it was going to be difficult to get by. Except for Amdo Yéshé, a Lhasa resident, most of those whose names were called out along with my own were in a group that had come from Shika-tsé prison. Most of them had been officials working for the Chinese during the so-called Democratic Reform period who were accused of misappropriating property and other management errors. They used to say, "We may have made some mistakes in economic matters, but we are not counterrevolutionaries like you who rebelled against the Party and the People's government," and since they consistently oppressed us politically, the prison officials had quite a different attitude toward them. Thus it was clear that once we got to Powo Tramo we would face not only problems with basic needs but also discrimination, bullying, and recrimination among the prisoners. This was a prospect I particularly dreaded.

As those of us whose names were on the list had a special opportunity to send messages to our families informing them that we were to be transferred and asking them to visit beforehand, I sent a note to my family right away. My middle sister Losang Chödzom was home at the time, and using her skill in procuring from others what she could not provide herself, she came to see me the same day, bringing *tsampa*, wheat flour, meat, and butter, as well as a change of clothes and even 20 *yuan*. That was the largest food parcel I had ever received in prison, and since the official who supervised our meeting that day was one of the better ones, it was relaxed. Still, there was nothing else we could talk about, and finally my sister told me to look after myself and encouraged me to write as soon as I could. As we parted, it occurred to me that if anything were to happen, that would be our last meeting. I could not erase the resounding impression made on me by hearing about the large number of prisoners who had died in Kongpo, and my sister was similarly affected. Even now I can clearly recall her looking back again and again as she walked away, and waving to me.

Then they divided the thirty of us into three groups of ten and made ready for departure. The next day a large truck came, into which they loaded the first group, together with the work tools, and sent them off. For the next few days, those of us in the remaining two groups of ten rolled up our bedding after breakfast and waited in readiness, but no truck came for us. Fortunately, it turned out that on the way to Powo Tramo we were first going to the Drikung valley, an area under Medro Gongkar county. Whatever the differences between the two places in terms of workload and living conditions, the latter was much closer to Lhasa, and since it would be much easier for my family to reach me there, I became less gloomy. Suddenly one day about a week later, around midday, two large trucks arrived, which were the ones taking us. We had to leave hurriedly, without a chance to eat the midday meal. Then we crossed the Kyi-chu bridge east of Lhasa, and as we passed through Lha-dong Shenka, Tsé Kungtang, and beyond, there was nothing in my mind but the misery of watching the glorious gilded roofs of the Potala palace receding in the distance, and on we went, reaching Medro Gongkar as it got dark.

During that part of the journey we had no problems at all because we were on the main road from Chengdu to Lhasa, and as this was the supply route for the Chinese garrison in Lhasa, there were workers permanently engaged in maintaining it. The road from there to Drikung, however, served only the local villagers, and since it was irrelevant to the needs of the Chinese, it received only haphazard maintenance. In particular, there was no bridge for crossing the Medro Pu-chu [river] on the way from Medro Gongkar to the village of Ka-tsel, and you had to find your own way across. The driver followed previous tire tracks, but as it was the coldest time of year the water was frozen, and one of the wheels of our first truck broke through the ice and got stuck. We immediately got down and tried to pull the wheel out by breaking up the ice around it, while some pulled on a rope tied to the front of the truck and others pushed from behind, but despite our many attempts, we not only failed to extricate the wheel but also made it sink in deeper.

Meanwhile, night had fallen and there was a very bright moon, for it would have been something like the twelfth or thirteenth day of the lunar month by Tibetan reckoning. Everyone was hungry, as we had left Drapchi that day without eating the midday meal, but as that spot was cut off from nearby villages by deep water, there was nowhere to go looking even for some hot water. The four guards and one official with us, irritated by hunger, ordered us to hurry up and pull the truck out. If we could have pulled it out quickly, of course we would happily have done so, but since all of our strength combined was insufficient, we had to go about it more patiently. We took turns crawling under the truck to break up the ice with our iron bowls, and scooping out the broken ice by hand. I was hampered by the big fleece jacket I was wearing and had to take it off, but as soon as I did so, the cold became unbearable. Because I dipped my arm in the icy water while wearing my jacket, the right sleeve became soaked right up to the shoulder, and as soon as I took a break it froze and the arm became extremely painful with cold. In any case, although we younger ones worked through the night with our swollen fingers in the ice, we were still unable to move the truck as the moon set behind the western horizon.

Then it became so dark that, far from being able to work, we couldn't even see the person we were standing next to. Finally, the guards decided that one of them should stay behind while the prisoners put their bedding and other necessities on their backs and headed off in the dark, under the supervision of the others, through Ka-tsel and toward Drikung. But then, although our drivers had been told where exactly in Drikung we had to go, they had stayed behind with the trucks, and the official and guards not only had no detailed directions but didn't even know which side of the river to walk on, and in the pitch dark there were no local people to ask and all we could do was guess which way to go. After a while, dawn broke and we found ourselves in a village called Medro Lha-dong-gang. We asked the villagers where the Drapchi prisoners were working on uncultivated land, and they replied that they had seen or heard of a few prisoners' tents on some vacant land near a place called Trong-nying (*Drong nying*) on the north bank of the river, but weren't sure if they were from Drapchi or not. As that seemed to be the right place, we headed on to the coracle ferry at Tang-kya, reaching there soon after sunrise, but the boat was on the far side, and though we kept calling, there was no response. A villager told us that at this coldest time of the year, there were chunks of ice floating down the river in the morning, and the coracles could ply only after midday.

"You'll have to wait until noon," he said. We asked if there were no other ferry, but he replied, "Everyone knows that this Tangkya coracle ferry is the main one. Local people sometimes cross in other suitable places, but that's hardly going to help you. The river is frozen at Drikung Rongdo and you can easily cross there, but that's half a day's march away."

Apart from a cup of tea the previous morning before leaving Drapchi, we had had no chance to eat anything and were desperate. Our guards had been very feisty that morning, making us march in order under strict control, but as they had likewise had to go without food, they gradually started to lag behind us with hunger and fatigue.

As we marched on toward the ford at Rongdo, we asked for black tea or boiled water in the villages we passed along the road, and some brave people shared what they had with us, but as we were more than twenty people there was no way to cope with us all. Although many of the villagers were willing to help us quench our thirst, they were under political pressure not to associate with prisoners and the like, and so avoided us out of fear. Anyway, having taken only one meal in two days, we reached a village called Bamda, on the way to Drikung Rongdo, at about five o'clock in the evening, and opposite there, on open land on the far side of the river, were some military tents that belonged to the Drapchi prisoners' camp. But as there were no coracles or boats at all in that stretch of the river, we faced the tiresome prospect of having to go on to Rongdo, still several hours' walk away, and then all the way back [on the other side of the river]. Then two shepherds, one elder and one younger, told us that this was a particularly cold winter, and that in a place nearby where the river had never frozen before, they had been able to drive their flocks over on the ice. "As long as you don't all cross together, but go a few at a time," they said, "you can get across without having to go up to Rongdo," and that is what we decided to do.

The first one to go across was Pema Dorjé from Lho-drak, who said he had experience of walking on the frozen surface of the Yamdrok-tso lake, and although the ice made a couple of cracking noises, he got across without difficulty. I went next, and for more than two thirds of the way everything was fine, but suddenly, as I was about to reach the far shore, there was a tremendous cracking noise and I fell over. I looked around, wondering what had happened, and saw a huge crack opening up in the ice just nearby. Those on the shore shouted at me to get up at once, but at first I panicked trying to disentangle the strap from the load of bedding on my back, which had gotten wrapped around my neck, and once free, my body went stiff with fear as I tried to get up, and I was unable to do it. Then Pema Dorjé, who had already made it across, untied the strap from his own load and threw me one end, and by holding on to that, I managed to get across the crack. But there was no way for the rest of the prisoners and the guards to come after us, and they had no choice but to go on to Rongdo.

When the two of us got to the tents of the Drapchi prisoners it was sunset, and the group of ten that was already there immediately boiled some tea and gave it to us. After drinking tea and eating *tsampa* dough, we rested and reflected on that day's hardships. The rest of the prisoners finally got there around midnight.

CHAPTER 10

The Trong-nying Prison Farm

THE VILLAGE OF Trong-nying is about four days' walk from Lhasa, in the Drikung area, which was now part of Medro Gongkar county. It was formerly the estate of a land-owning family called Doe-trong (*rDo grong*). Generally speaking, as Tibet used to be a vast country with a small population, the cultivation of fields in some areas was alternated year by year, and the areas cultivated were the easiest to irrigate, so a large amount of potentially fertile land was left idle due to the difficulty of irrigation. Since there was a lot of uncultivated land in the Drikung area, the plan was to use the Drapchi prisoners' manpower to construct an agricultural unit (*Zhing rva*), and that is what our three groups of ten were sent there to do.

In Drikung, there were pastures in the upper valleys and fertile agricultural land in the lower valleys. In some pockets there were forests of willow (*Glang ma*) and ash (*Khred pa*) where, before the Chinese invasion, many kinds of wild birds and animals roamed free. The mountainsides were mostly covered with bushes like dwarf juniper and rhododendron, rockspray and barberry, and the fallow land was full of thorn bush (*Tsher ma skya tsher*), so it was a place where people who were free to do so could easily find the means of livelihood. However, the inhabitants were quite miserable in appearance, physically weak and with little regard for their attire. The finest product was an edible [mustard] oil that was light and durable, and in Lhasa, where oils from many different regions were sold, Drikung oil was considered the best.

We put up our tents on the riverbank near the village of Trong-nying. There were three prisoners' tents, one for the officials, and two for the guards, six in all. Our task was to collect and stockpile brushwood in preparation for the arrival of a larger group of prisoners. The daily quota was two loads, which we were ordered to collect before midday. This was because during the twelfth month of the Tibetan calendar (January–February), there were often afternoon dust storms so fierce that people could not see each other even close up, and the guards feared that prisoners might be able to escape at such times. Since there was plenty of brush, it was not difficult to collect two loads, and we spent the afternoon doing so-called "political reeducation" inside the tent, so at first the work was physically undemanding.

After a few days, a group of us younger prisoners were selected to prepare the ground on an island in the river between Medro Gongkar county and a place called Dongpo-gang, where another Drapchi prison farm was planned. Being surrounded by water, the place was cold, and moreover could not be reached from any direction without crossing the water. At that time, we approached it from the north bank; the fast-flowing water was to the south, while the northern side was broad and shallow. It was evening when we got to the riverbank, and much colder than in the morning; but in any case, no one could stand the bitter cold of the river water in winter except a prisoner who was ordered to cross. That evening, we pitched the tent there and then, and slept. The next day we collected brushwood as before. As the place was surrounded by water, there was tamarisk wood (*'Om bu*) that we gathered with no great difficulty.

Early one morning a few days later, a messenger came from Medro Gongkar county to report that a team of trucks bringing equipment from Drapchi had arrived on the Medro side of the river and we had to come and collect it. We had to move at once, and Medro was on the south side of the river, where the water flowed fast. We looked for a fording place but found none. As we left the bank, the water was higher than waist level, and there were two or three channels to cross. It was sunrise, and the cold east wind that accompanies the sunrise during winter in Tibet started to blow. There were a great many sharp slivers of ice being carried along in the water, and on the way over, walking without loads, we tried to avoid them by dodging back and forth. When we climbed out of the water onto dry ground it was colder, and the first time, when we went barefoot, the sand and pebbles that stuck to our wet feet froze instantly, so that when we went to brush them off, skin and flesh came off together with the pebbles, which felt like burning.

When we reached the Medro bank of the river, just setting eyes on the huge quantity of equipment—work tools like picks and spades, ironware, kitchenware, and a new tent for the guards—made us despair. For the ten of us to transport it all across the river, there was no saying how many trips we would have to make. On each crossing, in addition to a full load, we younger ones also had to carry one of the guards over on our back, and unlike before, under the weight of the loads and the guards we could not avoid being struck by the shards of ice in the river. They left wounds when they hit our legs, and red streaks of blood could be seen running in the water. But the guards on our backs had no difficulties at all, and when we swayed too much, or especially when we came close to toppling over, they grabbed hold of our hair and even our ears, threatening us to steady up. On reaching the far bank, some of the better guards handed out cigarettes to those who had carried them over while others scolded their bearers for walking unsteadily, and some prisoners even had to endure beatings there on the riverbank.

Anyway, since we could not complete the job with only a few trips, we had to keep going for several days, making four trips a day. There was little time to take our shoes off for each crossing, it wasn't easy to walk across barefoot, and, especially in the morning, if we went without wearing our pants and shoes we would be wounded by the ice. Not only were we without a dry change of clothes, at that time we were sleeping in a place surrounded by water in a worn-out tent that gave no protection against the wind during the month when temperatures were 13 or 14 degrees below zero. The prisoners who had no relatives [to bring them essential supplies] and had to stay in their soaked clothes throughout those few days aggravated their colds, kidney problems, and other ailments, becoming too sick to get out of bed, while others became deafened by the water and wind, and all of those employed in carrying became physically depleted. With their sallow complexions and bags under their eyes, they looked like the prisoners dying of starvation in Drapchi earlier on. Since I was able to fortify myself with the generous supplies of meat, butter, and other provisions that my elder sister had brought before my departure from Drapchi, apart from undergoing the severe cold and being unable to sleep at night from the roar of the wind and water in my ears, I did not suffer terribly. A few days after the carrying work was over, a brigade of Drapchi prisoners arrived, but although it seemed that some of them were to stay in that place, a sudden announcement came that instead we were all to move back to the initial settlement at Trong-nying. Of course the equipment had to be carried by manpower just as before, but this time there were more of us and as it was the start of spring, the water was not so cold. This time, however, I encountered a special problem.

There was a team of plowing yaks that had been brought from the northern pastures some time before, when we were preparing to work at that location, that we were to use as pack animals on the move back. The yak herder was a former Drapchi prisoner whose sentence had been served and was now working as a prison employee, and another prisoner and I were appointed his assistants. This was because our remaining sentence period was less than the other prisoners', so we did not have to be accompanied by the guards. But I had no previous experience of loading yaks and had not even driven them before, while those yaks had never carried loads before. Worse still, as there were no saddles on which to tie the loads, we had to tie them onto their bare backs. First we had problems holding them still, then we had problems loading them as they bucked and shied away, and when we finally got going, they shrugged off their loads along the way, and especially in the water, so I became completely soaked [while trying to recover the equipment]. These exasperating difficulties were a special experience for me.

After moving back, our group of officials, guards, and prisoners stayed as before in tents near Trong-nying village, and as soon as the spring thaw came, we started digging up the empty land. There were about a hundred prisoners, and we just worked to the best of our ability, with no daily targets to meet, but soon a large number of additional prisoners arrived from Drapchi and we were divided into three groups. Thereupon, the officials allotted an unthinkably large area of land as our objective, which was to be dug, planted, and harvested within the space of a year, as well as the construction of a prison building and many subsidiary duties. Everyone had to undertake to complete all this work, and the work teams not only had to fix targets but were also ordered to compete with one another in exceeding them, so that the original workload of digging empty land was multiplied. In addition, we had to attend evening meetings for the criticism of those who failed to meet the set targets.

As a shortcut to achieve these targets, two or three like-minded prisoners would turn over one huge clod of turf at a time by digging together, which gave the superficial impression of great progress, but when we got around to breaking up the soil more finely, it gave us more work to do. In particular, at sowing time, groups of four or five prisoners had to pull heavy tractor plows over the field, and when they snagged on these unbroken clods or the roots of thorn bushes, the impact would make them fall over.

Anyway, that year we turned over enough wasteland to plant a thousand measures of seed (*Son khal* = approx. 28 lbs.) and harvested it, with only the prisoners' manpower, human labor unassisted by animals, not to mention machines. Agricultural labor tires both the body and the mind, and the traditional saying of the elders that the defilement of working the earth (*Sa grib*) ages one beyond one's years really seems to be true. One may get fatigued while doing other kinds of work but, so long as one is fit, the fatigue wears off with rest, whereas agricultural labor in general, and especially that task of cultivating wasteland, was not simply arduous in the moment; by the time we returned to our tents in the evening we would either collapse from exhaustion immediately or go into a kind of motionless torpor, sleeping with our eyes open, like fish.

During the year or so I was there, the prison diet consisted of a regular supply of *tsampa*, and there were no deaths from starvation. I myself received food parcels from my elder sisters through others visiting prisoners in that area, and one time my eldest sister Losang Chönyi-la got leave from the Penpo state farm where she was working on road construction to come and visit me and brought me some good, nutritious food, so there were mostly no problems of sustenance.

One time, three of us with the least time still to serve, Dra Yéshé Tokmé of Séra-jé, Chimé Dorjé of Éma-gang Shaka-dékyi, and myself, were given tools, baskets, and so on and sent together with two officials to a valley over a pass from Trong-nying called Drikung Tsa, to gather willow canes. It was during the fourth Tibetan month, and as we climbed toward the pass on the mountain behind Trong-nying, the azalea and rhododendron bushes were full of flowers, and the air was pervaded with their scent and the delightful sound of the cuckoo's call. There was a nomad family staying on the pass, and their yaks and *dris* (females) were like ornaments adorning that mountain. It had been nearly four years that we had been in the constant presence of prison guards, so that day, with just two Tibetan officials and none of those "henchmen of the lord of death" nearby, I felt relaxed and joyful. We boiled tea and took our midday meal with the nomad family. As we entered their tent, the nomad couple became extremely deferential as soon as they saw the two officials, and served them, as well as the three of us to one side, with nomad products like buttermilk and whey as refreshments. It was the first time in more than three years that I had gotten to eat such delicacies, and the delicious taste is something I can recall even now.

As we were coming down the far side of the pass, we passed a mountainside enclave that had been ravaged by fire and all the vegetation burned, and as we discussed discreetly among ourselves how this fire could have started, the horseman who had accompanied us from Trong-nying leading two pack horses carrying the officials' bedding and food supply told us what had happened. There was a People's Liberation Army encampment nearby, and they came here to hunt wild animals. The previous winter, a group of soldiers had used their machine guns to shoot grouse on this mountain, and the sparks from the bullets striking the rocks had ignited the dry winter grass, starting a fire. Local people had tried to put it out, but even from a distance the heat of the blaze was unbearable and they could not get near. Fortunately, after burning for a few days, it had died down by itself. It was said that the bones of many wild animals had been found in the ashes. In earlier times, there was a large herd of deer in the mountain willow groves above Drikung Tsa that used to come down in the summertime to feed on the farmers' crops and cause damage in the fields, and the villagers had to keep watch on their fields by night. Since the events [of 1959], they had been hunted by the PLA as well as the county and township (*Chus*) officials; those that had not been wiped out had fled over the hills to more remote places, and now none was left.

That is something I saw and heard in one locality, but generally speaking, it was around that time that the destruction of Tibet's natural environment began. Just like the saying, "Whoever associates with bad people may end up sharing their punishment," when the failed harvests in China led to famine in Tibet as well, soldiers and officials could destroy any kind of wild animal as much as they wished, and this was the most dangerous time of all for Tibet's precious wildlife. In the northern pastureland, for example, the Chinese army camps fitted heavy machine guns onto big trucks and chased after wild yak, wild ass (*kiang*), gazelle, and antelope (*chiru*), slaughtering them. Since there were great herds, they were not driven to extinction, but the fearsome wild yak is mostly solitary and never moves in groups larger than four or five, and being less plentiful than the wild ass and gazelle, it succumbed more quickly to excessive hunting. Similarly, after my release from prison I heard that the many deer and bears that once inhabited the mountain passes between Lhasa and the Drak and Trang-go valleys to the south were no longer to be seen.

We stayed happily for a few days in the monastery at Drikung Tsa, and ate together with the two officials at mealtimes. One day they took us to the upper part of that valley to scout for timber for the construction of the prison building at Trong-nying. The upper valley was largely forested, and on one side was a grove of mountain willow that had not been cut for generations and was said to be the residence of the local territorial deity. There was a small shrine to the deity in the grove, and many strips of wool and ornaments and so on hung in the branches of the nearby trees in offering. It was a place cherished by the local people. Nonetheless, a few days after we had returned from gathering willow canes, the prisoners were taken to cut wood in the grove.

At that time, the propaganda and newspapers claimed that in civil society there was freedom of religious belief and local traditions were respected, but the reality was that without even asking the local people, they cut and cleared that forest grove that had been preserved for generations, and within about a month they had destroyed it altogether. In the same way, all the commonly owned wooded areas on the mountainsides around Trong-nying were eradicated by the prisoners just as the hermitages and groves of trees north of Lhasa had been, and even the willow plantations belonging to individual households were destroyed. Village people who lived in the vicinity of a Chinese army camp or official settlement particularly suffered losses of this kind.

That summer was mostly spent collecting and transporting building materials for the new prison, and the greatest hardship was cutting and transporting the wood from Drikung Tsa, because to cross the high pass behind Trong-nying and return [with loads of timber] from the forested areas on the far side, we had to walk sixteen hours a day. Our evening political education meetings were devoted to a campaign for the selection of prisoners whose standard of work performance qualified for the "Six Excellences." It was said that if you were selected, your sentence would be reduced. The Six Excellences were excellence in thought reform, excellence in labor reform, excellence in self-criticism, excellence in exposing the faults of others, excellence in unity [with the group], and excellence in hygiene. Prisoners had to declare whether or not they had personally fulfilled these criteria and to admit those on which they fell short, and these were commented on at the group level. Of course, those who had already been through numerous campaigns of this kind knew full well that the real purpose was to mislead and create internal divisions among the prisoners, but there were times when everyone was obliged to do their best to comply. Therefore, people admitted to shortcomings in the least serious points, like unity and hygiene, but claimed to be sufficient in the others.

But they say that "people have a hundred thousand peculiarities," and some found ways of courageously declaring it a sham and a deception by speaking ironically. For example, one of our fellow prisoners, the former lay official (*Shod drung*) Latok Surkhar Ngawang Puntsok-la, was a person of courage and conviction. When he was called upon to assess himself in the course of this campaign, he said, "It was because of fulfilling the Six Excellences that I formerly held a position in the Ganden Po-trang government, when I wore a badge of distinction and my horse was garlanded with insignia. But with the changed circumstances my fate has been determined by others, and being without liberty even to go to the toilet, not to mention do anything else, I cannot qualify for even one excellence, only for [the proverbial] 'nine misfortunes.'"

Another prisoner, Nyi-dön the broadcloth merchant from Lho-ka Dra-nang, always wore a Chinese-style dust mask, regardless of the season, and people said it enabled him to do prayer recitation without being seen. When that suspicion was put about, he was subjected to frequent struggle sessions, but no matter what accusations were made against him, he remained totally silent throughout. When asked why he never said anything, he replied, "Because I make fervent prayers that through these struggle sessions I may absolve whatever harmful actions I have committed toward the sentient beings of the six realms, and since I only pray for all sentient beings to be happy and have no other bad thoughts, I do not hear what you are saying at all." He just took whatever was thrown at him, and not only during that campaign but all the time he was a target for victimization and recrimination.

At that point, I had no more than six months of my sentence to serve, and since I had learned how to avoid criticism and especially had gotten along with my fellow prisoners for some time, nothing was said against me during that period. I often used to be sent, unaccompanied by guards, along with the prison storekeeper and horse-cart driver to collect prison supplies like *tsampa* from places like Medro Gongkar county, Tangkya township, and Drikung Nyima Chang-ra township. The storekeeper carried our daily ration with him, so we could eat whenever we felt the pangs of hunger. The assembly halls of the monasteries were then being used to store *tsampa*, butter, edible oil, and so forth. In Tangkya township, for example, was the former Tangkya monastery, and the assembly hall was used as a granary. It was the same at the Dakpa Labrang in Medro and Drikung Nyima Chang-ra.

Except for places like Séra, Drépung, and the Lhasa Tsukla-khang, which retained an essential staff of monks, monasteries throughout the country had become like empty boxes, where not only the monks but also the statues on the shrines had disappeared. In the area around Medro Gongkar there had been a large number of minor monasteries and nunneries, and during the so-called Democratic Reform, the monks and nuns had not merely been forced to disrobe, but much more cruelly, issued one of a pair of lottery tickets and obliged to marry the holder of the corresponding ticket. Sometimes these couples were grossly mismatched in terms of age, but they were forced to marry regardless of any personal preferences. I had heard such stories from imprisoned former monks while I was in Drapchi and had not really believed them, but during my several trips around the Medro area on supply duty for Trong-nying prison I heard them again, and I would like to appeal to any of those forcibly married at that time who are still with us to put their experiences into writing.

It was around then that the flames of a war between China and India were being kindled on the Indo-Tibetan border, and just like people all over Tibet, the prisoners at Trong-nying had unbridled hopes [of an Indian victory] and failed to disguise this in their outward behavior, with results that will be described.

During 1962 our daily work at the prison, now known as Trong-nying "Lungtrang" [state farm], was tilling the fields. One day when we were digging wasteland on the riverbank below Trong-nying village, we saw a large number of horsemen on the far side of the river heading for Medro Gongkar county, wearing greeting scarves (*Kha btags*) and apparently having traveled a long distance. We assumed that they were delegates from some meeting or other in either Lhasa or Medro county. The Democratic Reform period was coming to an end, a new series of administrative organizations was being set up in the cities and villages, and work meetings were continually being held in the agricultural areas, so the local representatives (*U yon*) and new leaders (*Tsu'u krang*) had to come to Medro Gongkar county to attend meetings. The scarves around their necks, which they might have received at such a meeting, seemed to confirm it. But after the first day, these horsemen kept passing in the direction of Lhasa every day for almost a week, until we thought that every man, young and old, and every horse in the valley of Drikung must have gone and, no longer believing that they were all attending a meeting, we didn't know what to think. It did not occur to any of us that a war could have broken out.

Not long afterward, it was reported in the *Tibet Daily* newspaper that there had been "Indian expansionist incursions in different sectors of the Sino-Indian border," and we heard from the prison horse-cart driver, a former Séra monk called Wangdü who made frequent trips to Medro Gongkar county accompanied only by the storekeeper and without guards, that the word in society at large was that war had broken out, and the large number of horsemen we had seen recently heading from Drikung to Lhasa were going to the front lines on the border to support the Chinese army by transporting ammunition and other duties. For us political prisoners, this was wonderful news and our greatest source of hope. Apart from those like myself with four- or five-year sentences, the majority of the prisoners had sentences of more than ten years, like twenty, eighteen, or fifteen years, and in view of the prison diet and work regime, as well as lack of medical care and other facilities, they had no expectation of living that long. So most people felt that once the outcome of the war had been decided for better or worse, if things went well we could be liberated from our plight. While the newspaper represented it as a border conflict, we felt that in reality the Indians were going to use force to come to Tibet's aid and take back the entire country, wrongly believing that India had a better-equipped and stronger army than China. So with high hopes, we paid special attention to reading *Tibet Daily*, covertly exchanged views with trusted comrades, and waited for our wish to come true.

Normally, no matter how much the officials goaded us to study *Tibet Daily*, the idea of reading it during our spare time would have been out of the question, and even during the allotted evening study periods when one person read aloud, those listening would either fall asleep or make expressions of disbelief among themselves, and when the officials came around to check on us they very often found someone to scold or criticize. So when some people started reading the paper at their lunch break and even taking it with them to work, their way of thinking became obvious, and the prison officials could see that they "harbored empty hopes" about the outcome of the ongoing war. But the political education of the prisoners and even the discussion sessions continued as normal, as if nothing had happened. At that time, the prisoners used to idly gather on a sandbank by the side of an irrigation ditch running through the prison compound, where those who could read Tibetan explained to those who couldn't about the causes of the war and the relevant place names in the eastern and western sectors where it was being fought.

Then one day, while the prisoners were living in this state of anticipation, *Tibet Daily* announced that the "Sino-Indian border dispute" had been "resolved," and both sides had withdrawn to an agreed distance from the frontier. Before long, the local Tibetans who had been engaged in supporting the troops by transporting equipment and ammunition came home. Among them was the leader of Trong-nying village where we were staying; he came and gave a very long speech to the prisoners about how the "Indian expansionists" had been defeated, and even how many of the Indian front-line troops who had been taken prisoner had embraced the "humanistic ideology" of the Communist Party and did not want to return to their own country. Finally, he told us, "Some of you may have 'harbored empty hopes' about the war, but that is just a daydream. Instead, if you confide in the People's government you will receive leniency, for you have no other path to follow than offering your heart and soul to the Party and People's government and giving the rest of your lives to 'Reform Through Labor.'" The great expectations we had had for that war were an ignorant fantasy, and this was the disastrous outcome.

Then suddenly one day an extremely vicious Chinese leader called Ma Guocheng arrived at Trong-nying from Drapchi prison number 1, accompanied by two regular officials, and on the afternoon of the same day all the prisoners were summoned to a big meeting. Ma Guocheng began by summarizing the achievements of the Trong-nying farm during the year or so since it had been established, and the progress in labor and thought reform. He then stated the Party's policy for prisoners that all actions of thought, word, or deed contrary to the spirit of labor and thought reform that might have been committed since our arrival at the farm, whether by ourselves or others, direct or indirect, would be treated with leniency if confessed and with fierce retribution if withheld, that "worthy deeds" [of confession] were the best way, and so on. More specifically, he said that many of us had demonstrated by our behavior during the Sino-Indian war that we cherished empty hopes, and these would have to be cleared up during a forthcoming political campaign. It was called the "Great Winter Training Session" (*dGun sbyong chen po*) and would go on throughout the two winter months. All other work would be suspended for that period, and under the new regulations prisoners would be restricted to their own groups of ten and could only go to the toilet in line with the rest of their group, twice a day. Even within the group, conversation between two or three individuals was not permitted. If we wanted to make a confession, we could approach the prison official concerned or do so at a meeting of our group, or best of all, put it in writing and hand it in.

The campaign started from the end of work that day, and the prison became a more terrifying place than before. Of course, the prisoners' empty hopes for the war had been disappointed, but they had not foreseen the imposition of a political campaign of this kind, and before comrades had a chance to exchange words or encourage each other, contact was cut off. Nonetheless, during the four years since 1959 we had witnessed the attempts by the Chinese authorities to turn Tibetans against each other and test us in all kinds of ways. In particular, people knew very well that two prisoners involved in the same case were never kept together but confined separately, and during questioning they would tell both suspects, "Your friend has admitted everything and turned over a new leaf," so for a while, the prisoners tried to appear enthusiastic in thought and labor "reform," but resolutely denied anything about having empty hopes during the war. But then there was always the anxiety for those who had been involved in any incident that their colleagues would let them down, and except for examining the behavior of one's associates from a distance and winking at them in encouragement, there was no other way of alleviating the apprehension. Things went on like this for two weeks or so, until one of the prisoners made a confession involving a list of about forty names.

That person had been chief among those commenting on the newspapers and had behaved the most flagrantly. His name was Kyi-shong Jo-la A-nen, and he belonged to a family called Gyatru-ling Néchung from the Gongkar area in Lho-ka, whose members had traditionally been selected for government service. His level of written Tibetan was as high as could be, and he was an old man of wide experience who had gained familiarity with the situation of all social classes in the old society and could tell you about any place in Tibet, but especially about the south [where he was from]. Many people from Lho-ka were arrested and imprisoned in 1959, as happened throughout the country, and he was among them. He seemed to be a loyal Tibetan; he got along easily with others, both young and old; and it was extremely interesting to hear him talk about his varied experience, both in the past and more recently, which is why the prisoners used to go and listen to him talk in their free time. While at Trong-nying I also went frequently to listen to him. Fortunately, however, another member of the Gongkar Gyatru-ling Néchung family called Shérab Menbar, one of A-nen's relatives, was in my group, and he told me about A-nen's past and advised me not to associate with him. Because I had cut off relations with A-nen after that, my name was not on the list of those implicated in the wartime incident, but several of my close friends were in touch with him and were implicated.

Thus, having no chance to speak to or reassure one another, we were in a state of mutual suspicion. Fortunately, because work had been suspended for many days at a time and both the prisoners' and the officials' kitchens ran out of firewood, they had no other option than to send all the prisoners out on the mountain to collect more. The groups of ten could not be kept separate while on the mountain, so this was the best opportunity for people to talk with their comrades. I went after Géshé Dorjé Wenbar-la of Drépung Go-mang, who was my closest friend and confidant, and without looking at me directly he positioned himself to meet me surreptitiously. Géshé-la asked, "What have you said about us?"

"I only have two months left of my sentence," I replied, "and whether I get out or not is in your hands. I have consistently regarded Géshé-la [you] as a great spiritual guide (*dGe ba'i bshes gnyen*)."

These words pleased Géshé-la. "You are certainly the student of a fine teacher," he said. "I will keep my mouth shut. But for the earth and the sky, no one will find grounds for suspicion [of what was said] between us. I will pray that you get safely out of prison. Now go on ahead," and our mutual suspicion was cleared up. Then on the way back down I reassured Kun-ga-la, the steward of my comrade Dzasak Kétsul-la the military commander, and Chimé-la, a former officer in the bodyguard regiment, so we had no doubts about each other.

Still, the campaign continued to get harsher, and we could hear the noise of angry confrontation going on from about eight o'clock in the morning until midnight. The campaign was so harshly accusatory that even those who were not directly implicated would unanimously have preferred to continue with the normal regime of laboring to meet extreme work targets on scant daily rations, in the freezing cold, driving wind, or excessive heat. Most of the prisoners in our group of ten were former monastic officials from Lho-ka, such as abbots, chant masters, disciplinarians, managers, and so on, and there were a few laypeople from Lho-ka; since they were already well aware that A-nen was a troublemaker and well-known rogue and had not been involved with him, we were the least affected and did not have to face any specific accusation.

Then one day a Chinese official whose family name was Chang came to our group quarters, together with a Tibetan official called Nyima and two guards, and told us all to go outside. They searched my bedding, clothes, and possessions and those of my close companion Géndun Dondrup, a former monk of the Döl Sung-rab-ling monastery in Lho-ka, very thoroughly, and even removed the dried tamarisk bush stored under the earthen platforms on which we slept. I had thought that the several searches of the prisoners' bodies and possessions since that extraordinary campaign had begun were due to Chinese suspiciousness in general, but from this special search of both of our bedding it was certain that we had been accused by someone. Besides being in the same canteen group, Géndun Dondrup and I were close confidants who told each other everything, but if there had been any potential problem he had not mentioned it up to now, so I thought I was probably being falsely implicated in some other problem because my sentence would soon be over and they wanted a pretext not to release me on time. As I pondered these possibilities, they removed a sharpened shovel blade with no handle from among the tamarisk bush under the bed, and the officials and guards at once demanded of Géndun Dondrup, "What are you doing with this?" That relieved my fear that I myself was to be accused, but still my canteen group had been implicated, and all the members of our group were asked why they had attempted to conceal such a thing and not reported it, and told to unambiguously identify his associates. Yönten, the former chamberlain of the Samyé protector temple and leader of our group of ten, and Shérab Menbar were taken aside and asked who was his companion and to which other group members he was closest. And since I naturally came under suspicion, I was filled with anxiety that I would not now be released at the end of my sentence.

The inquiry into Géndun Dondrup began that evening. Although I really wanted to ask him about it, we never got the chance to talk at leisure. Géndun Dondrup had sharpened and hidden the shovel blade because, on his own admission, he had had great expectations of the Sino-Indian war and had believed that the talk of a dispute on the Indian frontier was to disguise the fact that Indian troops were coming to help Tibet. But he thought that in the case of an Indian victory, the Chinese authorities would deport us political prisoners to China, if not massacre us, just as had happened in Chongqing to the Nationalists trying to flee to Taiwan after the defeat of the Guomindang. Therefore, once the Indian forces advanced into Tibet, we would have to stage an uprising. This could be done on the frequent journeys we had to make across the pass from Trong-nying to Drikung Tsa; we would kill our guards and escape through Drikung into the ravines of Kongpo [near the Indian border]. When the officials asked him how many others were involved in the plan and who the leader was, he replied that he didn't know how many were involved, because the plan had circulated from one individual to another, and none of those involved knew who all the others were, not to mention who the leader was. He told them that Puntsok Wangdü had inducted him into it, but did not give any other name.

Puntsok Wangdü was the former treasurer of Dak-la Gampo monastery in Dakpo, and they were both serving twenty-year sentences. He was the first to tell the authorities about the plan and name other members of the group. Puntsok Wangdü had been an associate of A-nen and was among those named by him. In fact, it seemed quite obvious to me that he was someone who pretended to be courageous and distinguished, and the impression I had of his character when he repeatedly came visiting Géndun Dondrup was not favorable. In any case, he faced a lot of struggle after being implicated by A-nen, made confessions during that fierce campaign, and named other individuals besides Géndun Dondrup whom he had inducted, and since others also named him in their confessions, the whole story came out.

I had no relationship whatsoever with Puntsok Wangdü, but he told Géndun Dondrup, "Don't let your canteen group member Tubten Khétsun know about this. He is too young to be reliable, and since he is due for release soon, if he were to know, he could report it if he was worried about anything standing in the way of his release, so we need to be careful," so Géndun Dondrup did not let any of his canteen group know. But from the way he said, "No problem," [Puntsok Wangdü] could tell that Géndun Dondrup and I had the same political viewpoint, which he told the authorities, and because of that I became falsely implicated and had to face a lot of questioning both within our group of ten and separately from the officials. "Since I am due for release soon, I would have no reason to get involved in such a dangerous business," I said. "On top of that, as you can see, my family members have been doing everything possible regardless of the difficulty in order to look after me, and even if I were capable of betraying the People's government, I could never turn away from repaying the kindness of my beloved family. You may think that Géndun Dondrup and I were political allies, and even conspirators in this uprising, but if you cut my neck for that, only white blood will flow out" [a reference to a well-known story about the last words of Pönchen Shakya Sangpo, who was falsely accused of murdering Pakpa Rinpoché], I told them with an air of desperation. And since Géndun Dondrup told them that we had no other connection than being in the same canteen group and no one else said anything, they didn't take my interrogation any further.

After two months of numerous harangues over political problems during that campaign, the time for spring planting came around and we went back to work as before. No one knew what punishment those implicated in the problems would receive, but since most were already serving eighteen- or twenty-year sentences, it was anticipated that the lesser offenders would receive life terms and the others execution. When we went back to work, the authorities suspected that those people might try to escape or even kill themselves, and their groups of ten were given the responsibility of keeping an eye on them. When I got to ask Géndun Dondrup about the matter, he told me, "The reason I didn't tell you about this was not at all because I didn't trust you. Those of us with twenty-year sentences that will keep us in prison for the rest of our lives can only turn to such desperate acts. You are nearly out, so I didn't want to get you in any trouble. That's why I kept it from you. Then, I didn't know exactly who else was involved, although I knew from Puntsok Wangdü that A-bar-la of Purbuchok Labrang was one. We were going to introduce ourselves to each other when the time came. So far, I did not have to mention any other name than Puntsok Wangdü."

Anyway, during that so-called Great Winter Training Session we had argued back and forth [in struggle sessions] about what we had expected from the Sino-Indian war, about those who had insulted the Chinese government or made agreements with others to try to escape, and most serious of all, about the discovery of the plan by Géndun Dondrup and others to escape after massacring the guards. The fundamental reason for that discovery lay in our failing to stay calm when the war broke out and expressing our hopes in an obvious way, as well as the attempt by the despicable A-nen to lessen his own punishment by implicating many others. That was one outcome of the expectations we had for that war, which is still one of the most valuable lessons I have learned in my life.

Once the campaign was wound down, we started to prepare for spring planting. Since there was not much of my sentence left to serve and I had not been implicated in any problem, I tried to galvanize some of the ordinary officials in our brigade by reminding them that my sentence was about to end and I was due for release, but apart from writing it in their notebooks, I got no reaction. Then, after about a month, two higher officials came from Drapchi, a Chinese whose surname was Hao and the Tibetan Ba-pa Késang. They had come on account of the several political developments that had been taking place at the Trong-nying prison farm. I presented the copy I had of my sentence document to the official Ba-pa Késang and requested to be released on time. This Késang was one of the senior prison officials; he had a passive temperament and spoke and made judgments well. He told me, "This can be referred for approval, and we will know the answer before long." A few days later, they called me in and told me to pack up my bedding and other things to go back to Drapchi, and meanwhile not to make contact with any other prisoners. While I packed my things, one of the ordinary officials stayed with me in case I tried to speak to the others, so my earlier promise to my close friends that I would carry their messages or requests out if I was released was frustratingly reduced to empty words. They may have thought that I was being secretive in order not to jeopardize my release, but in any case, with no chance to do anything more, I was put in a truck that evening and sent to Drapchi.

It was about eleven o'clock at night by the time we got there, and I was put in cell 24. The prisoners were already asleep, but the leader of that group had them move this way and that to make a space for me to lie down. Then, since my release was virtually granted, my head was still spinning with various ideas about what I should do next when dawn came. As soon as the signal came for the prisoners to get up, I went out hoping to meet some of my acquaintances while washing my face and hands, but although the Drapchi regulations seemed to have eased a little since I was last there, those with whom I was familiar smiled at me but did not approach to exchange a few words. I wondered whether they were reticent because they had heard that many people had suffered during the political campaign at Trong-nying after being implicated by their fellow prisoners and assumed that I had been one of the informers. I was thinking that I should explain the situation clearly to my friends when the morning tea break ended, the prisoners lined up with their brigades to head off for work, and the officials in that brigade said that I should go to work with the others. Since there was no one I knew in that brigade, I found it particularly hard to pass the time that day.

After we had finished work, my closest comrade, the [former] monk official Jampa Tendzin-la, came looking for me. He told me that there was something I had to be told, but Losang Mönlam-la would do that. Likewise, when I went looking for my dear mother's associate Ri-sur Ama Yangchen-la, she showed no joy that I was about to be released, but told me with a heavy heart to let her know if I needed anything. Then, as I was thinking that I had to find out what was up, the [former] monk official Losang Mön-lam-la arrived. He was the son of Shölkhang Épa Yöndak Tendzin Dorjé-la, who had given me extra work tokens while I was at Nga-chen, had been a secretary at the emergency headquarters in the Norbu Lingka during the uprising, and after his arrest had contracted lung disease and stayed in the hospital. He took my hand, saying, "Dear friend, I have something to tell you, so prepare yourself. Recently your uncle the chief secretary was brought to the Detention Center here from the Tibet Military District prison. Not long after, he came to the sickroom with a stomach ailment, and on the second day of the new Tibetan year, he passed away. Of course you will be upset, and we are also very upset that one of the old generation of first-class government servants has gone, but it could not be helped. However, while he was in the sickroom I was nearby and was able to attend to him, sit with him, and tell him whatever I knew about what was going on. Likewise, many other former government officials and patriotically minded people in the prison came to see him both openly and covertly, and he very warmly gave us his encouragement. His death coincided with the Tibetan new year, and this year there was a special holiday in the prison with a cultural show that we were to attend, so there was some sense of observing the new year according to our own tradition, and we even wore new clothes instead of the usual ones. But as soon as that sad news circulated among us, we left the place where the show was being held and removed our festival clothes as a mark of respect. In short, we paid him the respect and veneration due such a veteran government servant of distinguished courage and altruism."

"What's the use of regret now?" he concluded by way of encouragement. "We just have to pluck up the courage to live if we have to live and to die if we have to die." For a while I couldn't formulate any thoughts of either joy or sorrow. Previously, when my elder and younger brothers and sisters brought me extra food, they would say that everyone was fine, and that they could go once a month to the TMD prison with extra food for our uncle the chief secretary and elder brother the palace steward and get a written note from them in reply, so I had figured that going to visit my uncle and brother would be the first thing I would do after being released. But with that unfortunate news, my anticipation vanished instantly. What really filled me with regret was that my uncle had passed away no more than two weeks before I got back to Drapchi.

During the next few days I stayed in Drapchi, and many friends came to offer their consolation and best wishes, until the morning of March 21, 1963, when the official Ba-pa Késang gave me instructions for my release, together with a batch of documents including my release certificate and letters of recommendation for a residence card (*Them tho*) and edible oil ration, and told me to go straight home. After I had hurriedly rolled up my bedding and effects, Késang escorted me to the main gate of the prison. It was the moment when most prisoners were lined up in the compound ready to leave for the morning's work and, inspired to see me being released alive and well, having survived that period of great danger and hardship in one piece, they waved at me in greeting. Thus I set out on a new life in changed circumstances, and whether or not the masses lived in happiness in the New Society as was constantly claimed by the Communist Party's propaganda, as far as I was concerned, as long as I was not at odds with its regulations and had food to eat and a place to live, I resolved that I would earn on the strength of my own abilities to repay the kindness of my loving elder sisters, and returned home in that spirit.

However, as will be seen, and quite contrary to those expectations, life in civil society involved great physical and mental hardship and, at times, suffering and terror even greater than I had experienced in prison.

CHAPTER 11

Back Home from Prison

ON MY RELEASE on March 21, 1963, I walked out of Drapchi prison with my bedroll on my back, and when I got to the east Ling-khor road I met an old childhood playmate who greeted me warmly and explained where my family was staying. He said that my youngest brother, Nga-nam-la, was in school and he would let him know that I had been released, and thus encouraged by such a spirit of cheerfulness among my contemporaries, I reached the Tara Khangsar house in Banak-shöl where my brothers and sisters were living. The house had two street entrances, back and front, but although I banged for a long time on the back door, no one came to open it. After a while, a schoolgirl told me to go in through the front door, and when I went around to the front and through the entrance I found my middle sister Losang Chödzom-la milking a cow. She was so overjoyed to see me that she shed tears as she welcomed me, and right away made some tasty, nourishing butter tea.

As I drank that delicious tea of which I'd so often dreamed, I felt that I had left behind the suffering of the past and the ordeal of months and years of hunger and privation, and was glad to have survived it all in one piece. To have managed to live through it was to recognize that the pleasant or unpleasant things that happened were the nature of cyclic existence itself, and I reflected on how miserable it was that so many people had died untimely deaths in prison due to various terrible conditions, and even worse, that some people had taken their own lives when the suffering was too much for them to bear. Then my youngest brother, Nga-nam, came in, having been told of my release and taken leave from school. He hugged my leg and sobbed for a moment, and I too was overcome with feelings of joy and sorrow combined.

My sister said that first of all I should report to the leader (*Tsu'u krang*) of our local subcommittee, and then report my release to both the Banak-shöl neighborhood committee (*Grong mi lhan tshogs*) and the East Lhasa sectional office (*Don gcod khru'u*). So I made my report to the leader, and was told to take my release certificate and letters of recommendation to the subpolice station (*mNgags gtong khang*) in the sectional office to finalize my residence card, and then to go to the food grains office (*'Bru rigs las khung*) to finalize my ration card. When I had my residence card and ration card after running up and down among the police station, sectional office, and food grains office a few times and got home again, Losang Chödzom seemed slightly more relaxed. She asked if I had gotten my documents and then asked, "Did the sectional office say you have a 'hat'?"

Not understanding her, I asked, "What's a 'hat'?"

"'Having a hat' means someone is deprived of political rights and has to live under the supervision and control of 'the masses.' Except for a few special cases, most prisoners who have been released after completing their sentences are given 'hats.' Having a hat makes things extremely difficult. Even to go to work as usual you have to report to your supervision subcommittee, not to mention for any other purpose. And when you come back in the evening you have to report that you are back. Every week you have to make a written report of your thoughts and hand it in. I hope you don't have a hat. Last night I dreamed that you arrived at the door of our old house with your bedroll on your back. I particularly noticed that you were not wearing a hat. I didn't take this to mean that you would come home today, but now that I think about the dream, there is hope that you won't have a hat."

When my sentence had originally been decided, I was to spend four years in prison doing Reform Through Labor with two years' deprivation of political rights, and they had even given me the sentencing document. Now that I had been released after the end of my term, my political rights were unclear, and when I had gone to get my residence and ration cards the sectional office and subpolice station staff hadn't said a word about it, so I was left in a state between hope and fear, wondering whether I had to wear a "hat" or not.

Then, when my other brothers and sisters came home after work that evening and we were all reunited, I started to hear about the devastating transformation of the lives of ordinary Tibetans since the "changes." To start with, maybe I should give a very brief account of what my own family members went through.

Five people from our household had been involved in the 1959 uprising, and except our mother, who was too ill to be conveniently arrested, had all been arrested and imprisoned during the Chinese suppression of the uprising. Our mother and siblings who had been left at home were given an allowance of immediate necessities, such as bedding and a small amount of food to last for a few days, and confined to an adjacent building. Our household was declared "reactionary," the door was sealed, and all our property was confiscated. The same thing happened to most households associated with the former government whose members had participated in the uprising.

At that time, my family had hoped that those of us at the Norbu Lingka had been able to escape into exile, but none of us had managed to escape and we were in custody under tight control, so those left at home were assailed by troubles from all sides. Like people all over Tibet, under the oppressive demands of the occupation they had no rights whatsoever and had to obey and accept whatever they were told. They had to look after those of us in prison by bringing us provisions, without letting us know how little they could afford it once their every possession had been confiscated, and since we were being held in different locations and provisions could only be brought at the time appointed by prison regulations, they continually had to cope with these nuisances. However, most of our former servants and tenants, as well as our neighbors, did whatever they could to help out of sympathy, and our family members were not subjected to struggle due to false accusation or condemnation by those who might have profited by or been compelled to do it. At the time of my release, even though there were tight restrictions on the interaction of the extended family (*Pha spun*), our servants and tenants secretly came to see us, bringing tea, and did whatever they could to help us through the political campaigns that followed. This was not generally the case, since Chinese official practice was for people in every group to be pressured as much as they had to be to recriminate and struggle against their relatives and associates.

In the Democratic Reform campaign that followed the suppression of the uprising, not just members of the government, noble families, and monasteries (*gZhung sger chos gsum*) who had participated in the uprising but all those even slightly associated with them had their wealth confiscated—the exceptionally precious riches of many generations, which were stockpiled by the Chinese government's so-called Office of Industry and Commerce (*bZo tshong las khung*) to be transported back to China. Their furniture, chests, tables, feather pillows, Chinese and antique Tibetan carpets (*gTsang rum*), and floor rugs were taken by Chinese government offices for their own use. Superb articles of clothing, the finery once worn by the nobility for state occasions, made of old brocades with their own distinguished histories, precious furs, and different grades of broadcloth, and many other exquisite and valuable accoutrements were traded by the Chinese officials among themselves. The three kinds of sacred images [statues, scriptures, and *stupas*] confiscated from the government, nobility, and monasteries were stockpiled by the so-called Cultural Relics Preservation Office (*Rig dngos do dam las khung*), and the historic books and especially rare, handwritten works were set aside and taken to China, where today they are kept in the so-called Nationalities Cultural Palace (*Mi rigs rig gnas pho brang*) in Beijing.

Among the collection of books from Drépung monastery taken to China at that time was the fabulous copy of the Buddhist canon (*bKa' 'gyur*) written in gold, known as "the single ornament of the world," which was kept in the main assembly hall at Drépung. But one of its volumes happened to be left behind, and the monks took this as a sign that it would eventually return intact. When it was returned to the monastery twenty-five years later under the so-called Liberalization policy, people were quite amazed. Anyway, at that time (1959–60), after taking the best of what the Tibetans had for themselves, the Chinese government and its officials carried out Democratic Reform by distributing useless clothing, worn-out bedding, farm tools, and such among the people, while shaking both sky and earth with propaganda that they were justly redistributing to the masses the goods that the "three feudal lords" [state, church, and nobility] had amassed through their exploitation and oppression of the masses in the past.

Not long after, they initiated the Three Rejections and Two Reductions campaign. The three things to be rejected were the three feudal lords, and the two things to be reduced were high-interest loans and property rents. They announced to the public that the "old society" had been terribly backward, cruel, dark, and barbaric, and pressured ordinary people into agreeing to speak out about how they had suffered under the old system. They convened daily meetings for the condemnation and ridicule of the former society, which of course involved servants subjecting their former masters to struggle, but students were also cajoled and threatened into struggling against their teachers and children against their parents, and for a while the noise of struggle could be heard continuously, day and night.

In Lhasa at that time [His Holiness's tutor] the great Kyapjé Trijang Dorjé-chang was a particular target of Chinese animosity, and they incited people against him by staging a special display of illicit items and arranging for a couple of [former] junior attendants to claim that these things had been found in his Lhasa residence (*Khri byang bla brang*). They obliged members of the families that had been his main sponsors, like Rampa and Kashöpa, to lead the denunciation, and they emphatically claimed at numerous public rallies that Kyapjé Dorjé-chang was an immoral person. They staged theatrical shows in many localities as a way of spreading propaganda against him, and drawings intended to insult or demean him were put up on the walls of many houses in the city. Even more cruelly, the remaining [senior] members of the monastic communities of Séra and Drépung and the upper and lower tantric colleges who had been inducted into an organization called the Buddhist Association (*Chos tshogs*) were especially forced and harassed into denouncing and rejecting Kyapjé Rinpoché, and many of those who had received his teachings and initiations and refused to denounce him were imprisoned. One of the best known, Géshé Yéshé Gyatso of Drépung Go-mang, who had served as chant leader of the lower tantric college, had to spend a long time in prison. Another example was Séra Lawa Géshé Jampa Chöpel, who, with a number of his students, had tried to escape due to this situation but was arrested on the road and put in prison, where he eventually died. In short, the most distressing part of all the false accusations being leveled at individuals in society was being forced to criticize and repudiate the lamas, teachers, and benefactors who had once been the kind providers of religious teaching or the material welfare of religious practitioners.

Then, in 1960 the Chinese started the Reexamination campaign, for the further investigation of rebels and [hidden] weapons. There were hunts for those who had been indirectly involved or had hidden weapons during the uprising in which many people were falsely implicated, subjected to struggle at mass meetings, and then imprisoned. That was the time when I was in Téring prison where, on a single night, about a hundred people from around Lhasa were brought in, as happened at other prisons. One way or another, most people were imprisoned during that campaign. In Lhasa, one could estimate that during the suppression of the uprising and Reexamination, about two thirds of the male population between the ages of seventeen and seventy were imprisoned: if you ask any three men of my age or older, two of them will have prison experiences to talk about.

Concerning economic life, since that was the time of failed harvests and famine in China, whatever essentials one could buy were rationed, and edible oil was especially tightly controlled. Lhasa citizens, whether old or young, employed or not, were entitled to 20 pounds (*rGya ma*) of grain per month, half a pound of butter, and half a pound of tea, while children got 5, 9, 13, or 16 pounds of grain according to age. As for livelihood, apart from a little trade, most people had to work as unskilled laborers in the construction of new Chinese buildings. In the Lhasa area, most of the young monks who had not been imprisoned were sent to Kongpo to do road construction. Otherwise, they were in the Buddhist Association, but there was no religious practice at all and they were obliged to support themselves by joining in collective labor, the elderly working in vegetable gardens and the stronger ones breaking rocks or making mud bricks. Even then, their income was lower than the city people's.

The main employment for [former] Séra monks at that time was bringing wasteland under cultivation in the Dromtö agricultural area east of Lhasa, and the elder monks were given the duty of gathering manure. The amount they had to bring each day was fixed, and if they fell short they would face criticism and struggle at the evening meeting. Therefore, they would have to set off for Lhasa before dawn to look for whatever human or dog excrement they could find, and it was even said that they had to mix it by hand, but whether that was so or not, they did have to pick up such things with their fingers and make up a load by wrapping them in bits of cloth to carry back to the fields at Dromtö. Not only were the monks deliberately subjected to this kind of hateful and demeaning task, but also, as part of a campaign for the eradication of insects said to "cause disease and damage productivity," both the Buddhist Association people and the ordinary citizens were required to kill one hundred flies per day and as many mice and sparrows as they could, and present the corpses to their group leader every evening to be checked.

My younger brother Jam-pun-la was a teacher at the East Lhasa People's School (*dMangs slob*), and since the schoolchildren each had to present a daily quota of dead flies, mice, and sparrows to their teachers, he used to bring them home so that our family members could reuse them to fulfill their own quotas. These were some of the torments that people in civil society had had to endure during the four years I spent in prison, which I heard about from my family afterward.

Concerning the state of Lhasa society at the time of my release: the executive offices of the Chinese administration and their branches were many times larger than the offices of the former Tibetan government had been. Within the Preparatory Committee for the Tibet Autonomous Region (PCART), the city government came directly under the Lhasa Chengguan-chu or municipality office, which included executive offices called sectional offices (*Don gcod khang*) for the east, north, and south parts of the city, and three more for the surrounding agricultural area, making six sectional offices under the municipality. Under each of these were four neighborhood committees (*Grong mi lhan khang*), making twelve committees in the city and then twelve rural administrative divisions (*Xiang*) in the nearby villages. The sectional officials were Chinese government employees, and the senior leaders at committee and *Xiang* level received the equivalent of half a government salary, while the rest of the leaders at that level were ordinary people who had to make their own living. Nonetheless, their status gave them a power sufficient to strike terror in the heart of any ordinary person whose dwelling they approached. Those were the offices involved in the direct governing of ordinary citizens, and besides them, there were numerous quotidian departments and enterprises whose workers and employees were roughly equal in number to the entire civilian population of Lhasa; among those, the staff of the Public Security Office (*sPyi bde las khung*) was then the most powerful and notorious.

In terms of commercial activity, there were a few privately run sweet tea shops and a few people who set up stalls along the main roads selling candy and cheap cigarettes from China. Fewest of all were those who managed to get permits to sell bread, and all the other shops in the marketplace had been closed and their occupants were now working as construction laborers. You needed a permit (*sPa se*) to buy anything in most of the state-run stores, and these were given as a monthly allowance to workers in government departments or factories. No such permits were given to ordinary citizens. They could only buy a fixed amount of provisions, on the basis of a ration certificate, from the small stores known as "refills" (*'Dzad sprod khang*) in each committee where, in the case of clothing, for example, there was no choice at all of color or size. Above all, since edible oil was extremely scarce and the monthly ration was inadequate for most people, who were engaged in heavy labor such as construction, their main concern was to try to get hold of supplementary food like bread, which is why there were always a great many people to be seen crowding around the bread seller's door. But the bread sellers could only get flour on a monthly ration, and baked no more than five times a month. There was never enough for all those waiting to buy, so they jostled and pushed, and sometimes they would spill over into the baker's room, clay pots and kettle stands would get broken, and uncooked bread snatched out of the pan.

Some people who were very shrewd in such matters would secretly manage to buy oil directly from farmers who had plenty, but then it was very difficult to use, for when they made butter tea they would have to wipe off the tea churn with a bit of cloth in such a way that no one noticed, or if they fried vegetables they would have to do it so that no one else could hear or smell them doing it. These things are hard for the present generation to believe, but those who lived through those times had many experiences that are not easily told, stories that excite both tears and laughter.

At that time, skilled laborers like carpenters and masons could earn 2.5 yuan per day, ordinary laborers earned 1.2 yuan if they were strong, while those with less strength, as well as tailors, spinners, and weavers, got only 0.9 yuan. Even if you could work all the time, your monthly wage would only be enough to cover the rationed essentials like edible oil, so households like ours whose entire property had been confiscated by the state had no choice but to sell off the few things they had been able to hide to so-called "Khachara" ("half-breed") members of Lhasa's Nepalese community for a nominal price. Just like the proverb "When the old horse is struck down by lightning, the old dog takes on a new shine," the Khacharas made more profit from the changed situation in Tibet than they had for generations.

The Chinese government itself had people buying up precious items like gold, silver, jewels, pearls, and coral, as well as fabulous artifacts and other valuables. Those former nobles and large or medium-sized traders who had not participated in the 1959 uprising, had avoided having their possessions confiscated, and still had precious goods and artifacts to sell were exchanging them directly for commodities of completely incommensurate value, such as sugar, tea bricks, and cloth, which had become extremely scarce. Coral of a weight that would currently fetch tens of thousands of rupees in Nepal, for example, was exchanged for 5 or 6 pounds of sugar, or enough cotton to make a pair of pajamas. Later, that government emporium acquired precious medicinal plants like ginseng (dKar po gcig thub) and caterpillar fungus (dByar rtsa dgun 'bu), and [animal products like] musk, pilose deer antler (Sha ba'i khrag rva), bear gall, and precious furs from ordinary farmers and nomads at similarly unbalanced rates.

In society at that time, incomes and purchasing power were completely out of proportion; a month's income was sufficient only for basic necessities rationed at government rates, and anything else had to be purchased illicitly at inconceivably high prices. To give an example from my own experience, the most important item of clothing in those days was shoes, and there was no way to buy according to choice. One time, someone I knew had three pairs of Chinese army shoes for sale, and since my younger brother and I were in great need, we had to buy them. At first, he wanted 40 yuan per pair, but in the end he reluctantly agreed on 100 yuan for all three, the equivalent of three months' wages for me at the time. Fortunately, we had recently managed to sell off one of our hidden possessions, so I was able to find the money.

Under such conditions, people were too frightened not to go to work. Even if one had had enough money and provisions, it was not permitted to stay home at leisure, and apart from the hour of the morning when everyone went to work and the evening when they returned, the city was empty and silent. Coming and going in the morning and evening, people wore torn clothing covered in patches, and since they had neither the means nor the opportunity to wash their faces and hair regularly, they looked exactly like down-at-the-heels characters in a play; not a single one of them looked clean or healthy. And except for having the chance to live with my dear sisters again after my release, [I found] the mental and physical stress at times even worse than in prison.

For a few days after my release I stayed home at ease, and since the pretense of freedom of religious belief was still in place and people were allowed into the Tsukla-khang temple for worship in the mornings and evenings, I had a good chance to do that. A few days later, as I was getting around to looking for work, the security chief and other leaders of our committee came repeatedly to demand whether I was going to work and what I thought I was doing. At that point, since everything we had had been confiscated by the state, I didn't even have pocket money to keep me going for a month and my only possession was the ragged bedding I had carried on my back when I came out of prison; there was no option other than to earn some money. It was not so easy to find a job on the spot, but I asked many of my friends to look out for something, and my relative Késang Déchen-la, a former teacher at the Drépung tantric college, told me there was work digging the foundations for some new houses and collecting building materials with the construction unit he had joined, which had been involved with building the new Kyi-chu bridge. Before long, I was fully employed in the carpentry workshop in that unit, cutting house timbers on an electric saw, and sometimes cutting huge logs by handsaw. While I was there, the highest wage for ordinary workers was 1.3 *yuan* per day. I worked conscientiously without shirking or cheating, so the Chinese carpenters in charge didn't give me such a hard time.

After nine months or so, they recruited a certain number of workers from each neighborhood committee to work on fixing the canal at the Nga-chen power station, and I was one of those who had to go. The wages were lower than at my previous job, and the work was heavier, particularly as I had to load rocks for the canal onto a truck, which was of course hard work but also caused frequent injuries and was very demanding with our inadequate nutrition and clothing. After four months the work force was reduced, and I was part of a group of workers sent on from there to the Lhasa cement factory. The wages were just as low and the work just as heavy, and I experienced for myself what they say about cement dust being extremely harmful to the health. I applied to the committee for permission not to work there anymore, but since they had not sent us there directly, they in turn had to get leave from Nga-chen.

It was no more than three weeks before I was able to leave and come back home. While I had been at the carpentry workshop I had learned to cut timber with a [two-man] handsaw, and the highest wages to be had in Lhasa at the time were with a group of private-sector Chinese workers cutting timber that way, where those employed in pulling the saw from below were all Tibetan. Someone I knew put me in touch with one of those Chinese saw workers. He was the brother of the number 6 Lhasa transport company depot manager and did his saw work at that depot. He paid 3 *yuan* a day, which was the highest wage in the city for any craft work, but he was just as nasty as could be. If I hadn't finished the amount of timber he wanted sawn in a day, he wouldn't let me go home even when it got dark. If something was even slightly wrong, he scolded me viciously, and at times was even ready to beat me. His income was at least 30 *yuan* a day, and even though I did most of the hard work, he gave me no more than a tenth of what he earned, but I couldn't find any other job so had to stay with him.

How was it that his income was so much greater than that of any Tibetan with the same skills? Generally speaking, carpenters and masons were paid according to the amount they produced on a sort of hire basis (*Bogs ma*), unlike other workers, and at that time the rate was 1.5 *yuan* per cubic meter, so you earned according to the amount of timber you could saw. But in reality, most of the people doing that work were individual Chinese entrepreneurs, and they used to bribe the managers of the offices that hired them to cook the books. In our case, for example, since the Chinese saw man's brother was the manager of the office where the wood was sawn, whatever was omitted from the accounts went straight into their pockets. This can be seen from the fact that the few Tibetans who were in that business did exactly the same work as the Chinese but earned far less from it. Before long, one of my former prison mates called Tubten Gyeltsen-la, who was also doing sawing work, took me on as his employee. There was no guarantee of earning 3 *yuan* a day, but at least I would not have to put up with a Chinese boss. I helped him with the saw, but he took care of the tools and finding the work, and we divided whatever we earned between us, but in terms of facilities, skills, and especially finding work, we were never able to do as well as the Chinese entrepreneurs.

Then, around the end of 1964, the Labor Affairs Office (*Ngal rtsol do dam las khung*) of the PCART issued a proclamation fixing the wages for all categories of workers in the city and forcefully prohibiting the contracting of labor on any other terms, effective immediately. The wage rates specified in that document were more or less the same as the going rates, but what was different was the strict specification that members of the former ruling class (*mNga' bdag*) and their deputies (*mNga' tshab*) as well as members of the "four categories" (*Rigs bzhi'i mi sna ie*: ruling class, ruling class deputies, counterrevolutionaries, bad elements) were to be paid no more than 0.9 *yuan* a day, regardless of their work or ability. All workers were to be issued a certificate specifying their line of work and class category with the stamp of the Labor Affairs Office and their local committee, which was to be the sole basis for remuneration in all places of work. Since I was in the ruling class category, had participated in the uprising, and had been released after serving a prison sentence, I could earn no more than 0.9 *yuan* a day, whatever work I did. So I quit the job I had been doing and looked for some undemanding construction work, spending a few months doing odd jobs on the restoration of a building in the hospital on the site of the former bodyguard regiment barracks in the Norbu Lingka. Far from being able to repay the kindness of my family members, it was very hard even to meet my own needs on a wage of 0.9 *yuan* a day.

It was around that time that people involved in trade were subjected to struggle at mass meetings for allegedly evading taxes and eventually forced to pay an unthinkably high rate of taxes, and many of them were given political "hats" and made to do Reform Through Labor under the supervision of the masses. During 1962, when Liu Shaoqi was China's supreme leader, he had promulgated a twenty-six-point document on economic affairs that slightly relaxed the restrictions on individual or voluntary economic activity, and trade had been permitted in Tibet in accordance with the conditions in each region. At that time many people got permits (*Lag 'khyer*) and engaged in trade, but the document didn't remain in force for very long, and more than two years had gone by since controls had been reimposed and the traders had gone back to doing various kinds of labor. However, when the tax campaign was launched [i.e., in early 1965], they investigated those who had previously held trade permits to see how much capital they had, and imposed a limit called the "profit margin" (*Khe slebs*) based on the

Chinese government's own estimate, which the former traders were forced to admit having crossed, and then taxed them accordingly.

The worst offender in our neighborhood was the former horse trader called Powo Tségyé, who was ordered to pay an astronomical amount in taxes. He honestly pleaded that he was an old man with absolutely no business assets or profits on which he might pay such a tax, but instead of listening to him, they threatened him with the statutory punishment of imprisonment for not paying. He decided to commit suicide by throwing himself in the Kyi-chu river, but his relatives found out and managed to stop him, and they had to sell everything in the house down to the butter tea churn to pay the tax. He was put in the "big trader" (*Tshong chen*) class category and had to do unpaid Reform Through Labor along with us members of the former ruling class, their deputies, and the "four categories" of people with dubious loyalties, forbidden to sit with the ordinary citizens in the meetings, and subjected to political abuse. Later on, when we ended up working in the same place, I heard Powo Tségyé telling how when they came to look into his assets, the high rate of tax they demanded was entirely based on the average standard set by the Chinese government, and he did not even possess a tenth of that amount.

CHAPTER 12

The Agitation by the Muslims of Woba-ling

I WILL JUST say a little bit about the agitation by the Chinese Hui Muslims, which began around 1961 and was coming to an end by the time I got out of prison. In the old days, there were two separate groups within Lhasa's Muslim community. One was the Muslims of Indian Kashmiri origin, who were businesspeople with shops around the Parkor market street and were referred to by Lhasa people as "Parkor Kha-ché." The other group lived in an area on the east side of town called Woba-ling, working as butchers, millers, and sometimes market gardeners; their ancestors had come from the Xining region, and they were known to Lhasa people as the "Woba-ling Kha-ché" and in official Chinese usage as the "Hui nationality." Although both groups practiced the same religion, their places of daily worship and their graveyards were separate, since their forebears had come to Tibet at different times from different places, were of different ethnic origin, and had been granted different areas of settlement by the Tibetan government. Although Buddhists were the majority and Muslims a small minority, both groups were treated without religious discrimination or animosity as equal subjects of the Tibetan government with full access to Tibet's resources. They had permission to pursue the trades in which they were skilled, and they were economically successful members of the community.

After the devastating events of 1959, which affected everyone in the country, there was no longer any provision for the Parkor Kha-ché to remain in Tibet, and they appealed to the Chinese government to be allowed to return to their country of origin. Permission was granted, and by 1960 or so they had departed for India. The Woba-ling Kha-ché, with their origins in Xining and Gansu, had had very close links with the Guomindang representative office (*Don gcod*) in Lhasa prior to the Communist invasion due to their racial affinity, and as soon as the Communists arrived in 1950, they welcomed and cooperated with them like a baby embracing its mother. At that time, it was the Chinese-speaking members of the Muslim community, as well as some of the Ba-pas from Kham, who became the most trusted associates and translators of the Chinese, leading to resentment between them and ordinary Tibetans.

When the uprising broke out in 1959, the Woba-ling Kha-ché anticipated trouble and took refuge in the Chinese military camp rather than staying in their homes, and during the subsequent violent suppression, many Muslim youths took up arms and accompanied the Chinese soldiers as translators, oppressing and terrorizing the Tibetans. Because of that, some Tibetans burned down the Woba-ling mosque in the course of the struggle. Once the uprising had been forcibly put down, not only the qualified ones among the Woba-ling Kha-ché but even the old folks who usually stayed home and working members of trading and artisan families went to work as officials with the Chinese during the Democratic Reform campaign. They were rough and hostile with the Tibetans then, and behaved with unlimited arrogance. They had nothing but praise for the Chinese concepts of "Motherland" and "common good," but perhaps they had not grasped exactly how the Communists operated, for apart from rewarding them for joining up as activists by granting state funds for the repair of their mosque, giving some of them exemplary appointments to purely ceremonial positions, and moderately commending their political stance, with regard to economic and all other aspects, the Communists made them put on the same "wet leather hat" as everyone else, and before long they had lost everything and bitterly regretted having sided with the Chinese. So when the Tibetan Muslims of Kashmiri origin got the chance to return to India, the Tibetan Muslims of Woba-ling started an agitation to also be allowed to go abroad.

Getting no response from the Chinese [authorities], most of the Muslims who had served as Chinese officials resigned their positions, complaining that their loyalty to the government had gone unrewarded, and settled their families all together in a compound at the foot of the mountain below the Purbu-chok hermitage [in Do-dé] to the north of the city, which was used as a Muslim graveyard. They began a kind of passive struggle for the Chinese government to respond to their demands, and they had resolved to pursue it come what might, so when the edible oil ration was introduced and grain ration cards were distributed to all city residents, they refused to accept their ration cards. The Chinese didn't make any forceful or aggressive response and did not brand the so-called Hui agitation (*Hud rigs*

THE AGITATION BY THE MUSLIMS OF WOBA-LING   151

kyi rnyog dra) with terms like "reactionary" and "counterrevolutionary," but presented it as a "contradiction within the masses" rather than a confrontation "between the masses and the enemy." They used the few Chinese Muslim officials still in service to lead reeducation meetings telling their people to take ration cards like everyone else and go back to their homes, but instead of agreeing, the agitators called those officials traitors and beat them up. After that, the Chinese authorities arrested and imprisoned some of the leaders of the movement and ringleaders involved in the attacks, but continued to hold the reeducation meetings.

This passive approach by the authorities proved just as fatal as physical repression. Since they refused their edible oil entitlement, the Hui had to buy oil on the black market at the rate of about 15 *yuan* per [*Khal* = 28 lbs.] of oil and 5 *yuan* per [*rGya ma* = 1 lb.] of butter, which meant steady expenditure while living without income. As their reserves ran out, one after another they were unable to see it through, and within a year or two most of those Muslims had to return to their homes and take ration cards. Even by the time of my release in 1963, a few families were still stubbornly refusing ration cards, and their children were among the beggars along the Lingkor path during the fourth month Purnima holiday (*Sa zla'i dus chen*) that year. Anyway, not only did the Muslim agitation achieve no results, it excited no sympathy whatsoever from any quarter. In the end, after the leaders had languished in prison for ten years, two of them were sentenced to death during the mass rallies of the "One Smash and Three Antis" campaign of 1970 and executed in the Shangtap ravine east of the city; a couple of others were sentenced to be executed after two years, and some were sentenced to life imprisonment.

CHAPTER 13

The Fall of the Panchen Lama

THE OPEN CRITICISM, denunciation, and struggle against the Panchen Lama took place during the fourth session of the PCART People's Assembly in 1964, when he was accused of having "opposed the Party, opposed socialism, and opposed the people's government." After that, he was taken to China and made to suffer untold misery for the next 10 years. The reason was that after the Chinese imposed full control over Tibet in 1959 and subjected the Tibetans to unthinkable and inexpressible oppression unlike anything else they had suffered in their long history, Panchen Rinpoché had personally traveled throughout the areas inhabited by Tibetans. While investigating the causes for this heavy-handed treatment, he had been told about the appalling sufferings inflicted on the common people and, in an effort to ameliorate this dreadful state of affairs, had compiled a report consisting of 70,000 Chinese characters divided into eight sections concerning the situation in the country and suggestions for how it could be better handled in the future, which was submitted to the central government. Although that report had been submitted in 1962, the Tibetan people did not come to know about it until two years later when Panchen Rinpoché was openly denounced.

That Panchen Rinpoché would have mounted such a criticism of the Chinese government on behalf of Tibetans was something that the people of Ü province, and Lhasa in particular, had not even imagined. This was because during the time of the [previous] ninth Panchen Chöki Nyima, the functionaries of the Tashi-lhunpo Labrang and the Ganden Po-trang government had taken different views about their respective responsibilities, and some of the chief Labrang officials suddenly decided to take the ninth Panchen away from his Tashi-lhunpo monastery in Tsang and travel

to China via Mongolia, accepting the support of the Guomindang government against the Tibetan Ganden Po-trang government. When the Red
Chinese took over the country, that Tashi-lhunpo group identified itself
with them and, using the tenth Panchen reincarnation, Chöki Gyeltsen,
then only nine years old, as their figurehead, they egged the Communists
on to invade Tibet, incited them, and offered their full assistance—or that is
what Ü people said at the time. Before the "liberation" of China as a whole,
the aim of Mao Zedong and the top Communist leadership was to "liber-
ate" the areas still under Nationalist control, but they had no fixed plan
for the invasion of Tibet. It was commonly claimed that when Mao Zedong went on a congratulatory visit to Russia after the establishment of Red
China, Stalin strongly encouraged the idea of immediately sending troops
into Tibet, which he saw as a strategic territory, and on the strength of that
and the appeals by the leaders of the "Panchen Nangma-gang" group, the
Chinese launched their invasion.

Of course one cannot put all the blame for the Chinese invasion on the
Tashi-lhunpo leaders, but such talk was not unfounded nonsense either.
For example, in his *Old Man's Tale*, Khémé Dzasak, one of the signatories
of the "Seventeen-Point Agreement on the peaceful liberation of Tibet,"
wrote that during the negotiations the Chinese government ordered the
Tashi-lhunpo and Ganden Po-trang delegates to sit together and resolve
their historical differences. In the course of the discussion, the Chinese
government representative Zhang Guohua became infuriated by an argument put forward by one of the Tibetan government representatives, the
chief secretary Lhawutara, and responded quite directly and unabashedly that the issue of the Tashi-lhunpo Labrang or Panchen group was the
main reason Chinese troops had to be sent into Tibet. And in the keynote
speech by Nga-pö (Ngawang Jikmé) to the second session of the fifth TAR
People's Congress on July 31, 1989, he said that although in the prelude to
the signing of the Seventeen-Point Agreement the discussion was solely
between the central government and the Tibetan government, the Chinese
had suddenly announced a new requirement, talks to solve the historical
dispute between Ganden Po-trang and Tashi-lhunpo. One of the most important points Nga-pö made in that speech was that while it was possible
that these discussions had been initiated by the central government, they
could well have been initiated by the [Tashi-lhunpo] Nangma-gang leaders. Panchen Rinpoché was only nine years old at the time, which clearly
shows [that it was] the Nangma-gang leaders inciting the Chinese government in that period.

In any case, after Chinese troops had forcibly entered Tibet, Panchen Rinpoché and his entourage reached Tibet via Xining with a Chinese military escort in 1952. While the Tibetan government made lavish preparations for his reception in the Dalai Lama's apartments in the Lhasa Tsuklakhang temple, the Tashi-lhunpo Labrang officials, emboldened by Chinese support, not only had their say in the matter but also, as this was to be their first-ever meeting, insisted that Panchen Rinpoché should not prostrate himself before His Holiness and that the two lamas' thrones should be of equal height, ignoring the accepted conventions of religious polity. The Chinese government representative in Tibet, Zhang Jinwu, also interfered in the arrangement of this meeting.

Then Panchen Rinpoché resided [at his monastery] in Shika-tsé up until the events of 1959, and in those years the Labrang officials used their position, riding on the shoulders of the Chinese, to increase their standing in relation to the Ganden Po-trang government in whatever ways they could, and the chief district administrations (*rDzong khag*) in Tsang under Shika-tsé's authority were given special treatment. Not only that, there were many incidents of the monastic and lay followers nurtured by the Labrang's leading figure, Dzasak Tanak Tétongpa Ché Jikmé, bullying and threatening subjects of the [Lhasa] government in the Shika-tsé area and even attacking them, so that the people lived in a state of apprehension. One of my prison mates called Losang was from Shika-tsé and had been working for some time in administering the Pa-ri trade tax (*Phag ri sho khral*) when it happened that one of the Tashi-lhunpo Labrang groups was slightly affected by that tax. One morning while he was in Shika-tsé, some youths recruited by Dzasak Tétongpa and so-called disciplinarians from Tashi-lhunpo suddenly barged into his house and led him away, without giving any reason, to the marketplace, where they gave him 100 lashes of the whip in public, then announced that this was the punishment for defaulting on a grain loan. That is just an example, but one frequently heard such stories, for the struggle between the Tibetan government and the [Tashi-lhunpo] Labrang gave rise to mutual antagonism among the common people and instances of bloodshed in many parts of Tsang, as I heard from fellow prisoners from Tsang.

In 1959, when the whole of Tibet rose up against the Chinese, the Tashi-lhunpo Labrang recruited people from the three main districts under its control, Lha-tsé, Ngamring, and Puntsok-ling, for a paramilitary organization entirely armed by the Chinese military, known as the "Panchen's bodyguard," which was one of the chief instruments for the suppression of the people during the uprising. In reward for having taken this stand in complete opposition to the Tibetan people, when the holdings of monasteries and monastic and noble estates all over the country were obliterated during the Democratic Reform campaign following the quelling of the 1959 uprising, Tashi-lhunpo and the Labrang officials retained their authority, received compensation for their monastic and private estates, and were appointed to positions in the Chinese administration. Moreover, they offered Panchen Rinpoché the position of acting chairman of the PCART in place of His Holiness, and built him a new residence called Dorjé Po-trang at Shuktri Lingka in Lhasa. Because of the Panchen's stand, people in Ü, and Lhasa especially, lost faith in him somewhat, and some openly criticized and resented him as a lama in name only, who was in the pocket of the Chinese. So the fact that Panchen Rinpoché had actually been single-mindedly looking after the interests of the Tibetan people with such great concern and without regard for his own position amazed people once they came to know about it, and those who had criticized him regretted what they had said, confessed their mistake with joined palms, and gained faith in him.

Before people found out about the 70,000 Character Petition, Panchen Rinpoché used to give weekly audiences at his Dorjé Po-trang residence in the Shuktri Lingka, which were attended only by old folks who stopped by on their circumambulation of the Lingkor circuit, and occasionally he gave a longevity empowerment in the reception hall. At such times, Panchen Rinpoché repeatedly joined his palms in prayer while uttering the name of His Holiness the Dalai Lama in devoted recollection, and when Lhasa people heard about this, they became more convinced that the earlier opposition to the government by his Labrang and support for the Chinese was only the doing of the Labrang officials, while the Panchen himself had unequivocal faith and devotion [in His Holiness], so more people started coming to hear his teachings and attend his audiences.

A little while later we heard that Panchen Rinpoché had gone on a tour of Kongpo, but in fact, in order to quash the 70,000 Character Petition, the Chinese had taken him to Kongpo with the intention of getting him to repudiate it. But Rinpoché had the welfare of his people at heart and bravely refused, so that finally, at the fourth PCART assembly in 1964, he was openly denounced, criticized, and subjected to struggle, and then taken off to China. In order to prepare public opinion for the denunciation of the Panchen Rinpoché, they set up an exhibition on the "crimes of the anti-Party Panchen clique" at Trungchi Lingka, the site of the present Tibet University, and each neighborhood committee in turn took people there to see it. I was in Lhasa at the time and was taken to see it, and an activist member of my subcommittee appointed to check on my reaction stayed right next to me throughout the tour, which was very trying. The exhibition featured rifles, cannon, a jeep, radio transmitters, and a "Vajra army" flag, which were presented as evidence that the "Panchen clique" was staging a rebellion. Some of the famous images from holy places in Ü district, including the Reteng Jowo, the Ra-tsak Dakini, and the Shédrak Acarya [Guru Padma], which the Panchen had collected and looked after, were also in the exhibition, and people jostled to get a closer look at them. The exhibition guides delivered a very harsh diatribe about how Panchen Rinpoché had been involved in violent opposition to the Party, had stolen national sacred artifacts for himself, and behaved despicably.

After the tour, we had to give an account of our feelings about it in the evening meetings of our subcommittees. The Chinese hoped that after seeing the exhibition, the people would vigorously oppose, denounce, and defame Panchen Rinpoché, but it didn't happen like that. One amusing instance was a fat Khampa trader from the Lhasa meat market who had not been obliged to see the exhibition since he was of poor [class] origin and chronically ill, and normally stayed home. However, the prospect of seeing the sacred images persuaded him to go, and when required to give his reaction at the evening meeting, he said, "Today's tour was really a great opportunity! Previously, to get to see these holy images you had to spend a lot of physical effort, precious time, and money, but this morning, due to Panchen Rinpoché's great kindness, we got to see them all there at once!" There were separate meetings for us "class enemies" to determine whether we had any involvement in the Panchen issue, and daily meetings in each Reform Through Labor group where we had to give our views, which made our misery worse.

CHAPTER 14

The Misuse of Education

IN 1964, THERE were three primary schools and one middle school in Lhasa, and a school for training teachers and officials. Most of the students training to be teachers and officials were from all over the country, and since they were being educated only for that purpose, they were all from poor class backgrounds. As long as they committed no major mistakes during their time as students, they were automatically given jobs when they finished, and schoolchildren from poor class backgrounds who attended [primary and middle school] for the requisite period were also given employment afterward, regardless of their results. But because so few Tibetans could speak or read Chinese at that time, even the children of politically ostracized parents could go on to middle school and find employment if their grades were good enough. Thus we all hoped that my youngest brother, Nga-nam, who was in the number 2 primary school, would get through school and at least become qualified rather than having to work as a manual laborer, and since he always attended class and worked hard at everything his results were fine, and in 1964 he took the middle school entrance test and felt confident of getting in.

Then one morning, as he was waiting for the list of new students to be announced, the middle school admissions subcommittee pasted up a list by the school gate from which the names of most of the diligent students who always attended and did well were absent. This was a peculiar development that had not been seen before. Nga-nam's name was also missing, and he came home in a very dejected state to tell us about it, but while we were all downcast, we felt that it was better to suffer our disappointment in silence than to go trying to find out what had happened, which would be like asking for trouble. Meanwhile, the other students who had not been accepted got together and requested the admissions subcommittee to explain whether it was because they had not achieved the required percentage on the exam or for some other reason, but the committee would only say that it had been decided at a higher level. Finally, it dawned on everyone that the pupils who had been denied entrance to middle school were the children of [politically] ostracized families, and had achieved much better exam results than the others.

The only possible conclusion to be drawn was that children from the ostracized social class were having the opportunity of education taken away from them. If that were so, there was no question of making amends with a payment, and it meant that this was an evil design to further long-term Chinese control over Tibet. Mao Zedong had said, "The more education a person has received, the more unreliable his character; the more books he has read, the less he can be relied on to take a stand." It is because educated people have the capacity to think for themselves and make up their own minds on any particular issue, and hence cannot be marshaled and exploited at the whim of [the authorities], that Mao said they were unreliable and dubious, and it was on the basis of this distorted view that bright students were being denied education due to their family background or their parents' political record. The reason those pupils who were denied entry to middle school got distinguished results was that the educational methods enforced by government policy led to different attitudes among the students and affected their willingness to study. As already mentioned, children of ordinary working families simply had to attend school for the requisite period in order to qualify for employment afterward and hence did not bother to study hard, while children from ostracized families had no surety of employment other than their actual results at school and were also encouraged at home, and so tended to get high grades. It need not be supposed that their performance was due to any other factor, such as inherent ability.

In any case, this was how middle school admissions were handled from 1964 up until the end of the Cultural Revolution, so the Tibetan officials holding key positions throughout this period were pawns of the Chinese who despised their own people and were no more able to think for themselves than donkeys in a herd, and the Tibetan people came to feel contempt for their own kind. Indeed, one cannot blame those [Tibetans and non-Tibetans] who have not understood the origins of the present situation in Tibet and those who point out that the struggle, recrimination, and cruelty inflicted during the years of intense suffering was done by Tibetans themselves. However, if you look carefully at how these things came about, you can see that they were the product of a long-term strategy for the imposition of foreign rule.

Anyway, the students who could not stay in school at that time had to make their living as manual laborers, and thus my youngest brother, Nganam, had to spend the next twenty years of his life working as a construction laborer under conditions of great hardship and with very low income, absolutely against his own wishes and those of his family.

CHAPTER 15

The Establishment of the Tibet Autonomous Region

WHEN THE TIBET Autonomous Region was formally established in September 1965, a group of central government representatives, led by one of the then vice premiers of the State Council and Public Security Minister Xie Fuchi, arrived in Tibet to attend a grand inaugural ceremony. Not long afterward, it was decided at an autonomous region conference that the Communist Party Tibet work committee and most of the main TAR departments would move to the Powo Yiwong region once the necessary construction had been completed. Thus, most of the construction units in the autonomous region departed for that place, and a large number of ordinary laborers were recruited from Lhasa municipality, Chamdo prefecture, and so on. In Lhasa, each neighborhood committee had to recruit a quota of workers—sixty in Banak-shöl's case—and if there were not enough volunteers, it was up to each subcommittee to designate candidates, and our subcommittee put down my name. My younger brother Nga-nam was working as a construction laborer at the time and volunteered to go with me. All of the recruited workers left Lhasa together in a convoy of ten trucks on September 26.

This was before the start of the Cultural Revolution, and the workers' parents and relatives came to see them off with tea and beer as is the Tibetan custom, and my brothers and sisters also came. As we set off, they put a greeting scarf (*Kha btags*) around my neck, which was the first time I had worn one since the [1959] troubles. For me, this was a chance to see the Kongpo and Powo regions, where I had never been before, which are quite different from Ü province and well known for their unique landscape, although the earlier news of the deaths of so many prisoners in those areas had left a strong impression on me, and there was a reluctance [to go] in the back of my mind. Once we got there, however, we found that it was an extremely beautiful place. After we passed Numa-ri, where Kongpo begins, six hours by truck from Lhasa, the mountains on both sides of the road were filled with a verdant abundance of flora, and we could see the famous Nyang-chu river surging into waves as it flowed southeast through a valley somewhat broader than a gorge, whose flanks were adorned by fields like ornaments, planted with various crops and terraced in some places, like the stepped base of a *stupa*. In the uplands there were said to be rich pastures where many nomads lived. It was September, and the fruit of the walnut and peach trees, which belonged to no one, was there for all to enjoy as they pleased.

The beauty of the area was such as I had never seen in the other parts of Tibet I had visited. However, it was because of these natural resources and environmental conditions that most of the Chinese business enterprises in Tibet at that time, both private and state-run, had been established in Kongpo. By the time we got there, only a few years had passed since the enforcement of Communist rule in Tibet, but in this area with the largest concentration of Chinese outside Lhasa, Chinese settlements both military and civilian were already to be seen in every corner of the valley, most notably logging teams and big timber yards, for the forests were being cut indiscriminately. However, the upper and lower reaches of the main valley were still covered with forest, and the scars left by logging had not yet become evident.

After crossing the Serkyim-la pass beyond Nyingtri, we reached Kongpo Lu-nang. There is a popular proverb, "If once you set foot in Kongpo Lu-nang, you will not think of your own homeland anymore": it is a broad valley bounded on either side by mountains capped with snow and covered with virgin forest in their middle reaches, sweeping down into lush meadows the color of parrots' plumage. The inhabitants are semipastoralists, for cattle thrive on the abundance of water and grazing, and the climate is pleasantly temperate. It is as fair a land as can be found anywhere in Tibet. It is said that most of the inhabitants are the descendants of Khampas who passed through on their way from eastern Tibet to holy Lhasa and other pilgrimage destinations in Ü, and were so taken with the area that they returned to settle there. There were a few Chinese army camps and a few road workers' camps, for the highway running through Powo was continually affected by landslides during the summer rains. Otherwise, there weren't many Chinese settlements there at that time.

Even as we went on toward Powo Yiwong the way was blocked by a landslide, and we had to stop in a road workers' compound. I well remember being in that place during the celebration of National Day [October 1]. Then we reached Powo Yiwong. According to local tradition, that area too was a special "hidden valley"; before reaching it one has to pass through a very narrow gorge, which gradually opens out into a broad river valley, covered with primordial forest, with a fabulous lake at its center that is supposed to be the talismanic lake of some protector deity. Beyond the lake to the north is one of the great snow mountains of ancient myth, a splendid peak known as Ngang-yak Karpo. According to the locals, there is a great cleft in the mountains on one side of the lake where iron ore is found, and that is smelted and worked to produce the famous Powo knives (*sPo gri*). Here and there, the land is adorned with level meadows like natural sports fields, and the crop cultivated in that area is a type of grain that ripens into a flower, which was in bloom as we arrived, so from a distance the scene really looked like something painted by a master artist.

However, the people's way of life was apparently primitive. Many of them had a poor physique, perhaps because of the plant life in the water; there were a lot of people with goiter and warts on their faces and hands; some had deformed limbs; and there seemed to be a high proportion of congenital idiocy. Their settlements were not concentrated in villages, but dispersed, and their main form of livelihood was forestry. As well as [the usual] wheat, barley, peas, buckwheat, millet, and so on also grew well, and the climate and elevation allowed for two annual crops. They had cattle such as *dzomo* [yak-cow hybrids], cows, and goats, and also kept hens and pigs. Most of the men liked to hunt, and they had different kinds of hunting dogs of which they were very fond. The most crucial imported commodity was salt, but although Tibet had salt in inexhaustible quantity, the Chinese government did not allow for its supply to such small communities, so evidently they had to find other sources.

By the time we arrived in Yiwong there were already many construction work sites, and the workers arriving from Lhasa were allocated to different ones. The workers from the four neighborhood committees under the East Lhasa sectional office were bound for a place called Chakar on the north side of the lake where there was a brick factory and a logging team nearby, and we were sent to the brick factory. The place we had to stay in, where the bricks were made, had just a roof to keep off the rain, with no side walls, and a hundred people were put there together, with a space assigned to each subcommittee. It was autumn, and with the warmer temperatures in that area the lack of walls was not a problem, for the breeze served as welcome ventilation to clear the stench of so many people living in a confined space.

There were different sections in the workplace, the adobe-brick makers and clay-brick makers, the brick kiln operators and those who cut wood for the kilns, while the most important [pieces of equipment] were the hand carts, and more important still were those who repaired them. Since I had a little experience of repairing such small vehicles from my time in prison, I was put in the vehicle repair division (*Tshogs chung*). The vehicle repair people were entitled to a skilled worker's wage, but since I belonged to the "ruling class" category, my wage level was among the lowest even for unskilled workers. Although there was not such an enormous practical difference between these wage levels, the indiscriminate exploitation of even our physical strength under the regulations of an oppressive political ideology was in itself offensive. However, since this construction work had been deemed one of the autonomous region's most important targets, some consideration was given to the workers' standard of living, and the provision of food and other necessities was no worse than for civilians in Lhasa at that time.

To judge from the scale of the construction work sites in Yiwong, they seemed to be engaged in a project that would be going on for at least five or six years, but after about four months the intensity of the work lessened, and we heard a whispered rumor that we were to be moved to Kongpo Nyingtri. Not long afterward an announcement came that our work group had to move on to Nyingtri, and the other work groups in Yiwong were also moved, to places in Kongpo and in Chamdo prefecture. I heard two different explanations why these large-scale construction units suddenly had to quit: some said that although in terms of the climate and landscape this was a suitable place for Chinese people to stay, a team of British geologists had earlier found that the area was flood-prone, and some Chinese geologists had recently confirmed this. Other people said that there had been several cases of spies being dropped by [foreign] aircraft in that area. Neither version was confirmed by the authorities, but the latter seems more likely to me. Anyhow, that great construction project was abandoned midway through, and later on, apart from a "secret" Party training school ("*Yid 'ong sbas tshon*") and a few agricultural units, no large-scale official complex was ever [built] there.

All the same, it was clear that they managed to devastate the forest in that area within a very short time. Obviously the proposed construction site had to be cleared and leveled, and timber provided for construction. Then, just to take the example of our brick factory, they needed 40 to 50 truckloads of firewood per day to fuel the kiln, and they used an unimaginable quantity of timber for the scaffolding alone when they set up a new kiln.

One of the logging teams nearby had about 400 or 500 workers, and if you work out how much they must have cut every day, it is frightening. Moreover, the sequence of the work was totally haphazard, with no thought at all being given to the regeneration of the forest, which was not the usual practice even in China, not to mention elsewhere. The only substantial outcome of the construction program in Powo Yiwong, then, was the tremendous damage inflicted on the surrounding forests.

Our work group moved to Kongpo Nyingtri early in 1966. We traveled back on the same road by which we had come to Yiwong and found that in the space of those five months the area had undergone great changes. A logging department and timber yard had been established in Kongpo Lu-nang and, most striking of all, the mountain slopes above Nyingtri leading up to Serkyim-la pass were full of logging teams. The largest of them was the team affiliated with Drapchi prison. All the trees near the passable section of road on that mountain had been cut, and now they were making inroads in areas not accessible by the road.

Our new factory was established on the site of a disused brick kiln, which we enlarged, on open land in front of Nyingtri township. The centerpiece of construction in Kongpo at that time was the so-called "Eight-one" [August 1] new town (*Ba-yi* in Chinese) in the area [formerly known as] Ba-chi, where a large textile factory, a power station, a match factory, and a paper factory were being built. Since our factory had to supply all those construction sites with bricks, tiles, and quicklime and the strength of our workforce and the required production levels were in inverse proportion, the work became extremely demanding. Less efficient groups of workers had to make up for it in their spare time. Things got worse not long after our arrival in Nyingtri with the launch of the "Four Cleanups" campaign (*gTsang ma bzhi*), when official work teams (*Las don ru khag*) organized by the TAR Party committee were deputed to each departmental division and a six-member official subcommittee arrived at our work site. The "Four Cleanups" were "clean administration," "clean thinking," "clean economy," and "clean conduct," and the main objectives concerned the Party organization and the leaders of our factory, but also involved "education" for the rest of us in the current political drive. Having to go to the meetings every evening before we could recover from the day's toil was one of the worst torments of the Communist system.

There were separate meetings for the few of us in the "ruling class" and "ruling class deputy" categories, where we had to account for our progress in "thought reform," and in the name of "labor reform" we were called on to clean up around the workplace, cut firewood for general use, and help in the preparation of a general meeting hall, playing field, and other facilities in the mornings and evenings, on Sundays, and whenever we had free time. One of the members of the official subcommittee was a short Chinese man who particularly had it in for me. He was always looking for any issue with which he could attack me, asking my fellow workers how I was doing, ordering them to supervise and criticize me, and ordering those in my dormitory to report to him on any rumors I might spread, any reactionary thoughts I might express, or any irregularity of behavior they could think of. When there was a political campaign going on, the work teams would politicize any incident they could find as an accomplishment of their mission, regardless of whether it was really a matter of concern, and that Chinese went to all possible lengths to stir up trouble for me. However, most of my fellow workers and those in my dormitory were kind and well-intentioned people, and they always let me know discreetly that he was vindictively looking for an accusation to frame me, and sincerely confided in me about how to stay out of trouble.

But there were always a few mindless ones who followed whatever the Chinese told them. Dönden, the cook in our communal kitchen, was one of them, and he handed in a "thought report" to that Chinese saying that I had been making exaggerated remarks about the virtues of the "old society" in order to corrupt the thinking of young people who had grown up "under the red flag." In the next meeting, the Chinese official told me several times while pointing his finger at me, "If you voluntarily confess your mistakes, the Party will treat you leniently," but I was not aware of making any mistakes and had nothing to confess. Finally, in an attempt to intimidate me, he told me very aggressively, "Unless you confess your crime of corrupting the thoughts of the youth who have grown up under the red flag, as well as your objective in doing so, you will have to face struggle at the general meeting and could end up going back to prison." Thereupon, I said that if anyone could testify or demonstrate that there had been any incident of my poisoning others' thoughts, they should please speak up, but none of the young people present so much as opened their mouths. Finally, the false accuser Dönden told the Chinese official privately that he had seen the young ones always gathering around me and listening to what I had to say, but since he could produce nothing more in support of his accusation and no one else came forward to confront me, he and the Chinese were confounded, and after they warned me to "think carefully about my guilt," the meeting came to an end.

After that, no one tried to sustain or repeat this allegation, but the official work team stayed on, and thereafter, with the issue of two successive central government policy documents, "The Dictatorship of the Proletariat Must Be Consolidated" and "Class Struggle Must Never Be Abandoned," those in the "ruling class" categories were cornered. We each had three individuals assigned to us as supervisors, and whenever we needed to go into town or any other place, we had to ask the "supervision subcommittee" (*lTa rtog tshogs chung*) for leave and give our reasons. And they made a rule that even if we were given leave, we had to be back within four hours.

It seems that at that time there was a fierce dispute within the central government over the direction of official policy, and there was one incident I clearly recall. They used to give a weekly film show in our factory, and one time, before the main film, they showed a newsreel of the central leaders meeting with foreign guests. I was sitting next to a Muslim fellow whose family name was Ma, and he asked me if I noticed anything in particular about the newsreel. I had not, so I asked him what he meant, and he replied that one of the leaders was heading for disaster. He knew this because the main concern of newsreel producers was to respect the status of the top leaders, so one could easily tell from those films who were the most powerful even though it was not actually stated. In the film we had just seen, Liu Shaoqi was not very evident and appeared only momentarily. You could tell from that, Ma said, that an internal dispute was going on, and he turned out to be right. Those documents on consolidating the proletarian dictatorship and continuing the class struggle seem to have been designed to influence an ongoing struggle within the central leadership, and the campaign known as the Great Proletarian Cultural Revolution was started shortly afterward.

The Onset of the Cultural Revolution

THAT THE HORRIFIC campaign known as the Cultural Revolution was one of the greatest catastrophes in the history of not just Tibet but China as a whole is admitted by the current regime. The reasons that led Mao Zedong to start it are popularly explained as follows: in 1957, even before the [disastrous] results of Mao's Great Leap Forward had become evident, a faction of the leadership, including the defense minister, Peng Dehuai, opposed him. The tradition of the personality cult had come to an end with the denunciation of Stalin in Russia after his death, and when all this led to a variety of views and positions among the Chinese leadership, Mao feared that his position as supreme leader was under threat. Meanwhile, unlike Mao, the President of China, Liu Shaoqi, took a favorable view of the development of the entrepreneurial economy, and when he implemented measures to that effect that won the support and approval of the people and the leadership, his position was strengthened. This displeased Mao, who then tried to popularize the view that by "taking the bourgeois road," the faction of the Party led by Liu was "reviving the corpse of capitalism" and leading China "back into darkness."

In any case, the campaign came into the open in June 1966, when some students at Beijing University wrote a big-character poster criticizing the leaders and teachers at the university and praising Mao; it called for "bombarding the bourgeois headquarters," and that was the spark that set it off At the same time, the central government's Cultural Revolution Committee was set up and initiated the campaign by issuing Directive 5–16, calling for a "Great Cultural Revolution" in which the "Four Olds," "old culture, old thinking, old habits, old customs," had to be destroyed.

I was still in Kongpo then, and not long after the announcement of Directive 5–16 in our factory, one of my friends who was working on the power station in "Eight-one" new town came to tell me that since the launch of the Cultural Revolution in Lhasa all the sacred statues, scriptures, and images left in the Tsukla-khang and other monasteries had been destroyed; people's houses had been searched and they were made to carry whatever sacred images or religious paraphernalia they had through the streets in public humiliation processions (*Khrom bskor*) and subjected to struggle. In consternation, I vividly recalled hearing from the elders how, during the spread of Communism in Russia, Mongolian monasteries, including the great temple of Urga (*Da khu ral*), had been completely destroyed and thousands of monks slaughtered. Now, as I contemplated how the Chinese had flung away the disguise of their "freedom of religion" policy and gotten down to the basics of Communist practice, I started shivering with anxiety as though I had caught malaria. One of the things I was most anxious about was my three elder sisters in Lhasa, who had entered the religious life as children and, despite having been at home since the troubles, still lived as nuns; with the thought of what maltreatment they could face in this campaign against religion and traditional culture, I could neither eat nor sleep. I was somewhat relieved when someone I knew from the factory returned early from a visit to his relatives in Lhasa and brought a letter for me saying that my sisters were fine. The reason he came back early, however, was that he had reached Lhasa just as the city was in the throes of that campaign, and had no wish to stay longer. He gave an account of the situation but could not say exactly whether my house had been searched, and I was still far from feeling reassured.

Then, one Sunday when I had gone to buy something in Nyingtri, I saw a group of so-called Red Guards banging drums and cymbals. They were leading a couple of elderly Kongpo people who had tall paper hats stuck on their heads, boards hung around their necks [like criminals] with SPIRIT MONSTERS (*lHa 'dre gdon bgegs*) and REACTIONARY BOSSES (*Log spyod phyug bdag*) and then their own names written on them, and religious scroll paintings tied around their waists like aprons, and they were made to pull a small cart loaded with scriptures and printing blocks and so on. Since I too was a "class enemy," there was no saying that the same would not happen to me, and when I envisioned this happening to my nun sisters during the terrible events taking place in Lhasa, the apprehension was unbearable. A few days later, some Nyingtri Public Security officials came to the factory to investigate whether anyone had seen or heard of the couple who had been led on the public humiliation procession or their children, and put up a notice requiring anyone who found out where they had gone to report it to the Public Security Office in Nyingtri or any related department. According to local people, the disappeared couple had acted as guides for many of those who fled to India in 1959, and since they knew all the secret routes it was believed that they must have fled the country. But a few days later, the bodies of that couple and one of their children were fished out of the Nyang-chu river below Nyingtri. They had tied rocks around their necks and drowned themselves.

Like everywhere else, our factory in its turn received the order to destroy the Four Olds, which meant whatever prayer books, *malas* [rosaries], blessing cords, and amulet boxes people had. Men with long hair and women both young and old had to cut their hair, and in accordance with the prohibition of Tibetan clothes like gowns and women's aprons, people could wear only [modern] Chinese-style clothes. There were women who valued their long hair so much that they wept with frustration at having to cut it, and those who felt that they were unsightly with cropped hair. But different leaders handled things in their own way, and while things remained calm in our factory, there were other work sites where carpets, cloaks, jewelry such as rings and bracelets, and even wooden bowls and leather bags were declared "old habits" and their owners obliged to destroy them. Then there were Red Guards who carried scissors around with them to cut off women's hair as they pleased, and branded workers in possession of religious objects "spirit monsters" and subjected them to public humiliation and struggle.

Once the campaign got going, more attention was paid to political education than to productivity, with particular emphasis on the study of the essential points from the *Quotations of Mao Zedong* and examination of the students' ability to recite them. There were continual meetings for the denunciation of "power holders in the Party taking the capitalist road" and dissemination of big-character posters. But they didn't say who these "power holders" were, and for a time, people didn't really know. Then the *People's Daily* published the names of three figures known collectively as the "village of three wicked households" who were representative of the "power holders within the Party," and they put up even more big-character newspapers denouncing them. Many films, books, stories, and songs categorized as having been tainted by their ideological poison were denounced and banned. Next, [office holders known to belong to] the "Liu-Deng tendency" were named as the biggest "bourgeois capitalist-roader power holders" in the Party, and it was announced that Liu Shaoqi and Deng Xiaoping were the principal stooges of capitalism. Mock resumes of their careers called them names like "reactionary," "traitor," "scab," "revisionist," and so on at will, and they were vilified by theater groups performing plays about Liu and Deng "reviving the corpse of capitalism," by artists painting caricatures of them on notice boards, walls, and roads, and more. Then the names of many senior members of the Communist leadership who had participated in the Long March and Revolutionary War were included, and they were repudiated and removed from their positions.

At that point, most of the ongoing construction projects in Kongpo were scaled back, and they announced a list of names of workers from our factory who were required to go and work on the proposed construction of a power station and cement factory in Chamdo prefecture. My younger brother Nga-nam was one of them, and he subsequently related that the power station and cement factory were being built as part of a planned factory for weapons and other military supplies in the Guru and Wa-yok areas [of Kham Dra-yab], with resources taken from pristine natural deposits, such as metal ore from Kha-kong and Kyi-tang, coal from Martsa-la, and timber from Chamdo. That vast building site was code named "Ground Plan Number 3 Construction Zone" (*Sa thig gsum pa'i 'dzugs skrun*).

In December 1966, the few of us from the "ruling class" category, the older and less physically fit, and those who had no political or physical impediments but had not distinguished themselves in conduct or outlook either, were sent back to Lhasa. By that time, things had become slightly calmer than at the outset of the campaign, when the house searches and public humiliation processions were in full swing, but there had nonetheless been changes since my departure for Kongpo. For instance, in addition to the regular leaders, there was now in every neighborhood committee a group of young Red Guards whose power had been greatly enhanced by the turn of events and who could inflict struggle and public humiliation on anyone who did not meet with their approval. There were [neighborhood] meetings every evening, and before they started, we had to recite from the quotations of Mao and sing songs based on them. Everyone, young and old alike, was required to carry the book of his quotations with them at all times in a small cloth bag made of any kind of red material decorated with a five-pointed yellow star, tied on with cord in a place where it could always be seen. Also, wearing badges with Mao's profile or slogans praising him on one's chest, and other visible marks of devotion to him, were among the most widespread practices. The Red Guards, boys and girls alike, wore blue trousers, military-style jackets with leather belts, and army caps, with or

Young Red Guards on their way to "destroy the Four Olds." *Used with kind permission from Woeser.*

without insignia. They rolled up their sleeves and trouser legs and wore red armbands bearing the characters "Red Guard" in yellow.

Among the ordinary people, even the Tibetan clothes worn by women differed from men's only in the pleat down the back [of the skirt], and in front they wore not the traditional multicolored apron, but one made of black cotton. At that time, the appearance and bearing of anyone you looked at was either rough and conceited or timid and downtrodden, according to their position, and it was extremely rare to see anyone with the cheerful look that comes from mutual trust and affection. Even entertainment shows were only about "class struggle" and "progressive struggle," and the style of presentation was so crude and violent that just watching them was enough to provoke an opposite reaction to that intended. That is what I found on my return to Lhasa from Kongpo.

My brothers and sisters and close friends told me that at the start of the Cultural Revolution campaign, when the searches and street parades were going on, our house had not been affected, but hearing about some of the things that had happened to others was comic as well as tragic. Take what had happened in our Banak-shöl neighborhood: the very next day after the proclamation of the above-mentioned Directive 5–16, the education, propaganda, and culture departments of the autonomous region initiated

Desecration of the Tsukla-khang in Lhasa, September 1966. *Used with kind permission from Woeser.*

the destruction of the Four Olds by obliging the students at the teacher training college and Lhasa middle school to destroy whatever sacred objects there were in the Tsukla-khang, Ramo-ché, and other temples and monasteries around the city, whereupon the local youth in the Banak-shöl area formed their own group and went to destroy the sacred images in the oracle temple (*rGyal khang btsan khang*) where local people worshipped their territorial deity.

The house of Chang-ngöpa Dorjé Ngödrup, a former government official, was the first to be searched. Since he had not participated in the uprising, the contents of his house had been spared, including old furniture, silver and gold jewelry, and the costume worn by officials of the former government. They listed all the items of precious jewelry, which had to be sold to the state, and dressed up Chang-ngöpa Dorjé Ngödrup in the tra-

A struggle session in Lhasa during the Cultural Revolution. *Used with kind permission from Woeser.*

ditional costume and his wife, Téchö-la, as a mockery. They also found a brocade drape (*sTan dkar rdo rje*) once used to decorate the throne of a high lama, and since it had a swastika design, they said it was a German Nazi flag. The next house they came to was Banak-shöl Changdong-tsang. The head of that household, Sonam Peljor, had been a bursary official (*Shod phyag nang*), and they took out the round hat (*Bog rdo*) worn by holders of that office and made him put it on. Among his possessions, they also found some British cavalry jodhpurs that they made him wear, and a ceremonial knife and bowl case (*rGya gri phor shubs*) that they tied around his waist, and they hung Chang-ngöpa's swastika throne drape on a stick like a flag and stuck it on Changdong-tsang Sonam Peljor. Then, together with members of other households who had been searched and dressed up in various garb, they were led out to be publicly humiliated, surrounded by the local officials and Red Guards to either side, front and back, and some mindless people in the crowd spat and threw dirt, or insulted and abused them.

One of the people in that procession, a woman called Pa-yong who had nothing to do with the former so-called "ruling class," was made to put on a horse saddle they had found while searching her house, and her daughter Jampa was dressed up in ridiculous clothing and sent with her. That girl had formerly been a member of the official drama troupe and was one of the actresses in the propaganda film entitled *Serf*. Later she was employed in the government-run bookshop, and was working there at the time, but still she was taken out in the procession behind her mother, like "both losing the reins of a galloping horse and getting dragged along behind," and as a result of that appalling mistreatment and abuse she lost her wits. People said that despite all the medical treatment her mother arranged for her, she went insane and later died.

So unbearable was the savage mistreatment that took place during the launch of that campaign that people killed themselves by drowning, jumping off heights, cutting their own throats, or hanging themselves rather than endure it. One of the most distressing cases concerned the couple who ran the Chokri-wö Chinese goods store on the south side of the Parkor and their three children. Faced with the torment of being labeled "spirit monsters," the whole family jumped to their deaths from the main bridge over the Kyi-chu river, and although the Chinese guards on the bridge tried to drag them out, since the river was swollen by the summer rains, they were carried off by the current and the parents and two elder children drowned. It seems that the youngest child was on the father's back, and instead of sinking, was carried toward the shore, and the Chinese foreman of a work team repairing the river embankment near Tsédrung Lingka, a mile downstream from the main bridge, swam out and managed to save the child.

Like the saying that "When the old horse gets struck down by lightning, the old dog takes on a new shine," there were also those few for whom the onset of the Cultural Revolution provided an opportunity for big financial gains. Some of the neighborhood leaders, for example, and some Red Guards used to pocket things that were easy to carry when they did house searches and took note of any valuable or special things they could not just pick up, which they would later come and requisition when they could pretend to do so with the authority of the neighborhood committee, and never return them. Likewise, the Khachara [half-breed] traders in Lhasa with Nepalese citizenship did not have to fear having their houses searched since they were considered foreigners, and many Tibetans who felt unable to dump their sacred objects and treasured heirlooms in the river preferred to leave them with such people. When they came to reclaim them, the Khacharas would say that they had been too scared to hang on to them and had ended up destroying them, and some would pay the owners a nominal price for the objects, while others, far from paying even a cent, would threaten the owners with reporting to the Chinese authorities that they had attempted to conceal such monstrous superstitious objects in the first place. Since sacred images and historic treasures were not valued at the time of the Cultural Revolution, it seems that they were not strictly controlled at the border checkpoints, and the Khacharas were able to take those objects entrusted to them by Tibetans to Nepal, and from there to the West, where they sold them for many *lakhs* of rupees. They were able to build multistory hotels in Nepal, and some of those are still said to be named after the temples and statues on whose proceeds they were built, like Tara Guest House, Buddha Guest House, and so on.

Lhasa people also threw many of their precious things in the river at that time out of fear, and there was a group of people who got rich by fishing them out again, but unlike the two categories of profiteers already mentioned, they did so with hard effort and disregard for the political and physical dangers involved. I later worked with someone who had recovered things from the river in that period, who told me that he and his wife quit their usual work as meat sellers for three weeks or so and stayed by the riverside with a hook for pulling things out. He also went in the water with a rope around his waist while his wife held the other end, and he dragged the hook this way and that. Sometimes they would spend a whole day without recovering a single thing, and other times they would find all kinds of things as soon as they got there in the morning. In those three weeks spent by the riverbank, he said, they recovered enough to keep a spendthrift going for four or five years. That is one story from the early days of the Cultural Revolution, a tale people will never be able to forget.

But to continue with my own story, I returned to Lhasa from Kongpo exactly at the time they were recruiting more workers for the construction of a new canal from below the Nga-chen power station to Lhasa, which had begun about three weeks earlier, and as soon as I got back I was instructed by the neighborhood committee to go and work there. Generally speaking, there was a big difference between finding a job for myself and being sent to work by the committee: whatever hardship and wages came with a job I had found independently, I did not have to put up with their coercion and felt a little more at ease, whereas being sent to a work site by the committee meant not only hard work and low wages but also suffering the rigors of the work site regime and its leaders. That canal construction camp was set up at the height of the Cultural Revolution, and I personally suffered more there than in all the previous time since my release from prison.

Concerning accommodation and hygiene, the camp was undertaken and administered by the Lhasa municipal authority (*Chengguan-chu*), which was an executive office, and did not provide accommodations or other living provisions for its workers. The workers' tents and communal kitchen equipment were arranged by each of the neighborhood committees involved, and all the committees had were the flimsy summer picnic tents made of linen and cotton that had been confiscated by the state during the Democratic Reform. The work camp was set up during the tenth Tibetan month, when [night] temperatures are sometimes 13 to 14 degrees below zero, and since that was all [the shelter] there was, we had to suffer never being able to sleep at night due to the cold. At the same time, with more than 100 people sharing one kitchen and only two or three copper tea urns, we could not get enough hot tea to drink. Individually we had neither the time nor the means to heat up the cooked food brought from our own homes, and since we were in the middle of a so-called "underlining class distinctions, class consciousness, and class solidarity" drive, those in charge of making the tea would not allow "class enemies" to heat up their food by the hearth. Thus the cooked food we had brought was as cold as food out of the refrigerators we have these days, but we had to eat it just to keep ourselves going, and in this way many "class enemies" gave themselves chronic stomach problems. During that period of intense cold, it was hard to get even a bit of lukewarm water to wash your face in the morning, and there was no other provision for hygiene, so many people caught colds, and while unable to sleep at night from the cold, we also had the grating noise of all those people coughing and hawking to endure. The standard workday for civilians specified by the Labor Bureau was 8 hours, with a provision for lengthening the work period in case of urgent necessity, but at that time we had to work about 12 to 13 hours every day, leaving our camp before sunrise and returning at nightfall. As for wages, my entitlement of 0.9 *yuan* was insufficient for myself alone to live on.

We were building a canal, and as in most Tibetan terrain, the soil was mixed with river rock and sand, which makes it one of the heaviest kinds to carry and one of the hardest to dig with picks and shovels. Because of the soil composition, it was occasionally necessary to dig three stories [6 yards] deep, and since the mounds of excavated earth did not spread out, it had to be hauled up a steep rise. In most places, before we reached the required depth of the canal it filled with water, and those digging with picks and shovels had to stand in the water, sometimes up to their knees. Those carrying baskets on their backs had to fill them with rock and earth from underwater, so their backs and trousers got completely soaked, they got chafing sores on their waists, and without dry shoes to wear, blisters on their feet, and had many other hardships in addition to the already hard labor. Because there was no time for the day's wet shoes and clothes to dry out before they had to be reworn, we had no dry clothes to put on when we got back from work. The worst job at that time was working with a pick, because you had to stand in water all day and dig, and where there was no water the ground was frozen hard and even tougher to dig. Because I was a "class enemy" and a young man, I always had to do the heaviest and most dangerous jobs, and at that time, they gave me a pick and told me to dig. Excavating underwater was a little easier, but digging the frozen ground, you had to swing the pick 20 times to fill a basket with earth. The earth supplying two or three groups shoveling it into baskets with spades had to be dug with the pick, and even if we slogged away for the whole day without once looking up, whenever the carriers idled waiting for loads, the supervising officials came and forced the diggers on, regardless of the terrain being dug, and in the evening meetings to discuss the progress of the work, the less energetic diggers were scolded and criticized.

During the workday we had two five-minute breaks, one in the morning and one in the afternoon, but we could not use them as we pleased and had to spend the time reading or reciting from Mao's quotations, and when we returned to camp in the evening we had to attend a meeting after we ate. The usual purpose of these meetings was to discuss the progress of the work, but we also had to study and discuss the proclamations on "class struggle" and "proletarian dictatorship" issued periodically by the central government and autonomous regional government. There were separate meetings for "class enemies" where we were supposed to recognize the crimes of our former way of life and resolve, over and above the performance of "thought reform" and "labor reform," to give our maximum effort and determination to fulfilling the spirit and goals of the work at hand. At that time, the leaders and so-called "activists" could easily turn anything they took exception to, even small things, into issues over which people were subjected to mistreatment like struggle, denunciation, and public humiliation. Regardless of whether you had knowingly committed any misdeed, once an altercation arose you would be in big trouble, and those who refused to go along with false accusations made against them would be labeled as having a "stubborn old-fashioned brain" and have to face numerous beatings and struggle sessions. On the other hand, if you admitted that such an accusation was true to get some temporary relief, you would be saddled with a huge burden of guilt, it would be written on your political record, and you would have to recount how you committed that crime and atone for it in each subsequent campaign.

Therefore I was constantly wary of the danger of being accused and always made as much effort in the work as I could, but at that time we had someone called "fat Tenchö" in our group, a bad character who got along with no one and strongly resented "class enemies." Ever since he'd joined that work camp, he had done whatever he could to bully "class enemies," and in the meetings he would always tell how they had failed in reform, and incite the young activists and people from "poor" class backgrounds to subject them to struggle and humiliation, or threaten them with punishments himself. At the time I was working with the pick, he said that I was making no effort and scolded me many times, saying, "You're a young man, but instead of putting your back into the work, you stand there like you had swallowed a pole!" and in the evening meeting with the leaders and activists, he insisted that I didn't work, that I was proud and had a bad attitude and should be struggled against, but fortunately the other activists and leaders didn't go along with his idea. Basically, most of the Banakshöl neighborhood officials were nonaggressive, and there were no struggle or humiliation processions in our work camp as there were in others. In particular, one of the rural neighborhood committees working on the canal conducted struggle sessions on the work site and were always parading those they called "class enemies" and "spirit monsters" in tall paper dunce caps even during the short morning and afternoon breaks, and there was no respite from the clashing of drums and cymbals and the shouting from their marches.

One of the most frightful humiliations carried out in that work camp involved Jampa Wangmo, one of a group of former Chubsang nuns in the Nyang-tren farmers team. Since she had been associated with Kyapjé Trijang Rinpoché, it was said that during the campaign to repudiate Rinpoché after the Democratic Reform in Lhasa, they made up a lot of false statements about him and forced her to admit to them and repeat them in propaganda shows, and she had been a principal political target in the Nyang-tren area ever since. It was said that Jampa Wangmo was forced to work so hard at that camp that she could bear it no longer and dropped a rock on her own foot; anyhow, the toes on one of her feet had been mangled. I don't know which demons the Nyang-tren leaders and activists were possessed by, but instead of showing her any pity they forced her to work just as hard as before with her foot in a bloody mess and continued subjecting her to struggle and humiliation and every other kind of misery. Those neighborhood officials from the rural areas around Lhasa protested that the city neighborhood committees were not pursuing "class struggle" hard enough and that "class enemies" and "spirit monsters" were being let off the hook. They worked their farmers sixteen hours a day and said that we should do the same, and announced a competition between the two groups, which made things worse for us too.

Those former government officials and "upper-strata figures" (*mTho rim mi sna*) who had not participated in the uprising and were "progressive" (*Yar thon pa*) members of the Chinese United Front had been subjected to house searches and public humiliations at the onset of the Cultural Revolution. After that they were put under the supervision of the neighborhood committees of the areas where they had previously lived or worked, who made them do Reform Through Labor, so some of the progressives from Lhasa were sent to work on the construction of that canal. These people had come from office jobs where the only labor was half a day of gardening or cleaning up once every two or three weeks and doing heavy physical work day after day was something outside their experience, so they were faced with a particularly unendurable ordeal when they were suddenly sent to that severe and arduous canal construction camp and put under the supervision and command of "the people."

When they first got there, some of them were self-confidently thinking that despite their background in the exploiting class, their basic political stance had been correct, and acted all enthusiastic about the revolution and socialist collective labor, joking with each other as they went to work and pretending to be brave revolutionaries unconcerned about having to do hard labor. Some of them, like Kashö Chögyel Nyima and Tétong Khen-chung Losang Namgyel, who were old men on the verge of death, sang revolutionary songs while they worked and ran races as they carried baskets of earth, and affected false camaraderie with the officials and activists. For impartial members of the public, however, it had long been recognized that despite coming from noble families that had prospered for generations on the goodwill of the Tibetan government, when the Tibetan people gave up everything to rise in revolt against the invasion, these people had sided with the Chinese and taken the path of betraying their country and selling out their people, and that it was they who were the real traitors. They were therefore mocked and spited in all kinds of ways, but at that time more than ever, people found their face-saving insincerity even more shameful, and their initial affectation of enthusiasm for labor only increased the punishment in store for them. Those from noble families who had participated in the uprising held a particular grudge against them, because in the past, before the outbreak of the Cultural Revolution, when they had occupied positions in Chinese government departments, they had refused to acknowledge not only former colleagues but even their own parents and relatives, in the cause of "taking a clear stance."

In fact, apart from a few "running dogs" and zealous stooges of the Chinese, most of those so-called "progressives" had qualified for their positions simply by having stayed in their homes during the uprising. They did not deserve to be trampled on now that they had fallen, and for my own part I helped them out at work by sharing whatever I knew from my own experience and did not act as though they owed us an apology, although in the course of conversation I did manage to embarrass Tétong Khen-chung Losang Namgyel by reminding him of the hectoring speech he made to us in the TMD prison. At first they had been confident that Reform Through Labor for them would just be short periods, after which they could go back to their offices, but as successive campaigns became more far-reaching, they had ended up doing full-time work under harsh conditions, going steeply up and down in water and mud, in freezing weather and miserable accommodations, facing hardship on all sides day after day. Within a few days of their arrival their façade had crumbled completely; not only were their backs raw and their feet blistered, they could barely walk even without loads, they had to suffer being unable to eat or sleep properly and in some cases not even being allowed to go to the toilet as they pleased. On top of that, they faced the prospect of being treated the same as other members of the exploiting class, if not worse, for as long as Mao lived, since during the conflict between the two rival Cultural Revolution factions they took turns leading formerly notable progressives in public humiliation processions every Sunday.

Around that time, Red Guards from each province and municipality in China started carrying the message of the Cultural Revolution around the country. Red Guards from several provinces in mainland China came to Tibet to spread the Cultural Revolution, and likewise a Red Guard group from the Lhasa middle school marched all the way to Beijing to publicize the Cultural Revolution, in emulation of the 15,000-mile Long March previously undertaken by the PLA. As these activities spread the campaign's influence beyond the center, the main aim, to "overthrow the power holders within the Party who had taken the capitalist road," began to affect the local chairmen and other top leaders of provinces, municipalities, and autonomous regions around the country. In Tibet, first of all the number three man in the CCP Tibet Work Committee, Wang Qimei, who led the first military advance on Chamdo [1950], was said to have committed the cardinal error of surrendering to the enemy and was taken for struggle at departmental staff meetings. Then, one after another, many other top leaders like the number two, Zhou Renshan, were branded "corrupt," "spies," "scabs," and so on, and began to face struggle.

But the cadres were not united in their opposition to those leaders. One faction upheld Wang Qimei as a faultless revolutionary and called for the overthrow of Zhou Renshan and others, while another defended Zhou and wanted to overthrow Wang, and out of these differences there emerged two factions. Those who claimed Wang Qimei as a true revolutionary and accused Zhou Renshan of being a spy for the Guomindang Mongolian and Tibetan Affairs Commission formed an organization called Nyamdrel, the "Great Revolutionary Alliance" (gSar brje'i mnyam sbrel chen po), and their opponents' organization was called Gyenlok, the "Red Rebel Faction" (dMar po'i gyen log shog kha). Since most of the ordinary cadres and most factory workers, students, and city people belonged to the Gyenlok at that point, their membership was much larger, but the differences between these two factions or viewpoints solely concerned their opposition to certain leaders and did not arise from any broader theoretical conflicts. A central government directive issued at that time called for carrying the Cultural Revolution forward through the full expression of views, holding thorough debates, and writing big-character newspapers, so the refutations and defenses of those leaders were argued over in all the government offices and on the main streets, the walls on either side of the so-called "People's Street" in Lhasa were plastered with hundreds of new poster-newspapers every day, and since the furtherance of the Cultural Revolution was taken to be a matter of primary concern for the promotion of national well-being, those employed in government offices and state factories and earning government salaries spent all their time participating in disputes, writing posters, and staging demonstrations, instead of attending to their immediate duties, and gave such political activities priority over the more ordinary demands of productivity. Thus our canal construction work camp became much more easygoing, the weather became warmer, and since the officials and people of "poor" class background were always off attending the meetings of the different factions, there was no one but "class enemies" left in camp and things were very relaxed.

Around that time, the Gyenlok faction set up a special Committee for the Overthrow of Local Emperors that was chiefly intended to bring down the most senior Chinese leader in Tibet, Zhang Guohua. They gave this organization great importance, and every Sunday there were meetings in the middle of the People's Street where they held demonstrations and burned effigies of Zhang Guohua and so forth. Next, the Gyenlok managed a nonviolent takeover of the main propaganda organs, the newspaper office and the broadcasting office, and within a few days they not only controlled the output of propaganda but also appeared to have gained the upper hand in most of the government departments in Lhasa. At this, the central government sent orders to the TMD headquarters to forcibly expel the Gyenlok from the newspaper and broadcasting offices, which was followed by a period of strict martial law in Lhasa when all propaganda output was under the control of the military. When the Gyenlok group came under attack, many people went over to Nyamdrel, and the discrepancy in size between the two groups' memberships came to an end. The Nyamdrel group had the support of the TMD, and it was said that its membership mostly consisted of the more educated and responsible members of each department.

From that time on, Nyamdrel was established as the more powerful of the two organizations. However, the factional divide had created problems for the continuity of ongoing construction and productive work, and like many other places of work both large and small, the labor camp building the canal from Nga-chen to Lhasa had to be shut down midway through, and the workers sent home. In view of the hardships of that camp, this was [a relief] comparable with getting out of prison, but since most construction enterprises in Lhasa had also been discontinued due to the current strife, and those that had not were contracted out to the municipalitywide Poor Laborers Collective that had been established in each of the city's sectional offices and in which "class enemies" were expressly prohibited from working, my attempts to find employment after returning from the canal camp were unsuccessful. Thus, together with two other "class enemies" under the Banak-shöl neighborhood committee who had been given "hats," Nyemdo Jampa Tendzin-la and the former Méru monastery disciplinarian Losang Jikmé-la, I ended up going to make adobe bricks in lower Sang-yip [near Drapchi]. The work was extremely hard, but earth and water were abundant, if there were many customers we could get a good income, and what was more, "class enemies" like us had the freedom to work unsupervised.

Before the outbreak of the Cultural Revolution it would have been hard for people like us to get to do such work, because we had to go wherever our neighborhood committees sent us, and even had that not been the case, everyone knew that brick makers had a good income and the neighborhood officials would never have countenanced the idea. At that time, when there was no other work for us to do, the committees did not stand in our way, but with so little construction work available and so many unemployed people turning to brick making, there was no way to choose a good place with plenty of earth and water in which to work. All the same, no matter how much harder we had to labor or how much less we were able to produce as a result of the site available, we had to do something, and started making bricks in pits left behind by others. A hard-working brick maker could make 1.5 *yuan* per day, provided that he could sell his product, but when the buyers who supplied the building sites came for adobe bricks, their main concern was to pick a location that allowed for easy transportation, and some of them would also ask questions about the class background of the vendor, so on that basis it was extremely difficult to sell our bricks. We worked in out-of-the-way earth pits already abandoned by others that did not allow for convenient transportation; then, if we were ever dishonest about our class background we would be guilty of "covering up class status," one of the most heinous political offenses there was, and if we were honest the buyers would be scared away. If for any reason our bricks were sold while bricks made by someone from a "poor" class background were left unsold, the buyer could be accused of having deliberately patronized "class enemies" and of having taken an insufficiently resolute stand on the class issue.

Anyway, after about two months of worrying that we would never be remunerated for the bricks we had worked so hard to make, we heard that a branch office of the Lhasa bridge construction workshop needed a huge quantity of bricks to build a boundary wall and paid the horse- and donkey-cart drivers around Lhasa to transport them to the building site. We immediately spoke to all the cart drivers we knew and managed to sell all but a few hundred of the bricks made by the three of us over the previous two months in one go, so our labors did not go entirely unrewarded.

Then I heard that a brick-making place near the village of Rinchen-tsel in the lower Nyang-tren valley was where they bought adobe bricks for military construction around Lhasa. Cultural Revolution factions were not allowed in the army and their building projects were going on as usual, so, thinking that we would have a better way of selling our bricks there, Losang Jikmé-la and I went to Rinchen-tsel to look for a place to work. But, like the saying, "Even the rich boy will be disappointed if he comes late," all the places where earth and water were available were so full of people working there wasn't even standing room. All the same, we did see a big army truck loading up with bricks, and as the brick makers didn't have many prepared, we figured they must be selling them regularly. There might be problems with the available resources of earth and water, but thinking that whatever bricks we made could be sold without a doubt, we dug a new pit in an out-of-the-way place and started the very next day.

During the few days before our bricks were dry, trucks came from all the army camps asking if we had any to sell, but we had just gotten started and had no dried bricks yet. It was the tenth Tibetan month [November/December] of 1967 when the two of us started working there, just when it gets really cold, and when building work usually comes to an end or at least is scaled back, and within a few days of our arrival even the army stopped buying so many bricks, and the few who came were picky about transport access and checked the quality of the bricks carefully. Besides being farther away than anyone else's, because of the type of soil, all our bricks froze and turned out not to pass any quality test, so except for sitting there hoping that eventually someone would come and buy them, there was not much else we could do. But we could not go without work either, for without the assurance of some kind of income there was no peace of mind, and the unemployed were continually called on to perform sundry duties for their local committee, totally unpaid. So regardless of whether there were buyers or not, we packed minimal provisions, a little *tsampa* and a Thermos of black tea, and went over there, partly to keep making bricks, but mostly to wait in the hope that buyers would show up.

On my initial release from prison I had vowed to take on the responsibility of being the main breadwinner in our household, but as it turned out, we "class enemies" were not rewarded in accordance with our efforts under the Communist system, and what I had been able to earn was barely enough to keep myself going; at times, when I could not earn even that much, I had to fall back on the support of my brothers and sisters. Mindful of the efforts I had to make when I went off to work, my three elder sisters did their best to look after me even when there was not enough to eat at home, and if they happened to come by any tastier or more nutritious food they kindly saved some for me, so I felt reticent when I went back home without being able to say that I had sold any bricks that day. As for my partner Losang Jikmé-la, he had been a genuine monk and was serving as a disciplinarian at Méru at the time of the troubles, when he was imprisoned and lost whatever possessions he had in his quarters. On his release from prison, he owned nothing more than his bedding roll and the clothes he was wearing, a single monk who depended on his daily wage for his daily meal. In this situation, if we had been able to sell even some of our bricks it would have made the difference between life and death, but in view of the ongoing developments, the prospect seemed quite hopeless.

At that time, the "full expression of views" and "thorough debate" between the rival Cultural Revolution factions turned violent, and knives, spears, slingshots, and so on were used, on the principle of "retaliation in self-defense." The Nyamdrel people took over the autonomous region [government compound], Gyenlok occupied the Yabshi Taktsér house, and the [activist] groups from each office, factory, and school joined one side or the other. In order to bolster their respective positions, they dismissed the official grain rationing and distribution system and spread some hearsay among the public that it was a legitimate target of the campaign. Then they said that everyone had to make up their minds and join one faction or the other, and whoever tried to stay in the middle would find nowhere to buy his monthly grain ration. Grain was as precious as life itself at the time, and most people believed it and unwillingly joined one faction or the other. "Class enemies" were expressly forbidden from joining either, however, and as it was they who were now supplying the monthly grain ration, we found ourselves liable to starvation.

My companion Losang Jikmé-la was a person of long experience with a highly philosophical approach to adversity. "Instead of worrying about things we can do nothing about," he used to say, "like having no way to work, not being able to sell our bricks, and the intensification of the conflict, if you reflect on the workings of karma, cause and effect, you will be free of worry. Alternatively, you could consider the whole course of this turmoil as the magical display of Tibet's protective deities. Either way, whatever we have to put up with meanwhile, if the Chinese don't bring this civil war to a swift end, everything could be torn apart, and that could be a chance for us Tibetans to slip off the leash." His positive outlook made me feel somewhat better, and since he could talk fluently about political and religious matters both past and present, we used to spend whole days sitting in the sun chatting, instead of working.

I remember when we ate our packed lunches of black tea and *tsampa*, my friend would always say that when we sold our bricks, we would go for a decent meal at the Kaochi restaurant (*Kaʾo ci za khang*). This was a government-run eating house in Lhasa where various meats, oil, and vegetables were available, and most of those doing heavy labor regarded it as a place where exhausted people could replenish their energy. At that time, the physical demands of the work and the nutrition we received were in inverse proportion, and our strength was depleted. By the end of the day we were constantly dislocating our calf muscles, and making bricks in the cold of winter with our hands in the mud, we could no longer feel them; they lost sensitivity and became so cracked and bloody they were unsightly. So we imagined that getting to eat in such a restaurant even once would bring us demonstrable physical relief, but far from going there, we didn't even have the price of our monthly grain ration and had to eke out the three winter months under those harsh conditions.

At that point, realizing that apart from karmic purification there was no other use in continuing to work there, we decided to stop for a while. Having no other choice, we piled up all our bricks and covered them to prevent damage during the summer rains, and left them in that empty spot. We took turns checking on them occasionally, and on my visits I saw that nearby villagers, cart drivers, and so on were stealing them little by little. Finally, during the summer of 1968 they were washed away by the rains, so the 30,000 or so bricks we had made with so much difficulty went to waste without earning us a single cent, which is something I feel bad about even now. After that, I stayed home, asking whoever I knew to look out for any kind of work that would bring in enough to cover my monthly grain ration and going to every corner of the city looking, but as I said earlier, most places had stopped work due to the political chaos, and in those that had not, employing "class enemies" was out of the question. Had it been summer, I could have gone cutting grass for our cow and had some recreation at the same time, like bathing and relaxing by the river, but since it was the first Tibetan month [February/March], before the cold season has ended, when the spring wind blows, I had to put up with staying home involuntarily, where I could be called on to do unpaid work for the neighborhood committee.

Having to stay home because I could not find work was like waiting to die. Like the proverb "Food is the meditation deity of the unemployed," I was overwhelmingly hungry, and with very little to think about and feeling unable to make sense of the tangled mess of problems that we faced, there was nothing to stop one going insane. But then I thought more positively that since firewood was no less indispensable than grain, and even more costly, I would go collecting firewood in the hills around Lhasa, hoping to overcome the need to buy any and perhaps even collect enough wood and dung to sell, and thus cover the cost of my grain ration. But the foliage on the surrounding hills was sparse, and after the Drapchi prisoners were forced to cut and uproot what little there was in 1959–60 it had been decimated, so there seemed to be nowhere to get fuel. That put an end to my hopes of finding wood to sell, but as our ancestors used to say, "Neither the mountains nor your parents will send you away empty-handed," and with determination I could always come back with some dung and twigs, enough to heat whatever meals I ate while staying home without work, and compared with the narrow focus of staying indoors, my mind was more at ease. However, since the only twigs and dung left to collect were on steep cliffs, when the spring wind got up, it was as much as I could do to come back alive, without thinking about finding fuel as well.

At that time, I went to gather wood on the mountains on either side of Bumpa-ri, on the south bank of the river. I would bring a little *tsampa* mixed with water in a leather bag to eat for lunch, and if the weather was fine, I would eat it while overlooking the Lhasa valley. From there, I could see from the mouth of the Tölung valley in the west all the way to Dromtö in the east, and got a clear picture of the extent of Chinese construction since their arrival more than ten years earlier. Formerly, it was the splendid Potala palace and the Tsukla-khang temple that stood at the center of the Lhasa Dharmachakra, and of Tibet as a whole, as the supreme field of merit for all living beings, blazing with the power of blessing, surrounded by the dwellings of the common people beautified with the characteristic features of their tradition, where agricultural and pastoral products were always plentiful, people were naturally easygoing and kind, of gentle disposition, constant, and ever concerned with benefiting their fellow man, so that anyone who lived in this city for any length of time would only want to stay that much longer, for it was a haven of peace. Now, the old city that had not been whitewashed for a long time but left to decay seemed dark and grimy; it had been encircled by ugly Chinese buildings with corrugated iron roofs and was filled with the ruins of destroyed monasteries and temples. Wherever you went, instead of seeing attractive people or hearing pleasant talk, there was only the din of killing, chopping, and beating, and the majority of humble citizens lived in hunger, fear, and fatigue. Whichever aspect one considered, it had become an unredeemed hell on earth, and seeing that brought on a profound sadness.

At that time, we heard nothing of world affairs, and particularly had no news at all of the activities of His Holiness, the focus of Tibetan aspirations, or the government in exile. Chinese propaganda stated as forcefully as it could that the so-called exile government had not gained the support of any country in the world and not only was Tibetan independence a daydream, but the internal religious and regional differences among the exiled Tibetans had intensified and were pulling the exile government apart. To enforce their control of the majority of Tibetans left behind under their rule, the Chinese had divided them into different categories and set them against each other everywhere, so that far from expressing solidarity among themselves, Tibetans were not even permitted or able to associate with each other. When no one trusted anyone else, people had to live cautiously, and we "class enemies" in particular were subject to constant political persecution and, without economic rights, had to suffer exploitation. At that time, no one would give paid work to a "class enemy," and they had to work in the name of Reform Through Labor for their local administrative committees or cooperatives, which is to say that neighborhood committee leaders and ordinary householders called activists could force them to work for unlimited periods with no payment whatsoever, and scold and brutalize them over any small thing, like coming late. Finally, we were not allowed to speak loudly or walk in long strides and had to act deferentially, like animals who understood human speech, and when I thought about living such a life, like the saying "It is preferable for sufferings to be shorter than for joys to be longer lived," it often occurred to me that I had no wish for it to be long.

When gathering firewood proved insufficient and I had to get some kind of work to cover basic expenses, having asked everyone I knew to look out for available work, I learned that our neighbor A-ché Sonam-la knew someone in the Tromsi-khang neighborhood committee who was in charge of a carpenters' cooperative and was looking for a worker who could saw timber. Fortunately, that was something in which I had some experience, so A-ché Sonam-la introduced me and he gave me the job. The daily wage of 2 *yuan* was very low compared with that of most saw workers, but finding work was so rare that such an opportunity was like life-saving medicine. By that time, the conflict between the two Cultural Revolution factions had become like a civil war with the use of military weapons, and at least four or five people were getting killed every day. Both factions used all means at their disposal to consolidate and increase their organizations, including political incitement and economic guile and trickery. For instance, they got hold of meat and butter from the northern pastures, which were very rare commodities, and sold them to their members at rates fixed by the state, and a lot more people joined the groups and their battles when they saw that such things were available, adding to the membership of both factions.

Most of the members of the carpentry cooperative where I worked belonged to Nyamdrel, and one group of youths there was none other than the Red Guards or armed fighters of one of the Nyamdrel constituent groups called Farmers and Pastoralists Command Headquarters (*Zhing 'brog si ling pu'u*), the head office of a citizens' organization. Thus the cooperative had to go to Nyamdrel meetings two or three times a week, and whenever fighting broke out here and there. Members were assured of their wages, but since I was a hired worker, I had to go without wages whenever the cooperative was closed. In such desperate times, though, it was enough just to have an income without worrying about how much it fluctuated. At that time, for example, the Gyenlok had a base in Lubu, on the west side of Lhasa, and the Farmers and Pastoralists Command affiliated with Nyamdrel were based in the Gyumé area north of the city, and they were continually fighting each other; for the ordinary people living in those areas, there was no question of going out to work when just trying to stay alive in the midst of it all was as much as they could do.

How had the factional combatants come by such weapons? Generally speaking, weapons and firearms are strictly controlled in Communist countries, and in Red China there was extremely tight control of guns, which could be kept only by those in charge of security in the key government offices and by no other officials, let alone regular citizens. When the battles of the Cultural Revolution factions first broke out, even the bullets for army weapons were tightly controlled, and soldiers were prohibited from joining any of the factions by strict order of the State Council and Central Military Commission, so the initial combatants had no access to firearms and had to use more traditional implements like swords and spears. But instead of dying down, the conflict intensified, and although the military personnel refrained from openly taking sides, individual commanders naturally sympathized with those with whom they might have lived or worked in civil society. For example, since Nyamdrel had defended the top commander of the TMD, Zhang Guohua, it became clear that the TMD was effectively supporting Nyamdrel, while it became well known that the number 11 army division stationed at Péding to the east of Lhasa was supporting Gyenlok. Anyway, there was no other source from which the later factional combatants could have gotten their weapons, and although it was said they had been seized in raids on isolated army bases, for the most part that was just a convenient story they agreed on to cover up the supply of military weapons to the two factions, and it seemed that anyone who wanted to participate in the fighting at that time could get hold of weapons without any trouble. Some mindless youths even carried their weapons around and used them to bully and intimidate ordinary innocent people by arresting, detaining, interrogating, and searching them.

Both sides also used to hurl devastating bombs made by packing gravel and explosives together in sacking, which fell like thunderbolts with no way of knowing from where or at what they had been thrown, so except by sitting inside motionless, like a hermit in meditation, there was no way to protect oneself from them. To launch them, they weighed down one end of a plank with sandbags and put another explosive under the free end, and the force of that explosion catapulted the bomb bag into the air. But they could only roughly estimate the direction and distance it would go, and instead of hitting any target, the bombs would often fall on the houses of innocent civilians, causing many deaths and injuries and destroying residential buildings. Similar losses were caused by the mines that both groups laid underground. One morning when I got to work, I noticed a circular trail of white powder under the sawing scaffold where I worked, and as I was wondering what it could be, people from the nearby houses called out to me that explosives had been buried there and I should not go near. Since the cooperative members were Nyamdrel fighters, their Gyenlok opponents had assumed that I was one of them, and came under cover of night to plant explosives. They were seen by the nearby residents, who marked the spot as a warning after they had gone. Had the good citizens not done so or failed to warn me, it would have meant nothing more than the loss of my life and the retaliatory killing of some poor "class enemy" performing compulsory labor for the Gyenlok side. Fortunately this did not come to pass, but until someone with the necessary experience to remove the explosives could be found, I had to go without work for a couple of days, which seems like much longer when you are starving.

CHAPTER 17

The June 7th Massacre

JUNE 7, 1968 was one of the most brutal and chilling massacres of all, and one the Tibetan people will never be able to forget. As the conflict between the two Cultural Revolution factions became increasingly bitter with even the military taking sides, the TMD forces gave all kinds of support to the Nyamdrel and in their hatred for the Gyenlok faction, they were ready to confront them on any convenient pretext. On the morning of May 27, 1968, the corpse of a Chinese member of Gyenlok and employee of the Tibet long-distance telegraph office, who had been secretly detained by Nyamdrel a few days earlier, was found dumped outside Nangtsé-shak [the former courthouse] on the north Parkor street. I actually saw that shrouded corpse on my way to work that morning. From what people said, the body not only bore the signs of torture but also had nails driven into the crown of the head and soles of the feet. Word spread that it had been brought by two members of Nyamdrel's Farmers and Pastoralists Command on the back of a bicycle and dumped there. The Gyenlok were furious and held an emergency meeting where they announced that debts of blood should be repaid in kind, the loudspeakers on the roofs of the Gyenlok bases started to play mourning music and rallying songs, and people were fearful as they heard the rumble of preparations for retaliation coming from those bases. Ordinary citizens tried to buy their provisions in the morning, since by noon the two factions started hurling insults and accusations through loudspeakers and shooting at each other, and no one went out in the streets. At that time, the Tsukla-khang temple was occupied by Gyenlok, and since the place where I worked was nearby, I could clearly hear their loudspeakers roughly cursing Nyamdrel over the murder.

Then, on June 7, I heard the sound of gunfire and the occasional grenade being thrown during the morning, paid no attention, and went on sawing timber, but by three o'clock in the afternoon when the noise of machine-gun fire and grenades exploding around the Tsukla-khang intensified, the foreman of the timber yard told us to pack up our tools at once and go home. Even before we had packed up, the gunfire became louder still. Walking through the Parkor on my way home, I did not see a single other person, and as I headed apprehensively toward the meat market, I clearly saw bullets fired from the rooftop of the old Surkhang house hitting the door panel of a shop. When I got to the meat market there was a crowd of people standing and looking back toward the Parkor. I tried to ask what had happened in the Tsukla-khang, but learned only that there had been a violent battle and did not get any of the details.

Sometime after I got home and the noise of gunfire around the temple could no longer be heard, the relatives of a neighbor of ours, a meat seller, whose cousin was among the Gyenlok faction occupying the Tsukla-khang together with the spouses of two of our other neighbors, gathered in an agitated state, and we wondered what had happened. Then, just as it was getting dark, the cousin arrived with his mother leading him by the hand. A little while later, when the sound of weeping came from our other neighbors, it was apparent that their spouses had been killed, wounded, arrested, or come to some other kind of harm.

It is inevitable that people get killed and wounded in conflict and that one side prevails over the other, but on that occasion, rather than wondering which side had won, people found the events too dreadful to contemplate, so a terrifying story went around that the PLA had slaughtered Tibetans in the Lhasa Tsukla-khang. A few years later it happened that Tubten Lodro, the cousin of our meat seller neighbor, and I were in the same group of workers breaking rocks, and he told us in detail the story of how he had survived the hail of bullets when Chinese soldiers launched an attack on the temple. This was his account:

> We had gathered in the Tsukla-khang at that point because it was occupied by the propaganda subcommittee of the Gyenlok number 4 command (*Si ling pu'u bzhi pa*), and the reason we insisted on occupying it, against the wishes of the Lhasa people, was that the Tsukla-khang is the tallest and the most central building in the city, and loudspeakers positioned on its roof could be heard in all quarters, which was an important advantage in the propaganda war. While the two

factions were locked in confrontation, one of the main objectives in the struggle was to destroy or capture [the opponent's] propaganda departments and equipment, and Gyenlok had mounted several attacks on Nyamdrel's Farmers and Pastoralists Command based in the former Gyu-mé monastery, which was one of their propaganda units. Nyamdrel made loud boasts that they would destroy the Gyenlok propaganda subcommittee in the Tsukla-khang, and in their announcements they repeatedly threatened us with annihilation and in particular made threats against some of our propaganda personnel.

Therefore, the main reason for gathering at the Tsukla-khang was to defend our propaganda subcommittee, and there were also many taking refuge there because they could not remain at home in the face of their threats. However, in terms of arms and other resources, we were no match for the Nyamdrel because they had the support of the TMD and most of their members held positions of political and economic power in government departments. Some of the Gyenlok were schoolteachers, but most were just ordinary workers, and except for a few teachers from people's schools (*dMangs btsugs slob grva*) and a few leaders of city neighborhood committees who belonged to the Gyenlok side, those gathered at the Tsukla-khang were just ordinary citizens. Only a few were armed and there were many women. Moreover, we did not announce or call either directly or indirectly for any other agenda than the defense of the Cultural Revolution, the defense of Red political power, national unity, and Chairman Mao's thought, and while we were aware of the possibility of an attack by Nyamdrel's Farmers and Pastoralists Command on our propaganda subcommittee, none of us would have believed that the PLA itself would come and crush us mercilessly. That is something I find incredible even now.

Anyway, on June 7, Nyamdrel began firing continuously into the Tsukla-khang from neighboring buildings like the old Samdrup Potrang, Do-ring, and Jutéling houses so we could not get out onto the roof and had to stay on the middle floor. A little after midday, when the noise of gunfire had subsided a little and we went out onto the roof, PLA soldiers came jumping across the rooftops of adjacent buildings, Méru-nying, Ga-tro-shak, and Jam-khang, and in an instant there were soldiers all over the roof of the Tsukla-khang. We were in no position to take on the army, and even if we had been able to do so, opposing the army would have been contrary to our revolutionary stand.

At the same time, we were confident that as long as we did not oppose them the army would not just attack us at will, so those of us in the temple stood together holding up the *Quotations of Chairman Mao* and chanted slogans from the *Quotations* in unison, like "Revolution is no crime, to rise up is justified" and "The people respect the army, the army looks after the people." It did us no good. One of the army commanders fired his pistol in the air, whereupon the soldiers fired machine guns and whatever weapons they had straight into the group standing there. Some of us were hit and fell to the ground, and others fled to either side.

I fell to the ground and pretended to be dead, and after the soldiers had kicked us a few times, they went after those who had scattered and fled, throwing grenades or shooting at anything at all in the darkness of the temple, and for a while the air was filled with the noise of their shouts, explosions, and gunfire. Lying there on the ground, I felt something wet and cold on my cheek, and when I touched it to see what it was, my hand became red with blood. I assumed I must have sustained a serious wound, although I felt no pain, which I thought was because of being so terrified, but in fact the blood on my face had dripped from the dead bodies on either side and I had not been injured at all. The soldiers went through all three floors of the temple, arresting the Gyenlok supporters and beating them as they led them away, even the wounded. Those who were wounded screamed from the pain, and some of them called out pleading to be killed rather than endure it. Once the soldiers had carried out their suppression and gathered all their [detainees] together, the Nyamdrel supporters came and beat them again, and some who had not been seriously wounded so far were crippled by the beatings they were given at that time. Most horrific of all was a girl who had been shot in the abdomen and was sitting with her hand covering the wound to prevent the intestines spilling out, until the Nyamdrel kicked and stamped on her belly and her intestines poured out into her lap. I too was kicked and struck with rifle butts many times, and seeing the behavior of the soldiers and the Nyamdrel, I never imagined that I would survive. Later on when things had calmed down, the family members, spouses, children, and parents, of those occupying the temple gathered outside the door, and after the soldiers gave permission, a group of us went back to our homes accompanied by our relatives. My mother came and took me home.

He told us stories of that episode more than once, in a voice choked with emotion. In any case, the soldiers slaughtered a total of fifteen Tibetans on that occasion, both men and women, and many more were wounded so severely that they never recovered. The bodies of those killed were taken to the Lhasa Mentsi-khang [hospital] together with the wounded, and the corpses were left there until the central government's Cultural Revolution Subcommittee reached a decision concerning the incident. Since it was summer, the corpses rotted and residents in the vicinity of the Mentsi-khang were exposed to an unbearable stench.

Differing accounts of that military crackdown circulated in society at large. According to one that enjoyed wide currency, the method used by Nyamdrel and the TMD to defeat and eliminate the Gyenlok faction was to produce allegations that could justify a crackdown on the grounds that they were endangering the security of the southwest border of the Motherland, which the army was responsible for safeguarding. Thus, the earlier incident of the murdered corpse dumped in the Parkor was intended to provoke the Gyenlok, but when no extreme reaction was forthcoming, the second step was to take advantage of popular resentment against the Gyenlok propaganda subcommittee occupying the Tsukla-khang to do something even more daring: massacre the occupants on the pretext of expelling them by public demand. They were confident that this would provoke an extreme reaction from the Gyenlok, which would allow the [military] to crack down on them once and for all.

While there may have been differing standpoints and objectives among the actual members of Nyamdrel and Gyenlok, since in general both factions stood for the defense of Red political power and Mao Zedong's thought, the differences between them excited no sympathy among the Tibetan public. Nonetheless, to mercilessly slaughter a group of ordinary Tibetans without any warning in the course of securing a strategic objective was to treat Tibetan lives as less valuable even than the lives of beasts, something to be disposed of at will, and that is why Tibetans referred to this incident as the "June 7th massacre." For some time afterward, the Tsukla-khang was occupied by Chinese soldiers who used several of the chapels as toilets and pigsties, and the main temple hall (*dKyil 'khor mthil*) was turned into a slaughterhouse where yaks, sheep, goats, pigs, and chickens were butchered.

Then people focused all their attention on the decision the central government's Cultural Revolution Subcommittee would reach concerning the incident. If they were to exonerate the army's massacre of Tibetans and declare Gyenlok a counterrevolutionary organization, Gyenlok was not going to lay down its weapons and bow down in homage. The character of the organization could change if it were to be excluded [i.e., not designated counterrevolutionary], and then there would be an excuse for those alienated from the Chinese government to stage an uprising, and some hoped that this would happen. But the subcommittee ruled that a couple of the army commanders involved in the incident had made errors, and a few of the leaders concerned were transferred to positions elsewhere. Both factions were recognized as revolutionary organizations, those who had lost their lives in the Tsukla-khang were lauded as "fallen revolutionary heroes," and their rotten corpses were put in a tomb in one corner of the Chinese mausoleum (*Dur khang*) west of Lhasa with a tombstone inscribed, MAY FALLEN HEROES NEVER DIE. Their relatives were awarded compensation of 2,000 or 1,500 *yuan* according to the number of children in the family, and the wounded were given medical expenses and nominal compensation, so the anticipated confrontation between two factions divided over substantial issues never came to pass.

As there was no subsidence of the ongoing conflict, the Gyenlok, having learned their lesson, preempted a further offensive against them by concentrating their fighters and weapons at bases such as Yabshi Taktsér, old Yu-tok, Mentsi-khang, and Tengyé-ling. In this deteriorating situation, most of the people at the carpentry cooperative where I worked went to fight with Nyamdrel, while the remainder, the elderly and the few individuals capable of thinking for themselves, could not face the prospect of staying where they were and moved the cooperative's work to a printing workshop in the TMD headquarters west of the city, so I went along with them. Inside the army base we were at no particular risk from the conflict, but there were repeated outbreaks of heavy fighting around Lhasa, and even the main commercial street, known as the People's Street, where we had to go every fortnight or so to collect our *tsampa* ration, was impassable. Once when we got there, we found some construction workers and a few others, unable to proceed and wondering what to do next. Finally, with all the builders carrying their gear and wearing battered straw hats, aprons, and gloves, and together with the children, women, and old people, we walked straight onto the main street. At the lower end, to either side of the main entrance to the TAR government compound, were the Nyamdrel fighters carrying various firearms and hand grenades, occupying sandbagged barricades, while at the upper end of the street, on either side of the Mentsi-khang, were similarly armed Gyenlok fighters. A few armed men approached us menacingly and angrily demanded, "Which side do you belong to?"

"We are class enemies," we replied with an air of desperation, "with no opinion either way."

Some of them even showed concern, saying, "How do you dare enter such a dangerous place? You'd be better off keeping a low profile."

For several weeks during the Chinese military anniversary that year, there was no way to go into Lhasa even to collect rations, and we had to wait to be given the army's leftovers. All the same, apart from the difficulty of those supply trips into Lhasa, being able to work in the safety of the army compound during those months of fierce fighting and have an income, I was doing better than I had been for several years.

Sometime after, there was some respite in the factional fighting in China, which had been the principal factor behind the fighting in Tibet, and the central government Cultural Revolution Subcommittee summoned representatives of both factions in Tibet to address them on the need to bring the conflict to an end. At the same time, the chairman of the central government's Tibet Work Committee, Zhang Guohua, whose status had been the main issue over which the factions had divided in the first place, was posted elsewhere in China, and the past errors committed by a few leaders such as Wang Qimei were acknowledged. Military leaders like the TMD political commissar Ren Rong and general Zeng Yongya were put in charge of the Tibet Work Committee and the autonomous region [government], and the fighting gradually died down.

The Cultural Revolution campaign itself was still not over, however, and those workplaces that had closed down remained closed, so employment was as hard to come by as before. Moreover, since overall productivity, transportation, and so on had been severely affected during the troubles, apart from stockpiled commodities, everyday necessities were extremely scarce, and on the occasions when the shops had sugar, molasses, cigarettes, soap, candles, and so on for sale, the shop staff would clandestinely inform their relatives and friends that such and such an item would be available on a certain day, and they in turn would inform their own friends and associates, so word traveled from one person to the next and when the day came there would be a big crowd waiting at the door. The quantities of the commodity on sale were never sufficient for all the people who came to buy, so inevitably they would jostle with each other, the glass display cabinets and tables in the shop would get broken, many people would lose their purses, and children and the infirm would be injured in the crush. After that, the shops had to start dispensing such commodities through a small window opening onto the street, so as not to have a ruckus inside.

The item in greatest demand was lighting. In the old days, electricity was not widespread in Tibet, and people used kerosene lanterns, candles, or oil lamps, according to what was available. These things had to be brought from India by traders, but they could be readily bought in the shops at any time of day. After the imposition of Communist rule, once the Nga-chen power station was completed, houses in the city were wired to receive electricity, but it was only for show. While the Chinese compounds always had electricity, ordinary dwellings in the city got a very weak supply for no more than ten days a month, and often none at all during winter and spring when the water level was lower. Candles and kerosene were nowhere to be found, and if lamp fuel was especially needed it would have to come out of the monthly ration of half a pound of edible oil. We had no choice but to use the thick lubricating oil meant for vehicle maintenance and engine oil dregs and suchlike, although the smoke not only covered everything in the house in black soot but also went in our lungs, so the phlegm we coughed up turned completely black. It was rare to find Tibetans in good physical health at that time, and this was one of the reasons. The construction of the Nga-chen power station was one of the main examples used by the Chinese in their claim to be developing Tibet and improving living standards, but if a detailed account of how Tibetans suffered and lost their lives in the construction of that power station were to be given, who could fail to be shocked? In reality, all the power stations, bridges, highways, and hospitals in their list of development achievements benefited only the Chinese themselves, and the fact that Tibetans benefited not at all can clearly be seen from the difficulty we had in being able to light a lamp after dark.

The next stage in the conflict between the two factions was a competition to expose "counterrevolutionary organizations" and "undercover spies," and those among us "class enemies" with bad political records, and especially those who were formerly in contact with foreigners, were rounded up at once by Nyamdrel and detained in a so-called "study group" in the Pabongka Labrang. Gyenlok then immediately detained a similar group of "class enemies" in Tengyé-ling, and both sides tried to uncover underground groups and spies by investigation, interrogation, and intimidation. Not only that, but during the two or three months they were there the detainees had to have food brought to them by family members, so their families also had to bear the hardships and expenses of their mistreatment.

Since the start of the Cultural Revolution, the category of people to be prosecuted under the slogan "Strengthen the proletarian dictatorship" had been widened, legal criteria [for prosecution] had been suspended altogether, and the implementation of any leftist agenda whatsoever went ahead, so courts and prisons everywhere were filled to capacity and the investigation, detention, incarceration, and punishment of alleged offenders was permitted. Since any criticism was "opposing [Party] policy" and would result in the critic being "hatted" for "lacking commitment," no one could say anything. The neighborhood committee leaders who treated the "class enemies" in their charge with utmost cruelty had the confidence of the higher authorities, and the more zealous ones made their "class enemies" stay in the evening political education meetings until midnight on the pretext of "class struggle" and "proletarian dictatorship" and made them do unpaid work during the day, for which they had to bring their own provisions.

To give a general list of the unpaid jobs they were given: first, in early spring when everyone did willow planting, the "class enemies" had to spend many days cutting the willow shoots in advance, then of course they had to join the ordinary people in planting them, but they also had to make up for all the planted shoots that failed to take root, so just the spring willow planting gave them about a month's work. Then there was "helping out" with the spring sowing, starting with clearing out the irrigation channels and spreading manure on the fields, then weeding, watering, and so on, which added up to about three weeks. During the summer rains they had to fix the leaking roofs in the committee building and clear the drains in the streets, and in the autumn they had to "help out" with the harvest, from cutting the crop right up to storing it in the granary once the threshing was over, which added up to two or three months. All year round, cleaning and sweeping up inside and outside the committee building and washing the streets was a task imposed on "class enemies," and for a time, so was emptying the toilets in each committee area. Similarly, it was their duty to make black borders and canopies on the house walls where Mao's slogans were painted, repaint them after the summer rains, and maintain them. This was a much more onerous task for "class enemies" in the countryside than for those in the city: there are still slogans like MAY CHAIRMAN MAO LIVE FOR 10,000 YEARS and Mao's quotations written in Chinese characters on the mountainside using white stones that can be seen from several miles away, which was something small groups of "class enemies" were forced to do. Similarly, the walls erected on either side of the highway, half a mile apart in some places, inscribed with Mao's quotations and finished with black borders and rain canopies, were certainly the compulsory work of "class enemies" in that area. Otherwise, they were continually obliged to perform various occasional unpaid tasks in the name of "helping out the community," such as repairing the leaders' own houses or cutting firewood, and this practice of obligatory unpaid work went on more or less until the time of Mao's death.

Since those were the prevailing conditions at the time, some brazen characters who called themselves "the laboring masses" would tell any "class enemies" in slightly better accommodations than themselves that they had to swap. According to their own whim, using the threat of force, and regardless of whether the occupants agreed or not, they would set a deadline to vacate their houses. They would move their own things into the houses of individual "class enemies" and simply take possession of items like storage trunks that the occupants could not move out immediately, just like bandits. In our Banak-shöl neighborhood committee there were many cases of "class enemies" being forced to swap houses, something made possible by the policies of the Chinese Communists.

CHAPTER 18

A Disastrous New Year

THE FIRST DAY of the Tibetan earth monkey year, 1968, was a new year's day to go down in history. Every society has its own way of celebrating the beginning of a new year, and in Tibet both the government and the common people used to stage very elaborate ceremonies with strong historical associations. Although the official celebrations had come to an end with the events of 1959, popular celebrations and some religious observances continued. With the start of the Cultural Revolution in 1966 and the forceful prohibition of the Four Olds, however, not only was there no question of celebrating the new year, but "class enemies" who stayed home at that time could very well be accused of wanting to celebrate, so we definitely had to be at our places of work and act as normal. Still, it is difficult to do away with people's ideas all at once, like cutting them off with a knife, and most Tibetans celebrated the new year at home before dawn, and discreetly greeted their trusted acquaintances with a "Tashi délek" [new year greeting] when they got to work.

But in 1968, Tibetan new year fell on the same day as the Chinese new year spring festival, and as it was the government's practice to grant everyone several days off for that occasion, they could not prevent Tibetans from having their own new year holiday. So that year Tibetans started saving up the things they needed to celebrate the new year months in advance, and we also put aside whatever foodstuffs we could. At that time, my younger brother Jam-pun was one of the teachers at the People's School in east Lhasa who, unlike most people, bought their monthly rations from the officials' ration store, and he got some very good quality *tsampa* in the month before the new year that we mixed with butter and discreetly stored in the cupboard together with other foods, ready for the holiday. The first day of Tibetan new year dawned with beautiful weather and bright sunshine, the queen of the heavens honored Tibetans with a special new year greeting, and people were enjoying the boon of the Chinese and Tibetan calendars coinciding on that lovely sunny morning. We had no idea of the disaster about to strike.

After our family celebration on new year's day, I was in the courtyard watching our neighbors' children play a game of dice when A-ché Tendzin and Lulu, Gyenlok leaders in the Banak-shöl neighborhood committee, and a few young Red Guards came into our apartment. It was normal for the neighborhood committee security personnel to patrol and check on "class enemies" or other suspicious people on special days, and I assumed that was what they were doing, but when I did not see them come out again, I wondered what was going on and went back inside to find them searching our cupboard. It was as if the fine weather had suddenly turned into a raging storm. That apartment had an inner and an outer room separated by a door curtain, and in the inner room we had lit a butter lamp as a new year offering. In one cupboard in the outer living room was the first-poured cup of tea (*Ja phud*) and a porcelain bowl containing new year sweet rice (*'Bras bsil*), and in the other a bowl of dry rice, a plate full of candies and other things, and a plate full of buttered *tsampa* dough. Lulu the Gyenlok leader looked through both cupboards and took out the plate of dough, shouting, "Who put this 'spirit monster' stuff here?"

While they were searching the cupboards, my elder sister Losang Chönyi-la went behind the curtain into the inner room to extinguish the butter lamp, and the smoke from the doused wick floated out. At this I got scared, thinking that there was no other explanation for it than as a religious act, but it seemed that the younger ones had grown up "under the red flag" and the older two had no knowledge of what religious offerings were, so none of them noticed the smell of the extinguished lamp. Meanwhile, Lulu kept demanding in a snarling voice to know who had prepared the *tsampa* dough. When I told him I had done it, he said, "You bring this and come with us," and making me hold the plate of dough, with one of their people on either side, they led me off to the neighborhood committee building, where Gyenlok had their base. There was another "class enemy" with a new year offering plate of dry rice, a plate full of sweets, and so on, as well as a scorpion-shaped piece of fried dough, which is traditionally made as an offering to the *naga*s when frying new year pastries (*Kha zas*). They put my plate of dough together with the other confiscated items, and told me, "You should think about what this means. This matter will be decided later; meanwhile, stay home and behave properly," then sent me back.

I returned to find my brothers and sisters in a state of anxiety. They told me that after I was taken away, our "class enemy" neighbor A-ché Sonam-la and Ama A-tra, a member of our group who had a "hat," had been led away by Nyamdrel leaders accompanied by Red Guards and had not returned. Although I had been allowed to come home, having been told to think and await judgment, I could not relax for the rest of the new year holiday. I had already agreed to visit one of my friends, who lived by the entrance to the Banak-shöl neighborhood committee, on the first day of the new year, and as I passed there I saw Nyamdrel Red Guards leading in many "class enemies" holding new year offerings of buttered *tsampa* (*phye mar*) and barley beer (*chang phud*), butter lamps, plates of pastries, and so on. I assumed that they would be sent home again as I had been, but a little while later the Banak-shöl Nyamdrel leaders and Red Guards led them around the Parkor in a procession with drums and cymbals, shouting, "'Spirit monsters' must be eliminated." This scared me and, thinking that my case could be decided at any time, and that if they called me and I was not home they could take my elder sisters instead, I hurried home to wait for Gyenlok's summons. But I did not have to join any humiliation procession that day, nor did anyone call on me during the four days of the Chinese new year holiday.

In fact, it seems that the Nyamdrel headquarters called Farmers and Pastoralists Command under the Lhasa municipality was responsible for carrying out that vicious plan on new year's day, and as soon as some of the Gyenlok units got wind of it they set out to do the same, but since they came late, the Banak-shöl Gyenlok caught only three of us—the former secretary of the Tibet military command, Pema Norbu; the treasurer of Tsawa Ösér Labrang, Dondrup Tséring; and myself—and were unable to stage a great parade as the Nyamdrel had done. Not only that, but I heard that since the central Gyenlok command had not approved of the plan to conduct house searches that day, the neighborhood-level Gyenlok units involved were accused of imitating Nyamdrel and this led to some internal criticism.

But the Nyamdrel led people from each neighborhood committee around the Parkor in humiliation processions that day, subjecting them to various kinds of mistreatment, and those whose offenses they considered more serious were not sent home again but kept in detention. They took our neighbor A-ché Sonam because they found her with a porcelain cup full of *chang*. As for Ama A-tra, she wore a "hat" and was in one of the "four categories" [of undesirable people], and in addition all her neighbors were neighborhood committee leaders and activists, so she had to be particularly careful and always kept up the necessary appearances. It seems that they could find no particular reason for making her join the humiliation procession that day, but the Nyamdrel brought a photo of Liu Shaoqi with them that they claimed to have found in her house, and led her away together with her son-in-law, an employee of the long-distance telegraph office.

The people taken in procession that day were made to wear various kinds of clothing and to carry their traditional new year *tsampa* boxes (*Gro so phye mar*), butter lamps, *chang* offerings, pastries, etc., and paraded up and down the Parkor for almost the whole day. Some mindless people in the crowd of onlookers who did not understand the significance of what was happening showered them with dirt and spat or flicked mucus at them, jeered, and subjected them to absolute misery. Among those in the parade were two eminent lamas under the Tromsi-khang neighborhood committee, the former abbot of Séra-jé Lhundrup Tapké, and another senior Séra-jé scholar (*mTshan zhabs*), Ngo-drup Tsoknyi, who had been marking the occasion with some ceremony, apparently quite oblivious to the danger of something like this happening. Red Guards had burst into their quarters that morning and found them conducting religious ceremonies dressed in full monastic robes, and they were led in procession in their robes and carrying a wooden tray with *vajra* scepters and ritual bells and other religious paraphernalia. It had been many years since anyone wearing the full uniform of the noble *sangha* had been seen in our country, and many of those who witnessed the procession that day spoke of experiencing a sensation of joy at seeing those robes, mixed with the unbearable sorrow of the circumstances in which they had come to light.

Then, on the fourth day of the Tibetan month, I got the summons from Gyenlok to come to their meeting hall at seven o'clock that evening. When I arrived, there was a sign pasted above the door reading STRUGGLE MEETING AGAINST "SPIRIT MONSTERS," which meant that I was going to be subjected to struggle. Until then, I had never been singled out as the target for a group struggle session, and in the current campaign there had been cases of a few morons among the public crippling people with their gratuitous beatings. Of course I was concerned about getting severely injured myself, but also about the kind of difficulties my family members could face, and as I waited there for the crowd to assemble my mind raced with such fears and I started shaking in terror. As I waited, an old tailor who used to live in our compound came and handed me a large cup full of strong *chang*, which I knocked back in one gulp, and that gave me courage and gradually stopped the shaking. *Whatever happens*, I thought, *there is no need for regret*, and my

Public humiliation of Dr. Lhundrup Peljor, former headmaster of the Nyarong-shak school, and his son and daughter. *Used with kind permission from Woeser.*

fear subsided. Once the Gyenlok participants had assembled, I was called into the hall. As soon as I entered, a loud voice led the crowd in chanting, "Never abandon class struggle" and "Clean up the 'spirit monsters,'" as I was led in front of the stage and made to stand with my head lowered. When the meeting began, I was told, "You, Tubten Khétsun, a reactionary oppressor who participated in the uprising, have indulged in superstition, without regret for your former crimes. You should make a full confession in front of the masses of your intention in making religious offerings!"

"It was just buttered dough, not an offering," I said. "I have always liked eating it, and since before new year my younger brother received a ration of good quality *tsampa* and I had an extra half-pound of butter for the spring festival, we had the ingredients to make some dough, so that's what I did.

Whether in terms of its shape, color, or anything else, that dough was nothing like a religious offering."

One of the Gyenlok leaders called Jampa Lung-rik had once served as
chairman (*Kru'u ren*) of Séra monastery and before the uprising had studied debate at Séra, so he was an assiduous interrogator who knew not to
make his maliciousness evident. He now challenged me: "Tubten Khétsun,
you should speak honestly. It was a form of offering. The manner of making
offerings can differ according to the situation. Since you class enemies are
very deceitful, you disguised it as food, but in reality you were determined
to celebrate Tibetan new year!"

As soon as he had spoken, the other leaders and activists took up the
cry, "It was an offering!" "He's holding on to the empty hope of bringing back
the old society!" "Making prayers to the Dalai and Panchen, do you want to
restore their power or not? Tell us clearly!" and they bullied me a lot, pulling
me up by the back of the neck, pushing me down again, and so on.

"Why would I hope for the restoration of the old society?" I said.
"Since our country did not produce so much as a needle, there is no reason
to have any attachment to such a backward social system. I have no 'empty
hope' whatsoever."

Then Jampa Lung-rik said, "Instead of just saying that the old society
was backward, why do you not enumerate its faults? If you say the old society was merely backward, you avoid listing the crimes of the three big oppressors to which you belong. The whole world knows that the old society
in Tibet was extremely dark, extremely barbaric, and extremely cruel as
well as extremely backward," and then they all shouted at me at once, about
things that had nothing to do with the original accusation, and told me
threateningly that this was not the way to make a confession. Even worse,
having to stand bent over for a long time without putting my hands on my
knees made my waist hurt and my face swell up, and as I had a cold at the
time, I was constantly dribbling, which worsened the suffering. But I no
longer felt the anxiety I had before the session began.

I had to stand like that for a long time while they brought up many
unrelated things while refusing to let me give any answer in my defense,
until some more kind-hearted youths in the crowd who could stand it no
longer stood up and, acting as if they were very tough, lifted my head by the
scruff of my neck and said, "Now you must confess." Then, after a few more
slogans were shouted, the inquisition abated, and when they lifted my head,
ostensibly to "show my face to the masses," I got some relief from standing
bent over for so long. The youths kept chanting slogans and making a lot

of noise, which passed the time, and finally around eleven o'clock at night, I was told to come back with a clear statement in writing and the struggle meeting came to an end.

I certainly met with misfortune on that occasion, but I was lucky not to have been taken by Nyamdrel: since the plan to search houses on new year's day was not prepared in advance and they only caught three of us, they could not stage a humiliation parade as Nyamdrel did, and since they were criticized by the Gyenlok headquarters for imitating Nyamdrel and staged the struggle meeting in order not to lose face, I was not badly beaten at all, and the case was resolved that same night. Nonetheless, I would have to account for the incident during subsequent political campaigns, and it was put on my "reform record" (*bsGyur bkod bya rim gyi yig cha*).

CHAPTER 19

Old *Tsampa* in Old Méru

FOR SOME TIME the assembly hall of the Méru Nyingba monastery in Lhasa was full to the brim with stale *tsampa*, which [the authorities wanted] to use up by selling it as the citizens' monthly grain ration. Although very old, that *tsampa* was basically of a good quality that was supplied to the officials' grain shop or *tsampa* store for officials' rations, but it was said that when the *tsampa* was delivered from the different mills they did not bother to distinguish between the old and the new, and once they had accumulated a stock that was too stale for the officials to eat, it was sold to the ordinary citizens. There was another story that for a time, Chinese military rations included a special convenience food that was *tsampa*-based but had many nutritious things like butter, mushrooms, nuts, and so on added to it, but since it contained butter it could not be kept for long periods, and later they stopped making it. When the stocks of that special *tsampa* in the army food processing factory went stale and they could find no other use for it, they sold it in the citizens' edible oil supply store.

In my opinion, the stale *tsampa* came from the military ration stuff, because the officials' edible oil supply store didn't have enough outlets to have accumulated such a huge quantity. Either way, it had a very damaging effect on the health of Lhasa citizens. When they went to buy their monthly ration, people used to pray that whatever quality of *tsampa* they were given, it would not be stale. That *tsampa* was so old that it would just stick to a cotton bag, and getting it out was like digging earth with a pickaxe. To say that the stink of stale *tsampa* filled the whole city would be a slight exaggeration, but it did pervade the area for some distance around Old Méru. That stale *tsampa* was supplied to each of the three administrative divisions in Lhasa city in turn for monthly distribution, so everyone ended up buying it [at least] four times a year, and [even at that rate] it took about two years to get through it all.

Since grain oil was tightly controlled at the time, if you wanted to buy slightly superior grain direct from the farmer, it cost over 20 *yuan* per [*Khal* = 28 lbs.] at least, and it had to be done with the greatest secrecy. If the authorities came to know about it, they would condemn it as "black mar-keteering" and "economic vandalism" and both buyer and seller would be prosecuted. Thus there was nothing to do but close your eyes and swal-low the stale *tsampa*. So mealtimes became depressing occasions, but how much more so for those with small children, because in Tibet *tsampa* paste is the only food for suckling infants, and their refusal to take to stale *tsampa* paste was an unbearable hardship for parents. Likewise, having to eat stale *tsampa* for long periods gave many people stomach pain, and many of them went to the hospitals for treatment. Indeed, if one were to list the various types of illness at that time, stale *tsampa* would definitely account for the highest percentage, but there was no way for anyone to say that it was a cause of illness.

There were four hospitals under the so-called TAR Health Bureau ('*Phrod bsten las khungs*), and patients were allocated strictly according to the administrative division of the city they belonged to, regardless of preference or suitability [of the facilities], which deprived people of any entitlement or say in their medical treatment. In any other country in the world, it is considered fundamental that the patient himself chooses which hospital and doctor to go to. In Lhasa at that time there were facilities for Western medicine and traditional Chinese medicine, as well as Tibetan medicine in the Mentsi-khang, and normally one would opt for Western medicine in the case of critical illness, injuries such as broken arms and legs, and operations, while traditional Chinese or Tibetan medicine would be preferred in the case of noncritical and chronic illnesses. But under the regulations there was no choice, which was just like treating the foot when it is the hand that hurts.

Even worse, under the hospital allocation regulations, citizens were is-sued a medical identity card, which was red for ordinary people and black for "class enemies." The significance of this was that ordinary people did not have to pay for treatment or medicine while "class enemies" did, and the different-colored cards were supposed to make hospital administration simpler, but in reality, in a situation where it was not actually stated that "class enemies" had no entitlement to medical care whatsoever, the black pass served as an indication to the doctor that the bearer's life was of no value. "Class enemies" were commonly told by the Chinese authorities, "One less of you people is one less mouth for the state to feed." It was also said that one reason "class enemies" were allowed into the hospitals at all was that black pass holders who needed operations could be used for the practical training of students, and the well-being of those patients was of no more concern to them than an animal or a corpse. That is what was said in society at large, and there is no way of knowing that it was not so. Most doctors in all the hospitals at the time were Chinese; generally speaking, the Chinese regarded Tibetans as very inferior; and on top of that, they saw "class enemies" as something abominable.

Anyway, in my own case, after the medical pass system was introduced, I never planned on going to any official Chinese hospital, and through the mercy of the Three Jewels I never had any medical problem serious enough to require treatment in a hospital.

CHAPTER 20

The Sino-Soviet War Brings Increased Oppression

THERE HAD BEEN ideological differences between China and Russia for some time when, in 1969, confrontation flared up on the border and, at Chenpahao island in China's northeast, heavy fighting broke out. Russia had one of the most powerful armies in the world and in terms of strategy, training, or any other aspect it outmatched China, so Tibetans had high expectations of the outcome. Of course no one likes war, and especially for us Buddhists the hope of gaining anything from armed conflict is totally unwarranted, but the Chinese were perpetrating unbearable cruelty on the Tibetans after successfully occupying our country unopposed by the international community, and with no other means to prevent our being wiped out altogether, we were desperate.

It goes without saying that the outbreak of war meant greater oppression for ordinary people on both sides: Mao Zedong's slogan for the crisis was, "Dig deep tunnels, stockpile grain all over, the enemy shall not pass!" and after that grain became even more tightly controlled than before, and people everywhere had to dig underground tunnels and shelters for war preparedness. In most places in China the soil has a high clay content, allowing for tunnels to be easily dug without the risk of collapse or, unless they are extremely deep, water seepage, and because of that the Communist guerrillas were able to dig tunnels during the war of resistance and inflict defeats on the Japanese. But Tibetan soil is different, and at least in the Lhasa area it is mixed with gravel and sand, a composition that does not allow for the digging of tunnels like those in China; if you dig deeper than one or two yards your hole fills with water, which makes things even more difficult. The Chinese government, however, paid no heed whatsoever to soil composition, and under the rubric of "Four Unities," "unity of planning, unity of command, unity of action, and unity of pace," they made people in Tibet dig tunnels like everyone else, causing great misery.

In the case of Lhasa city, the hardship imposed on the people differed greatly according to the disposition of the neighborhood committee leaders. For example, our Banak-shöl leaders regarded the digging of tunnels as a matter of appearances only, and were satisfied with having the "class enemies" dig under vegetable gardens and patches of vacant land in the neighborhood, without causing much harm to people's dwellings or livelihood. In the Shöl neighborhood committee, by contrast, they imposed great hardship by having both ordinary people and "class enemies" work many days without payment digging tunnels at the foot of the Potala palace, and used large amounts of explosives in doing so, and because of those explosions cracks opened in the palace walls, which have had to be repaired recently. In the Kamdong Tro-khang neighborhood committee in east Lhasa, they had the "class enemies" dig a kind of burrow running underneath the houses, with a central entrance passage, for which many people had to move out of their houses, and most houses lying along the route of the tunnel were damaged. The "class enemies" were conscripted to work on that continuously for several months, which prevented them from earning their living, and constantly working in muddy water seriously affected their health.

Once the tunnels were dug, they held air-raid drills, signaled without warning by sirens in the TMD compound, when everyone had to take shelter. We had to behave strictly according to the organization and code of discipline enforced by our neighborhood committee or work cooperative, and were told that any infringement of this code of discipline would be treated as a military matter. Those drills were sprung on us in the middle of the night on several occasions. Since there were strict orders for everyone to participate, even the bedridden and women in advanced stages of pregnancy had to go into the shelters. It was winter as well as being night, it was wet inside the tunnels, and we had to remain there for about two hours at a time, so many people became ill as a result. But gradually, the Sino-Soviet border war that had raised our hopes was heard of no more.

Not long after, in January 1970, a group of military commanders including the TMD commander, Zeng Yongya, TMD political commissar, Ren Rong, a few leaders of the central government Tibet Work Committee who had survived the purges of the Cultural Revolution, and leaders of the two factions established the Tripartite Revolutionary Committee (*Phyogs gsum mnyam sbrel gsar brje u yon lhan khang*). When the leaders selected their preferred appointees to head the organization, it was believed that most of them favored Ren Rong for the top post, but in any case that appointment was seen as a potential cause of fresh unrest. However, when the committee was inaugurated, it was General Zeng Yongya, the candidate supported by the Gyenlok faction, who was appointed leader by the central government, which surprised everyone. In fact, this was a maneuver by Prime Minister Zhou Enlai, the head of the central government's Cultural Revolution Sub-committee, intended to prevent the Gyenlok, who had suffered setbacks like the military assault, from feeling excluded and starting more trouble. Once the revolutionary committee had been established and the organizational strength of the two factions had naturally dissipated, Zeng Yongya was appointed elsewhere in mainland China and Ren Rong took over.

Gradually, so-called "military representatives" were sent to all government offices, factories, and people's organizations to look into the cases of murder, as well as "beating, smashing, and looting," allegedly committed during the years of turmoil, and those judged responsible were withdrawn from their positions and detained in groups called "reeducation classes" where they faced investigation and castigation. One group was sent to the Kongpo-Powo region, where they were detained for several months and subjected to such an unrelenting inquisition that the more sensitive among them could not bear it and committed suicide. Meanwhile, the Chinese central government issued a new ordinance, as will be described.

CHAPTER 21

The "One Smash and Three Antis" Campaign

THE NEW ORDINANCE called for the urgent propagation of the "One Smash and Three Antis" campaign (*gCig brdungs gsum rgol*). During the period of factional fighting, there had been political revolts of various kinds against the central government and the state economic system had been disrupted; with the breakdown of the state-managed supply of essential commodities, some people had been indulging in practices such as speculative hoarding, violating stable commodity prices, which was one of the tenets of socialism, so the purpose of this campaign was to rectify these problems. "One Smash" meant smashing present-day counterrevolutionaries, and the "Three Antis" were antiprofiteering, anticorruption, and antispeculative hoarding.

The definition of "present-day counterrevolutionaries" differed from one region to the next, and in Tibet the main target was anyone struggling for the Tibetan cause. During the chaos of the Cultural Revolution there had been violent uprisings in support of the Tibetan cause in Nyémo county in Lhasa prefecture, Pelbar county in Chamdo prefecture, Biru county in Nakchu prefecture, and so on. In Nyémo, what had apparently begun as a revolt by a local Gyenlok faction turned into a full-fledged popular uprising against Chinese rule that was bloodily suppressed by the army. Many were killed, and those who survived were imprisoned, along with anyone associated with them. There was a hunt for people connected with that movement in other parts of the country, and in many places, including Lhasa, they discovered posters with slogans calling for Tibet's independence, wishing for His Holiness to live for 10,000 years and for the Chinese invaders to be driven out, as well as pictures of Mao Zedong with the face crossed out or with horns drawn on the head.

In one of the more amusing incidents, a picture of Mao smeared with excrement was thrown into the street in the main Tromsi-khang market in Lhasa one night. The street sweeper who came across it next morning immediately informed the Public Security Office, which considered it a most serious offense and called in an investigation team. They concluded that the person responsible for defaming the chairman's portrait had eaten chilis and turnips the day before. When posters were discovered they used to take handwriting samples from the "class enemies" in each district, but on that occasion they investigated what the "class enemies" had eaten the day before.

Political incidents were regarded as the most serious, and while the authorities put strong pressure on government departments and the general public to report them, there were nightly meetings for "class enemies" to "confess their own crimes" and tell whatever they had "seen, heard, or suspected" of others. They came down particularly hard on neighborhoods or offices where posters had come to light, leading to some serious incidents, as happened in one of the stone-quarrying units in the TAR construction company when a FREE TIBET poster was put up on the wall of the toilet. After all the workers had been interrogated, a young man living in the Samding house in number 3 neighborhood committee in north Lhasa was identified, and when he eventually confessed and they grilled him on his objectives in putting up the poster, whether he was part of a secret group, and who his friends were, he had to give the names of many other young people. With another underground organization among the workers at the Lhasa cement factory, and one other Lhasa youth organization, there were three major cases of underground groups involving young people, all of whose members were arrested. There were struggle meetings every night in all areas of the city for those accused of any political discussion against socialism and the government, defaming Mao or in support of His Holiness and the exile government, or about plans to escape, and all you heard people talk about was who had been arrested that day.

At that time, an official from the Public Security Office came to address our meeting group of "class enemies" in the Banak-shöl neighborhood committee. He repeatedly threatened, "Unless those few among you who have committed crimes confess, you will be isolated." There was no way of telling whether he was just bluffing or a few of us were implicated in something, but we were all told to think it over, and although I personally knew nothing of any underground group, I was concerned that someone could bring up something I had said among friends concerning the hope for Tibetan freedom or against the Chinese government and Mao Zedong.

The most serious concern was that about a year earlier, I had asked to borrow a small booklet of His Holiness's collected speeches and another small booklet about the "Future Constitution of Tibet" from a friend of mine.

He told me, "I promised the owner that I would only read them at home and not lend them to anyone else, so you can look at them, but you can't take them home with you. However, we have a duty to make the speeches of His Holiness and the documents of the exile government available to concerned Tibetans, so I could copy them, and you could help me," to which I agreed, and whenever we had spare time I helped copy them. Not long after, when I went to an army camp to make adobe bricks, one of my fellow workers told me that the Chinese had found out about those booklets. When I asked him whether they had found out what my friend had done with them, and in particular that it was I who had copied them, he said, "What they found out about is the books you copied, and the person who told them has also been arrested. But that person doesn't know that you copied them, and as soon as this thing happened he managed to burn everything, so you don't have anything to worry about."

Nonetheless, it had become a serious matter, and the person who had told the authorities about it was still in custody. Although that person had no connection to me and the books had been burned, in the circumstances of the ongoing campaign, the story was liable to be blown up into something bigger under repeated examination and could end up implicating me. In view of the seriousness of the case, it was not just a matter of being arrested; more worryingly, it would not be sufficient [for my friend] to admit that he had copied the booklet, for they would demand to know where he had gotten the original and many other things. If he refused to tell they would inflict unbearable torture on him, and in order not to suffer that, he would have no choice but to inform on many others, including me.

At that time, political charges as minor as disrespect for Mao brought the death sentence at public rallies. To give one example, there was an old woman in the Banak-shöl neighborhood who belonged to the "poor" class category; she was about seventy, lived alone, and was so poor that she used to wear a hat like a stove lid, so people called her Grandma Stove Lid. For a time she was given the name Chief of the Poor, and during the launch of political campaigns when the work teams toured each district, she was the person of "pure" class origin with whom they stayed, following the Communist practice of "eating and living alongside the poor." Later on, when that title was given to someone else instead, it is said that she got angry and cursed Mao, for which she was arrested, and after a couple of months, she was executed at a mass rally. By those standards, if any question of my involvement with copying the booklet had arisen, my head would have been very close indeed to hitting the ground, and so the threats issued by the Public Security official were a cause of great anxiety for me. However, those threats turned out to be a warning to two others in our group of "class enemies," Namling Chökyi-la and Trin-pun-la, and not long after they were arrested for other matters and imprisoned for about ten years, but I never had any trouble over the things I had been worrying about.

Also at that time, there were periodic waves of house searches all over the city by fully armed soldiers looking for undercover spies, weapons, secret telegraph communications, and so on. They would come and search without warning during the night, guided by Public Security or those in charge of local neighborhood security. Even tougher, they used to send troops into the city around midnight to impose a blockade lasting three or four hours, and during that time anyone moving around the city, male or female, with or without a legitimate reason, would be seized, and it was said they had the power to shoot anyone who failed to respond when addressed.

The business of checking people's residence papers (*Them tho*) took half an hour, while they searched every household in the courtyard. Soldiers wearing white armbands for identification would suddenly pound violently on the main entrance door to the courtyard and push their way in. In courtyards where the doorkeepers took their time in coming or were unable to open the door quickly enough, they would break it down, or sometimes come in over the rooftops. In any case, twenty-plus Chinese soldiers would enter the courtyard and then split into groups of two or three to check each household and the residential papers of the occupants. Anyone inside not listed on the residence papers or registered as a visitor would be taken away, and if any listed member of the household was absent they would demand to know why. They would look over every corner of the house, groping or kicking at any object they considered suspicious.

Each time they conducted these inspections, they would find between 50 and 100 people who had not registered as visitors at the relevant sectional office, who would be detained at that office there and then, without being given an opportunity to explain themselves. About 80 percent of the unregistered people detained on these occasions were from rural areas and had come to Lhasa seeking medical treatment for ailments so severe that they had no time to apply for permission to travel from their local authority, and without such permission there was no way for them to register when they got to Lhasa. Even though it was quite obvious that they were invalids, the regulations required them to be taken in; those unable to walk had to be pulled in handcarts or carried on the backs of their hosts or companions, and on those nights the sectional offices took on the appearance of emergency battlefield sick bays for wounded soldiers. Because of the fear and the trauma of being moved back and forth, many of these invalids who had come to the city for medical treatment became worse. Some of the unregistered visitors were children (registered elsewhere) who happened to be staying with their parents, or parents staying with their children and so on, but in the case of the Tibetans, even if they were suffering from life-threatening illnesses or were members of the same immediate family, it was not considered a good enough reason and they were treated as criminals. In the case of the Chinese, however, most of their households in Lhasa at that time claiming residential grain rations had illegal members with no residence papers, but they were not checked at all and were free to stay there as they wished. Doesn't this show how very unequally the Tibetans and the Chinese were treated in every respect?

Anyway, One Smash and Three Antis was the most vicious political campaign of its kind so far, and until it came to an end, fully expecting to go back to prison, I exchanged promises and words of encouragement with trusted friends, destroyed any papers or possessions that could be considered suspicious, and remained in a state of heightened apprehension. And although no harm befell me during that campaign, many of my comrades who were patriotic and committed Tibetans did come to grief, and in particular, many, like the people of Nyémo and the young people of Lhasa, were executed at mass rallies.

CHAPTER 22

The "Great Massacre"

ABOUT A YEAR after those Nyémo people and the Lhasa youths were arrested, and after their crimes had been investigated, they were executed at a public rally attended by many people. Numerous countries in the world practice legal execution, but they differ widely in the degree of cruelty used to actually carry it out. As for the cruelty with which it is practiced in the so-called People's Republic of China, and particularly in the case of political offenders, I will just say something about the execution of the people from Nyémo county, which I witnessed and will never be able to forget.

There were mass executions of those involved in the Nyémo uprising on two occasions in Lhasa; seventeen were executed on the first and more than twenty on the second. A few days in advance of each execution rally, they put up posters with unrecognizable photos of those who were to be executed with Xs drawn through them in red ink and their names and crimes written underneath, on the walls of many houses in the city, along busy streets, and in the marketplace. The night before, there were general meetings in each neighborhood committee where we were told forcefully that the execution rally to be held the following day had to be attended punctually, even the sick and the elderly had to come—everyone except children too young to understand, and we could not just show up informally but had to go as a group. We "class enemies" and "hatted reactionaries under the dictatorship of the proletariat" were divided into groups along with those assigned to supervise our behavior, and there were orders for "class enemies" to be put right in the front of the crowd.

On the day of the rally, at the appointed time, citizens assembled at their respective sectional offices and lined up to be led to the place where the rally was held, the People's Stadium, where they stood in the lots designated for each administrative division of the city. On the stage and to either side were banners of black cotton with white paper lettering reading GENERAL MEETING FOR THE SUPPRESSION OF PRESENT-DAY COUNTER-REVOLUTIONARIES BY LEGAL SENTENCE and COUNTERREVOLUTION MUST BE ANNIHILATED, and loudspeakers played excerpts of Mao's quotations put to music and other songs chosen for the occasion. On the stage were members of the Revolutionary Committee, the city government, the TMD command, and so on, as well as the People's Court and Public Security Office. On either side of the stage and on patrol all around the assembly were military and Public Security guards brandishing weapons, to intimidate the public.

Then the leading official announced the beginning of the meeting by reading out the program, after which the loudspeakers repeatedly blared the slogan "Present-day counterrevolutionaries must be annihilated," chanted by loud male and female voices in Chinese and Tibetan alternately. The first point on the program was a speech by an official of the TAR Higher People's Court about the just nature of the meeting, after which he called in a harsh voice, "Bring the guilty before the court." Thereupon, several trucks carrying fully armed Chinese soldiers, followed by several more that each carried three of the badly beaten Nyémo prisoners surrounded by soldiers, with a final truck full of soldiers in the rear, drove in slowly and pulled up in front of the stage. The Nyémo people had black placards hung around their necks with their names written on them and crossed out in red. Those placards were said to weigh ten pounds apiece and were tied around the neck with a thin knotted rope, as a way of stopping the prisoners from shouting out. Their hands were tightly bound behind their backs and tied to the rope around their necks, and as the Chinese commonly do to prisoners about to be executed, they had wooden boards affixed to the back of their necks[, sticking straight up], which are said to be driven in under the skin. The soldiers guarding them on either side kept pushing their heads down, smashing their faces against the side of the truck so that their teeth were broken and their tongues cut, and blood dribbled out of their mouths. Having been tortured in this way, they were kept in front of the public for the three hours or so that the meeting lasted, and finally, after the crimes of each one and their death sentences had been announced, the procession of trucks again drove slowly around the assembled crowd in a gesture of intimidation, and eventually proceeded to the sand embankment near Séra monastery, north of Lhasa, where they were shot and dumped in the graves that had already been dug for them. There was a kind of festival of executions

Execution parade for the Nyémo rebels, Lhasa, 1969. *Used with kind permission from Woeser.*

Execution of the Nyémo rebels outside Lhasa. Taken from an official photo exhibit. *Used with kind permission from Woeser.*

that day, as similar numbers of prisoners were put to death in many counties all over the TAR.

Normally at mass rallies and other general meetings, the "class enemies" had to behave as they were told, ordinary people generally stood around in groups of two or three chatting, and went back and forth to the toilet and so on, while the leaders and activists joined in chanting slogans in loud voices and raised their fists to demonstrate their enthusiasm for "class struggle." But on that occasion, all the Tibetans were stunned and stood there like statues, unable to move. At the beginning of the meeting, the activists appointed to supervise us "class enemies" were performing the task diligently and showing a fierce attitude of "class solidarity," but as they watched fellows of their own flesh and blood being not only slaughtered but also tortured beforehand, they started to feel anger and disgust, and far from keeping watch on our reactions, the facial expressions of the activists themselves completely changed as their feelings became so strong that they could not help showing them.

Although people had heard many stories about Chinese massacring Tibetans before, that was in the past and such things were no longer going on in front of their eyes, but ever since the crushing of the [1959] uprising, official policy had gone from bad to worse, and now they could see for themselves something even more brutal than they had heard about before. Many of those watching could well have found themselves in the same position, since under these campaigns people were being executed not for any substantial offense but just on the basis of political remarks they were alleged to have made, as has already been described. Among the people from Nyémo there were a few with the title "Lama," and when their crimes were announced it was apparent that they had not actually participated in the revolt. It may have been that some incident had taken place in their locality, but they were executed for "practicing superstition" just because they had that title, and there was no more serious charge against them. Contemplating how it would be if we too had been implicated in the revolt gave rise to an unbearable anxiety, and with profound commiseration we uttered prayers of yearning that neither ourselves nor anyone else should meet with such a fate and that the victims might abide in the merciful embrace of Arya Mahakarunika in all their future lives. By the end of the meeting, everyone wore a downcast expression; there were no smiling faces to be seen among the onlookers, and those who cheerfully greeted their comrades in the bustle of the crowd did so only in order to encourage each other to be brave.

The Lhasa youths were executed about a year after that [October 1970]. I did not witness it because I was working in Kongpo at the time, but for the majority of Lhasa people who did, it was a terrible and unforgettable event. They were put to death even more cruelly than the Nyémo people had been, brought before the execution rally with their arms bound so tight that their shoulders were dislocated; their eyeballs were bulging out, their faces were swollen to an unusual size, their tongues were lacerated, and blood trickled from their mouths, eye sockets, and nostrils. A few of them had already stopped breathing as a result of these tortures by the time they reached the rally. Just hearing about it was more than one could bear, not to mention actually having to watch. Nonetheless, their parents, siblings, and grandparents were obliged to come and watch, and after the rally, meetings were held for all citizens, and especially for the relatives of the youths, at which they were forced to state that the torture and execution of their beloved children was just and necessary, and to thank the authorities for doing it. The official statement of their sentence said, "These present-day counterrevolutionaries have committed the heinous crime of opposing the Communist Party, the Nation, and the People. If they were not executed, the anger of the masses could never be satisfied, and we have executed them in accordance with the demand of the masses," thus shifting the blame for their cruel misdeeds, unheard of in the outside world, onto ordinary people.

There were several more execution rallies after that, at which five or six people were killed each time, including two of the leaders of the 1961 Tibetan Muslim agitation. There were also unpublicized killings of political prisoners in the jails, and it was said that a large number of prisoners were put to death at an execution rally in Drapchi prison for which inmates from all the other prisons were summoned. By that time, if there were no more than two or three executions at one of these rallies, we compulsory spectators would consider it a good day, as so [relatively] few people had been killed. In summary, the largest number of public executions took place in the course of that campaign, between 1969 and 1970.

Around that time, the Lhasa municipality government issued an order that every household in its jurisdiction, in both urban and rural areas, had to install a loudspeaker. There were already loudspeakers fixed on many of the higher rooftops that blared in our ears three times a day, but this was deemed insufficient, and in the name of "bringing Party policy to the doorstep," every household was obliged to buy and install its own contraption. In this period when Tibetans were being tormented by Chinese oppression and undergoing economic hardship, a great many people suffered ill health as a result, and it was widely reported that the condition of those with heart disease (*sNying rlung*) worsened as a result of having to endure the din of the loudspeaker for long periods in their houses.

What they used to broadcast was how great the production achievements were under the leadership of the Communist Party, how fine the nation looked, how powerful China was, how the imperialists and reactionaries had been defeated, and how class struggle had to be relentlessly pursued, without a single word of real news. Many households from the "poor" class category cut the wires to their loudspeakers before long to shut them up, and pretended that they didn't work anymore, but for "class enemies" there was no question of deliberately sabotaging our loudspeakers, and we even had to make sure that they didn't stop working, lest we be accused of sabotage and lack of enthusiasm for the Party's policies.

CHAPTER 23

PLA Soldiers Destroy the Fruits of the People's Labor in the Marshes

WHEN LHASA PEOPLE could no longer make a living even as construction laborers because of the civil war during the Cultural Revolution and their hardship was greater than ever, the marshes west of the city gave them a way to survive. First, I should say a few words about that marshland: it lies on the north side of the Kyangtang Naka meadow, [which used to stretch] to the west of Lhasa, where many generations ago it is said there was a small lake from which, according to folklore, lake-dwelling cows (*mTsho glang*) and horses (*mTsho rta*) magically appeared. As the lake waters gradually receded it turned into a marsh, and until the Chinese invasion it was a peaceful sanctuary of beautiful water birds such as cranes, geese, and swans, and was one of the natural ornaments of the city as it used to be. After the suppression of the uprising, the Chinese set about destroying Tibet's natural environment and wanted to turn marshes like this into agricultural land. They built drainage ditches in the marsh, and as the water level went down, the feathered occupants vanished and it became a field of swamp grass. When the clumps of turf formed by the roots of that grass were dug up and dried, they could be used as a kind of fuel, which we call "*la-ma*," and it gave Lhasa people an opportunity both to supplement their own supply of heating fuel and to sell it to others.

Generally speaking, the use of machinery was not widespread in Tibet, and we did not have the kinds of fuel used in developed countries, such as coal and coal gas. Moreover, there was not much forest in the Lhasa region, so traditionally, dried cattle dung was used for fuel. The farmers used to buy it from pastoralists in the neighboring highlands and supply it in turn to the city dwellers, an exchange from which all three communities benefited greatly. After the implementation of Democratic Reform, all the farmers and pastoralists had to join "mutual aid groups" (*Rogs res tshogs chung*), followed by the people's collectives (*Mi dmangs spyi khang*) of the commune system, in which individual economic activity was forbidden. Moreover, all kinds of crop fertilizer were controlled under the terms of the so-called "Eight-Character Directive on Agriculture" (*Zhing las yig 'bru brgyad kyi rtsa don*), which forced citizens to surrender their supplies of dung fuel for use as fertilizer, while under the core agricultural policy farmers were prohibited from selling any of their resources or products in the city. The Chinese met their own fuel needs by cutting the forests in the valleys of Kongpo, east of Lhasa, as much as they pleased and transporting the wood to Lhasa in truckload after truckload, without giving any thought to the needs of ordinary people. So it was that many poor households in the city ended up having to burn old bones and plastic and such things, the clear skies over our fair city were contaminated with acrid black smoke, and the high plateau air was filled with a foul stench. If the physical health of citizens at that time could have been analyzed with the kind of equipment we have today, it would undoubtedly have shown that many of them were adversely affected by this.

Because of the difficulty with lack of heating fuel, and especially when there was so little employment, the marsh became like a grant and a benefactor providing work for the citizens. At that time I too had no work, and no choice but to go and harvest turf in the marsh. Only people who had no other work did that. I was a young man who had spent four years after 1959 doing forced labor in prison and even after my release had to continue doing supervised labor, so since that is what I was used to, doing any other kind of labor should have been no great difficulty. Nonetheless, that work brought me no end of physical and mental hardship from the start.

To give a rough account of what it involved: to begin with, you had to look around the whole area to find a suitable place to work, not too wet, with a broad space for laying the stuff out to dry, and near enough to a road that was passable for vehicles, because the carrying distance from where the turf was cut inside the marsh back to dry land could only be covered by human effort; not even beasts of burden like horses or mules could go, much less wheeled vehicles, so if you failed to choose a good spot it made a huge difference in the amount you were able to harvest. After deciding on a spot, you came back the following day bringing a shovel with a good sharp blade for digging, one long and one short rope for carrying, and something to eat in the middle of the day. On arrival people would put markers around the space in which they intended to work. Then, after marking out similar-sized squares of about ten clumps [of turf] each with the shovel, they spent the next few days digging them out, and every so often laying them out in the sun to dry. The clumps had to be turned over after a few days, and when they had more or less dried, you brought the strongest members of your household to help carry them to the nearest roadside. The hardest part of the whole process was the carrying, and that day was like the Tibetan saying, "Those with strength need all they've got and those without suffer like hell," [but] as long as there was no problem with the weather, doing it that way worked well enough.

The going rate for one clump of turf was 0.2 *yuan*. Although I was counted among the strongest workers, I could not earn more than 2 *yuan* a day, so even though one clump of turf that took so much effort to harvest was worth so little, everyone who did that work used to feel very upset if a single one went to waste. Yet once the piles of turf were stacked up on the side of the main road, quite unthinkably, people came during the night and set fire to them. The next day, the marsh workers stood around the pile of ashes discussing what kind of villains could have done such a thing. Those to whom the burned turf belonged had arrived that morning with rented carts to transport it back to their homes, and naturally felt even more angry and upset. At that point, they all assumed that the culprit must be one of the harvesters, since there had been arguments among them over territory, especially spaces by the roadside, so those who had argued were mutually suspicious and remained wary of one another. However, the burning didn't end there but happened again and again, and when those suspected of responsibility had their stock burned too, people were even more amazed. A big pile of about 300 pieces that my colleague, the former disciplinarian of Méru monastery Losang Jikmé, and I had stacked up nearby got burned at the same time.

As we had no other place to stack our harvested turf, we had to put an end to this somehow, so all the marsh workers agreed in bitter resolve that regardless of the wind, the rain, and the cold, we had to get to the bottom of the matter by catching the culprit red-handed and producing the incontrovertible proof of an eyewitness to establish who was responsible. However, as those who stayed to watch the harvested turf by night concentrated only on getting their own share home as quickly as they could, no one could say who the arsonist might be. At that time, an old man called A-shang Chokdrup with whom I had been in prison had to spend two nights in the marsh guarding turf for the Tromsi-khang neighborhood committee people, and found out for sure. When questioned, he said, "It would be better not to look too closely into this business. The main thing is just to ensure that you don't have to leave your turf there overnight. Searching for the arsonist and pouncing on him would amount to suicide, so keep quiet."

But no matter how quiet you try to keep something, as the saying goes, "Water can be contained in a vessel, but no vessel can contain the spoken word," and eventually we found out that it was PLA soldiers who had burned our turf. This was something really unimaginable, and I myself couldn't quite believe it at first. Of course I had gained quite a deep impression of the army's attitude toward Tibetans and their capacity for cruel behavior since my time in prison, but I had not thought it possible that they could have set fire to the harvest for no reason at all, and anyone who had not been in close contact with the army and was familiar only with their propaganda would certainly have doubted it. But without following secondhand stories and by checking again, we found this to indeed be the case, and as the news passed from one person to the next working in the marshes, everyone knew it. Young people in Lhasa even coined a saying, "Uncle-all-yellow has made the turf all red," whose meaning was as follows: schoolchildren were supposed to call the soldiers "Uncle Liberation Army," so "all-yellow" was a reference to their yellow uniforms, and "all red" meant setting the stuff on fire.

Anyway, at that time those who worked in the marshes as well as their family members and dependents found themselves staring into the western sky as soon as they got up in the morning to see if there was any smoke in the direction of the marshes, in much the same way that farmers watch the sky for signs of dreaded hail as their crops ripen. It was a hazard against which we had no defense, and like the proverb, "If the lord of the manor becomes your enemy, flight is the best option," some gave up in absolute desperation.

As for the reason the soldiers burned the fruits of the people's sweat, blood, and toil, A-shang Chokdrup finally explained it to me directly: the road where we had stacked up our turf was the only motor road giving access to the artillery base at Pa-ri-ku, north of Lhasa, as well as some of the army's vegetable gardens in that area. The road was rather narrow, and piling turf along the sides made it even narrower, so when big trucks came that way they would have to drive slowly and make turns here and there to get by, and because of their refusal to put up with this, the soldiers flicked lighted matches and cigarette butts into the piles and burned them down. Those who have not used turf for fuel might think it impossible to set a big pile of it alight with something like a cigarette butt, and in a domestic hearth it is indeed one of the slowest kinds of fuel to catch, but outside in the driving wind a whole pile can burn down in a few minutes from just a spark of fire. But even with proof of this crime of destroying the fruits of the people's labor, not only was legal redress out of the question, if the Chinese even caught wind of such talk they would heap a mountain of accusations of defaming the "glorious Liberation Army" on those who said so, rather than offering any compensation for the burned harvest, and in certain circumstances it could result in heads rolling.

These things took place around 1969. Even the commanders of the troops involved knew all about it, but far from putting a stop to it or compensating ordinary people for their losses, they went even further in order to cover up these misdeeds, and decided that the entire marsh should be divided among the different army camps under the TMD and turned into an experimental farm. The army camps ordered people to stop harvesting turf and gave them a deadline of a few days to remove their existing stock. It wasn't easy to pack up that work in the space of three or four days, and as the battle between the Cultural Revolution factions was still not over, very little construction work was going on and alternative employment was scarce. Moreover, citizens had no other source of fuel, so there was no choice but to carry on.

At about that time, I was sent by the neighborhood committee to join a power station construction site in Tölung, west of Lhasa, and did not have to do that work anymore. Nonetheless, a few months later I was sent back in a group of young men to collect turf for the construction site's communal kitchen. By then, most of the harvesters were unable to continue where they had worked before and had moved nearer to Pa-ri-ku. We also picked a spot in that area, and as we were a team, we pitched a tent near the marshland rather than go back home in the evenings.

Meanwhile, the mistreatment of the marsh diggers by PLA soldiers had become widely talked about, but I would not be describing it here if I had not seen it for myself. The most depressing episode during the time we stayed there concerned a woman of about forty with three sons, who used to leave her tools and cooking pot in our tent overnight. Her eldest boy said he was fourteen, which I remember even now because we used to carry our turf along the same path as them, and when we gave little gifts to the children and asked them their names and ages, the eldest said that his mother told him he was born after the Democratic Reform, but couldn't say even that much about when the younger two were born. When we guessed their ages we thought the eldest really could have been fourteen, but in fact all three of them were no older than primary school age, and it was because they had to do such hard work alongside their mother that they looked older. Every day they cut and carried as much turf as they could manage, and every evening they filled up their handcart and dragged it back home. For clothing the eldest at least had a top and a pair of pants, albeit in rags, but the younger two just wore adult-sized shirts that served to cover their legs as well. The sunburned faces of mother and children alike were blackened by the mud from the swamp grass, which stuck to the sweat on their brows, and except where it had been washed off by fresh trickles of sweat, the only thing showing through the caked dirt was their white teeth. Pus and blood constantly oozed from cracks in the skin on the boys' hands and feet. Such was the poverty of this mother and her children whose hard-won produce was destroyed by soldiers using a tractor.

Whenever we heard the soldiers starting up their tractor, our foreman, Powo Tarchin, went to check whose turf they might be driving over, and one time as we were eating our breakfast in the tent he came rushing in, telling us, "Come quick! The army tractor is bulldozing the children's harvest, come and help them!" and by the time we got there about a third of their turf had been driven over. Some of us pleaded with the soldiers while others started gathering up the remaining turf. The boys' mother was down on her knees in front of the tractor, pleading, "Kind sirs! I have many children! I belong to the laboring masses!" in a mixture of Chinese and Tibetan, while her children tried to pull her back in fear that the tractor would run her over.

In addition to the two soldiers driving the tractor, there was an officer (*Phad krang*) in charge who seemed to be of slightly senior rank, and whose face was creased into an expression of haughty anger. His uniform jacket with red insignia was unbuttoned down the front, his left hand was planted on his waist, and in his right hand he held a thin willow cane, which he thrust aloft. Over the uniform cap emblazoned with the five-pointed star he wore a broad-brimmed straw sun hat that had a phrase from Mao's quotations, "In the service of the masses," inscribed on it in red ink. He had dark glasses on, and he was directing the two soldiers driving the tractor. The more we all pleaded, the more incensed he became, and he swore at us with whatever curses he could think of. My young fellow workers sang the Liberation Army song of the "Three Great Disciplines and Eight Responsibilities," and backed it up by chanting the slogan from Mao's quotations that says "Without the people's army, nothing could be achieved on behalf of the people," but although they were written on paper and used to fool the masses, those codes of discipline and sayings of Mao Zedong had not even a single sesame seed's chance of being put into practice, and chanting them only made the soldiers more determined. The song and the quotations with which my companions hoped to stop the wrecking had quite the opposite effect, and as if to spite us, the two drivers crushed what was left of the harvest in an instant.

At that, the woman slumped her head down on her knees and wailed, "Alas! Whatever have we done to deserve this? For mercy's sake!" while the children stood by her side weeping, and we tried to console them by saying that we could go and dig in some other place. The youngest boy asked his mother, "Are they Guomindang?" to which she replied, "Whoever they are, they've destroyed our harvest. Now if it weren't for you cursed children, there would be nothing to do but go and take my own life."

This incident is just one example of the state of affairs that drove many people to desperation. The little boy probably asked if those soldiers were Guomindang because the propaganda films often showed Nationalist soldiers inflicting harm on ordinary people and the Communist army defending and caring for them. Meanwhile, having reduced the mother and her children to misery, the two soldiers went back to their quarters with an air of self-satisfaction, as if they had just accomplished a tough mission, mimicking the woman's pleas as they went and laughing about it between themselves. For our part, we felt downcast that we had not only failed to save the harvest but made things worse by trying, and even rebuked one another for singing the song and chanting the slogan, but apart from consoling the mother and her children and picking up the few pieces of turf that were still usable, there was nothing we could do. If a photograph could have been taken of that scene, it would now serve as a very special testimony to put before the people of the world, but not only are there no such things, I never even got to know the woman's name or where she lived, which is quite frustrating. So I would like to call on anyone who has seen that marshland and is capable of drawing an artistic reconstruction of the event to please do so as a reminder for future generations.

There was another army camp near our tent that was a branch of the artillery camp, and when the cows owned by the Pa-ri-ku farmers came to browse on their vegetable patch the Chinese soldiers would beat the animals like anything, and the marsh diggers used to say that on occasion they had seriously wounded and even killed them. On either side of that army camp's vegetable garden were a few compost pits several yards deep and two or three yards across, lined inside with stone walls smoothed over with a layer of cement. Once when several of us were passing nearby with loads of turf, we saw some of the Chinese soldiers grab one of the Pa-ri-ku farmers' cows that had strayed onto the vegetable patch and dump it in one of those pits. If no one had seen them do it and it had been left there, the animal would surely have died within a few hours. In real terms, a cow was a farmer's sole possession, because apart from the division of the annual grain harvest by the cooperative, it was up to individual households to provide themselves with such things as butter or oil, and since cows were the only possible source, they were as dear to the farmers as their own children, and they were the most valuable resource left in the hands of individuals.

Fortunately on that occasion, a few of us saw the soldiers throw the cow in the pit. We were not going to ignore it and looked for a way to get her out, but the pit was deep, and as it wasn't filled with green manure or silt but human and pig feces, going in any deeper would have been unpleasant, and we were also too few. So some of us went to inform the Pa-ri-ku farmers, while others went to call those working in the marsh to come and help. Once we had summoned a large number of people and were setting about getting the cow out of the pit with the ropes we used to carry the turf, the Chinese soldiers saw us and came to expel us from their vegetable garden. We tried to explain how valuable the cow was to the farmers and that we had to get her out, but not a single one of us could express himself in Chinese. After explaining in a mixture of Chinese and Tibetan, we waited there while some of us went to explain the situation to the camp office, whereupon one of their officers came out with a Tibetan soldier to interpret. After a lot of discussion back and forth between the soldiers who had thrown the cow in the pit and the officer and interpreter, the officer told us through the interpreter, "We need [to talk to] the owner of the cow. We made this compost pit because it's important for the vegetable garden, and it's not our fault if a cow comes along and falls in. We want to know who its owner is, and the people digging the marsh should not interfere."

One of the marsh diggers among us replied, "The owner is a farmer. The cow may have fallen in by itself or it may have been deliberately thrown in, but in any case, it's everyone's responsibility to safeguard the people's property. Since the army is the people's army, it's their responsibility as well. If the owner doesn't come and the cow is left there, it's going to die."

"Are you saying that our soldiers deliberately threw the cow in?" the Tibetan translator demanded threateningly.

"I don't know," he replied. "All I saw was the cow in that pit, and if we don't get it out fast, it's going to die."

At that, one of our group of workers collecting turf for the power station construction site, a Muslim youth, pointed at the soldiers who had thrown the cow in the pit and fearlessly blurted out, "They threw it." At once the officer became furious, took out a notebook and pen from his jacket pocket, and asked the youth his name, age, neighborhood committee, class category, and so on. Our foreman, Powo Tarchin, got scared and said, "We had better not stay around here," and he told me with genuine concern, "Since you're a 'class enemy,' you will have a problem if the neighborhood committee finds out you were involved in this." So our group went back to work. Around midday, a junior leader of the Pa-ri-ku farmers' cooperative arrived at the army camp vegetable garden and managed to get the cow out of the pit, but when he got into an argument with the soldiers about the incident, they beat him and held him in the barracks for about two hours.

After that, our group of workers gathering turf for the power station construction site moved to another place on the south side of the marsh, the site of Lhasa's present coal-fired power station, from where the carrying distance was slightly shorter. Nearby was another military vegetable patch tended by two squads of Chinese soldiers, and they had put up a barbed-wire fence around it to keep animals out. However, sometimes the cows of the farmers in the Lha-lu area, as well as the horses and mules that pulled carts belonging to the local farmers' cooperative, managed to get in, despite the fence. When we saw animals like cows, horses, and sheep in there, we used to chase them out, in order to prevent them receiving the kind of abuse visited on the Pa-ri-ku farmers' cow, although, at least while we were around, the soldiers working on the patch also chased them out in good humor, without resorting to vicious behavior.

Then, one Sunday, most of us went home for a day off, leaving Powo Tarchin to watch the tent. When we came back on Monday morning, there was a dead horse with a bloated stomach lying near the army vegetable patch. We reckoned the soldiers must have poisoned it with insecticide, but Powo Tarchin told us that when the soldiers figured there was no one in our tent, they had electrocuted it. The horse belonged to the Lha-lu farmers' cooperative, whose sole means of income to buy renewable commodities came from providing horse cart transport for hire outside the peak agricultural season in spring and autumn, so the loss of a horse or mule was as serious for them as the loss of a cow for the Pa-ri-ku farmers. In fact, the value of all the vegetables in the soldiers' garden did not equal even half the value of a draft horse. The Three Great Disciplines and Eight Responsibilities of the PLA discipline code put great emphasis on safeguarding the people's property, and included such phrases as "not taking so much as a needle from the people," but in practice it was just the opposite.

Whether people in China would have put up with this dereliction of military discipline or not, I can't say, but in Tibet, even if crimes against ordinary people's property were committed in broad daylight for all to see, there was no appeal to justice. Even though our claims rested on a mountain of evidence, they would be disregarded, just as pointing out that soldiers had thrown a cow into a cesspit resulted in our names, ages, addresses, class categories, and so on being recorded and threats of reprisal made against us. All this followed from the loss of our freedom, and demonstrates the truth of the saying that "By losing freedom you lose everything." In any case, of all Tibetans living under Chinese occupation, it is especially those living in the vicinity of army camps who have suffered the most grievous losses and deliberate cruelty, as these stories show.

CHAPTER 24

The Systematic Destruction of Ganden Monastery

UP UNTIL 1970, the Yangpa-chen chapel at Ganden monastery, which contained the precious golden reliquary *stupa* of Jé Rinpoché (Tsongka-pa Losang Drakpa), as well as the great assembly hall, the Shar-tsé and Jang-tsé colleges, and other assembly halls, was used as a granary by the food grains department in Lhasa, just as Séra and Drépung monasteries were. But that year, quite suddenly, I heard that the leaders and managers of the neighborhood committee refill stores and the Lhasa East Wind boot and hat factory, as well as the tailoring cooperatives around the city, were going to Ganden to buy up materials. Carts from the Lhasa transport cooperative commonly went up to Ganden to transport the department's grain supplies, but I had never heard that there were warehouses for commodities other than grain, and I had been wondering what was up when one night a close friend came to my place saying he had something to discuss.

He told me that the great golden reliquary in Ganden Yangpa-chen had been emptied, along with other reliquary *stupas*, and the preserved bodies (*dMar gdung*) they contained were to be burned and the ashes used as fertilizer. However, the former monks still working at Ganden had managed to substitute the preserved body of Jé Rinpoché with another one, and had left it in a corner of the chapel. Since there was apparently no security watch on the Yangpa-chen chapel before and after working hours, we had to find a way to go and rescue it. My friend was determined to go but would not be able to manage it by himself, and the other comrades he had approached so far were too scared and did not dare get involved. "What do you say?" he asked me. "We have to do it. But first, I have requested friends of mine who have gone to Ganden to buy materials to check carefully whether it is really the genuine remains of Jé Rinpoché and exactly where it has been left. They will make contact with the monk-caretakers and report back without delay in the next day or two, and if it is the real thing that has been spared I will call on you at once to come and help me, so please prepare yourself for that eventuality."

It was a terrifyingly dangerous enterprise at the time of a severe crackdown when the One Smash and Three Antis campaign was in full swing; if the Chinese government found out, they would not have regarded it as a minor offense. All the same, it would have been extremely unheroic of me to back out. We were comrades, and I had often boasted to him that I would be prepared to sacrifice whatever I had if things became critical, so now there was not much else I could do. But before making up my mind, I asked him more about how the plan would be carried out, and he told me, "These days they are selling off a lot of antique stuff to the production cooperatives and to individual buyers, and lots of people are going to Ganden every day for that purpose, so the two of us can go there on that pretext and have a good look at where the precious body has been put and what route we can take and so on. Then in the evening we can hide in a crevice of the mountainside near the monastery, and sneak back into the Yangpa-chen chapel during the night to pick it up. If we get it, we will hide it in some inaccessible spot in the mountains, and then gradually we will find a way to get it out to Dharamsala in India."

That evening, with my mind racing, I thought how excellent it would be if the plan succeeded, and even if the authorities found out and I were arrested, I could quite legitimately insist that I had acted only out of intense devotion for the holy lama and had no political objective whatsoever, and might thus avoid being executed, so I decided to go. But my friend came back the next morning having received the unequivocal message that Jé Rinpoché's precious remains had already been burned, and we were both consumed with regret.

A few days later, the people from the neighborhood committee refill store came back, having bought lots of things other than sacred images and scriptures from the monastery, which they sold off to poor people in the neighborhood, while some of my friends gave me blessed objects of reverence that had been retrieved from among the contents of the looted reliquary, such as ashes and fragments of bone from the cremation pyres of great lamas, fragments of robes, and so on. The Lhasa East Wind boot and hat factory used the blessed vestments that had dressed statues at Ganden to make linings and soles for boots, and the tailoring cooperatives used the brocades to make quilt covers and bicycle seat covers and other things for sale, and for a while Lhasa was awash with things made from the offering vessels, the robes of statues, and the assembly hall cushions and pillar covers from Ganden monastery. Once the people from the agricultural communes around Ganden had dismantled the empty buildings and brought the painted and varnished timbers to Lhasa for sale, these too were to be seen at all the horse cart depots in the city, like the Tromsi-khang market and the Sungchö-ra courtyard.

A great many people both inside and outside the country did not realize the actual circumstances in which Ganden monastery was destroyed and cannot be blamed for believing the widespread fallacy that Tibetans themselves were responsible, or at least suspecting that that was the case. Because Ganden is situated on a mountainside two hours' drive away from Lhasa, city people had no way of checking what actually went on there, and the Chinese authorities deliberately took advantage of that fact in order to shift responsibility for their crime onto the local farmers. As for the real story of how Ganden monastery was destroyed, I heard it told in full at a meeting of the Tibet branch of the Chinese Buddhist Association (*Chos tshogs*) held in Lhasa in 1982, by a courageous monk who had served as the monastery's chairman (*Kru'u ren*).

As mentioned already, Ganden had been in the same position as Séra and Drépung until the sudden visit of a group of Chinese leaders from the finance department of the Lhasa city government, who made an inspection tour of the great golden reliquary. Not long after, another group of officials arrived, led by an officer of the Chinese government emporium [a division of the finance department, in the former Drupkhang Labrang on the Tromsi-khang street], a red-faced woman with long hair who dealt in the acquisition of precious commodities like gold, silver, turquoise, coral, agate, pearl, and so on. First they removed all the jewels ornamenting the *stupa*. Then they stripped off its gold covering. Finally they emptied the receptacle of its contents, going through them in meticulous detail, and all of these fabulous things went into the Chinese government's pocket. Whatever was left over after the looting of the jewels and gold, such as the frame and the preserved body that could not be readily disposed of, was burned and the ashes spread on the fields, on the pretext of following the Cultural Revolution imperative of destroying the Four Olds. In this way, the priceless sacred wealth of the great Ganden monastery and the reliquary of Jé Rinpoché at its center were systematically removed. After that, the leaders of the farming communes around Ganden, under Taktsé county of Lhasa prefecture, were instructed that if they took down the monastery buildings they could use the pillars, beams, and rafters for the construction of a new public hall for their commune, or sell them and distribute the income among commune members as an annual bonus. Thus the commune leaders directed their people in the dirty work of destroying the empty monastery buildings by tying ropes around the pillars to pull them down and so on, and used the timbers as they had been told by the government.

This amounted to the government inciting the commune leaders to achieve their own objectives for them, and the commune leaders ordering their members to carry out the destruction. But because most Lhasa people only saw the farmers bringing the timbers of Ganden into the city, it was assumed that they had destroyed the golden reliquary *stupa* in the same way that Red Guards destroyed the contents of the Tsukla-khang temple in Lhasa at the start of the Cultural Revolution, and they cursed them for it and held it against them. In reality, it was a case of "Mr. Wolf taking the tasty cut of meat and leaving Miss Vixen to take the blame," because the Chinese government had systematically stripped the golden reliquary to start with, and later had the local people destroy the empty buildings and take the blame for everything. The destruction of sacred images and objects by the Red Guards at the beginning of the Cultural Revolution and the destruction of the golden reliquary were quite distinct in nature: the destruction at the beginning of the Cultural Revolution was the expression of a political ideology, while the golden reliquary was destroyed with the sole intention of appropriating its gold and jewels. It seems to me important to make a clear distinction and to convey this to others in order that the fallacious version of events at Ganden not be perpetuated.

Not long afterward, the wind of that destruction threatened to blow away everything in its path, when the municipal government ordered that each neighborhood committee had to run its own communal dining hall, which would first have to be built, and indicated that they should get the necessary timbers by dismantling decrepit buildings at the Séra and Drépung monasteries. Thus each of the three sectional offices in the city picked groups of young able-bodied workers from among the "class enemies" in their area for the purpose. I was trying to earn a living harvesting turf in the marshes at the time, but my name was selected as one of those who had to go dismantle monastery buildings. I personally did not have the fortune to have contributed a single stone or clod of earth for the construction of those monasteries in the first place, and the idea that now I was going to accumulate the evil karma of destroying them brought me considerable anguish, but there was no way of getting around it, so reluctantly I prepared myself to go.

Meanwhile, however, an auxiliary construction unit under the TMD general command in charge of building a large weapons and ammunition storage facility in an area called Trenma, near Nyingtri in Kongpo, found itself short of construction laborers and was recruiting one group from the pastoral area of Damshung county under Lhasa prefecture and another from the city itself. Each neighborhood committee selected candidates to be sent, and I was among a group of young "class enemies" chosen from our neighborhood, so fortunately I did not have to accumulate the negative karma of demolishing a monastery. However, the work of dismantling those buildings was brought to a stop before it had been completed because of concern for the impact on public opinion.

CHAPTER 25

Sent to Kongpo for the Second Time

THERE WERE ABOUT four hundred of us on the list to be sent from Lhasa to join the construction of the Chinese army weapons depot in the summer of 1970, and over a few days we all went for a medical examination at a clinic in the TMD headquarters. Those who passed were then taken to a timber yard in an army camp at Lha-dong Shenka on the other side of the Kyi-chu river, where we had to stay for about two weeks at the height of the rainy season. Each of us was questioned on our personal history since age eight, our social background, and so on, and the information we gave was scrupulously checked with our neighborhood committee officials. While that was going on, some of the activists from that workplace organized us into groups to study Communist thought, chiefly the *Collected Works of Mao Zedong*. It was a suffocatingly restrictive environment in which we had to give an account of our own thinking, exactly as I had had to do in prison. The subject matter was "class struggle" and "proletarian dictatorship," and we had to account for our own thoughts with reference to our immediate situation. In my case, that meant having to regularly recite that I belonged to the former ruling class and was guilty of participation in the uprising, but that due to the correct policy of the Communist Party, I now had the opportunity to participate in this noble work of construction, and in recognition of this great kindness I was going to thoroughly complete personal reform and sincerely strive to contribute my utmost in the construction of the New Tibet.

During that period of investigation, it seemed that I would not qualify to be sent to Kongpo, but when they made the final announcement, there was only one person from our east Lhasa sectional office group who had a social background problem (Téring Ten-nor-la, whose parents had fled to

India and whose mother even worked for the Tibetan broadcasting service of All-India Radio in Delhi) and was therefore excluded, as well as a few others from poor class backgrounds whose behavior was considered undesirable. Coming from a higher class category was not a bar in itself. Being selected to go to Kongpo spared me from having to destroy monasteries in Lhasa, but as I was the only one from the "former ruling class" (*mNga' bdag*), I was worried that that would make me a principal target in future political campaigns.

When we got to Kongpo, because our workplace was in a military area, we had to follow the same daily routine as the soldiers. The work was hard and the civilian workers were paid less, but there was no discriminative treatment of higher and lower class categories in terms of work, wages, or bullying. We could buy military clothing, for summer or winter as appropriate, of a quality scarcely available in society at large, and it was a season of fine weather, so we got to supplement our diet with a variety of fruits and other foods that grew wild thereabouts. We took our daily meals in a common kitchen with no discrimination of access or fixed grain ration, so people could eat to satisfaction. Since they subtracted about 12 *yuan* per month from our wages for food, the monthly wage was insufficient when we had to buy clothing as well, but if you managed it economically it was certainly enough to live on.

The political education classes differed from those for civilians in that we had to study directives issued by the Central Military Commission, as well as routinely reciting Mao's quotations. Occasionally they would hold events for the whole camp known as "Recall Past Misery, Reflect on Present Happiness" (*sDug dran skyid bsam*), when people had to "remember the misery of the old society and appreciate the joys of the new one," and while I was there they had one lasting a week, during which they constantly played the song of mourning for revolutionary martyr Lei Feng, called "The Misery of Class [Society]," no cultural events were held, and people were supposed to wear ragged clothes and avoid looking cheerful. The kitchen served nothing but a plain, watery soup, and in the daily political meetings we had to sing the class misery song and condemn the suffering of the "old society," but the "class enemies" among the workers were not singled out for attack. Quite contrary to the fears I'd had on arrival, this was the most easy-going work site I had been sent to so far, and was just like the proverbial "sparrow's nest sheltered by a hawk's nest."

Lei Feng was one of the army's role models, and at that time the main figures in the central leadership wrote messages in his memory. Mao Zedong said, "We must learn to be like Comrade Lei Feng," and Prime Minister Zhou Enlai wrote, "In firm solidarity with the working class, clearly distinguishing between friend and foe, putting words into action with revolutionary courage, Lei Feng was a perfect Communist who spurned his own personal advantage in favor of the common good, and whoever wishes to further the proletarian struggle without regard for his own life should study and follow his example." "Learning from Lei Feng" was repeatedly propagated throughout society, but particularly in the army and in primary schools.

Although the One Smash and Three Antis campaign was being vigorously implemented in Lhasa, life had been going on normally within the army, but one evening about four months [after my arrival there] they held a general meeting to announce the already mentioned revelation of a secret youth organization struggling for Tibetan freedom, at which the sentencing document from the public execution was read out and posters with the photos of the executed offenders were put up everywhere. Afterward, there were group meetings to discuss the case and oblige participants to state their views about it, and since many of the workers in our group had relatives among the arrested youths, there were emotional scenes in many of the dormitory tents, and I feared that would lead to a campaign being launched in our own work camp. When we showed up for work as usual the next morning, those of us from Lhasa were told to assemble on one side, and a list of names was read out. The names were all those from the "middle trader" class category upward, and we were told that we would be going back to Lhasa the next day. Meanwhile our movement was restricted, and we were not even permitted to conclude any transactions we might have had with local people.

At four o'clock the next morning we left in a convoy of military trucks and drove for eighteen hours, stopping only for the drivers to relieve themselves, which they had to do in unison, reaching Lhasa that same night. Each truckload had half a sack of *tsampa* to go around and no liquid to mix it with, so we had no choice but to eat it dry, whereas on the outward journey we had taken three days and been given sleeping quarters in military truck stops along the way and plentiful servings of rice, steamed buns, and vegetables at mealtimes, just like the Tibetan saying, "Welcomed in and booted out." The reason for our suddenly being sent back before the completion of the construction work was the renowned suspiciousness of the Chinese: most of the workers sent from Lhasa were the children of "class enemy" families, as were the members of the secret organization exposed in Lhasa in our absence, and they seem to have suspected that some of us might have been implicated, particularly as we were working on a military project and could have tried to sabotage it.

For a long time during my stay at that work camp I was given the job of transporting building materials, and therefore got to visit many side valleys and other spots in the Nyingtri area, where I had been before, and had a chance to learn my way around and familiarize myself with the landscape. When I had come there to do construction work four years earlier in 1966, the Kongpo landscape was a brilliant green in all seasons, and although the forest was being cut along the north bank of the Nyang-chu river, the ancient forests on the south bank were unaffected and retained their natural splendor. By 1970, however, all the forest on the accessible mountainsides along the north bank had been cut down, leaving a denuded wasteland in their place, while a large number of bridges had been built across the Nyang-chu for the exclusive purpose of transporting timber and the forests on the south bank were being felled. There seemed no doubt that at that rate, Kongpo would be nothing but bare rock within a couple of generations. I found out from local people that the climate had changed, and although the weather was fine while I was there, when a strong wind picked up it would bring a dust storm like those we get in Lhasa.

When a forest is wiped out, a whole variety of other benefits is lost simultaneously, but at that time I had no idea how many useful forest resources there are besides timber, or of the importance of forests to the people and economy of the country as a whole. And I assumed that whether the timber being extracted from the valleys of Kongpo was benefiting Chinese or Tibetans, it was being used within Tibet. Not until I got to the processing factory described next did I realize that the lion's share was being transported to China as soon as it had been processed.

CHAPTER 26

The Xichao Dachang Timber Yard

THE CHINESE WORDS *Xichao Dachang* mean Western Station. It was the chief depot for military trucks plying the Qinghai–Tibet highway and was administered by the Qinghai provincial military headquarters. There was an enormous army base at that depot, which included a nearby timber yard, a vegetable garden, an orchard, and a food processing plant under its management, as well as a large dairy farm in the Chang Yangpa-chen area. Since the nonstaple food items produced were regularly available for sale to its staff, many people were eager to get themselves employed there in order to be able to buy otherwise scarce Chinese consumer products like cigarettes and sugar on a monthly basis.

One of my friends was working in that timber yard, and through him I managed to get a job there. Most of the work involved splitting huge tree trunks on electric sawing machines, so except for those cleaning up or sweeping up sawdust, the workers really had to be strong. It was said that the sawing machines in that workshop had been used by the Japanese during their occupation of China's northeast. Most had labels showing that they were made in America and a few were Japanese-made, and I had never seen timber being produced on such a large scale before. An average of 300 military trucks passed through the Xichao Dachang every day. Those truck teams were responsible for carrying military supplies in time of war, but usually they just carried timber, and normally they delivered loads of whole tree trunks from Kongpo to the timber yard two or three times a week. The quantity was so great that the trunks had to be stacked by crane so that they didn't completely cover the vast yard, until they formed a pile so tall it could almost be seen from Lhasa. Within two or three days they were sawn on those machines according to the Chinese system of measurement into 8″-wide planks, which were then transported elsewhere by another team of trucks. Three hundred truckloads of raw tree trunks from Kongpo made approximately 100 truckloads of sawn planks, and the by-products of processing, such as tree bark and sawdust, were sold to army camps and government departments in the area for use as firewood, fencing material, and so on, and I reckon the income from that alone must have covered the factory's running costs, including the workers' and officials' wages.

At first, I assumed that the processed timber was being transported to construction units at army bases in other parts of Tibet, but the officials working there told us quite openly and unambiguously that no more than 20 percent was used for building material at other truck stops along the Qinghai–Tibet highway, while fully 80 percent of it went to the Chinese provinces of Gansu and Qinghai. At meetings the factory boss (*Khrang krang*) always used to tell us, "Ours is a glorious workshop because in addition to assisting the construction of the New Tibet, it serves our brother provinces as well," shamelessly presenting this villainy as a virtue.

I didn't discover the fact that the valuable bulk of the timber was being shipped off to China through any special investigation but simply stumbled over it while trying to earn my living. If you had actually gone looking for such information throughout the country, who knows what you might have found? While at least 40 percent of the Tibetan forest decimated so far was undoubtedly being transported to China, the remainder that was being used within Tibet benefited no one but the Chinese themselves while the Tibetans, the rightful owners of the land, were not entitled to so much as a twig. As I mentioned already, when the neighborhood committees in Lhasa needed building materials for the communal dining halls ordered by the municipal government, they forced the "class enemies" under their control to go and dismantle the former monastic buildings at Drépung. Not only was timber not available to Tibetans for building houses, they could not even buy scraps for firewood but had to burn animal dung and turf and, in the poorest households, trash like old plastic and bones. By contrast, neither Chinese offices nor workplaces ever burned dung or turf for fuel, and to find an individual Chinese household [in Tibet] doing so was as rare as seeing a star in daylight. Those Tibetans on intimate terms with the Chinese, however, bought timber and firewood from them discreetly.

In much the same way, although there was a lot of new development and construction, like the housing blocks in Lhasa and other cities, factories, highways, and bridges, it was exclusively related to Chinese interests, while in out-of-the-way rural areas inhabited only by Tibetans the old donkey tracks were not replaced by any motor roads or modern bridges, as will be seen. In any case, the destruction of Tibet's forests is an irreparable loss, and in my view, if reversing it is not made a concern of the utmost priority, when the time comes for Tibet to be returned to Tibetan hands, it will be like inheriting an empty, derelict house.

Anyway, I was employed by the outfit that transported the timber to China, which did not fall under the economic regulations stipulated by the TAR and TMD authorities, so all the employees regardless of their class categorization received an extra sixteen pounds per month of either rice or wheat flour in addition to the grain ration, and were entitled to buy a monthly allowance of very scarce consumer goods imported from China, like cigarettes, sugar, soap, etc., as well as butter, meat, and fruit. In addition, if we had the money, we could buy more food products and military clothing on the quiet from individual soldiers, so from my own immediate point of view it was a comfortable position, given the prevailing conditions.

Later in 1970, after I had been working there for two or three months, they started to mine coal from a deposit at the head of the Yab valley in Tölung, west of Lhasa, and recruited workers to build an access road. When that group of workers required reinforcement, the neighborhood committee summoned me and I had to go and help. By the time I got there, most of the hard work had already been done and the road-building team had moved down to the mouth of the Yab valley to work on the last segment, which was completed in about a month. But after that, the workers were not sent home because their labor was needed to start on a large project in the same area, the construction of a total of six hydropower stations between Tong-ga in upper Tölung and Dongkar [below Drépung monastery]. And so, in the early spring of 1971, I had to go and work at the power station construction site in Tölung.

CHAPTER 27

The Tölung Power Station Construction Camp

AS SOON AS the coal mine road was finished in the early spring of 1971, the workers moved on to Ka-tak, farther up the Tölung valley, to start on the power station canal. It wasn't the coldest time of year, but there were brisk spring winds, and the only tents and other equipment we had were those the neighborhood committees had provided, the cotton summer picnic tents and screens confiscated all those years ago. They had since been used by a great many work camps and worn to shreds by the sun and wind, so one of the hardships of working on the coal mine road and the power station was staying in tents that offered no protection against the winter winds or the summer rains. Also, as this was the most extensive construction project since the start of the Cultural Revolution and the workers were not participating voluntarily, the municipal government specified that they should be organized into groups under the direct supervision of local officials from the sectional offices and neighborhood committees to which they belonged, and follow the regular discipline. That meant work meetings as well as political education classes every evening, and performing the daily labor in a state of apprehension.

During the nearly six years I spent on that construction site, I did a variety of jobs: first I worked on the canal like everyone else; then for a while I went up the mountains to collect firewood for the camp kitchen; then I was harvesting turf in the marsh, also for the kitchen fires; and when they began construction of the power station building, I was first transporting building materials and then cutting rocks. After that was done, I had to do maintenance and supervision work on the canal. Initially, during the hard work of digging the canal and building, because of the effects of the Cultural Revolution we were singled out for abuse, given the hardest and most dangerous jobs, the lowest wages, and the worst tents, and suffered badly from the unequal treatment. Later on, after the work camp administration building was completed and the workers got new tents, our condition improved, and after the power station was finished and I went on to do maintenance work, things became a little more relaxed, at least while there were no problems with the canal. However, due to the lay of the land in that area, the canal was dug into the mountainside, above the local farming villages and their fields, and during the excavation we were working on a strict deadline so that the main point was to finish in time, and no one paid attention to doing a good job. Thus, when water flowed into the canal it started to leak uncontrollably all over the place, damaging the fields and village houses, and especially the Qinghai–Tibet highway that ran alongside, and some of us "class enemies" had to risk our lives trying to stop it.

The most memorable incident was after the completion of the number 6 power station at Dongkar. A few days before, a ceremony was to be held to mark its inauguration. In order to prevent any mishap on the inaugural day, water was to be released into the section of the canal leading to the new power station as a test, so all the workers on hand spread out along the canal with their tools, having arranged to send a signal to close the sluice gate upstream in case of any leaks. But one stretch of that canal passed within the boundary wall of the petroleum storage depot at Dongkar, and all such installations were guarded by the army. The administrative office of the power station project had not informed the soldiers of their intentions, so when we came to check on the stretch of canal inside their boundary wall, they not only denied us entry but would not even let us come close and trained their guns on us. As the power station office and the guards were discussing how to handle the situation, the canal inside the depot's boundary wall started to leak.

At that point, the workers were allowed inside to try to fix it, but the canal was positioned above the petroleum storage tanks and in an instant, before anything could be done about it, water rushed out of the canal and overturned an enormous metal canister containing one hundred tons of fuel, which started to roll downhill. Those of us workers already inside the boundary wall dug up nearby rocks and earth and showed off all the skills we knew trying to stem the flood, but it did no good at all. A telephone call had already been made to the head of the canal telling them to redirect the flow, but since it took almost a day's walk to cover the length of the canal between there and Dongkar, it could not be cut off instantly, and meanwhile the water swept many more storage tanks down as far as the Dongkar number 2 brigade's threshing ground, burying their harvest in petroleum and mud. The highway was also flooded, blocking a large number of trucks, and in accordance with the traffic department regulations prohibiting even momentary man-made obstructions on the highways linking Lhasa with Qinghai and Chengdu, there were angry phone calls from the TAR Public Affairs Department (*gZhung don thing*), the traffic department, and TMD headquarters one after the other to the power station office, and the traffic department sent an investigation team.

Under unbearable pressure from their superiors, the office leaders had no choice but to take emergency measures, regardless of whether they would be effective or not, and summoned all their workers to the fuel depot. A group of those ["class enemies"] in no position to object were told to stand in the water and form two lines with our arms linked to fill the breach in the ruptured canal wall, while another group of workers were told to fill sacks with earth and pile them up in front of where we were standing, and the rest carried baskets of earth and rock to dump in there. The initial burst had occurred toward sunset, and it was nearly dark by the time we got into the water, so those dumping earth and rock could not see what they were doing and sometimes even emptied their loads on top of us. It was late autumn, and although the ground was not yet frozen, the mornings and evenings were very chilly, and we got so cold standing there in the water with linked arms for such a long period that some of the weaker ones started to collapse. But on the orders from above, we could not get out until the flow of water had abated, and ended up standing there for five hours. Only after midnight were we permitted to go back to our tents, and when we got out of the water our teeth were chattering so hard we couldn't speak and our limbs were numb and frozen stiff. Some of us couldn't even walk back to their tents and had to be carried.

Our teeth didn't stop chattering until long after we got back to our tents, and our bodies did not warm up again, yet as soon as the sun rose next morning the work of repairing the ruptured canal began with a meeting to announce that we must strive to complete the repair within ten days. First of all, the sacks of earth dumped there the night before, which had done nothing to hold back the water, had to be dug out of the mud, which caused us great hardship. The mixture of sand and earth coating the sacks scoured our hands, and by the end of the first day the skin on our fingers had split open. Things were a little better for those carrying earth and rock in baskets, who did not have to handle the stuff, but my job at the time was stone laying, so I had to work on the new stone lining for that section of the canal, and even touching the stone and cement plaster gave me heart pain and an unbearable burning sensation in my fingers. If the repaired canal wall was not perfectly durable and another breach occurred, it would mean problems of a greater order of magnitude, but it would have taken a month to make it perfectly durable and we had a ten-day deadline, so we were driven without an instant of respite from dawn to dusk. The ordeal of those ten days is so unforgettable that I can still vividly picture that canal wall.

This is just one example, but every time the canal was damaged by heavy rain in summer or ice in winter, we "class enemies" were driven harder than prisoners to repair it, with no more concern for our lives than if we were inanimate things. In prison, all the inmates were treated with equal harshness, whereas the "class enemies" in civil society could be pushed around by everyone else and made to do the jobs they couldn't or wouldn't do themselves. When there was tough work like that to be done, we were under orders so strict it was as if even falling sick or dying was prohibited, and although everyone worked in the same camp, "class enemies" were given the hottest place in summer and the coldest in winter. In brief, "class enemies" downtrodden by the two slogans "Reform Through Labor" and "Proletarian Dictatorship" were like the tormented underlings of the wrathful deities, who have the merest whims of their masters visited on their flesh. Notably, many of the "class enemies" mercilessly put to work in water or humid environments on that power station construction site and others like it ended up suffering from kidney disease and hemorrhoids, as can be attested by those of us who have survived until now.

CHAPTER 28

The Lin Biao Affair

A FEW MONTHS after the construction of the power station canal began in 1971, news of the attempted coup d'état by a faction of the military led by the central committee Vice Chairman Lin Biao became public. When the attempt failed, the leaders were arrested; Lin Biao and his wife and son fled toward Russia in a military aircraft that was shot down by a missile, and their remains were recovered from the site of the crash, on the border between Inner and Outer Mongolia. For most people, this was something unimaginable: Lin Biao was the only leader in the history of Red China to have been acknowledged in Party literature as Mao's successor, and it was normal practice in official recitations to refer to the Party central committee "led by Chairman Mao and Vice Chairman Lin." People had to memorize and recite Lin Biao's introduction to Mao's quotations, "In Praise of Mao Zedong Thought," also known as the "Preface to the New Edition," even more than the quotations themselves, and for a time, Lin Biao was an even more prominent figure than Mao himself.

Thus the incident could not be announced to the public simultaneously, and the news spread gradually in ever-widening circles. Since the Party's hold over hundreds of millions of people was at stake, there must have been particular strategies for the prevention of outbreaks of unrest [for different regions], but in the case of Tibet, they initially sounded out the Party leaders at county level and above, then announced the news to rank-and-file Party members, government officials, local government workers, and finally ordinary people. "Class enemies," however, were not told. At our canal work camp at that time, they always held separate meetings for "class enemies," and we were told as usual about "cherishing the Party central committee led by Chairman Mao and Vice Chairman Lin" and continued to recite Lin's "Preface to the New Edition," while in the ordinary meeting they were sounding the war cry against "Lin Biao's anti-Party clique."

Meanwhile, a number of differing accounts of the failed coup were circulating in society at large. Some said that Lin Biao's exaggerated praise of Mao was designed to ensure that by constantly being forced to sing his praises, ordinary people would naturally become fed up with him. Others said that during the revolution, many of Lin's former comrades were accused of being "counterrevolutionaries," "Party factionalists," "warlords," "capitalist roaders" and "revisionists," removed from office, and expelled from the Party, and ingratiating himself with Mao was a way of ensuring that this did not spoil his own career. It was also said that Lin Biao's intention was to free China from the misery it was then enduring, but only because when one political faction tries to overthrow another it always purports to have nobler aims.

Later on, when the military leaders who had conspired with Lin were brought to trial, their statements of confession printed in the *Tibet Daily* said that they had planned for two scenarios. In the first, when Mao went on a tour of the provinces they planned to take the opportunity to assassinate him, denounce him to the whole nation, and seize power. In the second, in case of failure, they would divide the country by establishing a principal base in Guangzhou in the south, from where they would carry on a civil war. Perhaps because Mao Zedong's karmic potential and fortune were not yet exhausted, neither plan was realized, and all those involved lost their lives. As far as we Tibetans were concerned, if the second scenario had come to pass and China had been split up, it could have provided Tibet with a welcome opportunity, and whatever had motivated Lin Biao's group, we were disappointed at least that their back-up plan had failed.

In the wake of the Lin Biao affair, the authorities increased their oppression of the people, and "class enemies" in particular, by launching the "Oppose Lin Biao and Confucius" campaign (*Lin khag Kong khag*). In the meetings for "class enemies," we constantly had to express our thoughts about the Lin Biao case with reference to our own progress in "reform," and sometimes submit them in writing. Ordinary people also had to write denunciations of Lin Biao and Confucius and post them on the camp notice board, but although the people working there had attended school in the period since Democratic Reform, those were schools in name only, and in practice most of them did not know how to write a single word of the denunciations regularly demanded of them. Since we "class enemies" knew how to write, we had to do it for them whenever we had spare time, and even during mealtimes. However, if what they said could not be put into writing exactly, some people found this unacceptable and got angry, and a few made false accusations that their words had been deliberately misrepresented. Likewise, during the fortnightly breaks from the work camp when we were allowed to return home, the neighborhood committees had us write denunciations to be posted on the walls of the alleys in their area, which was a very onerous addition to our regular burden. To tell the truth, I felt embarrassed that my written Tibetan was not good enough, despite what I had been able to learn as a child thanks to the kindness of my good parents, and this was obviously because I had had to spend my time working like a beast of burden at the age when I should have been studying, something I regretted bitterly.

The reason for the denunciation of Confucius, the founder of the Chinese cultural tradition who lived thousands of years ago, was that Lin Biao was a devotee of Confucius and quoted him in many of his writings, so Confucian thought was identified as the source of Lin's alleged wrong-headedness.

CHAPTER 29

The Defamation Campaign

AROUND THAT TIME, quite suddenly, two members of the Lhasa city branch of the Chinese People's Political Consultative Conference (CP-PCC), Dulwa Khensur Tubten Tséring and Kung-ru Shindram Tulku, both from Drépung's Go-mang college, were sent to make speeches at public meetings of each neighborhood committee defaming and insulting His Holiness the Dalai Lama. Generally speaking, successive political campaigns since the time of Democratic Reform had encouraged people to criticize and reject His Holiness from the political standpoint of "uprooting the evils of the old society," and at the many meetings held to elicit the views of the common people a few perverse individuals would indulge in defaming Him, but the majority avoided saying a single word about it. Some would describe the senior members of the former government (*bKa' shag srid gz-hung*) as the root of the "evils of the old society" while doing everything they could to avoid the heinous sin of vilifying His Holiness; thus none of those campaigns produced any results in this regard. The Chinese recognized that if they did not succeed in undermining the Tibetans' faith in and devotion to His Holiness, their control of Tibet would not be complete, so in view of their failure to encourage defamation from the political angle, they tried maliciously to undermine the Tibetans' faith in Him with false slander against His religious and ethical integrity, and cajoled those two religious figures into spreading it.

First of all, Kung-ru Shindram Tulku said that he himself had been recognized as an incarnate lama and was therefore in a position to know that this was a completely false notion, and maintained that His Holiness was an ordinary person like any other. Dulwa Khensur Tubten Tséring pretended that as he had formerly enjoyed the rank of retired abbot (*mKhan zur*) at one of the great monastic universities, he had accompanied His Holiness on visits to India and thus had the opportunity of close contact, and told the huge lie that because he'd had the status of a close attendant, he had found out that His Holiness was given to immoral behavior. Having been put up to make shocking and outrageous speeches at public meetings during the earlier vilification drive against Trijang Rinpoché at the time of Democratic Reform, he was deluding himself that he was about to reap big rewards in the present campaign, but the people of Lhasa did not believe a syllable of his oath-breaking lies, and the resolute ones who had gotten wise to the situation in the past were not going to be taken in this time around.

As for Kung-ru Shindram Tulku's assertion that he himself was not an incarnate lama, the public were quite prepared to accept it, because it is always possible to make mistakes in the process of recognizing reincarnations. But on the main question of Dulwa Khensur's false accusation of improper conduct against His Holiness, in previous accounts of his personal history Dulwa Khensur had never mentioned accompanying His Holiness, and he was also guilty of covering up his past. When he was subjected to struggle and told that first of all his past record would have to be clarified, it is said that a flustered request was made on his behalf to the relevant neighborhood committees to exempt him. These two speakers had addressed no more than a couple of neighborhood committee meetings when the Chinese authorities realized that the deception was not going to work and called it off.

If anyone at those meetings had gone along with the attempted defamation, it would have led to all the CPPCC figures being forced to make similar false accusations in accordance with their own particular circumstances, and the launch of a thoroughgoing campaign to repudiate His Holiness all over Tibet with the aim of influencing international opinion. Had that been successful, it would have meant the arrest of a large number of Tibetans, as well as suicides and other untimely deaths, while international opinion would surely have been affected. Once it had fortunately proved ineffective, some members of the public stuck threatening messages on Dulwa Khensur's door and accosted him in the street, warning him to desist if he valued his life. After several such demonstrations of public anger toward him, he became concerned enough to inform the authorities, and for a while they had to provide him with clandestine bodyguards.

Dulwa Khensur Tubten Tséring was one of those who were arrested and imprisoned for participating in the uprising and then released by the first general meeting of the public sentencing tribunals in 1960 to set an example of lenient treatment for those who confessed their crimes. After several years of civilian life, he was eventually inducted into the Lhasa city CPPCC and groomed for service in such ventures [as the defamation campaign]. In 1964, before he joined the CPPCC, he and I were together in the Nga-chen power station canal work camp. Since he was physically strong and a genuinely energetic laborer, and did not appear to be someone who flattered others to save his own neck but rather was always cheerful and liked to joke, his fellow workers liked to have him as a partner. Later on, after he joined the CPPCC, when I occasionally passed him in the street we would exchange greetings and chat for a few moments. Even after he made speeches defaming His Holiness there was no need for me to turn hostile, and I used to greet him just as before, but his cheerful demeanor had been replaced by one of severe regret and apprehension, and he would just smile at me from a distance and keep going. And who can blame him? His participation in the heinous business of defamation was in no sense voluntary or unprompted. All Tibetans at that time felt loyalty to their people and were united in their devotion to and faith in His Holiness, but at the same time those unable to renounce personal reward and even attachment to their own dear lives had no option but to reluctantly comply with the Chinese pressure on them to tell such lies.

Dulwa Khensur was among the first of many CPPCC delegates to succumb to this treatment, and when his vitality was affected as a result, he had to be withdrawn. Because he lacked courage to thoroughly renounce his attachment to this life and the frailties of the physical body, he was unable to resist Chinese intimidation, and there is no doubt that he uttered those soul-destroying lies involuntarily. Thereafter he was wracked with remorse, and passed away not long after.

CHAPTER 30

"Socialist Transformation"

IN 1974, WHILE a campaign called "Cleaning Up Class Categories" (*Gral rim dpung khag gtsang bsher*) was being carried out in official organizations like government departments, schools, and factories all over Tibet, ordinary people had to participate in a campaign called "Socialist Transformation" (*sPyi tshogs ring lugs kyi bsgyur bkod*). This involved ascertaining the class categorization of citizens on the basis of their former income, and further collectivizing and cooperativizing economic and productive activity. It appeared gentler than the other political campaigns, for there were no slogans calling for the assault and downfall of offenders, but in reality, although less visible, it was no less aggressive. It caused dissension within households and destroyed trust even between parents and children, resulting in a state of mutual suspicion.

After the Democratic Reform of 1959, people all over Tibet were divided into many different class categories on the basis of their former income. In Lhasa, there were six categories: former ruling class, ruling class deputies, big traders, middle traders, small traders, and the poor. Later on, those who suffered during the Cultural Revolution had been given other labels such as "spirit monster," even if they belonged to the poor class category, and categorized politically on an individual basis, which further distanced people from one another within the Tibetan community. Although nearly twenty years had passed since the introduction of all these labels to facilitate official control of the population, they were still considered temporary and had yet to be fixed definitively.

Thus, for the recategorization carried out under the Socialist Transformation campaign, people had to give proof of their status in the interest of their own future prospects, and if the individual concerned was not present at the relevant meeting a decision would be taken on the advice of the local subcommittee to which the individual belonged, and no appeal would be heard. Thus, the campaign began with a general meeting calling on all those concerned to attend. Normally, political meetings were attended by the leading officials and activists, and the "class enemies" under the control of the "proletarian dictatorship," while ordinary people regarded them as a burden to be avoided as much as possible; those who did come sat out of the way in the corner or at the back, where they could not be seen, and it was extremely difficult to get everyone there on time. But the meetings during that campaign were better attended than ever; everyone arrived on time and did their best to get a seat near the front. This was because of the announcement at the initial meeting that each person had to make their own claim, and it was said that even people who had not showed up for compulsory labor or political meetings since 1959, while their children or relatives covered for them, came to those meetings in person.

As for the procedure for ascertaining class categories: in our case, the Banak-shöl area [neighborhood committee] was composed of 18 local subcommittees, arranged into three groups of six subcommittees each for meetings led by the officials running the campaign and a few representatives from the neighborhood committee. First, every citizen was called on to give a detailed account of their assets and livelihood prior to the imposition of Communist rule, so, for example, those who were traders had to say how much capital they had, what kind of business they did, and what fixed assets such as property, vehicles, or production tools they had. Then the total value was estimated, and if it exceeded 5,000 *yuan* they were considered "capital investors" and were classified as either "big" or "middle" traders according to their assets. All members of families formerly in government service were categorized as "ruling class," whether or not they were the head of the household, while in other cases only the leading members were considered family representatives and categorized that way. Thus, because of the fear of being saddled with "ruling class" status, there were many disputes in each subcommittee, even among close-knit families, over who should take responsibility as head of the household, with mothers putting responsibility on their daughters and sons and daughters-in-law putting responsibility on their parents, and so on. The most prominent such cases were said to have occurred among the members of the Gyantsé Tsongkhang and Tsona Tsongkhang families under the Tromsi-khang neighborhood committee.

In the case of my own family, we were considered a "ruling class" household that had participated in the uprising. Before that, my uncle the chief secretary, my elder brother the palace steward, and I had been in government service; thus although I was not the head of the household, it went without saying that I was categorized as a member of the "ruling class." My elder sister Losang Chönyi-la had been arrested during the uprising and imprisoned, and since her release had been included among the "ruling class" for the purposes of compulsory labor and political meetings, but as she had previously been a nun at Tsamkhung Gönpa and had less standing than the other children and no particular responsibility in household affairs, we hoped that she might be reclassified under the slightly less onerous category of "ruling class offspring" (*mNga' bdag bu phrug*). However, as the purpose of that campaign was to maximize the "class enemy" label in order to facilitate the oppression of the Tibetan population, my sister remained in the "ruling class" category and continued to suffer the torment of "labor and thought reform."

Anyway, during the Socialist Reform campaign Lhasa citizens were divided into nine class categories:

1. All former government servants, lay and monastic, were "ruling class" (*mNga' bdag*).
2. Those who had served in the palace or Shöl bursaries, or as the stewards, bursars, or estate managers of local governors and noble families, were "ruling class deputies" (*mNga' tshab*).
3. Those who had owned fixed or liquid assets in excess of 5,000 *yuan* were "capital investors" (*Tshong las ma rtsa can*).

   These three were the actual target of the so-called "Dictatorship of the Proletariat."
4. Traders with assets worth less than that amount were "middle traders" (*Tshong 'bring*).
5. Self-employed people such as artisans were "workers" (*Ngal rtsol pa*).
6. Oracles, fortune-tellers, and religious mendicants were "religious workers" (*Chos las pa*).
7. Beggars, pimps, prostitutes, and so on were "vagrants" (*Mi 'khyams*). These four categories were also required to do "reform," but were called "those to be won over through education."
8. Stall holders with very little capital were "petty traders" (*Tshong pa nyi tshe ba*).
9. Former servants and wage laborers were "poor citizens" (*Grong mi dbul phongs*). These two alone were regarded as supporters or suitable allies of the Communist Party.

In addition to these categories, there were also "ruling class offspring," which meant that a total of 70 percent of the city's population were given labels that qualified them for condemnation and servitude. Once these had been entered on their residence papers, members of the targeted "ruling class," "ruling class deputy," and "capital investor" categories had to undergo "comparative assessment" of their performance of "labor and thought reform" at the six combined subcommittee meetings, and subjected to struggle accordingly. At first, individuals had to give a detailed account of their own achievements or failings in "thought reform"; they were then challenged, criticized, or refuted by the "masses" and assessed on their performance in regard to three points: whether they had obeyed the laws, whether their attitude to reform was correct, and whether they had committed fresh offenses. This was recorded in their personal file.

At that time I was summoned from the power station work camp in Tölung to a comparative assessment meeting in Lhasa. The group of "class enemies" who had been assessed before me had been accused of some trifling infractions, exaggerated ones at that, and undergone interrogation and struggle every night for four or five days before their cases were decided, so I prepared myself to face several days of inquisition and accusation. The meeting to assess my case was attended by about fifty people, including a female official called Yangdzom. Unlike in the struggle meetings of the past, I did not have to stand bent over and was allowed to sit on the ground, but during the interrogation they cursed and shouted at me no end, just like before. I made a short address to the meeting, saying that I recognized that my earlier way of life had been mistaken, and that with heartfelt gratitude to the Communist Party for giving me the opportunity to make a new man of myself I was sincerely engaging in "labor and thought reform," and that the people's criticisms of whatever faults and errors I had not recognized so far would help me to fully reform my outlook. At that, some people in the crowd called out that I made it sound like I had committed no errors at all in "reform," and if that were so there would have been no point in summoning me to this meeting, that I was not speaking honestly, and many other things.

The specific accusation against me came from a woman activist from the neighborhood committee called Tséring Lha-mo. Sometime earlier, when "class enemies" from all over Lhasa had been summoned to do unpaid labor on the construction of an ornamental pool in the "Lhasa Cultural Palace," she had been our supervisor, and because at that time I had carried earth and rock together with a "hatted reactionary" under the same neighborhood committee called Kunsang Rikdzin-la, and we had spoken together, she pressed me to confess whatever false rumors and bad talk we had indulged in. I replied that we had just been chatting and had not said a single word against the Party or the people's government, and that since Kunsang Rikdzin was here she should please ask him for herself, but without stopping to listen, she insisted that I was refusing to confess and that the assessment meeting would not be concluded until I did. She expected this to lead to several days of struggle against me, but the official Yangdzom told me to think about it carefully that night and give a clear account the next day, and with that the meeting came to an end.

The next day, expecting the matter to be taken further, I waited apprehensively to be called into the meeting, but I was not called and another "class enemy" went in for assessment. By that time, the campaign was being wound down, and as in all the Chinese campaigns, it was strict to begin with and more lax at the end. During One Smash and Three Antis, for example, people were executed even for small things at the beginning, but toward the end there were some more serious cases punished with imprisonment or "hatting" and compulsory labor. Anyway, not only did I get away with just one evening meeting of interrogation during comparative assessment, but because the only incident I had been involved in since my release from prison was preparing a plate of buttered *tsampa* one new year's day, the committee's assessment of my reform record put me in the group of those who had obeyed the laws. Nonetheless, for about six months following that campaign, all "class enemies" had to undergo a fresh imposition of strictures similar to those imposed on "hatted reactionaries" before the process of assessment was over.

CHAPTER 31

The Banak-shöl Production Cooperative

ONCE THE BUSINESS of ascertaining class categories and assessing the targeted groups came to an end, the second stage of that campaign was the compulsory organization of nonaffiliated wage earners into institutions under the slogan of "Full cooperativization and collectivization of economic production." Although most working citizens already belonged to organizations in many different fields of employment, there were some who for a variety of reasons earned their living independently, and they were now brought together in newly established cooperatives under each neighborhood committee called production cooperatives (*Thon skyed mnyam las khang*), and the municipal government allotted each of them an area of open land near the city that they were supposed to cultivate for grain production.

I heard that a "Banak-shöl production cooperative" was organized with about a hundred nonaffiliated workers under the Banak-shöl neighborhood committee and one A-ché Tendzin, the committee's local Party leader (*Tre pu'u hru'u ci*), was appointed in charge, while the other leaders were elected from among the membership. As with any organization started without capital, there was no way for the cooperative's members to earn an income for some time, so they were bound to face some hardship, especially since the leader, A-ché Tendzin, was a brute of a woman who spoke only about "class struggle," "revolution," and "proletarian dictatorship" and had no enterprise management skills whatsoever. I was working at the Tölung power station camp at the time, and felt relieved that since I had been sent there by the neighborhood committee I would not have to join the new cooperative, but one day one of its leaders called A-po Tra-lo showed up at the power station with a horse cart to fetch the "class enemies" from Banak-shöl. That felt like being plunged back into darkness, since whatever conditions were like at the new cooperative, just the fact that A-ché Tendzin was in charge meant that it would be miserable, but reluctant as I was, there was nothing to do but roll up my bedding along with the others, get in Tra-lo's cart, and go back to Lhasa.

We were told to attend a meeting of the new cooperative the same evening, and arriving there we found only the leaders and no ordinary people. A-ché Tendzin addressed us at length about how the new cooperative had been set up and why "class enemies" in particular were being recruited into it.

"Our nation is devoted to the noble cause of socialism," she announced, "and under socialism there is no such thing as individual economic activity, only cooperatives and communes, so under the regulations introduced by the Socialist Transformation campaign, a new production cooperative has been established for those who have so far been working individually. However, since some members of the new cooperative are unable to come to work regularly because of various domestic difficulties, some are sick, then there are the elderly and the young, and of course the majority are women, we are very short of manpower. That is why we are recruiting you 'class enemies' into our cooperative with the permission of the sectional office and neighborhood committee, and in line with the undertakings you all made during the recent comparative assessment meetings to exert yourselves in reform, you will have to give us your best efforts. This will be the test of how well you have done in reform."

Thus whether the cooperative was going to work efficiently or not would depend on the efforts of the few of us "class enemies," which meant sucking our blood and sweat dry, for the other leaders were no less rough-mannered, work-shy, and loudmouthed than she. One of them, a brother-in-law of Chamdo Pakpa-la from Kham Li-tang known as Mi-sing, was said to have formerly been a well-known swindler, and when he was given responsibility for the cooperative's production work, he drew up numerous financial plans quite at odds with the officially stated program and confidently established numerous subcommittees dealing with various undertakings such as carpet weaving, carpentry, construction, and stone quarrying, supposedly as a temporary measure to raise funds for the cooperative's main task of agricultural production. Since the "class enemies" from the power station work camp had been working as stone layers, they were sent to the construction subcommittee, but I was allocated to the stone-quarrying subcommittee. I had spent a few months doing stone quarrying while in prison, but that had only involved dynamiting, and I had no experience in cutting stone for use in construction. When I explained to the leaders that I had experience in stone laying, not cutting, and asked to be sent with the construction group, they told me:

"The fundamental aspirations of this cooperative rest on making the stone-quarrying group our mainstay, and we have sent you there because we have higher expectations of you than of any of the other 'class enemies.' As for familiarity with the work, this can never be gained other than by actually doing it. For example, although you are someone who formerly lived by exploiting the masses while 'seated on a square carpet,' you have learned stone laying simply by engaging in that work. Although you may face difficulties initially, you have to put up with them. Anyway, what is required of you members of the exploiting class is to recognize how you bossed around the masses according to your own whims, and it is not your place to pick and choose." Some of the leaders expressed themselves more softly and some were more threatening, but either way they said the same thing: that I had to not only work for the quarrying subcommittee, but take responsibility for productivity as well.

Of the nine people in that subcommittee, three were women, two were elderly, two were school-age boys, and the only able-bodied workers were the incarnate Lama of Khardo, Ten-nor-la, and myself, so that was totally discouraging for a start. Then we had to find our own stonecutting tools and a suitable place to work. As far as tools were concerned, we had to make our own arrangements, but to buy decent tools would have cost the equivalent of two months' wages. Since I had been working as a stone layer at the power station camp I could rustle up a sledgehammer, chisel, and crowbar, but some of the others didn't even have an ordinary hammer. As for a work site, there was a stone-quarrying unit of the TAR construction company working at a place known as South Bank at the entrance to the Dodé valley, and by making a contribution to their kitchen and passing a gift to the foreman, we got an already overworked spot alongside theirs. They had quarried it for so long that only useless remnants were left, but our inexperienced leaders regarded it as a bonanza and sent us there with high expectations. We pitched our tent near their workplace and started off sharing their makeshift tool workshop, but if none of us had experience in cutting stone for building, we had even less knowledge of how to turn out tools like chisels and crowbars.

Then we had to bring down rock from the mountainside above using dynamite, but there were many cattle in the vicinity and a much-used motor road nearby, as well as our host work site, so if we used too much it could cause a lot of damage, but if we used too little the rock would not come down, and none of us even had experience in using dynamite. So according to circumstances and with great effort, some of us gathered fragments of quarried stone, others managed to loosen boulders with crowbars and roll them down without using dynamite, but far from earning any income for the cooperative, we didn't even make enough to cover our own daily rations. I explained our difficulties to the cooperative leaders and requested them to hire a stonecutter who knew about tool making and explosives, and after a while they engaged someone from the Banak-shöl Yukung workshop's farming cooperative to come and give us training. He gave us the rudiments of stonecutting, but didn't know tool making and had no experience with explosives, so our problems were not over. Then it turned out that one of the cooperative leaders, the one called Tubten Lo-dro who had survived the massacre at the Tsukla-khang during the Cultural Revolution, had experience in making tools and using dynamite from his days as a road builder, so he came to our work site for a few days to teach us, but as the deputy leader of the cooperative he had no time to stay with us.

In any case, there was no way to accomplish the work we had been given without learning how to make what we needed by ourselves, so in order to make our work easier and more productive, I determined to start making tools myself by taking the trouble to go to stone-quarrying units thereabouts and learn how to do it. For a while I was unable to control the red-hot iron with the tongs and occasionally touched it accidentally, and the burns on my hands came up in blisters. Then it took me so long to shape a chisel blade that I went through a large amount of charcoal, and moreover I endangered my own and others' safety trying to get the temper of the blade right, but after a while I got the knack of working molten metal and fixing the correct temper, and overcame the problem of tools. We still had problems getting rocks down the mountain, however, and occasionally, when we did manage to roll a boulder down and everyone gathered around to help split it, if we failed to strike the driving chisel head-on with the sledgehammer it would spin off to one side, and many injuries happened that way. One time when Khardo Rinpoché struck the driving chisel off-center it flew into my cheek and nearly broke my cheekbone.

We carried on in this way, ill equipped and ill prepared, for about a year, and rather than bringing in any earnings, the other workers in the group had to have their wages supplemented by the cooperative. At that time my daily wage was 2 *yuan*. By then, the other members of the stone-quarrying subcommittee moved on to work in other subcommittees since ours had not been successful, until only Khardo Tulku Ten-nor-la and I were left. However, with just the two of us working together we managed things very well: I prepared the tools and split the fresh rocks while Rinpoché did the dynamiting and broke the rocks I had split into small pieces, and we found that concentrating on our own tasks made the work easier and even quite productive. I had become adept in tool making, and of all the different kinds of work I had had to do, I came to like metalworking the best. Meanwhile Khardo Rinpoché had become a highly judicious explosives engineer, and was able to dislodge boulders yielding more than 300 cubic yards (*Kung spang*) of gravel with a single blast, more than the two of us could get through in a whole year.

Then the cooperative imposed a work target on us. We each had to produce 500 *yuan* worth of rock per month, while we received no more than 90 *yuan* per month each in wages and an additional 20 *yuan* per month to cover the cost of tool maintenance and charcoal, but our earnings still paid the cooperative leaders' wages. Stone was in short supply at the time, and the cooperative got benefits such as transportation and timber from the army camps that bought our stone, as well as supplies of otherwise rare commodities like meat, butter, tobacco, sugar, soap, packaged foods, and so on, so we really had become the cooperative's mainstay. Even so, we never saw any increase in our wages, and the profits of our labor were enjoyed by a few leaders. Such was the everyday reality of "democratic centralism" and the "unique characteristics of socialism."

CHAPTER 32

The Farmer's Life

DURING 1974, THE arrival in Lhasa of a large number of destitute villagers from places like Drikung in Medro Gongkar county of Lhasa prefecture and Uyuk valley in Shika-tsé prefecture led to some anxiety over the hardships being endured by the great majority of people in rural areas. At that time of heightened concern, we received a letter from my elder sister Yangdröl-la, who was living in Yakdé Khang-shung in Rinpung county, Shika-tsé prefecture, saying that since there had been no rain in Yakdé that season the harvest had failed, and asking us to procure whatever grain we could for her in Lhasa. Like the saying "One fallen yak brings down a hundred others," this caused even more shortage than usual for us as well, but the food shortage in my sister's household gave me a chance to meet her again after a long separation, and to find out about the hardship among the majority of Tibetans in the countryside. I had wanted to go and visit my sister's place for a long time, but we were still young and had been content to wait for a suitable occasion to present itself; however, generally speaking human life is impermanent, and in particular, resources of every kind were scarcer in the rural areas than in the city and life was harder, so with the food shortage in Yakdé making things even worse, I got the impetus to visit my sister as I had long been intending.

In the summer of 1976 I applied to the neighborhood committee for leave to visit my sister, explaining that we had not met for a long time, and since the main leader, Chö-nga Tenpa-la, was a person with Tibetan sensibilities, he granted the request without much delay. At once I packed up the few sacks of wheat *tsampa* that we had managed to gradually accumulate by economizing, and set out for Yakdé. By that time a lot of motor roads had been built in Tibet, but they were exclusively for the benefit of the Chinese and only served their main centers, so in out-of-the-way village areas like Yakdé there were only mule tracks, and the Chinese government had not provided so much as an arm's length of modern road. Also, the impact of Mao's command to "dig deep and stockpile grain underground" had not yet receded, grain was still strictly controlled, and county and township administrations appointed people to check on individuals buying and selling grain and transporting it here and there. If they found out you had saved any or were giving it to someone else, you could be accused of undermining the socialist market system, have your grain confiscated, and go to prison, so I made the journey carrying the little grain we had worked so hard to procure and save by thrift in constant fear of official confiscation, as well as having the difficulty of finding and paying for rides in trucks and then on pack animals. I eventually reached my destination one evening at dusk.

When I first saw my sister I didn't know it was her. She had the same features and manner as our kind mother, but she was so downcast in body and spirit I could not bear to see it, and became deeply saddened. She herself was moved with both joy and sorrow, and wept for a moment as she embraced me.

After we had greeted and consoled each other and it was late, we said good night and lay down to sleep, but all I could think of was the conditions my sister was living in. The dwelling was like a leftover pastoralists' corral with a roof stuck on top, in derelict condition, with no windows to let light in and no whitewash on the walls. Inside, there was no furniture except a couple of cracked earthenware cooking pots, a couple of worn-out tin pans, and some ragged mattresses. The two elder children had worked alongside their parents since they were small and did not have the physique of most primary school children although they were around that age. Moreover, because they had had no chance to study they were completely illiterate, and there was no saying that the same would not happen to the younger two who, for the moment, were looking after the family's few cattle as best they could. They had no shoes to wear and their hands and feet looked alarmingly like birds' claws caked in grime. In other words, the exaggerated poverty of this household looked like something out of the fake reconstructions of the "sufferings of the old society" in Chinese propaganda, and with the scene occupying my thoughts and many questions running through my mind, I couldn't sleep a wink that night.

Everyone has their own tales of what they went through after the devastating events of 1959 plunged the Tibetan people into a pit of unbearable misery, and as I recall those of my own family I sometimes start to cry and at other times laugh out loud, but most notable of all is the situation I came across during the week I spent in that area, the conditions in which the local people as a whole had come to face a shortage of grain, and the particular ordeal of my elder sister's household.

Generally speaking, while the imbalance between Yakdé's large area and its small population had long been an impediment to prosperity, before the Chinese invasion the villagers did not depend solely on agriculture; the men used to buy rapeseed from other areas and produce their own edible oil, and with the wool they bought from the neighboring Yamdrok area, the women used to manufacture a homespun cloth called Yaktér, much worn by ordinary monks at the great universities around Lhasa, as well as other woven items like women's aprons, on quite a large scale. The wealthy engaged in trade and, being at liberty to pursue various enterprises according to their ability, they could procure grain from elsewhere whether natural setbacks [to agriculture] occurred or not.

When the Chinese government imposed direct rule over Tibet in 1959 and implemented Democratic Reform, they took possession of all the land and established organizations with fine-sounding names like mutual-aid groups (*Rogs re tshogs chung*) and people's communes (*Mi dmangs kung hre*) that deprived the people of their liberty and required them to engage solely in agriculture. Other traditional forms of secondary livelihood such as trade and handicrafts were banned and all household looms were confiscated. During summer and winter when there was little work to do in the fields, the people were forced to provide labor for the construction of Chinese official buildings, roads, and bridges, as well as mining and other work, as a tax obligation, and received no more than 1 *yuan* a day in wages, usually much less. Likewise, when the time came to collect the harvest for which the farmers had risen early and retired late and worked harder and suffered more than animals to produce, they had to surrender the greater part as a tax known as "patriotic state grain" (*rGyal gces gzhung 'bru*), receiving not one cent in payment.

Officials from the county, township, and village-level administrations came to inspect the fields, first in early summer when the barley shoots were growing and a second time when the heads of grain had formed, and made an estimate of the amount of grain tax they expected to collect at harvest time, and the farmers had to render exactly the quantity fixed in advance, even if there had been losses due to frost and hail. Even in a good year, each person received a fixed allowance of ten measures [*Khal* = approx. 28 lbs.] of grain, with an extra nominal allowance known as "grain points" for working people. The remaining grain, known as "surplus grain for sale" (*'Bru lhag spus tshong*), had to be sold to the state at a very low fixed price. A few measures of each person's allowance were also set aside as a "famine preparedness" measure by the township and village officials, and once they had put their seal on it, people could not use it even if they had run out of food.

After the establishment of the so-called "people's communes," individual work teams could not even choose whether to plant barley, wheat, or peas, as this was decided for everyone by the local government. After grain production was increased in some parts of China by planting a crop known as winter wheat, they had large areas of that sown, regardless of the different soil and climate in Tibet, like "taking a shoe as the model to make a hat." Winter wheat was particularly inappropriate in Yakdé, which is a high and exposed territory, but, like the proverb "The king's command can no more be resisted than a boulder rolling down a steep mountainside," orders were orders, and it had to be planted. Fields planted with winter wheat had to be irrigated all year round, which required a lot of manpower; more seed was required than for other crops; and the straw it produced had no nutritional value, thus depriving the cattle, horses, and mules of fodder, a problem scarcely less serious than depriving people of grain. Unlike other grains, the flour made from winter wheat was harmful to people's health, causing kidney problems, pneumonia, and many other diseases. The disastrous results of planting winter wheat were hit upon very pertinently in a dramatized commentary performed by the Lhasa theater troupe after Mao's death, for during that period the practice had imposed a heavy burden of misery on the people, livestock, and resources in many rural areas.

At the same time, under the campaign slogan "In agriculture, learn from Dazhai and emulate the courage of the people of Dazhai far and wide," Tibetan villagers were made to construct useless terraces on dry mountainsides. Whether or not this was a way to increase grain production was apparently a matter of less concern than wasting a lot of their time and effort to see whether they could "emulate the courage of Dazhai." They were made to construct irrigation canals many miles long, most of which were so incorrectly surveyed and measured that they ended up reaching the intended fields at the wrong level and were therefore useless. Since the manpower and resources for these undertakings had to come from the local cooperatives, their members suffered huge losses in annual "work point" earnings, while the Chinese government technicians who planned these reservoirs and canals faced not so much as a word of reprimand.

Then the agricultural cooperatives were ordered to use chemical fertilizers on their fields, which had to be bought for a high price from the state supplier. These fertilizers made already thin, dry soil dry up altogether, and in moister conditions they made the plants grow without bearing fruit, causing more harm than good, but anyone who pointed out that they were inappropriate for local conditions was condemned for standing in the way of "scientific agriculture." Similarly, they organized groups of people to set off explosions in the sky in summertime, which was the "scientific" method of preventing hail, and they had to do this as soon as they saw the clouds massing, but whether or not it prevented hailstorms, the cost of the explosives had to be met out of the farmers' earnings and was one of the most onerous imposed on them.

Under such oppressive and exploitative conditions, farmers got only ten measures of grain per person per year even when there was a good harvest, and since all household necessities right down to the year's supply of salt and soda had to be paid for out of the grain allowance, it was not enough, and most people ran out of *tsampa* by early spring each year and had to satisfy their hunger by eating vegetation. Before their work brigade would lend them grain, they came to search the house, and if they found as little as four or five measures [*Bre* = approx. 1 lb.] of *tsampa* inside, the applicant was not only denied the loan but also taken to face struggle at a public meeting. Grain loans were generally granted to only a few households on political grounds, and most farmers had to go hungry for half the year, doing heavy agricultural labor all the while, which sapped their strength and left them vulnerable to disease. Since medical facilities were minimal, there was a high proportion of early deaths among the rural population as a whole, and even the young people often looked as if they were over fifty.

As for the treatment of "class enemies" in rural areas, my elder sister's household could serve as an example: during the Democratic Reform of 1959 they were classified as "ruling class deputies," and the head of the household, Démön Rikdzin-la, was condemned for involvement in the "reactionary uprising" and imprisoned. The family's fields and all the contents of their house were confiscated, my sister and her husband Palden-la, Démön Rikdzin-la's son, and their two children were given enough *tsampa* to last a few days, mattresses, and a few other nominal possessions and sent to live in a decrepit building little better than a pigsty.

The cultivable land that was redistributed on the basis of family size was the most marginal in the area, and although after my sister's younger children were born the number of family members increased to nine, there was no corresponding increase in the allowance. Although they were a family of nine living on an allowance of marginal land for only four, when the people's commune was established they were excluded on the pretext that they were "class enemies" and left to fend for themselves. During the period of drought, excluded "class enemy" families were not allowed to irrigate their fields until the irrigation of the commune's fields was finished, so by the time they got water their fields were already parched, and without the timely arrival of seasonal rains there was no way to grow any crops.

Then there was a continual obligation for able-bodied household members to go and perform labor on Chinese road- and bridge-building projects and so on, and in addition, the local township and village administrations called on the "class enemies" in their area to do miscellaneous dirty jobs, so my sister's husband, Palden-la, was kept extremely busy. Even during the agricultural seasons he had to drop everything and go when the local officials summoned him. The most tiresome of these duties was frequently having to deliver letters to the Rinpung county administration, some 30 miles away, on foot and within a narrow time limit, regardless of the weather or the time of day or night. Since both working members of the household spent most of their time and energy performing unpaid tax obligations, they barely had the opportunity to try to meet their own needs by tending the few poor fields allotted to them, and in this way my sister's family were reduced to the status of beggars who were neither able nor permitted to beg.

CHAPTER 33

The Death of Mao Zedong and Subsequent Developments

EVENTUALLY A NUMBER of the elderly Chinese leaders started to pass away, and during that year, 1976, Prime Minister Zhou Enlai, army commander-in-chief Zhu De, Vice Premier Tong Piwu, Politburo standing member Kang Sheng, who had risen to prominence during the Cultural Revolution, and Deputy Prime Minister Liu Pu-chun, all of whom were important contemporaries and colleagues of Mao Zedong, died one after the other. For some time before he drew his last breath, Mao himself was seriously ill, and when even the usual newsreel films of him meeting foreign representatives had not been seen for a while and there were many signs—such as an earthquake measuring seven [Richter] points in the city of Tianjin, near Beijing, which killed tens of thousands of people, and a meteorite falling on a province in northeast China—there was some anticipation among Tibetans that these signified that Mao's death was imminent. When his life ended on September 9, a fervent wish of the Tibetan people came true.

I was working at the stone-quarrying camp at the time, and as it was a beautiful autumn day and the last, according to the Puk-pa system of astrology, of the seven days of the *rishi* star when the earth's waters are purified, I bathed several times in the nearby stream. Still, as the waters of the Lhasa Kyi-chu river are supposedly endowed with the "eight qualities" [of perfect water: cool, sweet, light, soft, clear, odorless, harmless to the stomach, harmless to the throat] and superior to others, I had agreed with my work partner to go and bathe there too, and by three o'clock in the afternoon we had left work and were returning to Lhasa. By the side of the main road on the approach to the city, some workers digging a trench for laying lead pipe a half yard or so underground had stopped working and were listening to a radio. As we wondered what was up, the noise of the radio got louder and we could hear mourning music of the kind they typically played to mark the death of an important leader. My companion, Khardo Tulku Ten-nor-la, turned to me and said, "One of the 'Oms' has had it." "Om" was a kind of code word used by young people in Lhasa to refer to senior Chinese leaders. I put my finger to my lips at once, signaling him to be quiet, because at such critical moments actions can have disastrous consequences and one has to be particularly careful, but before we had discussed whether or not to change our plan to go to the river, we parted ways to return to our respective dwellings. When I got home, my elder sisters had heard the mourning music, but had not yet been told who had died. Then, a moment later, my younger brother Jam-pun-la arrived breathless with the happy news that it was Mao himself.

Strangely enough, while walking to work that morning I had been joined by the former Ganden monk Losang Norbu, one of the fellow prisoners at the Nga-chen power station who used to sell me extra work points, and he had explained that there was consternation among the Chinese because the eighth month of their [lunar] calendar that year happened to be an intercalary month. This was an extremely rare occurrence in Chinese astrology, and signified an extraordinary cataclysm such as national upheaval in China or some disaster befalling the emperor—or president. This could be seen from historical records, and the Chinese in the office where he worked were in a heightened state of apprehension. "So," he told me, "that old devil Mao Zedong is finished." In those days, Tibetans heard no news from outside, and with internal restriction and repression as tight as could be, people wondered in utter desperation whether the only possible way their misery could end might be for a war to break out in China using modern weapons, with which they would all kill each other. Many of the older people really believed that things would improve once Mao died, although they could never say so.

A little while later, Khardo Tulku Ten-nor-la came and called me to go to the river as we had agreed, and as we headed toward the riverbank on the south side of Lhasa, people were hurriedly leaving their offices and schools and other workplaces and going home, as if a war really had broken out. When we first got to the river there were a great many people who had also come for the last day of the *rishi* star period, but when the loudspeakers in every part of the city started playing funeral music and announcing the news of Mao's death they soon thinned out, and when soldiers started to spread out along the riverbank, we quickly finished our bath and went home too.

After I got back, the summons came for us members of the "ruling class" and "ruling class deputy" categories and the "four categories" [of suspect people] to attend a meeting at the neighborhood committee office, and I went there right away. The committee officials were joined by a Public Security official for the Banak-shöl area called Késang Tséring, who had been sent by the Public Security department to address the meeting. He told us, "As you are well aware, Chairman Mao passed away today. Since reactionary class forces always use any opportunity they get to stir up trouble, you must strive to abide by the law, and may not move around just as you please. Since the city government has ordered that 'class enemies' are to be put under the control of their neighborhood committees for some time, 'class enemies' under the Banak-shöl neighborhood committee will have to go to Lo Khangsar to help the Banak-shöl agricultural cooperative with the harvest for several weeks, starting tomorrow. You will report outside the agricultural cooperative office at nine o'clock tomorrow morning, and no excuses."

After him, the other officials repeated the same speech one after the other, to the effect that whether or not we had food supplies to last us for the next few weeks or were sick, or had any other problems did not matter— we had to go and that was that. Preventive security was tightened all over the city that evening, soldiers were on the streets, local militia (*Yul dmag*) were mobilized, and there were thorough searches of the houses of "hatted" members of the "four categories," "ruling class," and "ruling class deputy" families, and other suspicious people. The Banak-shöl neighborhood committee was regarded as the most lenient of the twelve neighborhood committees in the city, and although its officials had to be seen to be carrying out the orders from the city government to conduct searches that night, they actually searched only a few households that the committee leaders considered suspicious and contented themselves with casual inspections of the rest. Anyway, we passed that night divided between anxiety and hope.

The next morning, we "class enemies under the dictatorship of the proletariat" assembled punctually outside the door of the agricultural cooperative to be taken the seven-mile distance to the rural area called Lo Khangsar where we were to remain in exile until the mourning period for Mao's death was well and truly over. We had to work every day from five o'clock in the morning until around ten o'clock at night bringing in the harvest, with a short rest period after work, followed by an hour-long meeting. In the meeting we were required to recount whatever good or bad thoughts had occurred to us during the day, especially concerning the death of Mao. At that time, there were around thirty of us "class enemies under the dictatorship of the proletariat" doing "labor and thought reform" in the Banak-shöl area; some were as old as seventy and some suffered from serious long-term illnesses, and it goes without saying that they could barely endure having to do such work, and being unable to do anything for them except sympathize made the rest of us feel bad. Then there were those who ran out of food, and not being allowed to go and fetch more, they had to go hungry.

For almost a month we had to work hard sixteen-hour days, as well as keep up the appearance of being in mourning and take great care when conversing with our fellow workers, which made the situation highly restrictive. Nonetheless, there was some glimmer of hope in everyone's mind, and we all shared the same expectation that Mao's death would be followed by a civil war to seize power, or at least that there would be some change in the current state of persecution. At the same time, those with heartfelt faith in and devotion to Mao were tormented with foreboding and worried aloud that "the corpse of capitalism would return from the grave" or "Red political power would be set back," as Chinese official propaganda always warned.

September 18 was fixed as the national day of mourning, on which not only government offices, the military, and all state-run concerns from factories, farms, shops, and transport operators down to hospitals but also ordinary workplaces like agricultural, pastoral, artisanal, and construction cooperatives had to close, and their members had to participate in mourning ceremonies. These started at three o'clock in the afternoon, and for the next half hour, everyone who drew breath on land under Red Chinese control, with the sole exception of four-legged animals, was ordered to stand to attention in the pose of sincere bereavement, regardless of wind, rain, or anything else. We had our mourning ceremony in the fields for about an hour, after which we had to join once again in a meeting where we had to discuss what our thoughts had been during that period, and criticize each other for not being mournful enough and so on.

A few days after that, the restrictions enforced by the city neighborhood committees were gradually loosened, and since we had finished bringing in the harvest anyway, we were allowed to go back home. In the space of the three weeks we had been away, black banners had been put up along the sides of the roads and over the entrances of government buildings bearing messages in Tibetan and Chinese spaced out along them in letters made of white paper, while people, as well as roadside trees, vehicles, and even animals, had white paper flowers stuck on them as a sign of mourning, giving the impression of an unseasonal snowfall. Chinese people were also wearing black cotton armbands on their left arms, but most Tibetans were going around with smiles on their faces as if some auspicious occasion were being celebrated.

When I got home, I heard that on the day after Mao's death, when we were packed off, there had been house searches all over the city, and instead of entering the usual way the militia had stolen into people's houses through windows and skylights, and many of those who had so far managed to secretly continue their religious observances had no chance to hide their prayer books and *mala*s as usual, and they were snatched. Those found with deliberately torn or defaced pictures of Mao were taken into custody. One of the worst—and funniest—incidents occurred in the number 2 neighborhood committee of north Lhasa, when the auxiliary troops got hold of the diary of the former monk official and librarian Ngawang Khédrup, some said by climbing in through a skylight. His entry for that day read, "Went to work as usual in the morning. At 5 p.m. heard the good news of Mao's death." This was taken very seriously, and subsequently he was taken from one neighborhood committee meeting to the next to face struggle, before being imprisoned. He was released when the overall situation relaxed some time later, but by then he had been crippled by a stroke as a result of the mistreatment.

In the same vein, when a Muslim called Habib who worked as an official in the food grains department of Tölung Déchen county was told of Mao's death by a colleague, he replied, "I should think so. The Chairman is an old man now," and for that perceived impudence he was imprisoned. Then there was a monk resident at the Ka Shar-lho house in the Kamdong Tro-khang neighborhood committee in east Lhasa who suffered from a nervous disorder affecting his eyes and mouth that made him appear to laugh, and he was accused of laughing with joy at Mao's death and subjected to an inquisition. In another case, someone who had borrowed a lute before Mao's death and was on the way to return it during the mourning period following the announcement was accused of playing joyful music in celebration, and there were many more like him.

In our neighborhood committee, all of the "class enemies" had been sent into exile and there had been no particular incident. However, when two nine-year-old boys, the son of a Muslim man in our subcommittee who used to tend the vegetable garden and the son of Khampa Tséten Tashi, in charge of the east Lhasa horse cart association, drew a human figure on a wall and put an X through it, they were taken in by the neighborhood committee for supposedly crossing out Mao and treated as political offenders. They were released a few days later, but at the same time Tséten Tashi started suffering from heart disease and passed away soon after, and from what the neighbors said, it was the incident involving his son that brought it on. These are just examples, but while the official mourning for Mao's death was going on the situation was extremely tense, and quite a number of unfortunate people were implicated in baseless allegations and imprisoned, or given "hats" and placed under the supervision of "the masses."

The official mourning observance on September 18 was held at three o'clock in the afternoon Beijing time [approx. two hours ahead of Lhasa sun time] outside the so-called Cultural Palace that had been constructed on the site formerly known as Shuktri Lingka [after an open-air teaching throne (*Zhugs khri*) established there for the Seventh Dalai Lama]. Except infants and geriatrics, who were left to sleep inside, everyone had to attend the meeting, standing in their respective [neighborhood or work unit] groups. September corresponds with the seventh month of the Tibetan calendar, the first days of autumn when the sun can still be as hot as in midsummer, and that day there wasn't "so much as a bird's corpse" of cloud cover, so during the three full hours of the mourning address being read aloud by the senior vice-chairman Hua Guofeng in Beijing and broadcast in every province, people had to stand motionless under the hot sun, and a number of them fainted.

The main reason for this was that people rarely ate well with any consistency, and when decent foods were available people tended to eat them up all at once, which led to such imbalances as high and low blood pressure. However, whether the Chinese really imagined that people were going to collapse from genuine grief or for some other, more deceitful reason, they had organized first-aid teams to be on hand during the meeting, and they came and carried off those who fainted. As I later heard from some of those concerned, when they came to and found themselves being tended to, they felt embarrassed, because they had fainted from physical discomfort alone—grieving for the old devil was out of the question—and they hated to think that other onlookers might have had that impression.

When Prime Minister Zhou Enlai had died in January of that year, during the eleventh Tibetan month and the twenty-seven coldest days of the year according to the Puk-pa system of astrology, the official mourning ceremony began at eight o'clock in the morning, and people had to stand in line waiting for two hours beforehand. Moreover, in spite of the cold, people were ordered not to wear their mufflers, fox-fur hats, face masks, and so on as a mark of respect, and without them they got frozen. So people whispered jokingly to each other that when Mao died he had to suffer in the hot hells and when Zhou died he had gone to the cold hells.

Once the official mourning ceremony was over, government offices and cooperatives went back to work, although those with really heartfelt devotion to Mao, and those with something to prove, felt unable to discard their black armbands and white paper flowers. Most people, however, were expecting a destructive struggle for power to break out within the central government leadership in Beijing, and discussed these hopes among their own circle of friends. Such power struggles were commonplace in China's dynastic history, and the talk going around at that time was of two opposed factions, a "Shanghai group" and a "Beijing group." At this critical juncture the propaganda outlets were saying nothing in particular about anything and keeping a very subdued tone, even as people paid more attention to them than usual. Then, on October 16, all the propaganda organs made an announcement in unison: the Party central committee under the wise and sound leadership of [now] Premier Hua Guofeng had decisively annihilated the Gang of Four, and before they had a chance to take down all the trappings of the mourning observances for Mao's death, there was a spate of joyful processions with banging drums and clashing cymbals and celebratory meetings.

From then on, there were changes in the government's approach throughout China. The blame for the disastrous results of the Cultural Revolution was put squarely on the Gang of Four, and Deng Xiaoping started to emerge as the most powerful and renowned figure in the central leadership. Under a policy of "vindicating the falsely accused," victims of the Cultural Revolution had their names cleared, were restored to their former positions, and were compensated for their confiscated property. In Tibet, there was no fundamental shift in the exercise of power, which remained as rigid as before, but great advances began to be made with regard to the basic needs of the Tibetan population. For a start, the principle of "To each according to his labor" was adopted, so that people received income in proportion with the work they did. Nightly political education meetings were gradually scaled back, and those with "hats" who had been deprived of political rights were restored to equal status with the rest of the population. Similarly, the principle of "equality of all citizens before the law" was announced, and those imprisoned for political offenses in 1959 began to be released. Only then, when my elder brother was released after twenty years in prison, were all our family members reunited, which brought us much joy, and not long after that, Tibetans in exile got their first opportunity to return and visit their relatives. Thus the hopes with which Tibetans had anticipated Mao's death turned out to be fully justified.

CHAPTER 34

The Rewards of My Hard Work

WITH THE DEATH of Mao Zedong, a new chapter of history began, and in order to secure popular goodwill and support, the heads of government and incumbent officials made radical changes in their conduct of public affairs. In Tibet, as issues related to "nationality policy" became a focus of concern, Tibetan officials dedicated to the welfare of their people seized the opportunity and began to move ahead energetically on working for the reestablishment of Tibetan culture. In the field of education, knowledge of written Tibetan had hitherto been restricted to reading Mao's quotations, with no wider currency at all, and had greatly degenerated, so the task of reestablishing it was a most immediate and pressing concern. In order to improve the level of written Tibetan, ensuring the quality of schoolteachers was the initial priority, and when schools were on the lookout for qualified Tibetan teachers, I was identified by the directorate of the TAR teacher training college as a potential recruit; they approached me through the leader of my local subcommittee, Ama Sonam Drölma, to see if I was interested in working there.

This was something of which I had so far not even dreamed. In view of my situation at the time, I would have been content to be appointed as a sweeper at the teacher training college, not to mention becoming a teacher there. However, to be quite honest about myself, having learned basic reading and writing at a private school when I was a child, I joined the palace secretariat as a junior government servant for a brief period before the upheavals of 1959; I learned the official style of writing but never had the opportunity to study grammar and spelling [enough] to be able to teach others. Then I was imprisoned, and ever since I had done nothing but manual labor, so I replied frankly via the subcommittee leader that after such a lapse of time I had no confidence at all to accept a teaching position at the teacher training college, but I hoped to be able to make other contributions, such as helping to write examples for school textbooks. Nonetheless, the college directorate had a higher estimation of my abilities and two of its members, Lungtok-la and Tendzin Lekdrup, approached the east Lhasa sectional office and the Banak-shöl neighborhood committee with a letter of recommendation from the school, as was official practice, to request that I be released from my duties in order to work there.

The office and the committee were ready to oblige and approved my release, but my immediate masters, the Banak-shöl production cooperative, refused to release me, and A-ché Tendzin lied to the two people requesting it that I was badly behaved, that I had not done well in reform, and that I was not a hard worker, to put them off. They were not about to believe this, but in the Communist system you have to accept what the leaders say, so they just said some sweet-sounding words to the leader of my subcommittee that they would keep making efforts to get me released and left it at that. This was an apt illustration of the Tibetan saying, "After working as a servant you end up being unfit for anything else." In short, it was because I had worked too hard for that cooperative. As already mentioned, the income from the stone I produced not only paid the leaders' wages but also helped them establish a link with the army camps that brought them far greater benefits, which they feared they would lose. On top of that, they were not prepared to acknowledge that they were denying the request for my release because of the resulting loss to the cooperative, as this would mean revealing how hard I had worked, and even that was too great a concession for them to make.

It was a grave disappointment for me that a few leaders were prepared to spoil my future by making false accusations and perversely passing off white as black for the sake of their own profit. For the moment there was nothing I could do about it, but I resolved that one way or another, I would give up stone quarrying. As the general situation continued to improve, my work partner Khardo Rinpoché gave up stone quarrying and went to do carpentry, and I was left to work alone as solitary as a deer, but I still managed to get the month's workload finished within fifteen or twenty days unassisted. However, sometimes overturning boulders alone was difficult and dangerous, and I developed problems with the joints in my right forearm from doing that work, and because of my general unhappiness over what had happened, I used that as a pretext to stop quarrying. Because of the way things were going, the cooperative leaders had no means of thwarting me.

Since for the moment there was no other work, I joined the cooperative's construction group. Meanwhile, it turned out that there was a large collection of scriptures, originally confiscated from the monasteries and lamas' and nobles' residences during Democratic Reform, that had not been shipped off to China with the rest but left in the Shöl printery and Potala palace. The soldiers occupying the palace during the Cultural Revolution had removed all the cloth covers in which these books were wrapped for their own purposes and left the leaves in a disorderly pile, and now the TAR Cultural Relics Office was hiring people in the Lhasa area who could read and were familiar with traditional literature to put them back in order. Dompo Tubten Gyeltsen, one of my former work mates from the timber-sawing workshop, was one of them, and with his help, I was taken on. Judging that the prevailing wind was in my favor, I simply informed the cooperative leaders and without waiting for their approval, started going to work at the Potala. They couldn't find any way of stopping me, so they just demanded that I pay a percentage of my wages to the cooperative, which I did. That was in 1978.

CHAPTER 35

Working in the Potala Palace

THE MAIN REASON I got to work in the Potala was having a friend to introduce me, as just explained, but it was also because an ordinance had been issued by the Chinese government for the preservation of what remained of Tibet's destroyed cultural heritage. Apart from those piled up in heaps and crammed into some scrap-metal storerooms near Ramo-ché in north Lhasa, most of Tibet's looted precious metal statues had been transported to China, where they were melted down and used to manufacture bullets and many other things, and since the Cultural Relics Office now had orders to prevent the remainder from being used in the same way, they sent a group of young workers sorting scriptures at the Potala to go and pick out those worth saving. Since they were in need of more workers to help with this task, I was recruited into that temporarily, and then went on to join the group sorting out the books.

The broken statues we had to go through were graded by quality, and the great majority of those made of the finest materials, like bronze, had been taken to China, although a few survived, such as the upper half of the Jowo Aksobhya-vajra of Ramo-ché, which was later recovered in China. In the storeroom where I was working, there were mostly fragments of massive gilt-copper statues, but also many small bronzes that we picked out, and the least damaged of those were placed in the upper-story apartment of the Késang Po-trang palace in the Norbu Lingka. We came across copper utensils such as kettles, braziers, cooking vessels, and so on, right down to chamber pots, which had once belonged to ordinary Tibetan households, jumbled up with the debris of statues and offering vessels deliberately smashed during the Cultural Revolution, when these things were condemned as "spirit monster" paraphernalia. Household

objects had been looted and destroyed as much as possible in China during the Cultural Revolution, just as they had been in Tibet, and it struck
me that this showed how they had eliminated all traces of the fact that
Tibetan household implements were totally different from those in use
among the Chinese.

After we had finished sorting through the statues, I went on to reas-
sembling and cataloguing scriptures in the Potala. After a few months,
those workers who were more religiously minded, single, and childless
were taken onto the staff of caretakers at the palace, and I was one of those
put in charge of sweeping up and maintaining the Dalai Lama's apartments,
temples, and reception halls. This was an enviable position, and for me, it
meant the chance to start living a meaningful life. Initially, the older and
newer sweepers worked together on keeping these rooms tidy and receiving visitors, but soon after, when the palace was first opened to the public,
the newly appointed sweepers were each put in charge of a chapel. We assumed the duties of a sacristan, keeping the chapel in order and receiving
those who came for worship, something more significant than being just a
caretaker, in which I exerted myself with joy and devotion.

During my time in the Potala, there was an incident where one of the
statues in the meditation chamber of King Songtsen Gampo went missing.
The statue in question had been given by the king of Nepal to one of the
TAR leaders, Tien Bao, when he went to Nepal on a "friendship" tour. It was
made of rather ordinary gilt copper and was not at all ancient, but was considered valuable because of its significance to bilateral relations. As soon as
the loss was discovered, the palace officials got very flustered and reported
it immediately, as required by the Cultural Relics Office regulations. The
customs officials at the Nepal border were informed and started rigorously
searching anyone leaving the country, while Cultural Relics officials were
sent to the palace to investigate. At the time the statue had disappeared,
the caretakers were still working as a group, so there was no individual to
be held responsible, and we newer employees were still arriving, so most of
us had no idea which statue it was, how big it was, or what it was made of.
All the same, we newly appointed caretakers were summoned to a group
meeting with the Cultural Relics official Rikdzin Dorjé and told to give our
views about how the statue had been taken, who might have done it, and
whether we thought it was a Chinese or a Tibetan. Since this question was
political, no one said anything. The statue was said to have been one [*Khru*
= approx. 19.5 in.] in height, and at that time visitors carrying large bags
were required to leave them at the entrance in the Déyang-shar courtyard.

It would hardly have been possible for someone wearing a *chuba* [Tibetan gown] to carry it off, let alone someone wearing just jacket and trousers, so one would assume that the thief must have been wearing the long Chinese-style coat called a *dayi*. So I said that it could not have been concealed by someone wearing a *chuba*, and this could be seen by putting another object of that size in the folds of a *chuba* for comparison, so although I could not say whether the thief was Chinese or Tibetan, it was likely that he was wearing a *dayi*.

Rikdzin Dorjé made no response, but basically the Cultural Relics Office suspected that a Tibetan working in the palace was responsible, and it was said that they secretly investigated the social backgrounds and contacts of these workers. When one of us, a young man named Chungdak, went off to China for training, they came and searched his dormitory room. For the next two years, the palace workers were under constant suspicion, until it turned out that customs officials in Guangzhou had apprehended a Chinese man trying to carry the statue out to Hong Kong.

Not long after I started working at the Potala, I noticed an item in a bulletin published for Chinese officials saying that a delegation of representatives from the Tibetan exile government was coming to Tibet on an inspection tour, and this was announced publicly in due course. People were told that they would be allowed to make inquiries with the delegation about their relatives who had settled abroad, but nothing else, and that they should receive the delegates courteously and refrain from showing anger toward them by throwing stones or showering them with dust. The reality was exactly the opposite. From the Tibetan point of view, young and old alike saw the exile delegation's visit as a long-awaited moment that seemed to herald the dawn of a new and happier time. It was an opportunity to speak out about the sufferings endured by the Tibetan people up to now, to tell the truth about the prevailing situation and urge them not to be taken in by the false appearances put on by the Chinese, and especially for the delegates to understand the condition of the majority of Tibetans in rural areas, and I wonder if there had ever been such intense consultations and compilations of testimony in our entire history.

Most Lhasa people never learned when the delegation was supposed to arrive, but during the approximate period many of them stayed home from work in readiness to go and greet them in the traditional manner, by burning incense. The Chinese authorities, however, were being very cautious and kept the arrival date secret, as well as the name of the hotel where the delegation was accommodated, so that on the day of their arrival there

Lhasa 1979: from left to right, younger brother
Jampel Puntsok, the author, late younger brother
Ngawang Norbu, younger sister Tendzin Drölkar.
Author's collection

was no big public welcome. But when they went to visit the Tsukla-khang
temple the next day, Lhasa people gathered there immediately in their
thousands and made plainly evident the agony of the Tibetan people, their
unswerving devotion for His Holiness, and their loyal respect for His exile
government. Not since the popular uprising outside the gates of the summer palace and on the Drébu Yulka grounds at Shöl in 1959 had such a large
political gathering been assembled spontaneously and without the force of
intimidation or bribery.

I did not join the crowd in front of the Tsukla-khang that day, but when
the delegation visited the Potala, all of those working in the palace assembled
to welcome and greet them in the Déyang-shar courtyard and make our feelings known to them, just as had happened outside the Tsukla-khang. That
day, no one except the staff was allowed into the palace, and ordinary people
were strictly prevented from approaching any nearer than the stone pillar in
Shöl, so we got to meet them at ease, without the pressure of the crowd and,
while inquiring after His Holiness's health, to apprise them of the real situation in Tibet. At the same time, I found the opportunity to inquire after the
whereabouts of my own relatives. When I asked one of the delegates whom I
knew from before, the minister for security Taklha Puntsok Tashi, about my
elder brother Yéshé Khédrup-la, who had fled in 1959, it turned out that he
was a carrying a brief letter from Khédrup-la and a photograph.

For twenty years there had been no written communication between Tibetans inside and outside the country, and not knowing if each other were even still alive, they had abandoned hope of meeting again in this lifetime until the developments following Mao's death began to allow for letters to be written and people to travel in and out. Thus, a short while before the arrival of the delegation I had been told by an acquaintance that my elder brother was alive and living in America, but that wasn't much to go on. So with the letter and photo from the delegation to show that he was alive and well came the hope of seeing him again. More generally, when Tibetans who had been living under Chinese rule heard from the exile delegation about the activities of His Holiness and the situation of the exile government it gave them new hope and strengthened their resolve, and even those few who had believed the Chinese propaganda regained some confidence in their own people, changed their tune, and started to repent their views. On the individual level, families like ours that had been divided and had long remained in a state between hope and fear about whether their relatives were still alive had their doubts resolved one way or the other. The delegates had certainly accomplished the basic tasks given them by His Holiness and the exile government, even if some of what they had to say brought the people a few disappointments.

Apparently, after the return of the first Tibetan government delegation, the Chinese authorities held a review meeting, and one of the Chinese leaders declared, "We made two wrong assessments. First, we overestimated the members of the nonresident government, and second, we underestimated the Tibetan public." What this meant was that since the exile government's principal agenda was independence and its representatives were to openly discuss the two opposing perspectives on the history of Tibet, the Chinese side had taken them for qualified politicians with experience of a variety of social and political systems, familiar with domestic and foreign languages, and taken their reception very seriously, but they had not proved worthy of this assessment. This statement was probably a mandatory slight, but the underestimation of the Tibetan people was a serious error. Since they thought that most Tibetans held the Communist Party and the people's government in reverence and loved socialism, it had never occurred to the authorities that there would be such a huge welcome and manifest display of affection and loyalty for the delegation, and the entire responsibility for this miscalculation had to be borne by the current TAR leader, Ren Rong. He had not only rigidly adhered to leftist policies and failed to implement the central government's nationality policy but also was accused of having given the central government entirely false reports on every aspect of Tibet's actual situation.

Then, a group of central leaders including the chairman of the Party secretariat Hu Yaobang, Party central committee Vice Premier Wan Li, and chairman of the Nationalities Affairs Commission Yang Jinren came to inspect conditions in Tibet at first hand. When they made a tour of the Potala, Hu Yaobang just glanced briefly at a couple of the golden reliquaries and apartments of the Dalai Lamas and showed little interest in the structure or contents of the fabulous edifice, but when they climbed up onto the roof, he looked out over Lhasa with a pair of binoculars and asked with great concern about all the official Chinese compounds, pointing them out and asking which office was which. He pointed to a Chinese-style pavilion in the middle of the ornamental pool by the "Cultural Palace" in front of the Potala and asked what it was, and on being told that it had been built as a recreation facility for the autonomous region leaders, he demanded sarcastically, "Who is enjoying themselves in there?" In the special meeting held a few days later, he apparently used this as an example when he stridently criticized local leaders for "throwing the funds provided by the central government in the Yarlung Tsangpo river" by wasting them on such things of no benefit to the needs of ordinary people.

On his departure from Tibet, Hu Yaobang declared that apart from the 20 percent or so of the Chinese population usefully employed in the region, like medical and technical professionals, the remainder should be withdrawn. The most senior TAR leader, Ren Rong, was appointed elsewhere in China and obliged to leave there and then, together with the central government delegation, and Yin Fatang, an official with experience working in Tibet, was called in from China as his replacement. Other Chinese leaders working in Tibet were also transferred, some offices were reorganized, and the positions of those central government cadres who had come to Tibet with little justification, by explicit appointment or otherwise, were rendered untenable.

Therefore the Chinese cadre force in Tibet was overtly or covertly hostile toward Hu Yaobang, and although their offices were powerless to defy his orders, the [regional] government ruled that the withdrawn cadres should be awarded a percentage of the wages due to them according to their period of service in Tibet in the form of a fixed allowance of Tibetan timber. Although the returnees were organized into three successive phases, all of them did their best to lay their hands on the timber allowance at once and to make sure that it was of the finest grade for making furniture, and fearing the trouble these discharged cadres might cause if disappointed, the heads of department let them do as they pleased. The first phase of Chinese cadres withdrawn in accordance with Hu Yaobang's orders departed not long after, but the remainder who had laid claim to an allowance of timber ended up never having to leave.

The few who did leave took two or three truckloads each of possessions with them, and the timber and wooden chests they loaded onto those trucks were so heavy that they had to use cranes. At one point, a painted propaganda board in People's Street in Lhasa that depicted a Chinese wearing a straw hat with a bedroll on his back and a tin bowl and wash bag slung over one shoulder, with the legend COMING TO BUILD THE NEW TIBET, had another drawing added to it of a big truck being loaded with a trunk so heavy it was about to topple the crane, and the legend RETURNING TO THE MOTHERLAND, which aptly expressed the real situation. They left, taking all these possessions, in broad daylight and with an irreproachable air, as if they were being as good as gold. Meanwhile, local leaders allowed thousands more Chinese to come in under cover of night without having to bring even bedding or eating bowls. In any case, apart from a few words and measures following Hu Yaobang's visit, his instructions were never put into practice, and because of the timber allowance for the so-called returnees, Tibet's forests had to suffer even more heavily.

Not long after that, the second exile government inspection tour composed of five members—four heads of foreign representative offices and the head of the exile Youth Congress—came to Tibet, and were warmly welcomed by the Tibetan public. They attracted large crowds wherever they went and spoke forthrightly about the activities of His Holiness and the situation of the exile government, and their tour seemed to be even better received than the first, although they were suddenly required to leave Lhasa before completing their itinerary. There were several factors behind this, but the immediate reason was that when the delegation traveled to Ganden to attend the Siu-tang festival, the employees of the municipal government's handicraft sales center had put up a tent in the ruins of the monastery and arranged a reception for them; around a hundred vehicles came from Lhasa and thousands of people gathered there, and when the delegates addressed the crowd, the Chinese authorities panicked and obliged them to curtail their visit and leave early.

What I heard was that the then exile government representative in London, Puntsok Wangyal-la, made confrontational and accusatory remarks in his speech, to the effect that the neighborhood officials and activists who had served the Chinese by bullying and harassing their compatriots would have to be reckoned with in future. The young people sympathized with this and took the curtailment of the tour as a vindication, while many older people felt that his words had been quite ill judged and unwarranted, and by precipitating the delegation's early departure, he had prevented them from fulfilling their appointed task. In any case, because of the crowd and the speeches made by the delegates at Ganden that day, they had to leave ahead of schedule, the names of many of those in the crowd were registered by the Public Security Office, and it was said that plainclothes police noted the registration numbers of the vehicles present and informed the offices to which they belonged, who then harangued the drivers and confiscated their licenses.

Soon after that came the third exile government delegation, which was received as well as the earlier two and successfully completed its mission. The visits by the three delegations allowed Tibetans inside the country and in exile to gain a clearer understanding of one another's situation. With the impetus of the slightly improved conditions following Mao's death, special efforts were being made for the perpetuation of Tibetan culture, and the opportunity arose for many older people with better knowledge of the written language to become employed as schoolteachers or in institutions concerned with cultural life. At that time, I heard that researchers were being recruited to staff the newly established Tibet Academy of Social Science, irrespective of whether they had participated in the uprising or were former "class enemies," and I went to see the director, Amdo Puntsok Tashi, presented my credentials, and expressed an interest in joining. He asked about my background in some detail and told me to submit an application in writing, with my background and qualifications, so I wrote down my story from the age of eight until the present without concealing anything and handed it in. About three weeks later, I was called to take the academy's standard examination, which I did under the supervision of a few of the academy's staff, and before long I received a letter of acceptance.

From 1959 up until a couple of years before that, I had labored under the "proletarian dictatorship" like an animal without so much as a sesame seed's worth of personal freedom, obliged to run at the beck and call of others, but now, with the turning of the wheel of time, I had been included in the ranks of the salaried officials of that same state and government. But if my hardships were less than before, it was not as if I had been granted freedom of thought or speech. The very purpose of establishing that academy, for example, was to assemble documentation to show that Tibet was an inseparable part of China and that many aspects of Tibet's intellectual and material culture had been introduced by the Chinese princess Kongjo, and other propositions quite at odds with reality. We were still living with the same terror of persecution and incarceration if we tried to give voice to the real situation.

CHAPTER 36

At the Tibet Academy of Social Science

DURING MY TIME at the Academy of Social Science, it had not yet opened and was still in the preparatory stage. The few employees were engaged in copying rare texts on religious and dynastic history borrowed from the TAR archives for the academy's forthcoming journal, *Tibet Research* (*Bod ljongs zhib 'jug*), and copying the catalogues of the former printers of religious classics. A year went by in this way before the formal opening of the academy was announced, and social scientific research was allocated among six working groups. I was put in the archive group, which suited me best, because that was just the title they gave to the work of locating and seeking out required texts and copying them, and spared me the problem of actually having to write false interpretations of them.

Then in 1982, the academy sent me with one assistant to commission prints of the Buddhist canon from the printing house at Dégé in eastern Tibet. On the outward journey we flew down to Chengdu, where we met the chief of the Nationalities Affairs bureau there, Tashi Tséring, and sought permission to make prints from the Dégé blocks. He was a loyal Tibetan concerned for his culture, and wrote us the best letter of introduction he could. After spending a few days in Chengdu, we boarded a public bus and headed back toward Tibet, traveling via the Chinese town of Ya'an and crossing the Erlan Shan pass to reach Dartsé-do.

Since my companion had many relatives in that town, we spent a few days there. It would never have occurred to a newcomer in this place that it was in Tibet rather than China, as the old Tibetan town had entirely disappeared beneath newly built multistory Chinese buildings. Apart from the occasional sight of a few old locals in Tibetan dress, everyone, men and women alike, wore Chinese clothes, and everyone spoke Chinese, even to the point of pronouncing their own names with Chinese intonation. To give one example: the name of the chairman of the Xikang (Kandzé) Tibetan Autonomous Prefecture government in Dartsé-do was Lu-tung-da, which is not a recognizably Tibetan name, but he was in fact a Tibetan called Los-ang Dawa, a name the Chinese pronounce "Lu-tung-da," which shows the level of self-confidence among the local Tibetan population. If Tibetan was not understood even in shops and eating houses, how much less could it be used in government offices, at the bank, post office, hospital, bus station, or other such places that local people had to frequent? The officials and staff working there were not all Chinese, many of them were Tibetan, but their behavior had become indistinguishable.

Going on up from there toward Dégé, through Mi-nyak, Tawu, Drang-go, and so on, all the trucks we passed coming the other way were carrying timber. In the Tawu and Drang-go valleys in particular, the forests had been cut mercilessly and so many logs dumped in the river that the water itself was scarcely visible. When I asked my fellow passengers why these logs had been put in the river, they told me that they were being floated downstream to Ya'an, where they would be retrieved, and that this was a wonderfully satisfactory means of transportation that saved on money and labor.

After passing through Kandzé, Darjé Gön, Béri, and so on, we reached Dégé Gön-chen and showed the official letter from the academy, together with the introduction from the Nationalities Affairs bureau in Chengdu, to the county leader and officials from the county cultural office. Since we were prepared to make the customary payment for the prints we commissioned, both offices were happy to accept it in principle, but said that the final decision could only be taken after consulting the senior and junior leaders of the printing house itself, and when they were contacted, the senior leader, Ngawang Tséring, and junior leader, Tashi Dorjé, flatly refused our commission. Since the popular, voluntary reconstruction of destroyed monasteries across northeastern Tibet had begun, large numbers of people were coming to Dégé to commission the printing of new scriptures, and as it had become established practice to bribe the two leaders, they would not entertain anyone coming empty-handed.

My companion then sent a letter back to our office explaining the situation and received a reply telling us to obtain the prints by any means possible, so we were obliged to find a way. One of the most influential figures locally at that time was Yang-ling Dorjé, a TAR secretary who had formerly served as leader of the Dégé county administration and was said to have protected the printing house during the Cultural Revolution. Many local people told us that we could succeed with his support, so we wrote back to Lhasa for his instruction in writing, and after waiting there for six months in all, we finally got hold of prints of about two thirds of the wood blocks they had, including the Buddhist canon (*bKa' 'gyur*) and commentaries (*bsTan 'gyur*), the Nyingma Tantras (*rGyud 'bum*), the Sakya teachings on "path and result" (*Lam 'bras*), the "Seven Treasuries" of Long-chenpa (*mD-zod bdun*), and so on.

We left Dégé on October 2, 1982 for Chamdo, where we spent a few days. As in Dartsé-do, the former town of Chamdo could no longer be found amid the new Chinese buildings. Though it was within the so-called autonomous region, most of the buildings were multistory Chinese offices and residences, Chinese settlers made up the larger part of the population, and not only the officials but also most of the local people understood and used the Chinese language. Returning from there through Powo and Kong-po, I found the deforestation so advanced that the so-called "forested ra-vines of Kongpo" were beset with dust storms. There could be no doubt that within a few more decades the land would not only be robbed of its beauty but also be ravaged by a deluge of floods and other natural disasters.

After getting back to Lhasa on October 10 and handing over to the academy all the books we had managed to obtain, I made my application for permission to visit relatives living abroad, and it wasn't long before I received my foreign travel permit. I left Lhasa on March 8, 1983, heading for Nepal.

Leaving Tibet

I HAD NO particular difficulties along the way, and arrived in the Nepalese capital, Kathmandu, on March 13, 1983. I sought lodging with some relatives of my father's family and spent a few days applying for permission to visit my brother in the United States and touring the holy places. I was planning to visit Dharamsala to seek audience with His Holiness and hoping to find a traveling companion, when I heard that His Holiness was soon to travel to Mön Tawang to perform a public Kalachakra initiation. Hoping to meet Him before His departure, I decided to fly, but new arrivals from Tibet had to have a letter of introduction from the representative office in Kathmandu before proceeding to Dharamsala, which delayed me for several more days. I took the flight on the 19th and arrived in Delhi only to find that His Holiness had departed that same morning. This was quite a disappointment, particularly as He was due to remain in the Tawang area for the next six weeks, and I had no relatives and even very few acquaintances in either Delhi or Dharamsala. Fortunately, however, the senior tutor Kyapjé Ling Tri-chen Dorjé-chang was staying a few days in Delhi for medical treatment, so I got to meet with him.

While waiting for His Holiness to return to Dharamsala from Tawang, I went on a tour of the holy places in India, like Bodh Gaya, Sarnath, Kusinagar, and so on, and then spent the remaining time in Dharamsala. That is the seat of the exile government and the center of the exile settlements, so besides exploring the area, I got to know more about the exile community in general and the monasteries and schools they had established in particular, and to admire the efforts made by the senior members of the community under His Holiness's guidance. I was granted audience the very next

Family photo 2004: from left to right, Tubten Khétsun, his nephew Tendzin Gyeltsen Khédrup, and elder brother Yeshe Khédrup. In the front row, his wife, Palden Drölma Khétsun, niece Tendzin Losang Khédrup, and sister-in-law Tsewang Palmo Khédrup. *Author's collection*

day after His Holiness returned in early May, and fulfilled the wish that had kept me alive throughout the months and years of suffering.

From there I returned to Nepal, received my permission to travel to the United States, and arrived here on May 31. Meeting up with my brother after more than twenty years was just like the expression "reuniting with one long feared dead." Since then I have stayed here, and although spending the better part of my life without freedom has prevented me from achieving competence in other languages, and therefore from making any great contribution in either public service or private enterprise, I have remained a steadfast and sincere supporter of the correct policy of His Holiness, unswayed by the schisms undermining the unity of the Tibetan people.

Having thus gained the opportunity to write about how I spent more than twenty years of my life as a human being subjected to animal servitude by another people in my own country, I have made great efforts to do so during my spare time, which have resulted in this book. However, I am neither a person of importance, capable of shedding new light on historical events, nor a heroic patriot with tales to tell of joining battle with the enemy; nor is my story one of miraculous survival in the face of unbearable physical ordeals. This is simply the story of what an ordinary Tibetan suffered under the Chinese occupation, and although lovers of adventure will hardly find it thrilling, it is a testament of our experience that I hope will encourage others with more extraordinary tales to put them into writing, so that the sufferings my generation went through will not be limited to hearsay but hopefully become, as much as possible, documentary sources at the disposal of the historians of the future.

Writing years after the fact, with deteriorated mental, verbal, and physical capacities, it is hard to avoid errors concerning exact dates and correct sequence, and with a request for the reader's forgiveness of any such flaws, I conclude.

Signed: Gyatso Tashi Tubten Khétsun
21st day of the eighth month of the fire mouse or Tibetan royal year 2123
October 2, 1996

Index

Ngo-drup Tsoknyi, 204
nomads, 110–11, 123
Norbu Dorjé, 75, 79, 84, 85, 86
Norbu Lingka barracks prison, 53–56
Norbu Lingka summer palace, 31(photo);
    Chinese assault on (1959), 34–39; and
    March 10th uprising (1959), 24–33,
    26(photo)
Nyamdrel ("Great Revolutionary
    Alliance"), 181–82, 185, 188–90; and
    "class enemy" study sessions, 198; and
    June 7th massacre, 191–97; and New
    Year (1968), 203–7
Nyang-chu river, 161
Nyang-tren valley, 104
Nyarong-shak school, 9–10, 13
Nyemdo Jampa Tendzin, 182
Nyémo county uprising, 214–15; and mass
    executions, 218–22, 221(photo)
Nyi-dön, 126

oil, edible, 119; and civilian life, 141,
    143–44; and oil lamps, 198; and rural
    life, 269; and Woba-ling Kha-ché
    Muslim community, 151
oil lamps, 198
Old Man's Tale (Khémé Dzasak), 153
"Om" (code word for Chinese leaders),
    274
Om-Khang shed, 28
Ön Gyelsé Tulku Ngawang Losang, 92
"One Smash and Three Antis" campaign
    (1970), 151, 214–18, 236, 261
"Oppose Lin Biao and Confucius"
    campaign, 252–53

Pabongka Ri-trö, 104
Palden (sister's husband), 271, 272
Palden Drölma Khétsun (wife),
    286(photo)
Panchen Chöki Gyeltsen. See Panchen
    Lama (10th incarnation)

Panchen Chöki Nyima. See Panchen
    Lama (9th incarnation)
Panchen Lama (9th incarnation), 152
Panchen Lama (10th incarnation), xii,
    152–56; and Chinese invasion, 153;
    and Dalai Lama, 154, 155; denun-
    ciation and struggle against (1964),
    155–56; and 70,000 Character
    Petition, 152, 155
Panchen Rinpoché. See Panchen Lama
    (10th incarnation)
"Panchen's bodyguard," 154–55
Pao-pao, 99, 100
Pa-ri-ku farmers, 231–32
Parkor Kha-ché Muslims, 149
Pa-wang, 76–77
Pa-yong, 172
PCART. See Preparatory Committee for
    the Tibet Autonomous Region
pea flour gruel, poem about, 104
Pelbar county uprising, 214
Peljor (Langdün family), 41
Peljor (Losang Chöjor), 47–50
Pema Dorjé, 118
Pema Drölkar (mother), 1, 2–3; death
    of, 3, 83; and March 10th uprising
    (1959), 3; release from Tsémön-ling
    Reeducation Center due to illness, 53;
    telling sister about death of, 92–93;
    Tubten Khétsun's last sight of, 53
Pema Norbu, 203
Peng Dehuai, 167
people's communes, 269–72
"People's Hospital" at Pomsur-nang, 13
People's Liberation Army (PLA),
    ix; destruction of turf cut for
    fuel, 225–31; evidence for long
    preparation before outbreak of
    hostilities, 45; guerrilla attacks on,
    18; and June 7th massacre (1968),
    193–94; military actions after
    March 10th uprising (1959), 34–39;

"Three Great Disciplines and Eight
Responsibilities" code, 233–34;
vicious treatment of farm animals,
231–34; wild animals wiped out by,
124; wildfire started by machine gun
fire, 123
People's Street, 181–82, 196, 289
"petty trader" category, 259
pills. *See* blessing pills
PLA. *See* People's Liberation Army (PLA)
poems, 104
political rights of ex-prisoners, 138
Pönchen Shakya Sangpo, 133
"poor citizen" category, 257–59
Poor Laborers Collective, 182
Potala palace, 23, 187; broken statues,
283–84; missing statue incident, 284–
85; sorting scriptures at, 282, 283; and
tunnel-digging during Sino–Soviet
war, 212
Powo Tarchin, 230, 233
Powo Tramo, 115–16
Powo Tségyé, 148
Powo Yiwong region, 160–62
Preparatory Committee for the Tibet
Autonomous Region (PCART), 5–6,
16, 19; administrative system, 142–43;
and Panchen Lama, 155
prison labor: agricultural labor, 122–23;
brick making, 93, 106–7; burning
corpses, 45; cart accident at Téring
prison, 76–78; Chinese conventions
on following impossible orders, 102;
collecting clay for building, 75–
78; collecting corpse from People's
Hospital, 108–9; collecting firewood,
93–104; deaths from falling while
cutting firewood, 96; dismantling
barricades, 45; at Drapchi prison,
93–104; and "Fifty Days of Fierce
Struggle" campaign, 61; landslide at
Nga-chen power station construction

site, 65–71; at Nga-chen power station
construction site, 57–71; odd jobs, 44,
93; Reform Through Labor Prison (*see*
Drapchi prison); sewage removal, 44,
53; sorting valuables, 79–80; transporting rubble, 61–62; at Trong-nying
prison farm, 119–36
prison life: changes in treatment of
prisoners, 112–13; cold weather, 43,
64, 101, 102, 116–18, 121, 131; cruelty
of guards, 42, 78–79, 99–101, 121;
death from cart accident, 76–78;
deaths from falling, 96; deaths
from landslide, 65–71; deaths from
overeating, 109, 110; deaths from
starvation, 97, 106, 108, 111; execution
rally, 223; and famine, 95–98, 104–6,
109–10; and "Fifty Days of Fierce
Struggle" campaign, 61; food confiscated, 97, 105; food sharing, 105; and
"Great Winter Training Session," 129–
31; injuries, 61–62, 70–71; kindness of
guards, 82–84, 86, 98; lack of nearby
relatives as contributing factor in
death, 110–11; living conditions at
Drapchi prison, 90–93, 105; living
conditions at Nga-chen power station
construction site, 58–60; living
conditions at Téring prison, 74–75;
living conditions at Trong-nying
prison farm, 121, 123; Norbu Lingka
barracks prison, 53–56; reeducation
study sessions, 45, 46, 91–92, 119,
120; searches of possessions, 72, 80,
84, 88, 97, 105, 108, 131; sentencing of
prisoners, 75, 89; and Sino–Indian
border war, 127–34; sleeping between
corpses, 108; struggle meetings at
Drapchi prison, 91–92, 94, 97, 102,
107, 110; struggle meetings at Téring
prison, 88–89; struggle meetings at
Tibet Military District Headquarters,